THE ADAMS CHRONICLES

Prepared by arrangement with

the Massachusettes Historical Society,

The Adams Papers,

and Harvard University Press

INTRODUCTION BY *Daniel J. Boorstin*

DESIGNER: BETTY BINNS

PICTURE EDITOR: FLAVIA RANDO

The
*A*DAMS
CHRONICLES

Four Generations of Greatness

JACK SHEPHERD

LITTLE, BROWN AND COMPANY
Boston   Toronto

*This work was prepared in conjunction with
the production of a television series of the
same name by Educational Broadcasting
Corporation, assisted by grants from The National
Endowment for the Humanities, The Andrew W. Mellon
Foundation, and Atlantic Richfield Company.*

Acknowledgments of permission to reprint
excerpted material appear on page 437.

Third Printing
First paperback edition

LIBRARY OF CONGRESS CATALOGING IN PUBLICATION DATA

Shepherd, Jack.
    The Adams chronicles, 1750–1900.

    Bibliography: p.
    Includes index.
    1. Adams family.   2. Adams, John, Pres. U.S., 1735–1826.   3. Adams,
John Quincy, Pres. U.S., 1767–1848.   4. Adams, Charles Francis, 1807–1886.
5. Adams, Henry, 1838–1918.   I. Title.
E322.1.A28S53   973'.0992 [B]   75-34422
ISBN 0-316-78497-4 (hc)
ISBN 0-316-78501-6 (pb)

*Published simultaneously in Canada by
Little, Brown & Company (Canada) Limited*
PRINTED IN THE UNITED STATES OF AMERICA

*To my parents, Grace and John Shepherd,
who celebrate life and the newness of each
morning; and whose concerns have taught their
children and grandchildren the belief,
shared by our forefathers, that the purpose
of freedom is to create it for others*

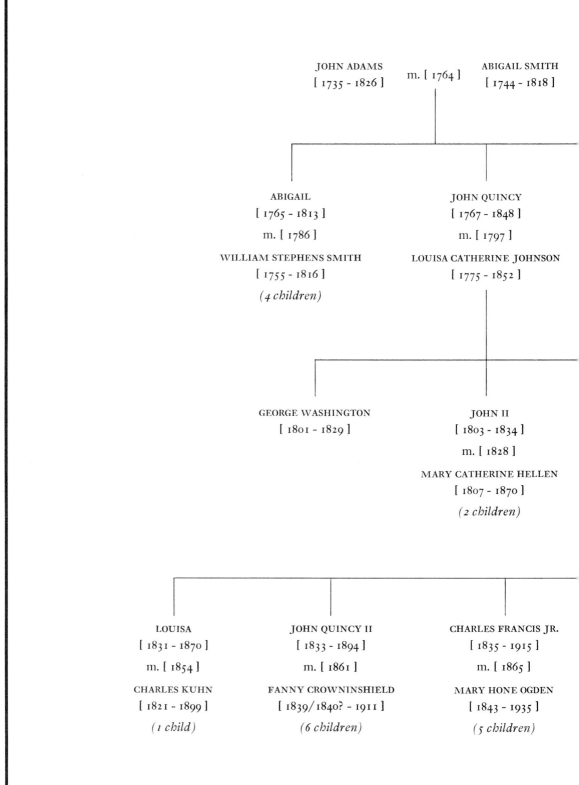

JOHN ADAMS
[1735 - 1826]

m. [1764]

ABIGAIL SMITH
[1744 - 1818]

ABIGAIL
[1765 - 1813]

m. [1786]

WILLIAM STEPHENS SMITH
[1755 - 1816]

(4 children)

JOHN QUINCY
[1767 - 1848]

m. [1797]

LOUISA CATHERINE JOHNSON
[1775 - 1852]

GEORGE WASHINGTON
[1801 - 1829]

JOHN II
[1803 - 1834]

m. [1828]

MARY CATHERINE HELLEN
[1807 - 1870]

(2 children)

LOUISA
[1831 - 1870]

m. [1854]

CHARLES KUHN
[1821 - 1899]

(1 child)

JOHN QUINCY II
[1833 - 1894]

m. [1861]

FANNY CROWNINSHIELD
[1839/1840? - 1911]

(6 children)

CHARLES FRANCIS JR.
[1835 - 1915]

m. [1865]

MARY HONE OGDEN
[1843 - 1935]

(5 children)

Four Generations of the Adams Family

SUSANNA
[1768 - 1770]

CHARLES
[1770 - 1800]

m. [1795]

SARAH SMITH
[1769 - 1828]

(2 children)

THOMAS BOYLSTON
[1772 - 1832]

m. [1805]

ANN HARROD
[1776 - 1846]

(7 children)

CHARLES FRANCIS
[1807 - 1886]

m. [1829]

ABIGAIL BROOKS
[1808 - 1889]

LOUISA CATHERINE
[1811 - died in
infancy]

HENRY
[1838 - 1918]

m. [1872]

MARIAN HOOPER
[1842 - 1885]

ARTHUR
[1841 - 1846]

MARY
[1846 - 1928]

m. [1877]

DR. HENRY P. QUINCY
[1838 - 1899]

(2 children)

BROOKS
[1848 - 1927]

m. [1889]

EVELYN DAVIS
[1853 - 1926]

Contents

A Family in the Public Service
by Daniel J. Boorstin

From the fortunes of the Adams family we can learn much that lies hidden in the lives of its separate members. The achievements of the individual Adamses are dazzling in their brilliance, gripping in their drama. But the family history moves in the long deep currents of American civilization. For four generations Adamses were leaders in the decisive battles of national life: the American Revolution, the movement against slavery, the Civil War, the railroad-conquest of the continent. If we can understand what the Adamses did for America, and what America did to the Adamses, we will witness, not merely the fortunes of a family, but the panoramic transformation of a nation.

The achievements of any one of a half-dozen Adamses would have sufficed to found a family — and to give an aura of distinction to children and grandchildren. John Adams was a principal architect of American independence — by organizing the Revolution at home, by pioneer diplomacy abroad — and he fatefully shaped the character of the new nation by insisting that George Washington be commander in chief and by naming John Marshall chief justice of the Supreme Court. Even if he had never been president he earned a place in the American pantheon by his profound and copious writings on constitutional law and political theory. John Quincy Adams decisively oriented American foreign policy and enlarged the definition of American independence by his authorship of the so-called Monroe Doctrine. Had he never sat in the president's chair, he deserved a chapter in the history of American letters for his treatise on rhetoric and a chapter in the history of American science for his founding sponsorship of the Smithsonian Institution and his role in celebrating the establishment of an American observatory at Cincinnati. His son Charles Francis Adams during the Civil War succeeded in one of the slipperiest tasks in American diplomacy — avoiding war with Britain and preventing British support of the Confederacy — and so played a decisive if too-little-sung part in the victory of the Union.

The fourth generation saw the achievements of the Adamses spreading out into the new industrial empire. Charles Francis Adams Jr. was perhaps the most articulate and self-conscious of the makers of the Railroad Age. And he pioneered in devising state regulatory agencies to protect the public interest. Henry Adams's classic *History of the United States During the Administrations of Jefferson and Madison* would have placed him in the top rank of American historians even if he had never written his *Mont-Saint-Michel and Chartres* or his *Education*. And, of course, these were not all the Adamses.

The Adams Chronicles depicts the dramas of these towering individual talents. But there was also an Adams Saga — an epic in which this all-star cast dramatizes the fortunes of a family. In this introduction I will try to sketch the outlines of that Saga. We will see how the relationships among the members of the family affected each hero's awareness of what was expected of him and what he expected of himself. I will try to show how America made the Adamses possible and how the Adamses expressed America. Incidentally we will discover why the family has not had its due in American history or patriotic lore.

Each of the achieving Adamses accomplished something that was neither trivial nor ephemeral. Yet their individual reputations eventually suffered from the grandeur of the achievements of the whole family. John and John Quincy set a standard and fixed a pattern that has led us to underestimate their descendants. By the third generation we are already wondering why Charles Francis was *not* elected president. As the generations pass, our temptation to underestimate them increases — just as the Adamses themselves come to measure themselves unfairly. A wry Harvard legend tells that Henry Adams used to wait in his study for someone to knock at his door to announce that he had been nominated to become another Adams president. Without such bizarre expectations how could Henry Adams plausibly have cast himself in the role of a "failure" and have recounted his impressive career as if it were nothing more than an "education"?

In the perspective of history, then, the reputation of the extraordinary individual members of four generations of overachievers has suffered from the excess of their family's talents. One Adams or another succeeded in showing that the family's resources were equal to almost every sort of leadership in American public life. (Only the army and the scientific laboratory lacked an Adams of shining eminence!) The family cast a long shadow. We find it hard to bring the Adamses of the fourth generation out of that shadow and measure the actual stature of latter-day originals.

The drama of the individual Adamses is well suited to the television screen. But the meaning of the Adams family in American life, and the large lessons of their chronicles for the role of a Family-Aristocracy in American Democracy, are not so easily portrayed. How did a changing America — and some unchanging features of American civilization — make it harder for their countrymen to put a proper value on them? What kept them from enjoying the satisfactions they had earned?

The political arena was where the Adamses first leaped to eminence. "Leaped" is the right word, for John's father was a farmer-shoemaker. In 1751, when John entered Harvard College, the first of his family to do so, his admission was evidence less of his family's distinction than of the readiness of the college even then to open its doors to young men of promise. In the ranking of his class, which *did* depend on social status, and which determined precedence in the assignment of rooms and of seats in the dining hall and in church, young John was placed fourteenth in a class of twenty-four. But political leadership in colonial America was somewhat less democratic than the makeup of the student body at Harvard College. The colonial legislatures and the governor's councils tended to remain in the hands of the well-to-do and the well-born. John Adams's rise to political prominence in Massachusetts illustrated the mobility of life in that colony. But his prominence came only after he had become a prosperous lawyer, including among his clients men like John Hancock, who was reputed to be the colony's wealthiest citizen. John Adams was accurately described as a "self-made aristocrat."

The eminence of the first three generations of Adamses — John, John Quincy and Charles Francis — was primarily in the world of politics. John and John Quincy were the only father and son ever to be elected to the presidency. Although members of the later generations possessed talents in some respects equaling those of their forebears, their talents did not take them to the pinnacle of national political life.

The scene of the Adams Saga shifts then from the White House and the Congress to other stages. We will find an explanation of this shift if we look more closely at the special virtues of John and John Quincy, if we see how the American political arrangements in that early age recognized their special virtues — and then how the democratization of American politics made it difficult or impossible for men of their stamp to reach the highest elective office. The transformation of American politics turned some of the Adamses' moral strengths into political weaknesses. The stoic virtues of self-made aristocrats would seem much less appealing under the vulgar spotlight of public opinion.

The proper attitude to public office, John Quincy Adams observed in December, 1808, should be "that which philosophers teach us should guide our views of death — never to be desired, never to be feared." Adams uttered this maxim after he resigned his office as United States senator from Massachusetts. By voting against the party line of the Federalists who had elected him, he had aroused the ire of his former supporters. "As to holding my seat in the Senate of the United States without exercising the most perfect freedom of agency, under the sole and exclusive control of my own sense of right, that is out of the question." Independence of partisan rule and of public opinion was an admirable — and thankless — Adams tradition.

During the nineteenth century the nation elaborated an apparatus of party discipline stretching from the grassroots precinct captain and the city boss to grand national party conventions and potent party caucuses in the Congress. And there grew beyond all precedent the means to articulate public opinion and to publicize the common view. Whole new industries developed to stir popular emotions and to inform leaders of the whimsies of current opinion, and new institutions arose for bringing recalcitrant statesmen to heel. Would national politics still have a place for Adamses? How could their steadfast refusal to speak for any but their own consciences fail to bring them discontent and frustration? Would the new millions at the ballot box vote laurels to men whose character required them to tell what the people did not already know and what they did not want to hear?

John Adams, the family's Founding Father, has become a national hero, but he was never a popular hero. If the American electoral process then had been as democratic as it later became, it is doubtful if John Adams ever would have been elected to anything. He was elected as a delegate from Massachusetts to the First Continental Congress in 1774 by the vote of the 129-member legislature of the colony. He was elected to two terms as vice-president not by popular acclaim but by the votes of the Electoral College when that small body was still functioning as the nation's Founding Fathers intended. When Adams was elected president in 1796, the electorate was still much restricted, and political parties had only begun to dominate the Electoral College by their instructions. In 1800, Adams was not reelected.

Adams's refusal to be a party man — even for the Federalist Party, which his political philosophy had helped to found — ended his career in national office. "I have never sacrificed my judgment," he insisted, "to kings, ministers, nor people, and I never will." His political adversaries had to recognize his independence. "He is vain, irritable," Jefferson noted as early as 1787, "and a bad calculator of the force and probable effect of the motives which govern men. This is all the ill which can possibly be said of him. He is as disinterested as the Being who made him."

The career of John's son, John Quincy Adams, showed a similar pattern. He described himself in his diary as "a man of reserved, cold, austere, and forbidding manners; my political adversaries say, a gloomy misanthropist, and my personal enemies, an unsocial savage. With a knowledge of the actual defect in my character, I have not the pliability to reform it." He was elected to the United States Senate in 1803, not by the whole electorate of Massachusetts, but by the state legislature. And when this Adams was elected president in 1824, it was not by the national suffrage but by the House of Representatives, which had the power in that year to elect a president because none of the four candidates had received a majority of votes in the Electoral College.

In 1828, John Quincy Adams, like his father before him, was not reelected; and his defeat by Andrew Jackson signaled the rise of populistic democracy. John Quincy Adams's second career — his seventeen years in the House of Representatives as a champion of antislavery and the right of petition — was made possible by the confidence of his friends and neighbors in the farming district of Plymouth, which sent him to Washington with 1,817 votes of a district total of 2,565.

His son Charles Francis was once elected to the House of Representatives, but after that no Adams was elected to an office in the national government. Although Charles Francis was active in party politics and was the Free Soil candidate for vice-president, his historic national service was his brilliant and subtle diplomacy as United States minister in London. In a letter to his son Charles Francis Jr., the elder Charles Francis summed up the family's political credo, and explained why, as partisanship and public opinion became more powerful on the national political scene, Adamses would be less conspicuous there. First among the qualifications of a statesman, he said, was "the mastery of the whole theory of morals which makes the foundation of all human society. The great and everlasting question of the right and wrong of every act whether of individual men or of collective bodies." He went on to explain: "In my opinion no man who has lived in America had so thoroughly constructed a foundation for his public life as your grandfather [John Quincy Adams]. His action was always deducible from certain maxims deeply graven on his mind. This it was that made him fail so much as a partyman. No person can be a thorough partisan for a long period without sacrifice of his moral identity. The skill consists in knowing exactly where to draw the line." In the next generation, the achievements of the family were to be of another order. How and where "to draw the line"?

The Adams passion for public service did not die, but it became difficult — or impossible — for Adamses to satisfy that passion by election to office. Of Charles Francis Adams's four sons, only John Quincy Adams II sought the favor of a large electorate. He was several times elected to the Massachusetts state legislature, and once received the nomination for vice-president on a splinter-party ticket, but he repeatedly failed in his bid to be elected governor. Charles Francis Jr. was among the first to sense that "application of steam to locomotion" was "the most tremendous and far-reaching engine of social revolution which has either blessed or cursed the earth": "I fixed on the railroad system as the most developing force and largest field of the day, and determined to attach myself to it." But as for politics, he remained "convinced that I have no aptitude, I lack magnetism frightfully, & have no facility of doing the right thing at the right time. I am frightfully deficient in tact; I never can remember faces or names and so I am by nature disqualified. I never could be a popular man." He saw this as a family trait, and complained, "I never could overcome my prenatal manner, and learn to say gracious things in a gracious way." This Adams had to find his path into the bustling railroad world through the genteel pages of the *North American Review*. He created a niche for himself in the public service by persuading the Massachusetts legislature to set up the first state railroad commission, and then he secured his own appointment to it by the governor. His work made it a model for the regulatory commissions that became a fixture of twentieth-century America.

Even if the Adams independence had somehow disqualified them for success at the national ballot box, the Adamses did not lose their instinct for the sources of power. Charles Francis Jr.'s vision of the new Industrial Leviathan was matched by his brother Henry's vision of the new power of opinion embodied in the newspaper press. In his autobiography, which he cast in the third person, Henry recalled his thoughts on his own career, when he was a young man in his mid-twenties: "One profession alone seemed possible — the Press. In 1860 he would have said that he was born to be an editor, like at least a thousand other young graduates from American colleges who entered the world every year enjoying the same conviction; but in 1866 the situation was altered; the possession of money had become doubly needful for success, and double energy was essential to get money. America had more than doubled her scale. Yet the press was still the last resource of the educated poor who could not be artists and would not be tutors. Any man who was fit for nothing else could write an editorial or a criticism. The enormous mass of misinformation accumulated in ten years of nomad life could always be worked off on a helpless public, in diluted doses, if one could but secure a table in the corner of a newspaper office. The press was an inferior pulpit; an anonymous schoolmaster; a cheap boarding-school; but it was still the nearest approach to a career for the literary survivor of a wrecked education. For the press, then, Henry Adams decided to fit himself, and since he could not go home to get practical training, he set to work to do what he could in London."

Returning to the United States after seven years abroad, Henry kept this focus for his ambition. "For large work," Henry observed, "he could count on the *North American Review*, but this was scarcely a press." The circulation of the *Review* then was about three hundred! Yet, he noted, "for fifty years the *North*

American Review had been the stage coach which carried literary Bostonians to such distinction as they had achieved." Well aware of these limitations, he knew that "what he needed was a New York daily, and no New York daily needed him." So, with characteristic indirection, he decided to go to Washington where, by writing occasional columns for "the Free-trade Holy Land of the [New York] *Evening Post* under William Cullen Bryant," he hoped to work his way up to a regular position on that height of potent heights — a New York daily.

It was by default then that Henry Adams later turned to history. And through lack of other, more contemporary outlets, he became one of the great American historians of the century. To him, historical writing was a convenient vehicle for expressing his indifference to passing fads and to the tyranny of public opinion. His most important work was a nine-volume history of the sixteen years of the administrations of Presidents Jefferson and Madison. "The author is a peculiar man," Charles Scribner the publisher wrote to a business associate in London explaining why he had not tried to secure the publication of those volumes in England, "and [he] don't care whether his book sells or not." Henry Adams's most widely read works, those on which his popular fame would rest — *Mont-Saint-Michel and Chartres* and his autobiography, *The Education of Henry Adams* — he had privately printed. The *Mont-Saint-Michel* (which Henry himself had had printed in an edition of one hundred copies) was nearly posthumous, for it was published under the auspices of the American Institute of Architects after the author had suffered an incapacitating stroke in 1912, which ended his writing career. The *Education* was posthumously published by the Massachusetts Historical Society.

Each of the Adamses, in his own fashion, preserved a posture of superiority to the verdict of the marketplace. At the same time, their instinct for power and their passion for public service bred increasing inward tension between their unquenchable sense of personal integrity and the compromising demands of an increasingly democratic America. An egalitarian nation, motley with recent immigrants, no longer acquiesced in genteel New England leadership. As American democracy advanced, the Adams posture of indifference to vulgar opinion somehow seemed to become a pose.

When Charles Francis Jr. turned from managing railroads to writing the colonial history of New England, he constantly wondered how many were listening. "If I could have heard that

20,000 copies of the 'Three Episodes [of Massachusetts History]' had been sold, my dearest ambition would have been satisfied; but I didn't hear it, and I never shall hear it." Henry Adams was anything but indifferent to the favorable reviews that the New York press gave to his *History*. How pleasant, he observed, to have "solid butter laid on with a trowel"! But how much more pleasant if the buying public had actually bought his books in large numbers. He compared himself to Gibbon and Macaulay, and resented the fact that the public did not do the same. In his *Education*, perhaps to conceal his resentment, he skipped over his work on the *History* (along with his marriage of thirteen years).

In nineteenth-century America, the sharp edges of the Puritan world were being dissolved. In that moral limbo called "Progress," the Ability to Get Things Done seemed the highest virtue. But the inherited Adams vision of a world of principles remained unclouded. In the eyes of the Adamses, God and the Devil had never ceased to battle. Neither the approval of the elegant few nor the plebiscite of the common millions could change ancient definitions of Good and Evil. "I believe," John Adams wrote to Jefferson in 1819, "no effort in favour of Virtue is lost."

This sharp moral vision did not promote practical success when the fittest had become confused with the best. And it is not surprising that the Adamses, who never lost their talent for intimacy, showed an equally remarkable talent for making enemies. "The Adamses have a genius," James Russell Lowell explained (and was quoted approvingly by Charles Francis Jr. in his autobiography), "for saying even a gracious thing in an ungracious way!" And they were quick to assume that the strength and obstinacy of their enemies might be a clue to the righteousness of their own causes.

Virtue, it seemed, must have a certain gruffness. "I cannot help suspecting," John Adams noted in Paris before the French Revolution, "that the more elegance, the less virtue, in all times and countries." Yet, at the same time, a democracy with no check on the whim of the populace was "the most ignoble, unjust, and detestable form of government." The Adamses' view of the world and of their own role in the public service thus made them peculiarly adept at casting others in the role of "enemies."

Personal independence meant being wary of dependence on *any*one's good opinion. "You recommend me to attend the town-meetings and make speeches; to meet with caucuses and join political clubs," the young John Quincy Adams wrote his father in April, 1794. "But I am afraid of all these things. They might make me a better politician, and give me an earlier chance of appearing as a public man; but that would throw me completely in the power of the people, and all my future life would be one of dependence. I had rather continue some time longer in obscurity, and make some provision for fortune, before I sally out in quest of fame or of public honors." Perhaps it was this fear of dependence along with a sometimes dyspeptic caution that led him to another "principle," which he said he had learned from a boyhood crush on an actress whom he had seen performing in Paris: "that lesson of never forming an acquaintance with an actress to which I have since invariably adhered, and which I would lay as an injunction on all my sons."

When his son Charles Francis was first elected to the Massachusetts legislature in 1840, John Quincy warned him against the "opposition and defeats and slanders and treacheries, and above all fickleness of public favor." And this same Charles Francis warned *his* son Charles Francis Jr. from London in November, 1861, against the demagogues who "become the mere sport of fortune. Today they shine because they have caught at a good opportunity. Tomorrow, the light goes out and they are found mired at the bottom of a ditch. These are the men of temporary celebrity. . . . Every civilised nation is full of them. . . . They sacrifice their consistency for the sake of power, and surrender their future fame in exchange for the applause of their own day."

This lesson was not lost, either, on the fourth generation of eminent Adamses. The tendency of public opinion to confuse moral issues bred in them a deep suspicion of democracy. "Like Henry," Brooks wrote in 1919, "I inherited a belief in the great democratic dogma, as I inherited my pew in the church at Quincy, but . . . I reverted to the pure Calvinistic philosophy." When President Eliot of Harvard, having heard one of Brooks's lectures at the Law School, observed that Brooks seemed to have little respect for democracy, Brooks retorted, "Do you think I'm a damned fool!"

The only eminent Adams who professed respect for popular opinion was the only one who had deserted the statehouse and the library for the marketplace. Charles Francis Jr. explained in 1878 that the purpose of the Massachusetts Railroad Commission, the pioneer regulatory agency which he helped create, was to serve "as a sort of lens by means of which the scattered rays of public opinion could be concentrated to a focus and brought to bear upon a given point." The foundation of his lifelong effort at railroad reform in the heyday of the railroad buccaneers was his faith in "the eventual supremacy of an enlightened public opinion." But he had contempt for his successful business associates. "Business success — money-getting," he remarked, ". . . comes from a rather low instinct. . . . It is rarely met with in combination with the finer or more interesting traits of character. I have known, and known tolerably well, a good many 'successful' men — 'big' financially — men famous during the last half-century; and a less interesting crowd I do not care to encounter. Not one that I have ever known would I care to meet again, either in this world or in the next; nor is one of them associated in my mind with the idea of humor, thought or refinement."

The compromising world of public opinion was not a natural habitat for Adamses. In their world of moral purposes, compromise was weakness, for the battle was between Virtue and Vice. "In every civilization," Brooks Adams concluded in 1919, "there are, as Saint Paul pointed out, two principles in conflict — the law, or the moral principle, and the flesh, or the evil principle."

In the mind of the fighting Adamses there was, of course, never any doubt of the side on which they were destined to be generals. "Your father and grandfather," John Quincy wrote to his son Charles Francis in 1840, "have fought their way through the world against hosts of adversaries, open and close, disguised and masked; with many lukewarm and more than one or two perfidious friends. The world is and will continue to be prolific of such characters. Live in peace with them; never upbraid, never trust them. But — 'don't give up the ship!' Fortify your mind against disappointments — *aequam memento rebus in arduis servare mentem* — keep up your courage, and go ahead!" This conviction of personal rectitude saved one Adams after another from the temptation to give public answer to enemies. They took a lofty attitude to those very electoral bodies whose favor they needed, they refused to build a patronage machine, and when slandered chose not to collect and publish the documents they possessed that would exonerate them. As a consequence, they bottled up their hatreds, and suffered in principled silence rather than sink to the level of their enemies. In the ceaseless war between Virtue and Vice, the defeat of any one generation of Adamses was only a minor skirmish.

Beginning with John Adams, the family constructed its own Rogue's Gallery of Public Enemies. John Adams could not tolerate Benjamin Franklin; he came to detest Hamilton; and his famous friendship with Jefferson matured only after both had retired from active politics. John Quincy Adams (then an unmellow fifty-nine) wrote in his diary for November 23, 1835, after complaining of the "conspiracy against me" at the conference at Ghent: "Among the dark spots in human nature which, in the course of my life, I have observed, the devices of rivals to ruin me have been sorry pictures of the heart of man. They first exhibited themselves at college, but in the short time that I was there, their operation could not be of much effect. But from the day I quitted the walls of Harvard, Harrison Gray Otis, Theophilus Parsons, Timothy Pickering, James A. Bayard, Henry Clay, Jonathan Russell, William H. Crawford, John C. Calhoun, Andrew Jackson, Daniel Webster, and John Davis, W. B. Giles, and John Randolph, have used up their faculties in base and dirty tricks to thwart my progress in life and destroy my character." Passionate enmities, though shifting from generation to generation, were an Adams inheritance.

It is not surprising, then, that John Adams's great-grandsons Henry and Brooks, who had given up the political battle, translated the penchant for personal enmity into cosmic terms. Brooks, who saw "the flesh . . . incarnated in the principle of competition . . . rooted in the passions of greed, avarice, and cruelty," cast bankers, the centralizing moneyed interests, in a Satanic role. Henry, too, fell prey to his own version of the Protocols of the Elders of Zion, and felt compelled to believe that the forces of Evil were well organized in some conspiracy. At the same time both Henry and Brooks in remarkable feats of intellectual acrobatics, balanced the dogmas of nineteenth-century physics on the dogmas of seventeenth-century theology.

The Adams tradition of public service was not built without cost. Different members of the family, according to their sex, their age, and their temperament, were all called upon for sacrifice. The least celebrated Adamses were, of course, the women. And if we ever doubted that women are the Forgotten Men of History, the Adams Saga should remind us. While the men of the Adams family were performing heroic deeds in public, the Adams women were doing a private work that required characters no less stoic and courageous. The democratization of American life in the four generations from John Adams to Henry Adams had hardly begun to change the place of women. The wives of the Adamses continued to pay a secret price for the advertised achievements of their husbands.

The only female Adams who has had anything like her due from historians is John's wife, Abigail (1744–1818). Still, despite the fact that she was one of the brightest, most public-minded, and most sacrificing of the family, she has been treated as little more than a mirror for her husband and the age. The entry for her in the concise edition of the authoritative *Dictionary of American Biography* sums her up in the single phrase: "Wrote distinguished letters containing vivid pictures of the times." Her personal contribution, and her essential part in the careers of her husband John and her eldest son John Quincy, have not yet had the spotlight.

"Our history," Charles Francis Adams complained in his memoir of his grandmother Abigail in 1875, "is for the most part wrapped up in the forms of office." And in explaining the sacrifices of Abigail he clearly revealed the institutions which confined her and hid her from view. "In every instance of domestic convulsions, and when the pruning hook is deserted for the sword and musket, the sacrifice of feelings made by the female sex is unmixed with a hope of worldly compensation. With them there is no ambition to gratify, no fame to be gained by the simple negative virtue of privations suffered in silence. There is no action to drown in its noise and bustle a full sense of the pain that must inevitably attend it. The lot of women, in times of trouble, is to be a passive spectator of events which she can scarcely hope to make subservient to her own fame, or indeed to control in any way."

Abigail Adams's accomplishments are doubly remarkable because in her youth, as she observed, "it was fashionable to ridicule female learning." In 1817 she recalled: "My early education did not partake of the abundant opportunities which the present days offer, and which even our common country schools now afford. *I never was sent to any school.* I was always sick. Female education, in the best families, went no further than writing and arithmetic; in some few and rare instances, music and dancing." The custom of the age condemned her to the private heroics of loneliness and long separations from those she loved. In the midst of her years of absence (1779–1784) from her husband during his long diplomatic mission to France and England for the new nation, she wrote (December 23, 1782): "I look back to the early days of our acquaintance and friendship, as to the days of Love and Innocence; and with an indiscribable pleasure I have seen near a score of years roll over our Heads, with an affection heightned and improved by time — nor have the dreary years of absence in the smallest degree effaced from my mind the Image of the dear, untitled Man to whom I gave my Heart. I cannot sometimes refrain considering the Honours with which he is invested as badges of my unhappiness. . . . Yet a cruel world too often injures my feelings by wondering how a person possessed of domestic attachments can sacrifice them by absenting herself *for years.*

" 'If you had known,' said a person to me the other day, 'that Mr. Adams would have remained so long abroad, would you have consented that he should have gone?' I recollected myself a moment and then spoke the real dictates of my heart: 'If I had known, sir, that Mr. Adams could have effected what he has done, I would not only have submitted to the absence I have endured, painful as it has been, but I would not have opposed it, even though three years more should be added to the number (which Heaven avert!). I feel a pleasure in being able to sacrifice my selfish passions to the general good, and in imitating the example which has taught me to consider myself and family but as the small dust of the balance, when compared with the great community.' "

During those lonely years she had heavy and diverse responsibilities: directing the family farm, recording prices current and rates of exchange and making up the invoices to keep the farm afloat, reporting political facts, playing both mother and father to the children at home, and instructing her absent eldest son in his morals and his duties.

She showed more than domestic fortitude. Later, when she rejoined her husband as the wife of the first minister from the United States to Great Britain, she endured the snubs of Queen Charlotte and the court, and helped the ministry of the United States, despite the strictest economy, cut a respected figure in London.

Even John Adams's presidency did not end the times of separation. While Adams was serving as president in the capital at Philadelphia, Abigail — partly because of her illness, partly because of the high cost of everything — remained for long periods at Quincy. In a letter to her in February, 1797, he explained the tribulations of the presidency:

"I hope you will not communicate to anybody the hints I give you about our prospects, but they appear every day worse and worse. House rent at twenty-seven hundred dollars a year, fifteen hundred dollars for a carriage, one thousand for one pair of horses, all the glasses, ornaments, kitchen furniture, the best chairs, settees, plateaus, &c., all to purchase, all the china, delft or wedg-wood, glass and crockery of every sort of purchase, and not a farthing probably will the House of Representatives allow, al-though the Senate have voted a small addition. All the linen besides. I shall not pretend to keep more than one pair of horses for a carriage, and one for a saddle. Secretaries, servants, wood, charities which are demanded as rights, and the million dittoes present such a prospect as is enough to disgust anyone. Yet not one word must we say."

On November 1, 1800, when he became the first resident of the White House, he asked "heaven to bestow the best of blessing on this house, and on all that shall hereafter inhabit it. May none but honest and wise men ever rule under this roof!" Abigail, hastening down from Quincy to join him, lost her way on the muddy paths from Baltimore to the swamps then called Washing-ton. They spent only an unhappy few months there, watching the nation refuse John Adams his hoped-for accolade of a second term, and incidentally preparing the residence for occupancy by a bitter enemy.

From about the time of her husband's election to the presi-dency, Abigail suffered an intermittent fever from which she never fully recovered. From 1801 until her death in 1818, she stayed at Quincy. Despite a series of family tragedies — a daughter lost in infancy, another daughter stillborn, a son who died in 1800, the death of her only remaining daughter in 1813 — she remained "a mortal enemy to anything but a cheerful countenance and a merry heart, which, Solomon tells us, does good like a medicine."

The other female Adamses, who lacked Abigail's epistolary eloquence, were left unsung, and almost unnoticed in history. Mrs. John Quincy Adams (Louisa Johnson Adams), born to an English mother and a Maryland father who was a merchant in London and later became the United States consul there, had lived her youth in France. On a meager budget, in extravagant St. Petersburg, she managed to maintain the dignity of a United States ministry. And while Napoleon was approaching Paris, she con-veyed her son Charles Francis across Europe toward their new assignment in London. But she remains a shadowy figure, now best remembered through Henry Adams's characterization. "Louisa was charming, like a Romney portrait, but among her many charms that of being a New England woman was not one. The defect was serious. Her future mother-in-law, Abigail, . . . was troubled by the fear that Louisa might not be made of stuff stern enough, to suit a New England climate, or to make an efficient wife for her paragon son, and Abigail was right on that point, as on most others where sound judgment was involved." Henry as a boy saw Louisa in her seventies "thoroughly weary of being beaten about a stormy world." To the boy she seemed "singularly peaceful, a vision of silver gray, presiding over her old President and her Queen Anne mahogany; an exotic, like her Sèvres china; an object of deference to everyone, and of great affection to her son Charles; but hardly more Bostonian than she had been fifty years before, on her wedding-day, in the shadow of the Tower of London."

As for Henry's own mother, Mrs. Charles Francis Adams (née Abigail Brown Brooks), he mentions her only twice in his *Education:* once, to note that she was one of the seven surviving children who shared the bequest of "what was supposed to be the largest estate in Boston, about two million dollars," and again, to observe that while his father was the United States minister "her success and popularity in England exceeded that of her husband" and that she "averred that every woman who lived a certain time in England came to look and dress like an Englishwoman, no matter how she struggled." On the subject of this devoted and long-suffering mother, Charles Francis Jr. is hardly more articulate than his brother. The only account of her in his autobiography recalls how she "at once fell into tears and deep agitation" when word was received in 1861 that her husband had been named minister to Great Britain. "My mother, in some respects remarkably calculated for social life, took a constitutional and sincere pleasure in the forecast of evil. She delighted in the dark side of anticipation; she did not really think so; but liked to think, and say, she thought so. She indulged in the luxury of woe!"

From his *Education* Henry entirely omitted his own wife, Marian Hooper, perhaps because he felt her death so deeply, and held himself partly responsible for her suicide. He did commission a memorial to her by Saint-Gaudens, which still stands in Rock Creek Cemetery in Washington, but he would not talk about her after she died, and was known to leave the room when her name was mentioned. Henry's attitude toward women remains a dark conundrum which conceals the women we would like to learn about through him. In *Mont-Saint-Michel and Chartres* he asserted with theological dogmatism the superiority of "Woman." At the same time he pontificated to his friend Mrs. Winthrop Chanler: "American woman is a failure, she has held nothing together, neither State nor Church, nor Society nor Family. . . . On the whole I think she is a worse failure than the American man who is surely failure enough." Since his view of women — he preferred to call them "Woman" — was so extravagantly theological and sociological, it is small wonder that he had problems with individuals. His romantic attachment, after his wife's death, to Elizabeth Cameron, the attractive young wife of Senator James Donald Cameron, is puzzling and impenetrable. He revealed a traditional Adams problem when he told her that "women are naturally neither daughters, sisters, lovers, nor wives, but mothers."

Brooks married "Daisy" Davis, the sister of Mrs. Henry Cabot Lodge, within a month after he met her. When he proposed, he warned her that he was "an eccentric almost to the point of madness" and that if she married him "she must do it on her own responsibility and at her own risk." This warning was one of the few understatements that the unstable Brooks ever uttered. Daisy, herself unstable, was expected to act as her husband's nurse, scapegoat, travel agent, guide, and psychotherapist.

The Adams Saga shows us how ill adapted to this New World civilization were the ancient institutions for accumulating distinction, for accelerating and increasing the motives of *noblesse*. The Old World maxim *noblesse oblige* meant that a noble inheritance required noble deeds. The Family, like many other of the most potent Old World institutions, was cumulative, while the civilization of the United States in every generation remained a miracle of renewal. America was an annual-model civilization — obsessively reaching for the latest and the newest. And Americans never ceased to be nervous lest the Good should prove to be the enemy of the New. Was not the willingness to experiment the grand modern — New World — virtue?

Even the extraordinary good fortune of being born an Adams might be peculiarly troublesome for an American. Inherited distinction created imperious community expectations and might nourish an unmerited sense of personal inadequacy. Becoming an American meant being willing to be measured, not against ancestors but against one's own hopes and possibilities. Charles Francis Adams Jr. noted the resentment that his father had come to feel. The "constant reference" to John and John Quincy "in connection with himself annoyed and at times irritated him. He could not habituate himself to it, nor learn to take it lightly and as matter of course, — at one time the commonplace utterance of some not unkindly man, devoid of good taste, and at another the obvious retort of a coarse and commonplace opponent, quick to avail himself of a telling personal allusion. For all such it was so very easy to refer to a noticeable family deterioration, — "sharp decline" was the approved form of speech — and the reference was sure to elicit a sneering laugh, and round of blockhead applause from the benches of the groundlings. . . . To have one's ancestors unceasingly flung in one's face is unpleasant, and listening to the changes incessantly rung upon them becomes indubitably monotonous."

The weight of the family inheritance accumulated through the century. "I must study politics and war," John Adams prophesied, "that my sons may have liberty to study mathematics and philosophy. My sons ought to study mathematics and philosophy, geography, natural history and naval architecture, navigation, commerce and agriculture, in order to give their sons a right to study painting, poetry, music, architecture, statuary, tapestry and porcelain." John Adams's generation was peculiarly posterity-conscious. Jefferson, too, was haunted by his duty to the future. But while Jefferson was preoccupied with man-in-general, Adams saw his own descendants as the representatives of a developing nation.

In societies less committed to judge each generation on its own merit, the accumulated glory of the Adams family could have provided an increasingly solid foundation for the public careers of later generations. But the United States was a nation of the uprooted. "We may consider each generation as a distinct nation," declared Jefferson, "with a right, by the will of its majority, to bind themselves, but none to bind the succeeding generation, more than the inhabitants of another country."

By the fourth generation, Adamses were paying a price for their family's distinction. They had become entangled in their past in a fashion characteristically un-American. Yet even then they tried — and largely succeeded — in making a national resource out of the family experience. They mapped the course of Adamses in American history, not to glorify the latter-day Adamses (quite the contrary!) but as a way of charting the career of a nation. A critic of Edward Gibbon's *Autobiography* once observed that the author tended to confuse himself with the Roman Empire. Readers of the scores of volumes of Adams letters, diaries, autobiographies, biographies, monographs, and historical treatises can see how closely the Adamses identified their fortunes with the destiny of the nation. The more we read of them and the more vividly we trace the Adams Saga, the clearer it becomes that their destiny was a measure of the nation.

As early as 1860, Henry Adams, who had been reading Gibbon, concluded, "Our house needs a historian in this generation and I feel strongly tempted by the quiet and sunny prospect." But even before Henry, the House of Adams had begun to chronicle the rise of the nation in the career of the family. Charles Francis Adams spent seven years editing ten volumes of the letters and papers of his grandfather John and writing a biography of him, and another ten years editing twelve volumes of the diary of his father, John Quincy. Charles Francis Jr. spent his last years writing about colonial Massachusetts, as well as a biography of his father.

The talented Adamses became hypersensitive about their own inadequacies. They became as unfair to themselves as John and John Quincy had been to political enemies. It is painful to see the able Charles Francis Jr. flagellate himself with unreasonable expectations. Overwhelmed by the distinction of his forebears, he reports in his autobiography the masochistic delight with which he disposed of the diaries of his youth:

"In those years I kept a diary. So doing was enjoined on me by my father; and I kept it from my Latin School days until the time I went into the army, in my twenty-fifth year. Later on I kept the volumes sealed up in a package, with directions that they should be destroyed in the event of my death. A few years ago . . . I opened the parcel, and looked through the volumes. I did this during my Sundays, passed in the house at Quincy while living in Boston — very charming Sundays they were, too. . . . During those days I exhumed the sealed package, and thirty years later, read over that old diary. The revelation of myself to myself was positively shocking. Then and there I was disillusioned. Up to that time — and I was then about fifty-five — I had indulged in the pleasing delusion that it was in me . . . to do, or be, something rather noticeable. I have never thought so since. . . . I saw myself in a looking-glass, and I said — 'Can that indeed be I!' and, reflecting, I then realized that the child was father of the man! It was with difficulty I forced myself to read through that dreadful record; and, as I finished each volume, it went into the fire; and I stood over it until the last leaf was ashes. It was a tough lesson; but a useful one. I had seen myself as others had seen me. I have never felt the same about myself since. I now humbly thank fortune that I have almost got through life without making a conspicuous ass of myself."

At the opening of the twentieth century, Henry Adams, referring to himself in the third person, fashioned his whole autobiography into an elegant new genre of literary self-deprecation. He was deeply pained when he read his brother Charles's biography of their father. "Now I understand," he exclaimed, "why I refused so obstinately to do it myself. These biographies are murder, and in this case, to me, would be both patricide and suicide. They belittle the victim and the assassin equally. They are like bad photographs and distorted perspectives. . . . I have sinned myself, and deeply, and am no more worthy to be called anything, but, thank my diseased and dyspeptic nervous wreck, I did not assassinate my father."

When Charles Francis Jr. the eldest of his generation, thought of joining the Union army to fulfill the family's patriotic tradition, he consulted his father. "My father, with the coldness of temperament natural to him, took a wholly wrong view of the subject and situation, did not believe in any one taking a hand in actual fight, and wholly failed to realize that it would have been an actual disgrace had his family, of all possible families American, been wholly unrepresented in the field. And I was the one to go!" When Charles Francis Jr. had put the question, his father had simply replied, "But none of his predecessors had been soldiers. Why should he?" To preserve the family's reputation, Charles Francis Jr. broke a family tradition. He served in the Union cavalry with bravery and distinction, reaching the rank of brevet brigadier general.

To reveal the special relations of Family to Democracy, the fourth generation — that of John Quincy II, Charles Francis Jr., Henry, and Brooks — is the most articulate. In that generation, men of large talents showed themselves conspicuously unable to come to terms with their noble inheritance. They spent themselves in quarreling with one another, in debunking their Puritan ancestry, and, finally, in maligning the human race. This is all worth reflecting on as a parable of the problem of *noblesse oblige* in a democracy. That fourth generation, it is also worth noticing, was actually the first in which all the family started with a comfortable money inheritance.

John Adams's talented descendants had become embittered — not only by what they felt to be their own inadequacy to the family inheritance but by the confusions of a democratized America. Henry and Brooks used all the apparatus of classical learning and modern science to document their frustration, to justify their pessimism, to prove that what went wrong was not just with the Adams clan or with America, but with the forces in the universe. Measuring themselves against the eighteenth-century eminence, they could not relax into a proper appreciation of themselves. Had not America — and perhaps the whole cosmos — abandoned the Adamses? Or had Adamses begun to abandon America?

What had become of the patriotism and the conscientious morality that had made John an enthusiast for the American Revolution and John Quincy a passionate opponent of slavery? The stoic and Puritan virtues no longer qualified an Adams for national political leadership. And their refined literary talents, ill suited to the newly potent mass-circulating books and newspapers, tempted them to withdraw into a literary world inhabited not by millions but by thousands. John Adams's great-grandson Henry Adams wrote to John Hay from Paris in 1900 that he cared "not one French sour grape how soon or how late this damned humanity breaks its neck."

American genius for renewal, American suspicion of last year's (much less last century's) model of *any*thing, including a family, stifled these latter-day Adamses with the distinction of their grandfathers.

The Adams Saga unfolded with a providential American irony. The nation's peculiar glory was its opportunity for a man to become a self-made aristocrat. John, the most American of the Adamses, had proved this was possible. But, the most distinguished American family inheritance, after only *four* generations (which would have been just a brief chapter in the chronicles of the Cecils, the Percys, the Churchills, or other distinguished Old World families) had already become a heavy burden to the descendants. In a nation which never ceased to idolize the self-made man, anything could be embarrassing that kept a man from standing on his own feet. And the civilization which Adamses had done so much to build would continue to flourish by finding ways for new John Adamses to spring out of each anonymous generation.

THE ADAMS CHRONICLES

1
Sensations of Freedom
[1758–1770]

FIRST there was the land, and then the people. Along the harshest coast they disembarked, erecting tiny seaboard settlements: delicate toeholds that barely held their grip. The land, the elements, repelled all but the hardy and stubborn and desperate. Why did they come? To escape old tyrannies and lost opportunities; to seek freedom and a fresh beginning. The New World offered them — perhaps for the last time in man's history — a new land and a new chance.

They entered the land at harbors that would become Boston, New York, Philadelphia, Charleston. As more immigrants from oppression and injustice, or of hope and fervor, arrived, the seaboard colonies grew. The people flowed onto the coastal slope, and farmed and traded. Who were these people? Early Puritans abused by the Church of England. Mennonites refused freedom of worship in Prussia. The Huguenots of France whose liberty was destroyed by Louis XIV. English and Dutch traders and merchants, discontented Germans, Scots from northern Ireland, Catholics and

Quakers. And the English poor unable to pay their debts and thrown into prison, only to be sent out to try their luck in Georgia. They named their new settlements after the past — Dresden, New London, Bryn Mawr, Havre de Grace, Dublin — or for the future — New Hope, Providence, Jericho, Beacon.

They pushed across the land, overflowing the Appalachian barrier, discovering the first of the great inland rivers, and the immensity beyond. Behind them, trade flourished, farms thrived, new schools and colleges were founded. And along the once-hostile coast, an upper class gathered wealth and self-confidence, and discovered its own eighteenth-century refinement apart from Europe.

To be sure, these early Americans were under England's rule. But they were already forming their own country. During a rapid half century of growth, from 1713 to 1763, their number increased fourfold; their colonies tripled in size. But most important, they gained a fast-emerging sense of the land, themselves, and their destiny. An empire was being born, and with it the growing awareness, spreading from northern mountains to southern swampland, that the land was theirs, and that they were, indeed, Americans.

Almost at the exact middle of this period, in 1735, John Adams was born in Braintree, in the Province of Massachusetts Bay. His family were farmers and preachers: strong people, resilient and stubborn. In the light of what happened later, he would need these characteristics and more.

His father, who was called Deacon John Adams to distinguish him from the son, was a farmer, shoemaker, tithingman, constable (tax collector), militia officer, and nine times a selectman, and for fourteen years a deacon of the North Precinct meetinghouse in Braintree. He was a quiet and calm man, firm in his opinions, "a typical New England yeoman" (as one of his grandsons later described him). It was not surprising that John Adams wrote upon his father's death in 1761, "Almost all the Business of the Town [was] managed by him for 20 Years together." As the father had managed a town, so the son would help mold a nation.

John Adams was a complex man who kept a diary and saved almost all of his correspondence — a practice his family

DETAIL: VIEW OF OLD BOSTON. PAINTING ON WOOD, ARTIST UNKNOWN, 1730–1740

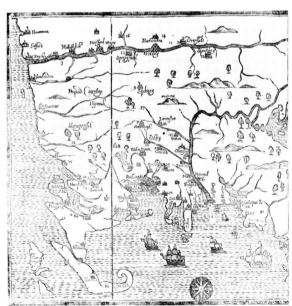

Settlers charted the coves and harbors of their new land. The earliest map (right) was a woodcut of New England. West is at the top and east at the bottom; Cape Cod to the lower left and Rhode Island off the coast—as an island. By 1740, Boston (above) was a major harbor that welcomed billowing ships of commerce.

DETAIL: WHITE HILLS MAP.
WOODCUT BY JOHN FOSTER, 1677

would maintain for four generations — thereby providing an overwhelming and valuable record of America's history. In his writings, Adams constantly analyzed himself and his time. "A Pen," he once wrote, "is certainly an excellent Instrument to fix a Mans Attention and to inflame his Ambition." Writing did both for John Adams, and perhaps that ambition, more than any other single thing, drove him to keep his record. Whatever the reason, there is nothing comparable from any other founder of the republic. Benjamin Franklin's writings of his early life in Boston and Philadelphia were the reflections of an old man. So, too, was Thomas Jefferson's autobiography, compiled when he was seventy-seven. George Washington kept diaries as a young man, but often recorded only the mundane — the weather, the state of the crops, distances — and ignored the profound.

Not so John Adams. His pen recorded his life from the age of twenty until, with interruptions, his last years. And his life, his generation, was unlike any other in American history, which measured and resolved serious and original political problems, and ignited the great beacons of American principles: the Declaration of Independence and the federal Constitution. His was a time of revolution and destruction, but also of creation and growth. A new federal state would burst forth from the old British Empire, and men like Adams would wrestle with and proclaim the first American ideas, and define the American character.

Almost symbolically, an early entry in John Adams's diary, one dated November 18, 1755, recorded "a severe Shock of an Earthquake" that caused his father's house in Braintree "to rock and reel and crack as if it would fall in ruins about us. Chimnies were shatter'd by it within one mile of my Fathers house." The seismic waves were felt on both sides of the Atlantic Ocean.

On August 6, 1755, at an early hour, a messenger from Worcester appeared on horseback at the Adams farmhouse on Penn's Hill, Braintree. He led a second horse, and spent the day resting. At sunrise the next morning he and John Adams started off and covered the sixty miles westward to Worcester that day. Adams was to be the town's new schoolmaster, a job arranged for him by his father and the Reverend Thaddeus Maccarty immediately after his graduation from Harvard four weeks before. He would teach fifty boys, aged five to fifteen, at the Center School, a one-room log house with fireplace facing the Worcester town green. His pay would be meager, but it included lodging with "one Green" and later with Dr. and Mrs. Nahum Willard.

Adams found his classroom small and crowded, the boys restless, the school-day long — from early morning until evening. He organized his pupils into clusters by age, much as his own boyhood school had been arranged, and soon the murmur of reading and memorization filled the little room. In winter, the room was also filled with the warmth of the fire and the stench of bodies "stitched" into their clothing until spring. Adams contemplated his position, and measured his ambition.

Worcester was a coarse frontier town, closer to the harsh realities of the French and Indian War than the established social life of Boston that Adams had known. Perhaps homesick, he began writing in his diary, thinking it an aid to self-cultivation. "A Journal," he wrote, "scrawled with Algebraical signs, and interspersed with Questions of Law, Husbandry, natural History &c., will be a useful Thing."

As his diary and his letters soon revealed, John Adams was a stubborn, warmhearted, self-important and impetuous young man — and a Yankee character. Benjamin Franklin would write about him in a letter to Robert R. Livingston in 1783: "I am persuaded that he means well for his Country, is always an honest Man, often a wise one, but sometimes and in some things, absolutely out of his senses." Ill-tempered at times, a hypochondriac, Adams came by his eccentricities naturally. He wrote of his parents' home in Braintree in 1758: "Passion, Accident, Freak, Humour, govern this House."

As a schoolmaster in Worcester, Adams fidgeted. Birth, money, position impressed him, and teaching at the edge of the American frontier promised little in the way of advancement or wealth. He was determined to improve himself, and his Puritan introspection and passionate self-questioning — traits later seen in his sons and grandsons to the sixth generation — filled his writings. He was twenty when he entered in his diary: "I can as easily still the fierce Tempests or Stop the rapid Thunderbolt, as command the motives and operations of my own mind. . . . My Brains seem constantly in as great Confusion, and wild disorder as Miltons Chaos. I have never any bright, refulgent Ideas. Every Thing appears in my mind, dim and obscure like objects seen thro' a dirty glass or roiled water. . . . Vanity I am sensible is my cardinal Vice and Folly, and I am in continual Danger, when in Company, of being led into an ignis fatuus Chase by it, without the strictist Caution and Watchfulness over myself."

Adams seldom enjoyed a triumph he did not later question and examine, often at length. At times, while chatting with his new Worcester friends, he fell to castigating the morals of gentlemen with laced clothing. Later, he would lash himself for his weakness and the looseness of his tongue. "I resolve never," he wrote in his diary, "to affect Wit upon lace wastecoats, or large Estates or their Possessors. I now Resolve for the future, never to say an ill-naturd . . . [or] an envious Thing concerning Governors, Judges, Ministers, Clerks, Sheriffs, Lawyers, or any other honorable or Lucrative offices or officers."

Such admonitions were mixed with self-doubts. Introspection, rather than slowing him, pricked him to new effort. One entry, written in his round hand, vowed: "I will Rouse up my Mind and fix my Attention. I will stand collected within my self and think upon what I read and what I see. I will strive with all my soul to be something more than Persons who have had less Advantages than myself."

And again he promised: "I am resolved to rise with the Sun and to study the Scriptures on Thursday, Fryday, Saturday and Sunday mornings, and to study some Latin author the other 3 mornings. Noons and Nights I intend to read English Authors. This is my fixt Determination, and I will set down every neglect and every compliance with this Resolution."

Fortunately, entries after these ardent resolutions showed him attending to the Worcester social life, such as it was, of teas and dinners and conversations. At one point, after four consecutive days without an entry, he noted only: "All Spent in absolute Idleness, or what is worse, gallanting the Girls."

In 1766, a young and unknown limner in pastel crayons, Benjamin Blyth, met John Adams during the lawyer's visit to Salem. Blyth, whose advertisements promised portraits "having good likenesses," did this work, the earliest-known portrait of Adams, when Adams was near his thirty-first birthday. The likeness, as advertised, was excellent. Adams was indeed chubby, with a soft, bland face that reveals little of the character that would later develop. He described himself as looking "like a short, thick fat Archbishop of Canterbury." And so he did.

JOHN ADAMS. PASTEL BY BENJAMIN BLYTH, 1766

He was young and passionate, and had an unusual New England sauciness. While he might scold about "Manners, &c." in others, he could also (later) advocate bundling, "tho Discretion must be used, and Caution."

He was not handsome, but short, balding, given to fat. He had "learned the Use of [tobacco] upon Ponds of Ice, when Skating with Boys at Eight Years of Age," and although he gave it up at certain times, most notably when he went abroad, he was, to his regret, a user of tobacco in several forms for sixty years. One of his earliest efforts to stop is recorded in his diary on Friday, March 12, 1756. He bet "a pair of gloves with Mrs. Willard that she would not see me chew tobacco this month." Whether she did or not isn't recorded, but it is clear that John Adams, throughout his life, struggled with Puritanic self-control.

Adams was determined to be more than a frontier schoolmaster. Near his schoolhouse on the Worcester green was the square white courthouse, from which three quarters of Worcester's residents took their living, directly or indirectly. There, country lawyers — and pettifoggers — met for the General Sessions of the Peace, and, four times a year, for the Court of Common Pleas, and, in October, for the Massachusetts Superior Court. Dr. Willard wanted John Adams to become a doctor, and the young schoolmaster liked the study of physics. But the actual business of being a doctor revolted him: as for cutting or bleeding a patient, Adams felt certain that as soon as he took scalpel in hand he would vomit. The Adams family, for its part, and most of John Adams's friends, thought he would become a minister. But "frigid John Calvin" did not attract him, and he had growing doubts about some "disputed points" of theological doctrine.

The courthouse, so near the school, drew him in. There he met and immediately liked James Putnam, a Worcester lawyer in his early thirties, witty and intelligent. On August 21, 1756, Adams contracted with Putnam to study law "under his Inspection for two years." The twenty-first was a Saturday, and on Monday the new student arrived at Putnam's house and "began Law." The decision had not been easy, or carelessly reached. "Necessity drove me to this

Determination," Adams wrote as he began his studies, "but my Inclination I think was to preach."

Adams's two years under Putnam prepared him well. But Worcester was not Boston. Adams longed to be where the action was. Besides, Braintree was home, and he missed it. On October 5, 1758, his law studies completed, John Adams returned to Braintree. He would start his practice, but he must also be admitted to the bar.

Three weeks later, Adams rode into Boston. His purpose was to seek admission to the bar through Jeremiah Gridley, a prominent Boston lawyer. Adams had been to Boston many times, most recently with his friend Samuel Quincy. He went to the courthouse, a building he knew well, but upon entering the courtroom he felt strange and awkward. It was ten-thirty in the morning, a case was in progress, and between the two presiding judges and the spectators was a large oval table with a green top covered with papers and inkpots. Around it sat a dozen lawyers, including Jeremiah Gridley, James Otis, Jr., and Benjamin Prat. "I felt Shy, under Awe and concern," Adams wrote in his diary for the day. The lawyers, he said, all "looked sour."

He correctly saw that this was not the time to approach Gridley about being admitted to the bar. He spent the day at court instead, and enjoyed Boston that night: "went to Consort with Samll. Quincy and Dr. [Silvester] Gardiner. There I saw the most Spacious and elegant Room, and the gayest Company of Gentlemen and the Finest Row of Ladies, that I ever saw."

The next day, Adams, still feeling timid, approached Gridley at his house and asked "what Steps to take for an Introduction to the Practice of Law in this Country." Gridley abruptly answered: "Get sworn." It wasn't quite that easy, and Adams soon found himself expounding and defending his legal study. Later, Benjamin Prat wanted to know if he had been sworn in Worcester.

"No," Adams replied.

"Have you a Letter from Mr. Putnam to the Court?"

The answer again was no, and Prat scolded the young Adams: "It would have been most proper to have done one of them things first."

OVERLEAF
When John Adams graduated from Harvard its campus in Cambridge appeared much as it does in the drawing on the next pages. This representation was engraved on copper in 1767 by Paul Revere. Harvard Hall, with cupola, stands in the center; next, to the left, is Hollis Hall and beyond it, Holden Chapel; Stoughton and Massachusetts halls, both eighteenth-century structures, are to the right. In 1775, the Massachusetts Provincial Congress asked Revere to engrave paper money, which he did by cutting this copper plate in half and using the back of it.

Josh Chadwick, del—

A Westerly View of The Co

A *Harvard Hall*   B *Stoughton*   C *Mass*

ges in Cambridge New England

ett   D Hollis   E Holden Chapel

A WESTERLY VIEW OF THE COLLEDGES IN CAMBRIDGE, NEW ENGLAND.
LINE ENGRAVING BY PAUL REVERE, 1767

Chastised, Adams finally persuaded Prat of his qualifications. Gridley, too, sponsored him, and stood up and spoke for him before the bar in Boston on November 6, 1758. (At the same time, Prat sponsored Adams's friend Samuel Quincy.) Adams was admitted. "I shook Hands with the Bar, and received their Congratulations, and invited them over to Stones to drink some Punch. Where the most of us resorted and had a very chearful [Chat]."

Getting a footing in Braintree was difficult for Adams. Cases were few for young lawyers. Almost all the local litigation revolved around strayed livestock, and one argument had resulted after a roan mare belonging to Luke Lambert got into Joseph Field's enclosure. Field had let the mare stay, enjoying his clover; he knew that after a week he could drive her to the public pound, as was the custom, and collect damages. But early in the second week, before he could do this, Lambert came to the pasture fence, stood on it to avoid trespassing, and waved his hat at his horse. The mare trotted out of the pasture, thus depriving Field of his damages.

Field brought suit and lost, but after a year or so, he decided to try again. Seeking out young Adams, he asked him to reopen proceedings and present a new writ that would win the argument. "The Writ," he warned Adams, "must be skilfully drawn."

Adams accepted the case, his first. Several preliminary hearings were held during the fall at the home of Colonel Josiah Quincy, an irascible New Englander whose son Samuel was counsel for the defendant. Adams fretted excessively about his performance and made long lists of "questions" arising from the arguments. In December, when the decision was handed down and Adams learned he had lost, he took the defeat hard, blaming himself and his legal preparation. "The Writt is defective," he told his diary. "It will be said, I undertook the Case but was unable to manage it."

But other cases came to John Adams, and quickly: Braintree folk sued with every season. He won a number of them, although they were hardly cases to cut a reputation on: a felt hat not delivered by the hatmaker; "an action for an old horse versus Samuel Spear." He argued many of his cases a second time in his diary and letters, noting mistakes and points to watch for in the future. He also struggled to control his sharp temper — inherited from his mother — that was only balanced by his keen New England sense of fairness. For him these were years of searching, of pondering his every step forward and backward in his quest. "Shall I look out for a Cause to Speak to," he asked himself, "and exert all the Soul and all the Body I own, to cut a flash, strike amazement, to catch the Vulgar?" Self-satisfaction eluded him.

Adams was a colorful, articulate lawyer. His courtroom style attracted courthouse buffs in Braintree. But he was also a learned man, well-read, intellectually growing, who placed great confidence in the bar and the legal system. He was vehemently opposed to the large numbers of wigmakers, merchants, shoemakers and other impostors passing themselves off as writ drawers and attorneys in Braintree. One day he had had enough, and, according to one account, the following took place:

Adams was presenting a case in the Braintree courtroom. His voice, high and full of anger, lathered the impostors who were representing Braintree citizens. "I would not have taken this case in the first place," he told the court, "if I had not thought it my duty to put down the pettifogging deputy sheriff who drew the writ.

"Good citizens have been defrauded," he went on. "Widows and orphans cheated of their rightful protection under the law. These are dirty and ridiculous litigations. Against this evil the very earth groans and the stones cry out." He remarked that the people of Braintree seemed to resort to lawsuits over any matter. "The village has become so petty quarrelsome," he said, "that a popular saying is going around, 'As litigious as Braintree.'"

Despite his outburst, the lawsuits continued. Indeed, the whole colony needed lawyers as tensions increased over property and sea rights between British and American merchants. Already the ablest graduates of the New England colleges were showing a tendency to go into law instead of theology.

Adams often visited Colonel Quincy to discuss legal questions; in fact, he and the colonel enjoyed one another's company. And, during the spring and summer of 1759, Adams began a long and sometimes painful wooing of Hannah Quincy, the colonel's daughter. Hannah could cut with her tongue, and was not above doing so. Adams was attracted and repelled, and wrote of "her saucy disrespectfull Expressions." She teased him with chat about long courtships, with lies about her correspondence with Dr. Bela Lincoln, and with her flirtations with Richard Cranch and Anthony Wibert. "This is bragging," Adams concluded, but he also worried that "she will drop such Hints, by and by, that I am in Love with her, and will tell others, that she aint obliged to take my meaning by my saying, but let me explain myself, and then I shall receive a Repulse."

Hannah, clearly, had the young men of Braintree dashing about that summer of 1759. Bothered by her guile as much as any, Adams lamented: "I dont know who has been plagued most, Mr. Cranch or I. I think I have as much Reason to complain of being plagued as he." Hannah had John neglecting his work, "out of Humour," and bothered by "Reflection, thinking on a Girl, ill Health, Want of Business, &c. [which] wrought me by insensible degrees into a peevish Mood."

He was, he later wrote in his *Autobiography*, always of an amorous disposition. "And very early, from ten or eleven Years of Age, . . . very fond of the Society of females. I had my favorites among the young Women, and spent many of my Evenings in their Company. . . . They were all modest and virtuous Girls, and always maintained this Character through Life. No Virgin or Matron ever had cause to blush at the sight of me, or to regret her Acquaintance with me."

Neither, of course, would Hannah Quincy. Their brief, but strong, romance that summer of 1759 soon ended.

In 1760, Hannah Quincy married Dr. Lincoln, but Adams still frequented her father's house. The two men dined and had tea together as usual. On June 25, 1760, they went out fishing in Boston Harbor in the colonel's canoe. Adams's account is rich and full of detail. The wind "died away into a Clock Calm," and then, when it turned and "blew afresh," the colonel became seasick. They had to put into Hangman's Island, where the colonel "vomited, very heartily, and then weak and faignt, and spiritless, he crawled up to the Gunning House, and wrapping his great Coat around him, lay down on the sea weed and slept." The day ended under a half-moon as

"THE REVD. WILLIAM SMITH'S HOUSE WEYMOUTH."
INK AND WATERCOLOR, ARTIST UNKNOWN, 1765–1800

In May, 1738, the Reverend William Smith bought this house for £45. His four children, including Abigail, were born here, and soon Smith had to spend another £100 for "Spouts," "Clab-boards," "Glass," "window Frames," "Painting," and the wages of housewrights to construct the ell behind the parsonage for his expanding family. In this house, John Adams courted Abigail and charmed her stern New England father (left).

THE REVEREND WILLIAM SMITH. ENGRAVING FROM, "THE CHAPPEL OF EASE," BY DANIEL MUNRO WILSON, 1890, AFTER A PAINTING NOW LOST

they "sailed" home. "We had none of the Pleasure of Angling, very little of the Pleasure of Sailing. We had much of the fatigue of Rowing, and some of the Vexation of Disappointment. However the Exercise and the Air and smell of salt Water is wholesome."

During this period, Adams also began visiting the Weymouth parsonage of the Reverend William Smith. Parson Smith's daughters failed to impress Adams favorably, at least on first acquaintance. The oldest, Mary, and the youngest, Betsy, then twelve, were more striking than Abigail, but still, thought Adams, lacking the "wit" and "tenderness" of Hannah Quincy. He found them "not fond, not frank, not candid."

But Adams was changing. At twenty-six, he owned a farm and a house (inherited from his father, who had recently died of "throat distemper"), and he could begin to count on some income from his law practice. He had "gallanted the Girls" mightily, especially Hannah Quincy. Now, he and his friend Richard Cranch discovered the charms and wiles of the two older Smith girls, whose mother was a Quincy. Cranch and Adams often saddled their horses and rode the four miles to Weymouth, which took half an hour, where they could combine legal business during the day with courting at night. Adams entertained the Smith girls with imitations of local dignitaries (whom they all knew), which brought roars of laughter. The attention was intoxicating, and soothed the bruises remaining from the Hannah Quincy romance.

John, after Hannah's wiles, was drawn to Abigail Smith's direct manner. Although nine years younger than he (she was seventeen when she first met him), Abigail was not afraid to speak her mind. She stood up to him, and he admired her for it. Even so, he tried to reform her — his drive to improve others as well as himself never faltered — but she would have none of it. She jabbed back and complained goodnaturedly that compliments were "a commodity . . . that you very seldom deal in." One time she wrote him that two apparitions had appeared in the Smith house. One of them resembled him. Why, she teased, would any apparition ever "assume a form like yours?" The directness only whetted his appetite for her.

After Cranch and Mary Smith were married, John for-

mally courted Abigail. Their love quickly became passionate
— and giddy. John arrived at the Smith's one evening carrying a letter for her, which demanded that she "give [the
bearer], as many Kisses, and as many Hours of your Company
after 9 O'Clock as he shall please to Demand and charge them
to my Account. . . . I presume I have good Right to draw
upon you for the Kisses as I have given two or three Millions
at least, when one has been received, and of Consequence the
Account between us is immensely in favour of yours, John
Adams." Abigail protested that John owed her for purloined
kisses, and John, playing the lawyer, advised her that she could
not sue for payment "unless I refuse Marriage; which I never
did, and never will, but on the Contrary am ready to *have you*
at any Time."

Once, when a severe storm prevented their meeting, he
called it "Cruel for detaining me from so much friendly, social
Company, and perhaps blessed to you, or me or both, for keeping me at *my Distance*." His ardor aboil, John knew that
"Itches, Aches, Agues, and Repentance might be the Consequences of a Contact in present Circumstances." To cool off,
he sometimes sought "noisy, dirty" Boston and its "Parade,
Pomp, Nonsense, Frippery, Folly . . . Luxury, Polliticks, and
the soul-Confounding Wrangles of the Law," all of which
would give him "the Higher Relish for Spirit, Taste and Sense,
at Weymouth, next Sunday. . . . Your — (all the rest is inexpressible) . . ."

Despite vows and passion, there was one long, forced
separation during the spring of 1764. A smallpox epidemic
broke out in Boston and Braintree. The disease was (and is)
extremely contagious and often fatal: during an epidemic in
Boston in 1721, some five thousand people fell ill and 844 of
them died. Later, during the war, of the eight thousand colonial militia who marched to Canada, more than two thousand
contracted the disease. The only preventive was inoculation, a
measure so highly controversial and dangerous that it was
banned at one time or another in almost all the colonies and
even in the Continental Army. Pus taken from a blister of an
infected person was introduced directly into the bloodstream,
thus causing what was hoped would be a mild form of the
disease. Either death or immunization resulted.

ABIGAIL ADAMS. PASTEL BY BENJAMIN BLYTH, 1766

Mrs. Adams, who had lost her husband through an epidemic fever, insisted that John take the risk and go to Boston for the long and painful treatment. Abigail's mother disapproved of it and forbade all her daughters to have it. So John went off without Abigail, but with a group of his friends, to Castle William in Boston harbor to be treated by a Dr. Perkins. They were shut up, five to a room, and denied bread and pudding. Adams was pricked, given powders, and inoculated. His head ached; he burned with fever, broke out, and triumphantly compared scabs with his friends.

Back in Braintree and Weymouth, John and Abigail tried as early as February, 1764, to fix a wedding date. Finally, on October 25, 1764, they were married in her father's house. Marriage hardly slowed Adams's work and business. His popularity, both as a lawyer and as a patriot, was increasing. For the year 1764, there are no diary entries at all. His practice had expanded so greatly that a note from him to Samuel Quincy lists almost forty cases Adams wished Quincy to enter for him in Boston. In 1762, Adams had begun traveling the Inferior and Superior Court circuits, and his circuit riding continued for fourteen years. During the years 1762–1766, Adams was also drawn, as were other prominent men of his time, into the growing turmoil between the colonies and England. Adams attended his first "Caucas Clubb," which met in Boston "in the Garret of Tom Daws." In 1761, he recorded arguments in Superior Court over the writs of assistance, which gave Crown officials the right to search at any time, anywhere, for smuggled goods. All the leading elder lawyers of Boston attended: Jeremiah Gridley arguing for the writs; James Otis, Jr., and Oxenbridge Thacher arguing against; and Benjamin Prat, refusing to argue at all, but observing from the audience. The writs were an attempt — and not the last — by the British to abrogate colonial "rights." For the first time, John Adams appeared as "secretary" for the coming Revolution. "Independence," he wrote, "was then and there born."

But as Americans began asserting their rights, Englishmen reminded them of their duties.

While young John Adams was riding circuit, tending his farm and beginning his family in Massachusetts Bay, another young man was also starting his career five thousand miles away. Both were loyal Englishmen of complex personalities and simple tastes that included farming. But both were also men of ambition, caught by swirling events that pushed Americans and Britons onto a collision course.

George of Brunswick, prince of Wales, heir to the throne of England, was three years younger than John Adams. He was precise and methodical, with a strong sense of duty and of politics. While John Adams drove himself with inner admonitions and questionings, Prince George often heard the voices of others: "George," his strong-willed mother frequently commanded, "be a *king!*"

In 1760, when John Adams was becoming a lawyer, Prince George, then twenty-two, became King George III. He set out to restore power to the Crown, diminished under his predecessors. His ministers came and went. The first, his personal friend Lord Bute, failed early in the game. The king then induced George Grenville to establish a ministry, and inserted personal friends at every level so that nothing could be done against the royal will. Grenville fell, not only because of the spreading rebellion in the American colonies, but also because he made the political mistake of trying to oust Stuart Mackenzie, one of the king's "North Briton" friends. The next ministry, Rockingham's, resigned rather than allow some of Mackenzie's colleagues into office. Finally, the king obtained the exact government he wanted, under his subservient friend Lord North. The power of the Crown was established at last.

For the first ten years of his reign, George III handled the colonists carefully, although not well. He ordered his friends in Parliament to vote for repeal of the hated Stamp Act. When Lord Hillsborough in 1769 argued for punishing Massachusetts for her Circular Letter of 1768 by altering the colony's charter, the king refused such an "odious measure" that would "increase the unhappy feudes that subsist rather than to asswage them." But the Boston Tea Party aroused his temper, and unwisely counseled, he was in great measure responsible for the Coercive Acts of 1774.

Whatever his private virtues and public faults, George III failed. He never understood men like John Adams, or others in the American colonies, who at the beginning were devoted, loyal subjects, attracted by his youth and personality. His best was not good enough; his perceptions were weak, his opportunities to reach out to his colonies and save his empire, ignored. The king's loss, of course, was the colonies' gain.

By mid-decade, 1765, Adams had established himself as a lawyer. His cousin, Samuel Adams, had already begun work with the Sons of Liberty, those early rebels. John Adams was far more cautious. He would be drawn slowly into rebellion. He would grapple — both privately and in public — with the new stirrings of a political problem older than recorded history: the balancing of liberty with order.

In 1765, with Jeremiah Gridley, Joseph Dudley and Samuel Fitch, Adams formed a lawyers' "Sodality" in Boston for the study and discussion of legal history and theory. What might have been just an esoteric platform for refining legal thinking became instead the honing stone of Adams's thoughts on the relationship between England and America. At this time he began making notes for an essay that later became known as "A Dissertation on the Canon and the Feudal Law." Revised and expanded, it was published without signature in the *Boston Gazette* in 1765 and subsequently in the *London Chronicle*. An examination of the widely hated Stamp Act, it marked Adams's opening, personal blow against the power of George III. Other essays against the actions of the king and Parliament followed quickly. There was much to write about.

In desperate need of funds for the empire, Parliament had begun to pass acts to gather revenue from the American colonies. The French and Indian War, after almost eight years of fighting, had created an enlarged empire for England. In 1763, France ceded her all of Canada, as well as Louisiana territories east of the Mississippi. But the victory was hollow: England's national debt had doubled. Added to this were the costs of expanded administration in two hemispheres. In America alone, the annual expense of maintaining civil and military establishments in 1764 was five times what it had

GEORGE III. OIL BY ALLAN RAMSEY, 1760–1770

been in 1748. In light of this, the chancellor of the exchequer, George Grenville, felt it only just and necessary that the American colonies increase their share of the burden. In 1764, he introduced into the House of Commons a series of resolutions for gaining revenue from America. So began the Sugar and Stamp acts.

The Revenue Act of 1764 — the Sugar Act — was the first of these measures. Besides providing revenue, its purpose was to tighten the mercantilist system by strengthening the Acts of Trade and Navigation. The American customs service was notoriously corrupt and sloppy: it collected less than a quarter of its cost of operation. The Sugar Act reduced from sixpence to threepence the duty on foreign molasses, but added duties on raw sugar and such luxuries as wine, coffee, silks and linens. At the same time, customs officers were encouraged to be more vigorous in enforcement, writs of assistance were authorized, and jurisdiction over revenue cases was given to the admiralty court if authorities chose to use it.

But New Englanders had been accustomed, for three decades, to ignoring duty provisions under the Molasses Act of 1733. Most molasses had come in from the French and Spanish West Indies. Rhode Island distillers, who made rum from molasses, imported less than one sixth of their molasses from English colonies. The smuggling was, of course, made possible only through the connivance of underpaid customs officers.

The interruption of this trade had profound repercussions. Molasses went from the West Indies to New England, and New England turned it into rum. The rum went to Africa for slaves, and most of the slaves went to the Caribbean — for molasses. This was the great triangular trade: molasses for rum for slaves. England wanted both revenue and preference in this lucrative trade for the English sugar islands. "It is no secret," John Adams wrote, "that rum was an essential ingredient of the American Revolution."

For men like Adams, the Sugar Act stirred up legal questions. Although the power of Parliament to tax colonial commodities for the regulation of the Crown's trade was universally acknowledged, the power of Parliament to levy such a tax for revenue was debatable. "One single act of Parlia-

A formal state portrait of the young and dashing king, who was just twenty-two when he ascended the throne in 1760. He ruled the most far-flung empire the world has ever known.

ment," wrote James Otis, Jr., "has set people a-thinking in six months, more than they had done in their whole lives before." Colonial lawyers found in the law the first intimations of "taxation without representation." It was, however, Grenville's next revenue measure that gave colonial opposition focus and voice.

The idea of a stamp tax did not originate with Grenville, but had been long prevalent in England. Other English ministers had rejected such a proposal; Pitt, for one, had "refused to burn his fingers with an American Stamp Tax." But Grenville pressed on. "No tax," he said, "appears so easy and equitable as a stamp duty." Unwisely, he revealed his purpose a full year before enactment, when American opposition was already aflame from the Sugar Act. On March 22, 1765, Parliament announced that revenue stamps costing (in specie) between a halfpenny and twenty shillings must be affixed to all newspapers, broadsides, pamphlets, almanacs, leases, commercial bills, notes and bonds, advertisements, legal documents and other such papers. The protests began.

The act aroused the most prominent and articulate men in the colonies. Merchants of New York, Philadelphia and Boston, whose every bill of lading would be taxed, organized for resistance and signed nonimportation agreements in an attempt to pressure Parliament into repealing the tax. Respectable men joined the Sons of Liberty forming in the colonies, and violence burst out: a mob, perhaps inflamed by Samuel Adams or the sermons of Jonathan Mayhew, marched through the crooked streets of Boston to the lieutenant governor's mansion and gutted it. On October 7, 1765, delegates from nine colonies met in New York City as the Stamp Act Congress to protest against taxation without representation; they stayed in session until the twenty-fifth. Business dwindled; trade with England dropped by £600,000.

John Adams recorded "the unconquerable Rage of the People," and wrote excitedly: "Our Presses have groaned, our Pulpits have thundered, our Legislatures have resolved, our Towns have voted. The Crown Officers have everywhere trembled, and all their little Tools and Creatures, been afraid to Speak and ashamed to be seen."

The colonies refused to comply with the Stamp Act.

This political cartoon depicts reactions to the Stamp Act. American supporters are being trampled and hung from the Liberty Tree.

OVERLEAF
American protests to the act brought a strong British reaction. Paul Revere's line engraving shows British troops landing in Boston and marching into the town on Long Wharf. Revere also inserted a rallying symbol: an American Indian princess (lower right) with her foot firmly on the chest of a prone British soldier. A rattlesnake coils around his arm.

DETAIL: A VIEW OF THE YEAR 1765. LINE ENGRAVING BY PAUL REVERE, ABOUT 1765

LAND AND BRITTISH SHIPS OF WAR LANDING THEIR TROOPS! 1768

.me up the Harbour and Anchored round the Town, their Cannon loaded,
.d. the fourteenth & twenty-ninth Regiments, a detachment from the 59th Regt.
. there Formed and Marched with insolent Parade, Drums beating, Fifes
.rounds of Powder and Ball.

A Long Wharf
B Hancock's Wharf
C North Battery

ENGRAVED PRINTED, & SOLD by PAUL REVERE, BOSTON.

A VIEW OF PART OF THE TOWN OF BOSTON IN NEW ENGLAND AND BRITISH SHIPS OF WAR
LANDING THEIR TROOPS! 1768. LINE ENGRAVING BY PAUL REVERE, 1770

One conservative response in Massachusetts was to close the courts because the officials, particularly Thomas Hutchinson, the chief justice, were afraid to proceed without the required stamped paper. Business fell off further, and Adams wrote on December 18, 1765, that he had "not drawn a Writ since 1st Novr." He was hard at work on his composition of the "Braintree Instructions" denouncing the Stamp Act and Parliament's authority to tax the colonies without consent. He, Gridley and Otis presented Boston's memorial against the closing of the courts; the argument was the opening stage in Adams's often bitter struggle with Thomas Hutchinson, who at that time was lieutenant governor of the province as well as chief justice.

Feelings in Boston were running high, and John Adams did not — perhaps could not — remove himself from the rising forces of liberty. On January 15, 1766, he wrote in his diary: "Spent an Evening with the Sons of Liberty, at their own Apartment in Hanover Square, near the Tree of Liberty. It is a Compting Room in Chase & Speakmans Distillery. A very small Room it is."

But its voice would become immense. British merchants, fearing loss of business, were influential in securing repeal of the Stamp Act on March 18, 1766. Adams recorded the "Rejoicings" over the repeal: "Bells rung, Cannon were fired, Drums beaten, and Land Lady Cushing [in Hingham] on the Plain, illuminated her House." But John Adams did not take part: he had to be in Superior Court in the morning, and his family was ill. Abigail Adams II, born on July 14, 1765, and her mother had whooping cough. Moreover, Adams's feelings had been pricked and he struck a theme that would recur in the family's history: the lack of public appreciation for their work. The town of Braintree ignored his role in pleading for repeal of the act. Heavily scratched out in his diary were the sentences: "I had [also] the mortification to see that while allmost all the zealous opposers of the Stamp Act [were caressed] by their Towns and chosen Representatives . . . I was liked to be neglected my self and that all my friends in my own Town were liked to be neglected too."

Some recognition did come, however. Adams was elected a Braintree selectman, replacing a man inclined to support the

The British occupied Boston and camped and drilled upon the Common. John Adams, along with other Bostonians, was displeased by a town "full of Troops" parading noisily. "Through the whole succeeding fall and Winter," Adams reported, "a Regiment was exercised . . . directly in Front of my house. The Spirit Stirring Drum, and the Earpiercing fife arroused me and my family early enough every morning, and the Indignation they excited, though somewhat soothed was not allayed by the sweet Songs, Violins and flutes of the serenading Sons of Liberty, under my Windows in the Evening."

DETAIL: PERSPECTIVE
VIEW OF BOSTON COMMONS.
LINE ENGRAVING BY SIDNEY
SMITH, 1770, AFTER A
WATERCOLOR BY CHRISTIAN
REMICK, 1768

GREEN DRAGON TAVERN. PEN AND INK WITH WATERCOLOR WASH BY JOHN JOHNSTON, 1773

"Radical Sam" Adams, John's cousin, could rally mobs or argue learnedly. He was one of the organizers of the Sons of Liberty, and here debates colonial rights in 1770 after the Boston massacre. Other radicals gathered at Boston taverns like the Green Dragon in the North End, where in 1773 the Sons of Liberty plotted the Boston Tea Party. Paul Revere lived nearby, opposite the Red Lyon Inne, whose sign he made. The lanterns that hung from the two holes in the sign were supposedly taken by Revere to use as warning signals that British troops were setting out for Concord and Lexington in April, 1775.

THE RED LION INNE SIGN.
MADE BY PAUL REVERE, 1770

SAMUEL ADAMS. OIL BY JOHN SINGLETON COPLEY, ABOUT 1770–1772

British Crown, in a vote that marked "the first popular struggle of the Revolution in the town of Braintree." He was pleased to have won, and ran again in 1767, but declined a third term. His law practice and his family were expanding: John Quincy Adams was born on July 11, 1767, his first son, who was "at the request of his Grandmother Smith christened by the Name of John Quincy on the day of the Death of his Great Grandfather, John Quincy of Mount Wollaston."

The remainder of 1767 was quiet, politically, until the end of November, when the Townshend Acts went into effect. They had been passed by Parliament to raise revenue by so-called external taxes: duties on English glass, red and white lead, paper, tea, and painter's colors. For Englishmen these new taxes on Americans had been the more welcome because they were designed to make up for some of the revenue lost through a reduction in English land taxes. For a more efficient collection of duties, the customs service was strengthened and reorganized. New customs officials and a board of commissioners of customs arrived in Boston by the end of the year. Unknowingly, two opposing forces were slowly moving toward collision.

As though drawn by the power focusing on Boston, John Adams and his family, in April, 1768, moved to the city "into the White House as it was called in Brattle Square." On December 28, his second daughter, Susanna, was born,* and in the spring of 1769, the Adamses moved again, this time "to Cole Lane, to Mr. Fayerweathers House."

John Adams still traveled monthly to the courts: in July, to Plymouth Inferior Court; in August, to Suffolk Superior Court; in September, to the Worcester Superior Court and Bristol Inferior Court; in October, to Plymouth Inferior Court and Bristol and Middlesex (Cambridge) Inferior courts; in December, to Barnstable and Plymouth Inferior courts. Life, however, was not all drudgery. On August 4, 1769, an entry in John Rowe's diary notes: "fine Weather Din'd at John Champneys on A Pigy with the following Company — John Hancock, James Otis, John Adams" and thirteen others.

* Life was still harsh for a newborn in the colonies, and Susanna died on February 4, 1770.

Such pauses were too few for Adams at the end of this pivotal decade. After the passage of the Townshend Acts in June of 1767, the merchants again boycotted English goods, and importations fell in Boston and Philadelphia by one half, and in New York by four fifths. Americans did without: men dressed in homespun, women found substitutes for tea, students used colonial-made paper. Only in Boston, where merchants deeply resented English interference, did violence again break out. And in three major cases, Adams revealed his stubborn desire to defend the cause of liberty *and* order.

In May, 1768, John Hancock's sloop *Liberty* was seized by the new customs officials, supposedly for smuggling wine. It was thought, however, that the officials had acted for two reasons: to enforce the Townshend Acts and to attempt to bankrupt Hancock, who was a well-known (and generous) contributor to the Sons of Liberty. Whichever, a Boston crowd grabbed the customsmen, roughly thumping them and destroying Crown property along the Boston wharves. Governor Bernard sent out word for two regiments of British soldiers to protect the commissioners, and the Crown was only too happy to put British troops into this recalcitrant American city. Two regiments sailed from Halifax, Nova Scotia, and British soldiers and officers quartered themselves upon the town of Boston, thus beginning an occupation of the city that steadily increased until the evacuation of 1776.

John Adams wrote a protest against the seizure of the *Liberty* for the Boston representatives to the General Court in June, 1768. But in August, Hancock's sloop was formally declared forfeit. He was brought to trial in November, and Hancock asked his friend John Adams to defend him. During the winter of 1768–1769, the short, fat lawyer from Braintree scuttled back and forth between his Boston house and the courts defending Hancock. "A painful Drudgery I had of this cause," Adams admitted. "There were few days through the whole Winter, when I was not summoned to attend the Court of Admiralty." Adams's argument was based not on Hancock's innocence, which was suspect, but on the legality of the Townshend Acts themselves, which denied Hancock the right to a trial by jury. After five months of litigation, Adams won, and Hancock went free.

Almost exactly a year after the *Liberty* was seized, another incident on shipboard brought Adams to the attention of patriot and Tory alike. On April 22, 1769, the British frigate *Rose* halted the brig *Pitt Packet* off Marblehead, Massachusetts. The smaller ship, manned by a crew of Irishmen, was carrying a cargo of salt. The British frigate sent over a boarding party, headed by Lieutenant Henry Gibson Panton, who went aboard the *Pitt Packet*, asked for the ship's papers, and began a search. Some of the Irish sailors, afraid of British impressment on the high seas, warned Lieutenant Panton from the forepeak that they would not be taken. One crewman, Michael Corbet, according to Adams's later accounting, drew a line in the salt on the deck, and challenged Panton: "If you step over that line, I shall consider it as a proof that you are determined to impress me, and by the Eternal God of Heaven, you are a dead man."

Panton calmly took a pinch of snuff, and very deliberately stepped over the line. He tried to grab Seaman Corbet, but Corbet held a harpoon, and drove it through Panton's neck, severing the carotid artery and jugular vein, "and laid the lieutenant at his feet."

A special court of admiralty promptly convened to hear the case, and John Adams (and James Otis, Jr.) rose to defend the sailors. The lawyers pressed to obtain a trial by jury, but were allegedly blocked by Lieutenant Governor Hutchinson's influence with his fellow judges: Governor Bernard, Governor John Wentworth of New Hampshire and Commodore Hood. Adams, citing the statute 6 Anne, ch. 37, sect. 9, which prohibited impressments of sailors in America by the British navy, and also arguing justifiable homicide, won his second major acquittal against the rule of the Crown. Corbet and his companions went free: the verdict was that Corbet and the others had acted in self-defense.

The trial of these young sailors and Hancock's case a year earlier aroused the people of Massachusetts and Boston, and pulled John Adams closer to the fervor of the rebellion. As he rode the court circuit or walked the streets of Boston, he was recognized as a "patriot" lawyer, and invited to dine and discuss the events sweeping the American colonies. He described one dinner "laid in the open Field" and attended by

"350 Sons of Liberty at Robinsons, the Sign of [the] Liberty Tree in Dorchester." There was much singing of "the Liberty Song. . . . This is cultivating the Sensations of Freedom. There was a large Collection of good Company. Otis and [Samuel] Adams are politick, in promoting these Festivals, for they tinge the Minds of the People, they impregnate them with the sentiments of Liberty. They render the People fond of their Leaders in the Cause, and averse and bitter against all opposers. To the Honour of the Sons, I did not see one Person intoxicated, or near it" — a remarkable observation. Some fourteen toasts had been drunk at the Liberty Tree in Boston, followed by forty-five at the dinner, each enumerated by the *Boston Gazette* of August 21, 1769.

Friction was increasing between the people of Boston and the red-coated British troops. Even Lord North was aroused to the point of calling Bostonians "the drunken raga-muffins of a vociferous mob." Recognizing the rising tensions, Adams, again working through the legal system he under-stood and trusted, wrote instructions in May, 1769, for the Boston representatives to the General Court (Massachusetts legislature) as he had done a year earlier. This time he recited lists of grievances suffered by Bostonians at the hands of British soldiers who were stationed in the town: "Common decency as well as the honor and dignity of a free legislative demands that the offensive Guards and Cannon be removed from our city. . . . An inquiry must be made into the Re-peated offenses and Violences committed by the Soldiery against the people of Boston." Things, however, were not so onesided.

On February 22, 1770, the British soldiers, in their bright red coats, were the objects of Boston's bitterness. Snowballs were thrown at them, and they were sometimes struck with canes and sticks. Fires were lighted at their quarters, and officers were taunted when they tried to investigate. Antago-nism between citizen and soldier flared repeatedly.

Christopher Snider and some other young Boston boys joined a mob shouting outside the home of a Boston mer-chant. The merchant, like a few others in town, had ignored the local nonimportation agreement, and was bringing in British goods and selling them. The mood of the people that wintry day was ugly; threats were made. But when the merchant did not respond, Christopher Snider and his friends marched to the house of Ebenezer Richardson, a customs employee and a representative of the Crown in Boston. The Snider boy's barbed taunts found their target, and Richardson stomped out his door. He was armed, and fired his musket once into the crowd of boys. Christopher Snider, just twelve, fell dead.

Four days later, John Adams, riding home from personal visits in Weymouth, encountered a large procession — the *Boston Gazette* placed the number of people at two thousand — near the Liberty Tree. Adams inquired, and discovered that this was the funeral "of the Child, lately kill'd by Richardson." He watched the procession as it quietly passed: "a vast Number of Boys walked before the Coffin, a vast Number of Women and Men after it, and a Number of Carriages. My Eyes never beheld such a funeral. The Procession extended further than can be well imagined.

"This Shewes, there are many more Lives to spend if wanted in the Service of their Country.

"It Shewes, too that the Faction is not yet expiring — that the Ardor of the People is not to be quelled by the Slaughter of one Child and the Wounding of another."*

Indeed, that "Ardor" would soon be fanned. For in the evening of March 5, 1770 — only eight days after Christopher Snider's funeral — a lone British sentry was standing his post at the Customs House on King Street. It was cold, there was ice and a light snow on the ground. Fires had broken out at various points around Boston that evening, and small clusters of people shouted at British soldiers on sight. One crowd stopped before the Customs House, and began yelling at the sentry. He sent for help, and six soldiers, a corporal and Captain Thomas Preston marched down to the Customs House from the Main Guard. They were pelted with snowballs and insults. Someone gave an order to fire, and the British soldiers stopped the taunts with musketballs. Five

The shooting of Boston citizens on King Street in 1770 immediately became grist for American propaganda mills. Henry Pelham, a young engraver, made a drawing of the incident, which he loaned to Paul Revere for his opinion. Revere, an astute businessman as well as patriot, used the drawing for this historically inaccurate line engraving of the "Boston Massacre." Pelham accused Revere of stealing his art: "When I heard you was cutting a plate of the late Murder, I thought it impossible as I knew you was not capable of doing it unless you coppied it from mine." Just twenty-three days after the shooting, Revere's engraving was on sale. Pelham's did not appear for another week.

---

* Ebenezer Richardson and George Wilmot, another customsman present at the shooting, were indicted and tried for murder. Wilmot was acquitted. Richardson was found guilty, but was pardoned by the king.

The BLOODY MASSACRE perpetrated in King—i—Street BOSTON ⋯⋯ 29ᵗʰ REGᵗ

BUTCHER'S HALL

Engrav'd Printed & Sold by PAUL REVERE BOSTON

happy BOSTON! see thy Sons deplore,
y hallow'd Walks besmear'd with guiltless Gore:
le faithless P—n and his savage Bands.
h murd'rous Rancour stretch their bloody Hands;
e fierce Barbarians grinning o'er their Prey,
prove the Carnage and enjoy the Day.

If scalding drops from Rage from Anguish Wrung
If speechless Sorrows lab'ring for a Tongue.
Or if a weeping World can ought appease
The plaintive Ghosts of Victims such as these;
The Patriot's copious Tears for each are shed,
A glorious Tribute which embalms the Dead.

But know, FATE summons to that awful Goal.
Where JUSTICE strips the Murd'rer of his Soul
Should venal C—ts the scandal of the Land.
Snatch the relentless Villain from her Hand,
Keen Execrations on this Plate inscrib'd,
Shall reach a JUDGE who never can be brib'd.

The unhappy Sufferers were Messᵗˢ SAMᴸ GRAY SAMᴸ MAVERICK, JAMˢ CALDWELL, CRISPUS ATTUCKS & PATᴷ CARR

Killed. Six wounded; two of them (CHRISTᴿ MONK & JOHN CLARK) Mortally

THE BLOODY MASSACRE PERPETRATED IN KING STREET, BOSTON ON MARCH 5TH, 1770.
LINE ENGRAVING BY PAUL REVERE, 1770

Americans fell, three instantly dead; a fourth died shortly thereafter, and the fifth in a few days.

Samuel Adams and Joseph Warren quickly spread the word of the shooting. John Adams found his cousin that evening "cooking up Paragraphs, Articles, Occurrances &c. working the political engine." Soon, word of the "Boston Massacre" was in every colony.

John Adams could have joined the popular outrage. Instead, he looked beyond the immediate moment to the likely repercussions. The British military authority didn't object to the arrest and confinement of Captain Preston and the seven soldiers by the civil authority. They would be tried for murder, and the question immediately was: who would defend them?

Preston requested Josiah Quincy, who refused unless John Adams would join him. Adams — this patriotic lawyer, friend of the Sons of Liberty, prosecutor against British injustice — accepted, which "occasioned a great clamor." Adams's reasons were clear: there would be liberty *and* order in Boston. If mob rule took control of the city and the colony, the other colonies would declare that there was a state of anarchy. Their alliance and support in the coming struggle would be lost. Moreover, if the mob and the radicals convicted Preston and his soldiers without trial, what could be hoped for the protection of any Massachusetts citizen? And under what law?

Adams and Quincy won their defense of the British soldiers. Preston was acquitted of the charge that he had ordered his men to shoot. Two of his soldiers were found guilty of manslaughter and, under the rules of that time, were branded on the thumbs and discharged from the British army. It was, on the whole, a lenient dismissal. But the law, a fair trial, and government by men, not mobs, had been upheld. Boston would not be abandoned to anarchy.

And so the struggle began. A man and his time had come. No longer could the British ignore John Adams, the once-loyal English subject, now an American turning his back to the Crown.

2
Thirteen Clocks Strike Alike
[1770–1776]

Now came a time of gathering clouds. For three years after the "Boston Massacre," political life in Massachusetts Bay quieted. The Townshend Acts except for the tax on tea had been repealed, and merchants grew fat. Northern New England was being settled rapidly; during the fifteen years before the Revolution, nearly one hundred towns sprang up in New Hampshire, seventy-four in what is now Vermont, and at least twenty in Maine.

While Paris held more than a million people and London about a million and a half, Boston, the center of the world drama into which John Adams was moving, had only fifteen thousand. In 1774 the total population of the thirteen colonies was about the same as that of London.

Fully as important as the question of expansion and development of the colonies was the question of who would rule them. Colonies like Connecticut were relatively democratic; others like New York were aristocratic in their social structure. Although the franchise was apparently fairly broad, class distinctions in the colonies determined social privilege and political power.

The colonial upper class consisted of merchants, landed gentry, clergy, lawyers and Crown-appointed officials. Although there was rivalry within this group, it controlled the colonial assemblies, owned most of the land, sat on the courts, directed the commerce, controlled credit (there being no banks) and set the social and cultural standards. Graduates of the nine colonial colleges filled the professions, and men like John Adams, son of a farmer and a scholarship student at Harvard, became gentlemen by virtue of their classical education. These people, though not born in England, were conscious of England and loyal to her heritage. Yet they also provided notable leaders for the coming Revolution: Otis, Adams, Hancock, Trumbull of New England; Jay, Schuyler, Livingston, Dickinson, Stockton of the Middle Colonies; Howard, Carroll of Maryland; Lee, Mason, Jefferson, Washington of Virginia; Jones of North Carolina; and Pinckney, Rutledge and Izard of South Carolina.

The middle class, sometimes sharing political power with these men (but not wealth or social status), formed the backbone of the colonies: farmers, city shopkeepers, master workmen in New England; the lesser planters and county-seat merchants in the South. They could read newspapers and follow politics, and produced such leaders as Patrick Henry and Benjamin Franklin. Less educated than those of the upper class, they were quicker to respond to emotional argument. It was in this group that Thomas Paine found his staunchest readers of *Common Sense*. While the upper class drank the tea, it was the middle class that dumped it.

Below them were people sometimes referred to as "the meaner sort" in eighteenth-century writings. Of the recent immigrants among them, a few halted at the seaports, where they became laborers, coastal fishermen and sailors, toilers and mechanics. Most pushed to the frontiers where land was cheap and hopes high.

This class was little interested in political theory or imperial organization; they would measure John Adams's writing not by what he said, but by how it appeared and *felt*. They cared much about — and would fight for — their

Mercy Otis Warren had little formal education yet she wrote for the Revolution. In 1805, her three-volume History of the Rise, Progress and Termination of the American Revolution *troubled John Adams, who thought it contained some errors "in those Passages which relate personally to me." Adams was particularly miffed at the line "his prejudices and his passions were sometimes too strong for his sagacity and judgment." He wrote Mercy Warren ten long letters in rebuttal, some running twenty pages or more. She conceded nothing, but replied with spirit and skill, and at much less length.*

MERCY OTIS WARREN. OIL BY JOHN SINGLETON COPLEY, ABOUT 1763

The silversmith and engraver appeared in workman's shirt-sleeves and vest for this portrait. His engraving tools, the burin and needle, lie on the table ready for use in engraving the teapot. As he proceeded, Revere would rotate it on the round leather pad under his hand.

PAUL REVERE II. OIL BY JOHN SINGLETON COPLEY, ABOUT 1768–1770

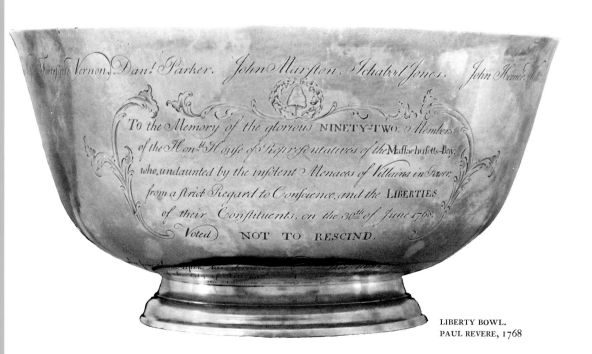

LIBERTY BOWL.
PAUL REVERE, 1768

economic welfare, religious liberty and political rights. These were simple, unschooled people, men of the mallet and wooden plow. They were religious, but not ritualistic, attracted to the Great Awakening of religious spirit.

Life in New England, even in the best of times, was harsh. The common man of New England suffered — the laborers, sailors, artisans, criminals, debtors and poor who built the roads, peopled the mobs, cast the cannon, and served in the ragtag army. Theirs was a life of twelve-hour workdays, rum, winters by the kitchen fire, one hot meal a day. Few women, although married young, lived a decade in marriage: pregnancies occurred every two years or so, and a rare woman survived her fifth childbirth. Laborers earned fifteen to twenty pounds a year, barely adequate if the men stayed healthy and single. It cost sixty pounds a year to support a family of four in Boston in the early 1770's, and inflation soon drove costs upward sharply.

The New England land, stubborn as the people themselves, yielded reluctantly. Those who did not farm were attracted to the sea and the offshore fishing banks, to shipbuilding and carrying goods for more prosperous neighbors. From every harbor in the New England coast — Falmouth (Portland), Maine; Portsmouth, New Hampshire; Salem, Marblehead and Boston; Plymouth, New Bedford, Providence, Newport, New London, New Haven — hundreds of brave men in little schooners, sloops and ketches put forth each year for coastal ports. Others in brigs and frigates put out for England, Europe, the Mediterranean, the Gold Coast of Africa and the West Indies.

Men like Hancock connected these sea traders with the shopkeepers and merchants of the interior. They set social standards by their wealth, patronized painters like John Singleton Copley and silversmiths like Paul Revere. When the British government regulated acts of trade, these men, and those dependent upon them, were directly hurt. This economic solidarity of the New England seaboard was a major reason why the four colonies of the region entered the Revolution as a single unit.

The religious, frontier and maritime interests of New England made it especially sensitive to almost every act of

Perhaps the most famous of Paul Revere's silver pieces is this punch bowl done in 1768. The Liberty Bowl, as it is known, honored the ninety-two men of the Massachusetts House of Representatives who supported the circular letter sent to the other colonies protesting the Townsend Acts and refusing to import any British goods.

Parliament. But Parliament and the king were unwisely insensitive to these Americans. Between 1770 and 1773, the chances for peace were never greater, nor less taken.

In Massachusetts after the Boston Massacre, the Crown seemed stronger than ever. "Men of fortune, men of the better sort" had been shocked to see their colony drifting under mob rule. New York, then Philadelphia and Charleston abandoned the Nonimportation Agreement. Isaac Low and Thomas Cushing argued that quarrels with England about taxation, colonial liberties and "high points about the supreme authority of Parliament" should end. John Hancock deserted the ranks altogether. He withdrew his legal business from John Adams and gave it to Samuel Quincy. Adams, stung, wrote in his diary: "Oh the Mutability of the legal, commercial, social, political, as well as material World! For about 3 or 4 Years I have done all Mr. Hancocks Business, and have waded through wearisome, anxious Days and Nights, in his Defence. — But Farewell."

Boston celebrated the queen's birthday with booming cannon and fireworks on the Common. Lieutenant Governor Thomas Hutchinson, a Crown appointee, saw his popularity returning, and he and the Olivers once more dispensed the king's favors. "We have not been so quiet these past five years," the governor wrote to England. "Our incendiaries of the lower order have quite disappeared. The people about the country have certainly altered their conduct, and in this town, if it were not for two or three Adamses, we should do well enough."

John Adams abandoned Boston and, he hoped, politics together. After a year as elected representative to the General Court (the legislature) from Boston, he moved his growing family back to Braintree in April of 1771. He and Abigail now had three children, including Charles, born May 29, 1770. The move to Braintree, Adams explained in his *Autobiography*, would improve his health and help him avoid continuous work. He had, at the time, "more Business at the Bar, than any Man in the Province." Although he kept his law office in Boston, the town was, he complained, bad for his health. Ten days after he moved out, Adams wrote in his diary: "I shall have no Journeys to make to Cambridge — no

In 1735, John Adams was born in the house to the right on his parents' farm at the foot of Penn's Hill. After their marriage in 1764, John and Abigail moved into the house on the left, which was John Quincy Adams's birthplace. Laundry flutters out back, and beyond lie the hills that were later destroyed by the Quincy granite quarries.

ADAMS BIRTHPLACES. OIL BY FRANKENSTEIN, 1849

general Court to attend — But shall divide my Time between Boston and Braintree, between Law and Husbandry. Farewell Politicks."

Complaining of ill health, Adams left by horseback on May 30 for a two-week trip to take the mineral springs in Connecticut. At Stafford Springs, he found "the Halt, the Lame, the vapoury, hypochondriac, scrophulous, &c." Still, the springs had helped some people and Adams, a practical man, was not going to waste his long journey. He "drank pretty plentifully" of the water, which tinged with a "reddish yellow Colour" whatever it washed, and swam in the pool. He emerged, gasping and shivering, and plunged in again — "but the 2nd time was superfluous and did me more hurt than good, it is very cold indeed."

Adams spent several days in Stafford Springs, and grew bored. "I begin to grow weary of this idle, romantic Jaunt," he wrote. "I want to see my Wife, my Children, my Farm, my Horse, Oxen, Cows, Walls, Fences, Workmen, Office, Books, and Clerks. I want to hear the News, and Politicks of the Day."

By June 17, Adams was back riding the eastern circuit. This was a time of hard work, and reflection. "Law and Husbandry" did take precedence; one entry in his diary contains a detailed "Recipe to make Manure." His Office Book for 1770–1774 shows that he took sixty-six cases in the July, 1772, term of the Suffolk Inferior Court, and his docket for the August term of the Suffolk Superior Court, which ran into September, listed seventy-eight continued and new legal cases. During one week in October, Adams tried nine cases before the Superior Court in Taunton.

This was a good time, at thirty-seven, for John Adams to take measure. His "little Farm, and Stock, and Cash" gave him satisfaction, although he did not think he had acquired much for a man his age. He owned the house in Braintree and some sixty-eight acres of farmland. He had paid off a debt to Colonel Quincy for twenty acres of salt marsh by the creek. The reasons that had made him leave Boston no longer existed: his health had improved, and Boston had been quiet for two years. Besides, John Quincy, his parents agreed, would eventually need the intellectual rigors of the Boston Latin School.

So, on August 21, 1772, John Adams paid £533 6s. 8d. to Shrimpton Hunt for a brick house and lot on South Queen Street (later named Court Street), "near the Scaene of my Business, opposite the Court House" in Boston. For the fifth time since 1768, the Adamses moved. Abigail's strength had returned after the birth of Thomas Boylston on September 15, 1772, and she, the three older children, the new baby, two maids and a houseboy arrived on Queen Street — followed by the farm cart with a load of firewood, pumpkins, onions and turnips — to join John Adams in late November.

Adams hoped that he had "profited by Retirement and Reflection" during the last nineteen months "and learned in what manner to live in Boston." If his health failed again, he would return to Braintree "and renounce the Town entirely." In order to live in Boston, he vowed: "I must remember Temperance, Exercise and Peace of Mind. Above all Things I must avoid Politicks, Political Clubbs, Town Meetings, General Court, &c. &c. &c." Like some of his other Puritan vows, this one did not last long — not more than five weeks, in fact.

Two major incidents pulled him into the thick of Boston politics. The British and Lord North decided in 1772 to reform the law courts of Massachusetts Bay, and the province learned that her judges of the Superior Court would be paid their salaries by the Crown instead of by the colony. Some colonists thought it a splendid idea. But others, like John Adams, remembered the words of King James I: "You make the laws. Let me make the judges."

Massachusetts judges were Crown appointees. The only control the people of the colony had over them was withholding their salaries. At a special town meeting in Cambridge in December, 1772, General William Brattle voiced his support of the move, and on the last day of the year published his reasons in the *Boston News Letter*. John Adams answered him in the *Boston Gazette* of January 11, 1773, and followed his article with six weekly pieces. The articles probed the nature of government, of empire, of the composition and procedure of English courts of law under free constitutional rule. Adams believed that judges paid by the Crown would lose all independence, and the people their liberty and safety.

He quoted from Bracton to Blackstone, he cited Latin,

and the articles grew in length until, at the end, the *Gazette* had little room for anything else. The printers reduced the size of the type. Adams himself wondered if the pieces might be "a trifle tedious." But their sheer weight swept down the Tory position. The very sight of the pages was overwhelmingly convincing.

When it became clear Chief Justice Peter Oliver would accept the Crown offer to pay his salary, the colony was at a loss for action. Adams, in a private conversation with friends, argued that the move struck at the very roots of the judiciary system and the law, and that there was but one recourse: "I said it was nothing more nor less than an Impeachment of the Judges by the House of Representatives before the Council." People were stunned: impeachment was without precedent in Massachusetts. But in February, 1774, after a series of delays, the Massachusetts House of Representatives, meeting in Boston, formally impeached Chief Justice Oliver. John Adams drew up the articles of impeachment, which he modeled after the English Parliamentary form. The proceedings failed, but their purpose, to remove Oliver from the bench, succeeded.*

Still, the British had an opportunity to let the colonies heal and prosper. "The people," wrote Connecticut's agent in England, "appear to be weary of their altercations with the mother country. A little discreet conduct on both sides would perfectly re-establish that warm affection and respect towards Great Britain for which this country was once remarkable."

But with a perversity only colonial power creates, Parliament decided instead to exploit the colonies. It granted to the British East India Company, in critical financial condition, the privilege of exporting tea directly to America. The company decided to sell its tea through its own agents, thereby enabling it to drop the price considerably. The tea, however, still carried the Townshend duty. Smugglers and honest merchants alike were undercut, and fearing that this new privilege of the

This 1774 satire, published in England, illustrated the punishment given a customs official who tried to collect duty in Boston. Under the Liberty Tree, patriots pour tea into the tarred-and-feathered man, while in the background a cargo of tea is dumped into the harbor.

---

* Samuel Adams in 1772 had organized committees of correspondence which began by writing from Massachusetts Bay towns to the Boston radicals "the sense of people concerning the judges' salaries." The idea for these committees, elected by each Massachusetts town, soon spread throughout New England, then to the Middle Colonies and the South, and were instrumental in bringing together the First Continental Congress in 1774.

THE BOSTONIANS PAYING THE EXCISE-MAN, OR PLIGHT OF LOYALIST AGENT. MEZZOTINT, ATTRIBUTED TO PHILIP DAWE, 1773

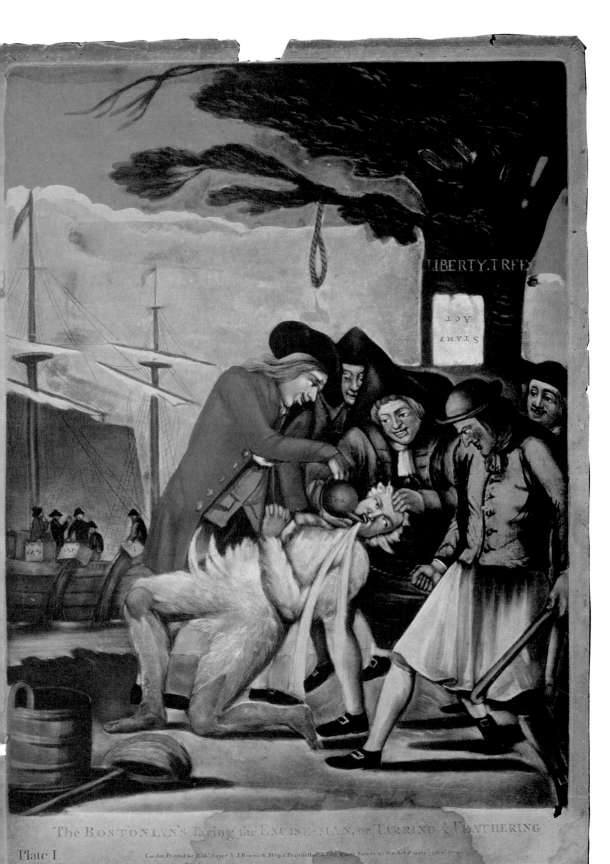

The BOSTONIAN'S Paying the EXCISE-MAN, or TARRING & FEATHERING

Plate I.

London Printed for Rob.t Sayer & J. Bennett, Map & Printsellers, No. 53, Fleet Street, as the Act directs, 25 Oct.r 1774.

East India Company might be expanded to include other goods, they quickly joined the American radicals.

Colonial reaction varied. In Charleston, the tea was landed but not offered for sale. In Philadelphia and New York, the tea was rejected and sent back to England. In Boston, the rejected tea was held on three ships in the harbor; the people of Boston would not let it be landed. Governor Hutchinson demanded that the tea be unloaded and the duty paid. Messengers from various committees of correspondence alerted the citizenry and organized several meetings. Colonists armed, and planned to toll church bells should the tea be landed. Abigail Adams wrote to her friend Mercy Warren of Plymouth on December 5, 1773:

"The Tea that bainfull weed is arrived. Great and I hope Effectual opposition has been made to the landing of it. . . . The proceedings of our Citizens have been United, Spirited and firm. The flame is kindled and like Lightning it catches from Soul to Soul."

On Thursday, December 16, 1773, a final appeal was carried by messenger to Governor Hutchinson at his house in Milton, about eight miles from Boston. By nightfall, several thousand Bostonians crowded in and around the Old South Church awaiting his reply. When it came — refusing clearance for the ships until the tea duty was paid — the people marched to the docks. A band of men, some disguised as Indians, rowed out and boarded the three tea ships, *Dartmouth*, *Beaver* and *Eleanor*, tied by long cables in the inner harbor at Griffin's Wharf. They dumped 342 chests of tea into the water, and destroyed some £9,000 worth of property. The next day, tea marked the edges of high tide on beaches as far south as Nantasket.

John Adams, in Boston, heard the news on his way home. His reaction was swift and strong, and, for a man who loved property and the law, surprising. He reasoned in his diary that there had been but three choices: return the tea, which the governor refused to do without payment of duty; land it, thereby "giving up the Principle of Taxation by Parliamentary Authority, against which the Continent have struggled for 10 years"; or destroy it. Adams's glee at the deed was almost boundless: "This is the most magnificent

Movement of all. There is a Dignity, a Majesty, a Sublimity, in this last Effort of the Patriots, that I greatly admire. The People should never rise, without doing something to be remembered — something notable And striking. This Destruction of the Tea is so bold, so daring, so firm, intrepid and inflexible, and it must have so important Consequences, and so lasting, that I cant but consider it as an Epocha in History."

But such a bold act, Adams knew, would not go unpunished. "What Measures will the Ministry take, in Consequence of this? — Will they resent it? will they dare to resent it? will they punish us? How?"

Adams and the other Bostonians would wait five months for their answer. Meanwhile, the Sons of Liberty, sensing the importance of this act, purchased and stored five hundred barrels of gunpowder in Boston and Charlestown arsenals. Militia companies were formed, or strengthened.

In a stroke, the Boston Tea Party scandalized moderates everywhere and heartened radicals. In England news of the Tea Party enflamed public opinion. Boston, said the *London Morning Chronicle*, was a "canker worm in the heart of America, a rotten limb which (if suffered to remain) will inevitably destroy the whole body of that extensive country."

On May 10, 1774, word reached Boston of Parliament's reaction to its Tea Party: a series of new laws. The first, the Boston Port Act, to take effect June 1, ordered the port of Boston closed to commerce until the tea was paid for. The second act, "for better regulating the Government of the Province of the Massachusetts-Bay," changed the colony's council from an elected to an appointed body. After August 1, 1774, no town meetings except for annual elections could be held anywhere without the governor's consent in writing. The third act, the Administration of Justice Act, allowed royal officials indicted for a capital offense while in line of duty to transfer their trials out of the province to ensure fair procedures. A fourth act, the Quartering Act, stipulated that housing for troops should be found close to trouble spots, not at distant Castle William.

On May 13, 1774, in order to enforce the Boston Port Act, HMS *Lively* sailed into Boston harbor carrying General Thomas Gage, commander in chief of British forces in

America. Gage landed in wind and rain on the seventeenth to relieve Governor Hutchinson, who sailed for England on June 1, the day the Boston Port Act went into effect. Three regiments of British troops followed Gage's arrival.

Instead of isolating Massachusetts, as planned, the Coercive Acts revealed a British power far more dangerous to liberty than mere taxation. In varying degrees, the twelve other colonial powers rallied to Massachusetts, and messengers from the committees of correspondence rode into Boston with reports. Christopher Gadsden wrote: "Don't pay for an ounce of the damned tea." He shipped rice to Boston from the planters of the Carolinas. From patriots in Norfolk: "Our hearts are warmed with affection for you. Be assured we consider you as suffering in the common cause and look upon ourselves as bound by the most sacred ties to support you."

On instructions from the Crown, General Gage removed the Massachusetts legislature (General Court) from Boston to Salem. On May 27, 1774, in Williamsburg, Virginia, a rump assembly, meeting in the historic Raleigh Tavern, sent out a call for a congress of all the colonies. In Salem, on June 17, the Massachusetts legislature, meeting behind locked doors for fear that General Gage would order the assembly dissolved, agreed to the congress "to consult upon the present State of the Colonies and the Miseries to which they are reduced by the Operation of certain Acts of Parliament respecting America." The legislature voted 120 to 12 to send five delegates as its representatives to Philadelphia in September: Thomas Cushing, Samuel Adams, Robert Treat Paine, John Adams and James Bowdoin.* With Gage's messenger pounding on the doors, it quickly appropriated £500 for the representatives' expenses. Then the delegates opened the doors, Gage's message ordering the assembly dissolved was read, and they walked out. It was the last General Court ever to convene in Massachusetts under royal authority.

John Adams heard of his appointment while riding the eastern circuit for the tenth and last time. "There is a new, and a grand Scene open before me — a Congress.

"This will be an assembly of the wisest Men upon the Continent."

* Bowdoin declined for family reasons to serve; he was not replaced.

Abigail and the children moved back to Braintree to live during his absences. Five British regiments encamped on Boston Common. Adams wrote James Warren: "Hampden died in the field, Sidney died on the scaffold, Harrington in jail, &c. Politicks are an ordeal path among red hot plough-shares. Who, then would be a politician for the pleasure of running about barefoot among them? Yet somebody must."

Farewell politics, indeed. The Adams family, for the first time, entered the stage of national and international politics. This son of a farmer and a shoemaker would soon take his place among men who, like him, were shaping their colonies' destinies: Roger Sherman, Joseph Galloway, John Dickinson, Peyton Randolph, George Washington, Richard Henry Lee, Christopher Gadsden, Patrick Henry, Philip Livingston, John Jay. They would be in the First Continental Congress, and debate the fundamental principles of government.

On August 10, 1774, accompanied as far as Watertown by sixty men on horseback to see them off, the Massachusetts delegates — Cushing, Paine and the two Adamses — left for Philadelphia.

"Clouds, indeed, and darkness," the great Edmund Burke warned Parliament, "rest upon the future."

The road from Boston to Philadelphia was one of the few good ones in the colonies. Along the way, especially in Connecticut, crowds greeted "the Boston committee" with enthusiasm. In New Haven, horsemen and carriages came out to meet them, bells were rung. "Men, Women and Children, were crowding at the Doors and Windows." Even Jared Ingersoll, Tory judge of admiralty and the infamous stamp master of '65, called on them "and made his Compliments very respectfully."

It was an impressive outburst. "No Governor of a Province, nor General of an Army was ever treated with so much Ceremony and Assidiuty, as We have been, throughout the whole Colony of Connecticutt."

By August 20, Adams and the others reached New York, where they stayed six days at the private house of Tobias Stoutenberg on Nassau Street near City Hall. New York troubled John Adams: it was a strongly conservative town, and its merchants were hostile to the plight of Boston. "This City," he wrote, "will be a Subject of much Speculation to me."

At this time, New York had about eighteen thousand citizens, slightly more than Boston, but the province as a whole had only two hundred thousand people, fewer than Massachusetts Bay. On his first day, after dinner, Adams walked to the Battery and enjoyed "a fine Prospect of Hudsons River and of the East River or the Sound and of the Harbour. . . . Between the Fort and the City is a beautiful Elipsis of Land, railed in with solid Iron, in the Center of which is a Statue of his Majesty on Horse back, very large, of solid Lead, gilded with Gold." Adams saw the shipyard, a stone hospital, the city prison, several markets, and "walked up the broad Way, a fine Street, very wide, and in a right Line from one End to the other of the City. . . . The Streets of this Town are vastly more regular and elegant than those in Boston, and the Houses are more grand as well as neat. They are almost all painted — brick buildings and all."

Adams never dined alone, and one day he and the others rode "three Miles out of Town" to have breakfast at John Morin Scott's home, "an elegant Seat . . . with Hudsons River just behind his House, and a rural Prospect all round him." (The Scott house stood on the present West Forty-third Street, between Eighth and Ninth avenues.) "A more elegant Breakfast, I never saw — rich Plate — a very large Silver Coffee Pott, a very large Silver Tea Pott — Napkins of the very finest Materials, and toast and bread and butter in great Perfection. After Breakfast, a Plate of beautiful Peaches, another of Pairs and another of Plums and a Muskmellen were placed on the Table."

Adams also spent an afternoon discussing politics with a group of New Yorkers that included Philip Livingston, "a great, rough, rappid Mortal. There is no holding any Conversation with him. He blusters away." Livingston worried about New England and its "Levelling Spirit" and "Hints were thrown out of the Goths and Vandalls — mention was made of our hanging the Quakers, &c."

Not surprisingly, Adams soon entered in his diary: "With all the Opulence and Splendor of this City, there is very little good Breeding to be found. We have been treated with an assiduous Respect. But I have not seen one real Gentleman, one well bred Man since I came to Town. At their Entertainment there is no Conversation that is agreable. There is no Modesty — No Attention to one another. They talk very loud, very fast, and alltogether. If they ask you a Question, before you can utter 3 Words of your Answer, they will break out upon you, again — and talk away."

In New York, Adams visited King's College (later Columbia University), "the Library, the Books and Curiosities," which included a class taught by one Dr. Clossy, "who was exhibiting a Course of Experiments to his Pupils to prove the Elasticity of the Air." Later, while crossing New Jersey during his trip, Adams also stopped at "Nassau Hall Colledge" in Princeton. "The Government of this Colledge is very Strict," he wrote, "and the Schollars study very hard. The President says they are all Sons of Liberty."

On August 29, Adams and his colleagues reached Philadelphia, then a city of thirty thousand, twice the size of Boston. As soon as he arrived — after a hot and dusty trip of nineteen days — he sent out his laundry: six shirts, five stocks, two caps, a pair of worsted stockings and one silk handkerchief.

The delegates of this first Congress were largely men of conservative temper, loyal to George III, and cautious. The delegates from Massachusetts Bay would be looked upon as radicals; Adams had been warned by Joseph Hawley to proceed with care. Accordingly, he held his vanity in check and made his own ability known while becoming acquainted with "a collection of the greatest Men upon this Continent in Point of Abilities, Virtues and Fortunes."

The first meeting began promptly on September 5. "At Ten," Adams wrote, "the Delegates all met at the City Tavern, and walked to the Carpenters Hall, where they took a View of the Room, and of the Chamber where is an excellent Library. There is also a long Entry, where Gentlemen may walk, and a convenient Chamber opposite to the Library. The General Cry was, that this was a good Room." In it, loyalty to the Crown did not prevent these fifty-five men from showing fidelity to conscience. Both John and Sam

Adams worked on the Declaration of Rights, and the Congress drew up Articles of Association, which amounted to a boycott of British trade.

Abigail, meanwhile, alone in Braintree, missed her husband deeply. She wrote him on August 19, 1774, shortly after he had left for Philadelphia: "The great distance between us, makes the time appear very long to me. It seems already a month since you left me. The great anxiety I feel for my Country, for you, and for our family renders the day tedious, and the night unpleasent. The Rocks and quick Sands appear upon every Side. What course you can or will take is all wrapt in the Bosom of futurity. Uncertainty and expectation leave the mind great Scope. Did ever any Kingdom or State regain their Liberty, when once it was invaded without Blood shed? I cannot think of it without horror. . . . I want much to hear from you. . . . I wish you every Publick as well as private blessing, and that wisdom which is profitable both for instruction and edification to conduct you in this difficult day. — The little flock remember Pappa, and kindly wish to see him. So does your most affectionate Abigail Adams."

What Abigail learned in John's return letters was that not all the important proceedings of the Congress took place in that agreeable "good Room." For the importance of the first Congress lay also in the simple fact of bringing together leaders of the thirteen colonies, who became acquainted, took measure of one another, and of the public opinion and leaders of other sections. The social gatherings were almost as important as the Congress itself. In his diary, John Adams entered:

"Dined with Mr. Chew, Chief Justice of the Province, with all the Gentlemen from Virginia, Dr. Shippen, Mr. Tilghman and many others. We were shewn into a grand Entry and Stair Case, and into an elegant and most magnificent Chamber, untill Dinner. About four O Clock We were called to Dinner. The Furniture was all rich. — Turttle, and every other Thing — Flummery, Jellies, Sweetmeats of 20 sorts, Trifles, Whip'd Syllabubbs, floating Islands, fools — &c., and then a Desert of Fruits, Raisins, Almonds, Pears, Peaches — Wines most excellent and admirable. I drank Madeira at a great Rate and found no Inconvenience in it. . . . In the

Life on the Adams farm was harsh and sometimes lonely. It never resembled the romanticized view held in the late eighteenth century, exemplified in this piece of needlework (right). New England farms were walled, fenced and often isolated, as the small drawing shows.

ABOVE: NEEDLEWORK PICTURE.
WOOL ON LINEN CANVAS,
BY MARY WOODHULL,
1775–1800

DETAIL: NEW ENGLAND FARM.
ENGRAVING FROM "TRAVELS IN
THE INTERIOR INHABITED PARTS
OF NORTH AMERICA," BY PATRICK
CAMPBELL, 1793

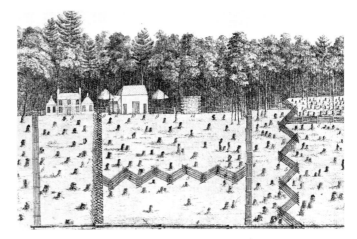

Evening General Lee and Col. Lee, and Col. Dyer and Mr. Deane, and half a Score friends from Boston came to our Lodgings. Col. Lee staid till 12 o Clock and was very social and agreable."

Adams met the Marylanders: "A mighty Feast again, nothing less than the very best Claret, Madeira, and Burgundy. Melons, fine beyond description, and Pears and Peaches as excellent."

On another day: "There is such a quick and constant Succession of new Scenes, Characters, Persons, and Events turning up before me that I cant keep any regular Account." In spite of terrapin, Madeira in great quantity and late hours, Adams's health was excellent.

While he was drinking Madeira, his countrymen were constructing embattlements on Breed's Hill. Tensions in Massachusetts Bay colony were rising daily, and on September 14, 1774, Abigail wrote John: "In consequence of the powders being taken from Charlstown, a general alarm spread thro many Towns and was caught pretty soon here. . . . About 8 o clock a Sunday Evening there pass[ed] by here about 200 Men, preceeded by a horse cart, and marched down to the powder house from whence they took the powder and carried [it] into the other parish and there secreeted it. I opened the window upon there return. They pass'd without any Noise, not a word among them till they came against this house, when some of them perceiveing me, askd me if I wanted any powder. I replied not since it was in so good hands."

Adams started home on October 28 "in a very great Rain, from the happy, the peacefull, the elegant, the hospitable, and polite City of Phyladelphia." It was not Philadelphia that filled him with such excitement, but Braintree — and the thought of seeing Abigail and his children. Only about three weeks earlier he had written: "Phyladelphia with all its Trade, and Wealth, and Regularity is not Boston. The Morals of our People are much better, their Manners are more polite, and agreable — they are purer English. Our Language is better, our Persons are handsomer, our Spirit is greater, our Laws are wiser, our Religion is superiour, our Education is better."

At home, Adams was elected an additional delegate to

the Provincial Congress meeting in Cambridge. During 1775, in reply to Daniel Leonard's MASSACHUSETTENSIS articles, he wrote a series of historical and polemical accounts of events leading to the First Continental Congress. The articles were signed NOVANGLUS and were published in the *Boston Gazette*. In them Adams denied the supremacy of Parliament over the colonies and insisted that the colonial legislatures were supreme in America. The colonies were not part of an empire but separate entities; regulation of colonial trade by Parliament was only by colonial consent. Adams kept his articles running every week until April 7, 1775, when fighting halted publication of the *Gazette*.

General Gage's duty was to halt rebellion in Boston and enforce the Coercive Acts. News that Massachusetts patriots were storing powder and arms at Concord set him into motion. On the night of April 18, 1775, Gage ordered a heavy detail of British regulars out of Boston to seize these stores. But Paul Revere and William Dawes aroused the countryside, and when British Major John Pitcairn, after a night of marching, brought his regulars out of the early morning mists into Lexington, he found a small knot of Minute Men lined up against him. Shots sounded, and eight Americans fell dead, ten wounded. When the British continued their march to Concord, "embattled farmers" at the bridge "fired the shot heard round the world." There could be no conciliation now. As the British regiments marched back to Boston, all along the road, behind stone walls, hillocks, barns and houses, the rebels made targets of the red coats. When the battered column staggered into Boston, it left behind seventy-three British soldiers killed, 173 wounded. "The Sword of Rebellion," said John Singleton Copley, "is drawn."

John Adams visited the American officers and rode to Lexington after the battle to ask the people what had happened. What they told him was "not calculated to diminish my Ardour in the Cause. They on the Contrary convinced me that the Die was cast, the Rubicon passed, and as Lord Mansfield expressed it in Parliament, if We did not defend ourselves they would kill Us."

Adams returned shortly to Philadelphia for the Second Continental Congress, which convened on May 10, 1775. The

OVERLEAF
The four prints of the battles of Lexington and Concord on the next pages were made from copper plates engraved by Amos Doolittle of New Haven. Within two weeks after the battles Doolittle, who had marched to Cambridge with the Connecticut Guards, visited the sites, made sketches, and took notes. His work is historically and topographically accurate, although the British were in more disarray at Lexington than Doolittle's engraving (at top) shows.

THE BATTLES OF LEXINGTON AND CONCORD.
LINE ENGRAVINGS BY AMOS DOOLITTLE, 1775

TOP: THE BATTLE OF LEXINGTON (AT THE BEGINNING
OF COMBAT)

MIDDLE: A VIEW OF THE TOWN OF CONCORD (AS THE
BRITISH MUSTER THEIR FORCES)

BOTTOM: THE ENGAGEMENT AT THE NORTH BRIDGE IN
CONCORD ("THE SHOT HEARD ROUND THE WORLD")

DETAIL: A VIEW OF THE SOUTH PART OF LEXINGTON (THE BRITISH HARASSED ON THEIR RETURN TO BOSTON)

war was spreading: on that same day, Ethan Allen and his Green Mountain Boys, along with Colonel Benedict Arnold, seized Fort Ticonderoga in a daring raid. This Congress was sharply divided between those Americans longing for reconciliation and those pushing hard for separation. Parliament was likewise divided. The factions debated similar issues on both sides of the Atlantic, with opposite results.

The prospect was peace, Edmund Burke insisted to his brethren in the House of Commons. But his voice of reason was lost in the din of the king's men seeking submission, not negotiation. "Conciliation failing, force remains; but, force failing, no further hope of reconciliation is left," Burke warned them on March 22, 1775. The next day, four thousand miles away, Patrick Henry allegedly told his Virginia brethren: "Gentlemen may cry, 'Peace, peace,' but there is no peace. The war is actually begun! Is life so dear or peace so sweet as to be purchased at the price of chains and slavery? I know not what course others may take, but as for me, give me liberty or give me death."

William Pitt moved in the House of Lords that the British troops in Boston, which were causing hardship and making a violent town a desperate one, be immediately withdrawn. "What is our right to persist in such·cruel and vindictive measures against that loyal and respectable people?" he asked. "You may spread fire, sword and desolation," declared the duke of Richmond seconding Pitt's motion, "but that will not be government." But Pitt's attempt at conciliation was overwhelmingly defeated.

So, too, did the American Congress debate, and with similar results, but from a differing viewpoint. John Adams, writing as NOVANGLUS, had said: "There is no avoiding all inconveniences in human affairs. The greatest possible or conceivable, would arise from ceding to Parliament power over us without representation in it." Adams was most impatient for independence. His fervor was not diminished by letters from Abigail.

In Braintree, with the "distressed inhabitants" of Boston fleeing past their farmhouse, and Continental soldiers being lodged and fed in her home, Abigail wrote John on June 16: "We now expect our Sea coasts ravaged. Perhaps, the very next Letter I write will inform you that I am driven away from our, yet quiet cottage. Necessity will oblige Gage to take some desperate steps. We are told for Truth, that he is now Eight thousand strong. We live in continual expectation of allarms. Courage I know we have in abundance, conduct I hope we shall not want, but powder — where shall we get a sufficient supply?"

With Massachusetts under attack, Adams fidgeted at the windy debates blowing through the Second Congress. Abigail asked: "Does every Member [of Congress] feel for us? Can they realize what we suffer?" And John answered: "No. They cant, They dont. There are some Persons in New York and Philadelphia to whom a ship is dearer than a City, and a few Barrells of flower, than a thousand Lives — other Mens Lives I mean." To Dr. Joseph Warren he poured out his frustration: "We find a great many Bundles of weak Nerves. We are obliged to be as delicate and soft and modest and humble as possible."

Abigail was John's most vivid and outspoken correspondent during these months. She knew the leaders of the Provincial Congress in Watertown, Massachusetts, from James Warren down, and carried on a spirited correspondence with Mrs. Warren, who was gathering material for her own three-volume *History of Massachusetts*. To John, she wrote of military actions, the coming independence, of politics and issues.

Abigail asked gently about John's health — he was having eye trouble — and spoke "ardently" for his return. And she gently pestered him for some domestic necessities. On June 16, 1775, she wrote: "I have a request to make of you. Something like the Barrel of Sand suppose you will think it, but really of much more importance to me. It is that you would . . . purchase me a bundle of pins and put in your trunk for me. The cry for pins is so great that what we used to Buy for 7.6 are now 20 Shillings and not to be had for that."

Sometimes echoes of Abigail's letters were heard before Congress. The radicals of this gathering opposed petitions to King George III for conciliation. What, they asked, were the surest conciliatory measures? "Powder and artillery," said John Adams.

GEORGE WASHINGTON. OIL BY CHARLES WILLSON PEALE, 1772

The Second Continental Congress was exquisitely split: on June 3, 1775, it named one committee to prepare a second petition for conciliation to the king, and another committee to find ways to borrow £6,000 to purchase powder to attack the king's men.

War, not conciliation, swept Massachusetts. General Gage was being besieged in Boston by the colonial militia that had formed an army with no legal basis for existence. Adams, and others, saw that Congress must adopt that army and appoint its commanding general. But who? The army was a New England — and largely Massachusetts — outfit. Intercolonial jealousies and rivalries still split the Congress. Bickering over the army and its command would paralyze the colonies at a time when they faced an increasingly bitter, and common, enemy.

On June 14, 1775, John Adams rose before Congress to nominate a commander. Hancock, as president of the Congress, faced Adams; and Hancock had very much wanted the post. As Adams detailed the state of the colonies and the army, and spoke of the gentleman "among Us . . . whose Skill and Experience as an Officer, whose independent fortune, great Talents and excellent universal Character, would command the Approbation of all America," he watched Hancock's face glow with smug vanity. But when Adams mentioned Washington's name, Hancock's expression quickly shifted. "I never remarked," wrote Adams later, "a more sudden and sinking Change of Countenance. Mortification and resentment were expressed as forcibly as his Face could exhibit them. Mr. Samuel Adams Seconded the Motion, and that did not soften the Presidents Phisiognomy at all."

It was a small delight for Adams, who perhaps remembered how Hancock had shifted his legal business to a Tory, and a wise move: Washington, a Virginian, would take over troops fighting in Massachusetts, and unite North and South in their common cause. On June 15, Washington was elected commander in chief, "an honor," he wrote, "I neither sought after, nor desired." Congress also elected additional officers, and, to raise revenue, voted $2 million in bills of credit.

On June 18, 1775, Abigail wrote John: "The Day; perhaps the decisive Day is come on which the fate of America depends. My bursting Heart must find vent at my pen." Dr. Joseph Warren, close friend of the Adamses', had been killed in battle. His body remained behind British lines. "Charlstown is laid in ashes. The Battle began upon our intrenchments upon Bunkers Hill, a Saturday morning about 3 o'clock and has not ceased yet and tis now 3 o'clock Sabbeth afternoon."

Abigail and John Quincy, then eight years old, climbed to the top of Penn's Hill behind the farm and watched the burning of Charlestown. John Quincy would later remember: "For . . . twelve months my mother with her infant children dwelt, liable every hour of the day and of the night to be butchered in cold blood, or taken and carried into Boston as hostages. . . . I saw with my own eyes those fires [in Charlestown], and heard Britannia's thunders in the Battle of Bunker's Hill."

At Bunker Hill (actually Breed's Hill) the British had won a tactical victory by driving the Americans from their embattlements on the hill with bayonets after twice being repulsed. But the cost was fearful: 1,054 British casualties out of 2,400 men.

On July 2, General Washington reached Massachusetts and took command the next day. Abigail met him and General Charles Lee, and reported to John: "The appointment of the Generals Washington and Lee, gives universal satisfaction. . . . I was struck with General Washington. You had prepaired me to entertain a favorable opinion of him, but I thought the one half was not told me. Dignity with ease, and complacency, the Gentleman and Soldier look agreably blended in him. Modesty marks every line and feture of his face. . . . General Lee looks like a careless hardy Veteran."

The Congress, meanwhile, tried to balance independence and conciliation. The impatience of John Adams was offset by the caution of John Dickinson, who, while fighting continued in Massachusetts, proposed the "Olive Branch" petition to George III. Dickinson was upset by New England's opposition to his conciliatory measures, and one time after a heated debate he encountered John Adams and upbraided him for his stubborn insistence upon independence.

But even this man sought redress. Dickinson and Jeffer-

This detail of a crude map, drawn in 1775, shows British and American positions in and near Boston. The number 14 (near the center) locates Breed's Hill; the number 13, Bunker Hill. In the surrounding countryside, reported a Loyalist mapmaker, "Not a Hillock 6 feet High but What is entrench'd, not a pass where a man could go but what is defended by Cannon; fences pulled down, houses removed, Woods grubbed up, Fields cut into trenches and molded into Ramparts."

OVERLEAF
When the great battle began, and the British shelled Charlestown before attacking Breed's Hill, the earth shook and the roar of cannon was so loud that it frightened Abigail Adams and her children in Braintree.

ATTACK ON BUNKER'S HILL, WITH THE BURNING OF CHARLES TOWN. OIL BY AN UNKNOWN AMERICAN ARTIST, 1783 OR LATER

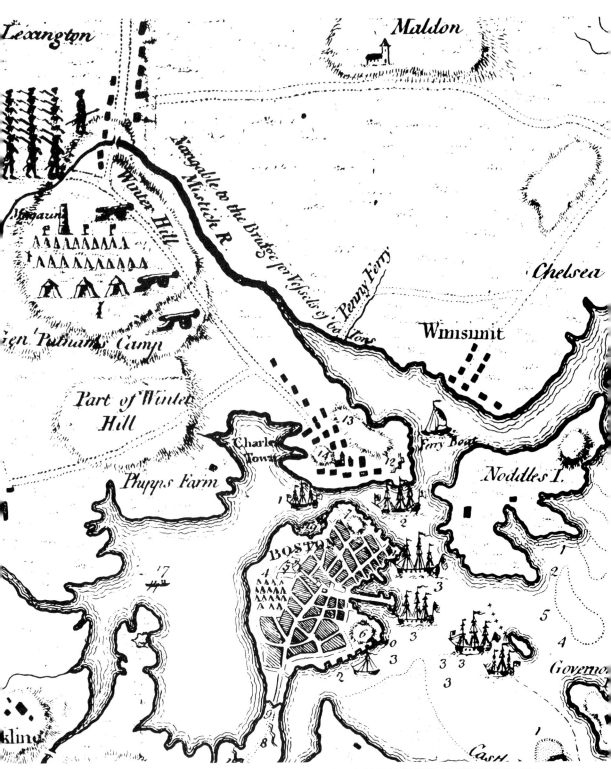

Lexington

Maldon

Chelsea

Winter Hill

Navigable to the Bridge for Vessels of 60 Tons

Mistick R.

Penny Ferry

Winisimit

Magazine

Gen' Putnam's Camp

Part of Winter Hill

Charles Town

Ferry Boat

Noddles I.

Phipps Farm

13

14   12

BOSTON

7

2

4

3

6   3

3

5

3   3   4

7

3

2

Governo

2

9

8

Cash.

kling

DETAIL: MAP OF BATTLE OF BUNKER HILL, TOWN AND HARBOR OF BOSTON, BY CHARLES HALL, 1775

son — a neat balance of conservative and radical — struggled to put together a "Declaration of the Causes and Necessity of Taking up Arms." Jefferson noted that the Pennsylvanian "was so honest a man, and so able a one, that he was greatly indulged even by those who could not feel his scruples." Dickinson could be driven to anger despite his hesitations. "While we revere and love our mother country," he wrote, "her sword is opening our veins." This collaboration between the two wings of the Second Congress succeeded. On July 6, 1775, Congress approved their statement: "We for ten years incessantly and ineffectually besieged the Throne as supplicants; we reasoned, we remonstrated with Parliament. . . . Our cause is just. Our union is perfect. Our internal resources are great, and, if necessary, foreign assistance is undoubtedly attainable. . . . The arms we have been compelled by our enemies to assume, we will . . . employ for the preservation of our liberties; being with our [one] mind resolved to dye Free-men rather than live Slaves."

Having done this, however, Dickinson insisted upon his Olive Branch. Half of Congress was outraged. Jefferson said: "The disgust against this humility was general." Adams agreed and called it "this Measure of Imbecility . . . [that] embarrassed every Exertion of Congress." Although the vote to accept the petition was unanimous, several members, including John Adams, signed the agreement with protest. Dickinson, noting that the assembly had inscribed its word "Congress" on the petition, rose and said: "There is but one word, Mr. President, in the paper which I disapprove, and that is the word *Congress*." Benjamin Harrison of Virginia countered: "There is but one word in the paper, Mr. President, of which I approve, and that is the word *Congress*." Franklin called the Olive Branch "another humble petition to the crown which, however, I think she has not sense enough to embrace." Indeed, George III refused even to accept the petition.

Dickinson's insistence upon conciliation and his slowness to see the desperation that John Adams saw — and heard about — in Massachusetts angered Adams. This led to a careless incident.

On July 24, 1775, John Adams wrote James Warren in a

mood of exasperation with John Dickinson, and alluded to Dickinson as "a certain great Fortune and piddling Genius [who] has given a silly Cast to our whole Doings." That same day, he wrote Abigail and complained about "the Fidgets, the Whims, the Caprice, the Vanity, the Superstition, the Irritibility of some of us," and the "Difficulty and Intricacy" of his work. Adams wrote that things were proceeding too slowly, and that "50 or 60 Men have a Constitution to form for a great Empire, at the same Time that they have a Country of fifteen hundred Miles extent to fortify, Millions to arm and train, a Naval Power to begin, an extensive Commerce to regulate, numerous Tribes of Indians to negotiate with, a standing Army of Twenty seven Thousand Men to raise, pay, victual and officer."

Both letters fell into British hands when the bearer, a young Boston lawyer named Benjamin Hichborn, was captured at the Conanicut Ferry near Newport, Rhode Island. The messages amused and outraged the British, who immediately had them printed in the *Boston News Letter*. Loyalists and British readers were especially shocked by the references to the colonies writing "a Constitution" and building "a Naval Power." Members of Congress exploded. Dickinson shunned Adams completely. Although Adams later said that publication of the letters did more good than harm by forcing Congress to discuss independence, that may have been a balm. As it was, he had been hurt by his impetuousness.

Congress also dealt with the small-bore matters of petty accounts, leadership rivalries, faltering loyalties, sectionalism. It was uncertain, divided, sometimes acrimonious, lacking money and struggling to understand and master the perils it faced. After adjournment on August 2, 1775, for a month, more than half the delegates headed north to see the army in Massachusetts — almost as though they were seeking physical proof of their own action. John Adams went home to Abigail — and brought her the requested pins.

Too soon, he returned to Philadelphia and stayed until December. In the records of this Congress, his name appears as chairman of twenty-five committees. He was also a member of many others.

That fall, while he was gone, Abigail once again looked

after the four children and the farm. Schools were closed and Adams's clerk, Nathan Rice, who had helped out last year, was now in the Continental Army. John Adams emphasized to Abigail the proper education of their children: "John [Quincy] has Genius and so has Charles. Take Care that they dont go astray. Cultivate their Minds, inspire their little Hearts, raise their Wishes. Fix their Attention upon great and glorious Objects, root out every little Thing, weed out every Meanness, make them great and manly. Teach them to scorn Injustice, Ingratitude, Cowardice, and Falshood. Let them revere nothing but Religion, Morality and Liberty." Abigail instructed her children, putting Nabby through the Latin *Accidence* and Tandon's *A New French Grammar* with her brothers.

Abigail had little trouble with the farm or the children. But she had good reason to fear what all people of that age feared: epidemic diseases. Abigail's home and family and the entire colony were swept by dysentery that fall of 1775, and by smallpox. John Adams's brother Elihu, in command of a company of troops at Cambridge, had died of dysentery in August. Abigail came down with it, and her children in succession. "Since you left me," she wrote John, "I have passed thro great distress both of Body and mind. . . . I was seaz'd with [a dysentery] in a violent manner. . . . Our Little Tommy . . . lies very ill now — there is no abatement at present of his disorder. . . . Our House is an hospital in every part."

The healthy tried to save the sick. "A general putrefaction seems to have taken place, and we can not bear the House only as we are constantly clensing it with hot vinegar." Abigail's mother came to the farmhouse every day to treat Abigail and Tommy. On September 25, she caught "the disorder" from them, and died six days later. "The Hand of God presseth me soar," wrote Abigail of her mother's death. "Tis a dreadful time with this whole province. Sickness and death are in almost every family."

It was a difficult time, too, for the cause of independence. The ostensible purpose of the two Continental Congresses was to get the Coercive Acts repealed, restore relations with England, and avert war and the trial of revolution. As late as the fall of 1775, the legislatures of North Carolina, Pennsylvania, New Jersey, New York and Maryland went on record against independence. Yet they could not profess allegiance while refusing obedience; moderates tried to persuade themselves that they were not opposing the king but the tyrannies of his ministers. They referred to the enemy as "ministerial," not British, soldiers. As late as January, 1776, the king's health was toasted nightly in General Washington's officers' mess.

But it was clear that independence was vital for military success; and military success was necessary to relieve the yoke of oppression. After so many had fallen at Bunker Hill and in the unsuccessful assault on Quebec in December, 1775, something permanent had to be established. Once again, the British helped. Not only did George III refuse to receive the Olive Branch, but also he and his Parliament ordered all trade and intercourse with the thirteen colonies halted on December 22, 1775. "It is," wrote John Adams gleefully, "a compleat Dismemberment of the British Empire. It throws thirteen Colonies out of the Royal Protection . . . and makes us independent in spite of all our supplications and Entreaties."

In January, 1776, Thomas Paine published his pamphlet *Common Sense*, which stated the case for independence in crisp language that appealed to the common man. It attacked George III, the British constitution and the empire, and restated the natural-rights philosophy that would form part of the Declaration of Independence. Strangely, John Adams did not like this call to America's common people, perhaps because he found the pamphlet too simplistic or extreme in the kind of broad democracy Paine advocated — or because Paine achieved instant national and international recognition while Adams labored obscurely. Whichever, John Adams wrote *Thoughts on Government*, in which he set forth his ideas for a checks-and-balances, bicameral government.

Events moved rapidly, almost inevitably. In January, 1776, Lord Dunmore bombarded and set fire to Norfolk, and patriots countered by firing Tory homes. Loyalists sought the protection of the British fleet. In February, embattled North Carolina farmers routed British troops and American Loyalists at Moore's Creek Bridge. In April, the North Carolina legislature authorized its delegates to the Continental Congress to join in the move to declare independence and form foreign alliances.

In Braintree Abigail suffered as much from being separated from John as from the war. Her letters, full of information, were also warm, reaching and sometimes passionate. In April, 1776, she wrote: "I miss my partner, and find myself uneaquil to the cares which fall upon me; I find it necessary to be the directress of our Husbandery and farming. . . . I hope in time to have the Reputation of being as good a *Farmeress* as my partner has of being a good Statesmen." And in the same letter she continued: "Write me how you do this winter. I want to say many things I must omit, it is not fit to wake the Soul by tender strokes of art, or to Ruminate upon happiness we might enjoy, least absence become intolerable. Adieu Yours." And in a postscript: "I wish you would burn all my Letters."

While John Adams was in Philadelphia working for independence, Abigail made declarations of her own for women's liberation. On March 31, 1776, she wrote John: "I have sometimes been ready to think that the passion for Liberty cannot be Eaquelly Strong in the Breasts of those who have been accustomed to deprive their fellow Creatures of theirs. . . . I am certain that it is not founded upon that generous and christian principle of doing to others as we would that others should do unto us. . . .

"I long to hear that you have declared an independancy — and by the way in the new Code of Laws which I suppose it will be necessary for you to make I desire you would Remember the Ladies, and be more generous and favorable to them than your ancestors. Do not put such unlimited power into the hands of the Husbands. Remember all Men would be tyrants if they could. If particular care and attention is not paid to the Ladies, we are determined to foment a Rebelion, and will not hold ourselves bound by any Laws in which we have no voice, or Representation.

"That your Sex are Naturally Tyrannical is a Truth so thoroughly established as to admit of no dispute, but such of you as wish to be happy willingly give up the harsh title of Master for the more tender and endearing one of Friend.

Why then, not put it out of the power of the vicious and the Lawless to use us with cruelty and indignity with impunity. Men of Sense in all Ages abhor those customs which treat us only as the vassals of your Sex. Regard us then as Beings placed by providence under your protection and in immitation of the Supreem Being make use of that power only for our happiness."

John Adams mulled this over in Philadelphia, and replied to Abigail on April 14: "As to your extraordinary Code of Laws, I cannot but laugh. We have been told that our Struggle has loosened the bands of Government every where. That Children and Apprentices were disobedient — that schools and Colledges were grown turbulent — that Indians slighted their Guardians, and Negroes grew insolent to their Masters. But your Letter was the first Intimation that another Tribe more numerous and powerful than all the rest were grown discontented. — This is rather too coarse a Compliment but you are so saucy, I won't blot it out.

"Depend on it. We know better than to repeal our Masculine systems. Although they are in full Force, you know they are little more than Theory. We dare not exert our Power in its full Latitude. We are obliged to go fair, and softly, and in Practice you know We are the subjects. We have only the Name of Masters, and rather than give up this, which would compleatly subject Us to the Despotism of the Peticoat, I hope General Washington, and all our Heroes would fight. I am sure every good Politician would plot . . . as he would against Despotism, Empire, Monarchy, Aristocracy, Oligarchy or Ochlocracy."

Abigail, dissatisfied with John's reply, wrote back on May 7: "I can not say that I think you very generous to the Ladies, for whilst you are proclaiming peace and good will to Men, Emancipating all Nations, you insist upon retaining an absolute power over Wives. But you must remember that Arbitrary power is like most other things which are very hard, very liable to be broken — and notwithstanding all your wise Laws and Maxims, we have it in our power not only to free ourselves but to subdue our Masters, and without violence throw both your natural and legal authority at our feet." Adams was unmoved.

In early March, 1776, Washington bombarded the British in Boston to divert their attention before assaulting and fortifying the heights on Dorchester Neck. Large numbers of cannon and local militia had been called up for the battle. The cannonading was continuous, and frightening. Abigail wrote John on March 3:

"I went to Bed after 12 but got no rest. The Cannon continued firing and my Heart Beat pace with them all night." Two days later she wrote again: "I went to bed about 12 and rose again a little after one. I could no more sleep than if I had been in the ingagement. The ratling of the windows, the jar of the house and the continual roar of 24 pounders, the Bursting of shells give us such Ideas, and realize a scene to us of which we could scarcely form any conception. About Six this morning, there was quiet; I rejoiced in a few hours calm. . . . To night we shall realize a more terible scene still. I sometimes think I cannot stand it — I wish myself with you, out of hearing as I cannot assist them." On March 10, she again shuddered to the cannonading: "I had scarcely finished these lines when my Ears were again assaulted with the roar of Cannon. I could not write any further. My Hand and heart will tremble, at this domestick fury, and firce civil Strife. . . . A most Terible and incessant Cannonade from half after 8 till Six this morning."

The struggle in Boston for Dorchester Neck and the heights controlling part of the city was successful. Bad weather and rough water prevented an assault by the British on the American fortifications, which got stronger by the hour. On March 17, General Howe evacuated Boston, putting all his troops and a thousand or so Loyalists on ships in the harbor.

Congress, seated on cushioned chairs within the white-paneled walls and high windows of the State House in Philadelphia, moved slowly to act. It opened colonial ports to all foreign vessels except those of England, and dispatched Silas Deane to France to purchase war materials and provisions. On May 10, it advised the colonies to form independent governments which "best conduc[e] to the happiness and safety of their constituents in particular, and America in general." Adams wrote the preamble to this recommendation, which one delegate called "a machine for the fabrication of independence" and Adams thought was independence itself.

"This day," he wrote James Warren, "the Congress has passed the most important Resolution that ever was taken in America." And to Abigail: "G[reat] B[ritain] has at least driven America, to the last Step, a compleat Seperation from her, a total absolute Independence, not only of her Parliament but of her Crown."

On Friday, June 7, 1776, Richard Henry Lee of Virginia proposed a resolution to declare the colonies free and independent of England. The motion was seconded, and debate raged that day and the next. Dickinson was in and out of the room, now arguing against Lee and the two Adamses, now across the hallway with the Pennsylvania delegates. Edward Rutledge wrote his conservative colleague John Jay, absent in New York: "I wish you had been here; the whole Argument was sustained on one side by R. Livingston, Wilson, Dickinson and myself, and by the Power of all N. England, Virginia and Georgia on the other."

The debate on Lee's motion was postponed until July 1. Delegates rode home to ask their assemblies for instructions to vote for or against. Meanwhile, both factions agreed that it would be wise to have a well-prepared declaration of independence ready, should the vote be affirmative. A committee of five was appointed: Jefferson, Adams, Franklin, Roger Sherman and Robert R. Livingston. They agreed on the broad articles of the declaration, and appointed a subcommittee of Jefferson and Adams to make the draft. In his *Autobiography*, John Adams wrote this account of his and Jefferson's meeting to write the most historic document in American history:

"Mr. Jefferson desired me to . . . make the Draught. This I declined and gave several reasons for declining. 1 That he was a Virginian and I a Massachusettensian. 2. that he was a southern Man and I a northern one. 3. That I had been so obnoxious for my early and constant Zeal in promoting the Measure, that any draught of mine, would undergo a more severe Scrutiny and Criticism in Congress, than one of his composition. 4thly and lastly and that would be reason enough if there were no other, I had a great Opinion of the

Elegance of his pen and none at all of my own. I therefore insisted that no hesitation should be made on his part. He accordingly took the Minutes and in a day or two produced to me his Draught. Whether I made or suggested any corrections I remember not."

Jefferson's account differs, but whichever, all in Congress agreed on one thing: they disliked the draft. John Adams claimed that it contained no new ideas. Richard Lee said it was copied from Locke's treatise on government. Others protested that it contained ideas that had already been discussed in Congress during the last two years. This was, of course, its strength: the Declaration proposed what everyone was thinking. "I turned to neither book nor pamphlet while writing it," Jefferson said later. "I did not consider it as any part of my charge to invent new ideas altogether and to offer no sentiment which had ever been expressed before."

Meanwhile, Adams's constituents wondered what was delaying Congress from action. "What in the name of *Common Sense* are you gentlemen of the Continental Congress about?" Benjamin Kent wrote him angrily. "Is it dozing, amusing itself?"

"Remember," Adams replied, "you cannot make thirteen clocks strike precisely alike at the same Second."

Opposition had been strong and vocal. Robert Morris, the merchant, held out against separation at any time. The Rutledges wanted South Carolina to set up its own government. Livingston was fearful that total separation would result in mob rule and a "democracy." Carter Braxton of Virginia (replacing Peyton Randolph, who had died of apoplexy), an aristocrat to his small-boned, ruffled wrists, argued that independence was "a delusive Bait, which men inconsiderately catch at, without knowing the Hook to which it is affixed."

Debate on Lee's motion began July 1. The day was stifling; the delegates sweated and fidgeted. John Dickinson had prepared — "with great Labour and ardent Zeal" — a long speech, which he delivered "with great Ingenuity and Eloquence," according to John Adams.

No one rose to oppose him. Adams looked about the room and "after waiting some time, in hopes that some one

Twenty years after the Declaration of Independence was signed, Edward Savage began his painting commemorating the event. Some of the men, like John Adams (standing, extreme left) might have been painted from life. Others, like Benjamin Franklin (seated, center) were from likenesses originally done by other artists. This engraving of Savage's work gives an accurate picture of the Assembly Room of Independence Hall where the signing took place.

THE CONGRESS VOTING INDEPENDENCE. STIPPLE ENGRAVING BY EDWARD SAVAGE,
STARTED AFTER 1788, UNFINISHED

RAISING THE LIBERTY POLE. COLORED ENGRAVING BY JOHN MC RAE, ABOUT 1820

The local taverns
rang with liberty
songs, and patriots
hung effigies of cus-
toms officials and King
George on the Liberty
Tree. One boisterous
ceremony was the
raising of the Liberty
Pole, sometimes
thought to be the first
Fourth of July cele-
bration.

less obnoxious than myself, who had been all along for a Year
before, and still was represented and believed to be the
Author of all the Mischief, I determined to speak."

There is no surviving record of what he said; he made no
preparation and never made an effort at verbatim recollection.
By some accounts, Adams began speaking about four o'clock
in the afternoon. During his speech a storm broke, and rain
poured down easing the heat. Adams had to raise his voice
over the thunder. It grew dark, and Hancock beckoned the
clerk for candles.

Before the final question was called and a vote taken, the
New Jersey delegation burst in, wet and dripping. Adams was
called upon to summarize the arguments for them. Afterwards, one of the New Jersey members, Dr. John Witherspoon of Princeton, ignoring the fact that he was new to the
Congress, stepped forward. His coat was still streaked with
rain; his clergyman's bib wilted on his chest. "The distinguished gentleman from Massachusetts," he said in his loud,
nasal voice, "remarked when we came in that the colonies are
ripe for independence. I would like to add that some colonies" — Witherspoon looked pointedly at the New York
delegation — "some colonies are rotten for the want of it."

On July 2, 1776, the vote for Lee's resolution was taken,
and it passed 12 to 0, with New York abstaining:

"*Resolved:* That these United States are, and, of right
ought to be, Free and Independent States; that they are ab-
solved from all allegiance to the British crown, and that all
political connexion between them, and the state of Great
Britain, is, and ought to be, totally dissolved."

John Adams had been instrumental in shaping his country's destiny. Of his work in getting Lee's resolution passed,
Jefferson wrote in 1813: "He was the pillar of its support on
the floor of Congress, its ablest advocate and defender against
the multifarious assaults it encountered."

Adams's persistence won. The ambition, intelligence,
skill which he honed daily saw its moment: on July 4, 1776,
after further debate, the text of the Declaration of Independence was approved. Indeed, thirteen clocks had struck as
one.

3

And Thus Are Kingdoms Obtained

[1776–1785]

*T*HE last leaf of the Olive Branch fell almost unnoticed. While Richard Henry Lee's resolution was being debated, Sir William Howe, after retreating from Boston on March 17, 1776, waited in Halifax until June 7 for reinforcements from England. He and his brother, Admiral Lord Howe, then sailed into New York harbor, Sir William landing July 2, and Lord Richard on July 12, 1776. These Howe brothers, Whig sympathizers, brought the Olive Branch with their swords.

Franklin, Edward Rutledge and Adams rode from Philadelphia to Staten Island to meet with Admiral Howe. On the way, Franklin and Adams shared a bed overnight at an inn in New Brunswick, and argued over whether or not to open the window: Adams feared the night air and the risk of a cold; Franklin held forth on his "Theory of Colds" and issued "an harrangue, upon Air and cold and Respiration and Perspiration" until they both fell asleep. The window stayed open. Once in Staten Island, the colonists heard Howe's offer from the king — granting clemency to the rebels if they would stop fighting, but no guarantee of future liberty. Adams and Franklin knew the chances for peace with Britain were closed forever.

Americans were not as united and determined as the ringing phrases of the Declaration of Independence suggest. The Revolution was fought with a lack of enthusiasm on both sides. George III had to hire mercenaries, his army was so widely engaged and his own subjects were so reluctant to enlist. British officers resigned their commissions rather than fight in America. On the colonial side, Washington's troops saw little need for continuous fighting: when New England was cleared, it was difficult to get Yankees to march to the aid of the Middle Colonies or the South. After the first enthusiasms of 1775, it was equally difficult to get southerners to march north. Few Americans would do any sustained fighting anywhere for their country: enlistments during the war totaled several hundred thousand; but Washington's standing army reached a peak strength of eighteen thousand men in 1776, and that fell to five thousand by the end of the year.

In fact, the Revolution was a civil war. The Loyalist minority helped prolong the fighting by whipping up enthusiasm in England among the British. Many of those remaining in the thirteen United States took up arms: New York furnished more soldiers to George III than to George Washington. It was John Butler's Tory Rangers and Guy Johnson's Royal Greens who, with Seneca and Cayuga Indians, committed the war's worst atrocity: the Wyoming massacre in northern Pennsylvania. In the South, the Loyalists and patriots fought bitter, personal feuds.

Supplying the rebel army was a problem, for Congress was weak and, until the Articles of Confederation were ratified, it had only moral authority. Congress made requisitions on the states for so many recruits for so many months or years of service. To get arms and munitions, it turned to supplies from France, captured matériel, and local enterprise. No battle was lost for want of arms or powder; but Continental soldiers did march barefoot to surprise and defeat the Hessians at Trenton on Christmas Eve, 1776, and left bloody footprints in the snow.

Congress that year, after the signing, spent much of its time fleeing the British. On December 12, 1776, it had adjourned in Philadelphia as Howe's army drove Washington's through New Jersey to the Delaware River. Congress reconvened at Baltimore, went back to Philadelphia until Howe occupied that city in September, 1777, then went off to Lancaster and York, Pennsylvania. John Adams dutifully followed, and presided over the Board of War and Ordnance, which handled military operations, recruits, defenses, prisoners, supplies, courts-martial, the rank of officers, and such. Adams knew at first hand that the American army was understaffed, undersupplied and decimated by illness.

He also knew, through Abigail, the hardship in the colonies. Congress, attempting to pay for the war and its supplies, had issued national bills of credit (the famous Continental currency), made requisitions on the states for money and kind, and contracted domestic and foreign loans. It was for this last purpose that it had sent Silas Deane of Connecticut to Paris. At home, both the state bills and the Continental bills depreciated rapidly; prices rose sharply as the currency devalued. Rioting broke out. Abigail wrote of one incident on July 31, 1777:

"It was rumourd that an eminent, wealthy, stingy Merchant (who is a Batchelor)* had a Hogshead of Coffe in his Store which he refused to sell to the committee under 6 shillings per pound. A Number of Females some say a hundred, some say more assembled with a cart and trucks, marchd down to the Ware House and demanded the keys, which he refused to deliver, upon which one of them seazd him by his Neck and tossd him into the cart. Upon his finding no Quarter he deliverd the keys, when they tipd up the cart and dischargd him, then opend the Warehouse, Hoisted out the Coffe themselves, put it into the trucks and drove off."

During this difficult time, Abigail gave birth to a stillborn daughter, a loss both she and John felt for a long time. In early August, she wrote her husband somewhat ruefully: "Tis almost 14 years since we were united, but not more than

* The bachelor was thought to be Thomas Boylston, a cousin of John Adams's mother.

half that time have we had the happiness of living together."

When Adams went home in November, he had strong reasons, as he put it, "to decline the next Election and return to my practice at the Bar." On January 3, 1778, the Massachusetts General Court paid him £226 6s. 2d. "in full Satisfaction of his Services & Expenses as a Delegate at the Continentale Congress for the Year 1776." It was hardly enough. In fear, as friends warned him, that he "was losing a fortune every Year by my Absence," he returned home and resolved not to run for reelection. "I had been four Years in Congress," he reasoned, "left my Accounts in a very loose condition, my Debtors were failing, the paper Money was depreciating, I was daily loosing the fruits of seventeen Years industry, my family was living on my past Acquisitions which were very moderate, for no Man ever did so much Business for so little profit. My Children were growing up without my care in their Education: and all my [pay] imoluments as a Member of Congress for four Years, had not been sufficient to pay a labouring Man upon my farm."

But during a trial at Portsmouth, New Hampshire, Adams learned that on November 28, 1777, Congress had elected him a joint commissioner with Benjamin Franklin and Arthur Lee to represent the United States in France. Adams's habit of seeing possible evils in events did not lighten his decision. "After much Agitation of mind and a thousand reveries," he wrote in his *Autobiography*, he announced his acceptance in a letter to Henry Laurens, president of the Congress.

Abigail and John decided that ten-year-old John Quincy would sail with his father on the *Boston* on February 13, 1778. Abigail soon wrote that she had lost not only her "better Half," but also "a Limb lopt of[f] to heighten the anguish." She implored her husband about John Quincy: "Injoin it upon him Never to Disgrace his Mother, and to behave worthy of his Father." She needn't have worried.

The sea voyage to Europe was, like many during the eighteenth century, harrowing: John Adams and his son passed through a four-day gale, the main mast cracked both above and below deck, they were chased by an English vessel and captured another. Adams only briefly got seasick, and in

JOHN QUINCY ADAMS. ENGRAVING BY SIDNEY L. SMITH FROM
The Studio, MARCH, 1887, AFTER THE PASTEL
BY ISAAC SCHMIDT, 1783

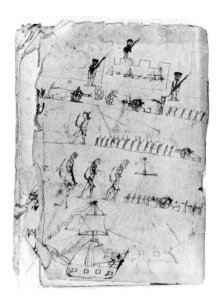

ABIGAIL ADAMS'S LOCKET

DRAWINGS FROM THE
DIARY OF JOHN QUINCY
ADAMS, 1780

fact strutted about the deck checking the ship's condition. Just thirteen days out of Boston, he made an eight-point list of "Observations" that ranged from the small amount of space between decks to "the Practice of profane Cursing and Swearing" among the officers and sailors. The next day he wrote about the "Irregularity of Meals. There ought to be a well digested System, for Eating, Drinking and sleeping. At Six, all Hands should be called up. At Eight, all Hands should breakfast. At one all Hands should dine. At Eight again all Hands should sup. It ought to be penal for the Cook to fail of having his Victuals ready punctually." Adams wasn't above sharing these views with the captain. "I am constantly giving Hints to the Captain concerning Order, OEconomy and Regularity," he wrote.

After six weeks at sea, the *Boston* put into Bordeaux. John Adams and his son traveled a hundred or so miles a day for five days before reaching Paris. The next morning they went to Passy, a semirural suburb now engulfed by the city of Paris, where Dr. Franklin, his entourage and Arthur Lee lived. It was to be a short and abortive stay for Adams.

For one thing, there was no real work to be done. The Franco–American treaties of alliance and commerce had already been concluded. For another, Adams found the commission in a chaotic mess: no official letter books were kept; finances were in bad shape; a plurality of American agents had been appointed by the various commissioners, and each tried to execute the same business and draw funds from the American ministers. "Public Business," Adams wrote, "had never been methodically conducted. There never was before I came, a minute Book, a Letter Book or an Account Book." Adams started them.

The commissioners, already squabbling among themselves, were unable to agree on anything, let alone get the French to agree on whatever they might propose. They fought about every matter, even a Fourth of July celebration.

Silas Deane had spent several vital years in France negotiating for a French loan and French supplies. Secrecy had been imperative if France were to avoid open war with Great Britain, and, in a marvel of stealth of the sort still employed today, Deane conducted all business with France through a fictitious "cover" firm by the name of Hortalez & Cie. When Franklin and Lee arrived with congressional appointments to work with Deane, friction began. Lee accused Deane of fraud with intent to embezzle, claiming that the French had offered supplies free — an unlikely prospect. There were, too, rumors that Deane had dabbled in English stocks and outfitted privateers. Deane's recall and replacement with Adams did little to settle matters. Adams found Arthur Lee and Benjamin Franklin still squabbling. Indeed, Lee was also irritating the French, while Franklin was wooing them, and being wooed.

Deane had lived in high style in Paris, and Franklin followed his pattern. The good doctor was at the pinnacle of his powers. The French loved him. By contrast, John Adams was snubbed continually by Louis XVI, then twenty-three and always dull, after being presented to him at Versailles. Adams, his New England juices churning, struggled to accept the luxuries of Paris and the attractions of Europe. He lived in Franklin's large house in Passy, drove no carriages and employed no private secretary. This was the beginning of an abrasion that would rub for a decade. Perhaps, as historians have suggested, John Adams's psychological struggle with European values was manifested in his actual disputes with Franklin, the Europeanized American.

Whatever, the affairs of the commission bothered Adams greatly. Unable to write officially to Congress, he wrote instead to Samuel Adams. He strongly advised that Congress distinguish between ministers and commissioners, that one of the former would be far more efficient — and far less costly — than three of the latter; that a specific allowance for salary and expenses, strictly accounted for, be substituted for uncontrolled expense accounts. Adams was, in effect, signing his own recall. Congress acted on his recommendations, except that it never asked him to come home. On September 14, 1778, it dissolved the American commission in France by electing Franklin the sole minister; these instructions didn't reach France until 1779. The congressional Committee on Foreign Affairs did not recall Adams but rather vaguely told him to stick around and look after things, especially "the Subject of our Finances."

HÔTEL DE VALENTINOIS. GOUACHE, ARTIST UNKNOWN

When Adams arrived in Paris in 1778, replacing Silas Deane, he took quarters in the mansion, where Benjamin Franklin and the other commissioners lived. The Hôtel de Valentinois rested on the heights of Passy and had two wings, formal gardens and "a wonderful view of the Seine and its shady banks."

Meanwhile, letters from Abigail, sometimes lost at sea and always delayed several months, pulled at him. She accused him of holding back his expressions of love and affection. Her need for him overflowed. "In the very few lines I have received from you," she wrote in October, 1778, "not the least mention is made that you have ever received a line from me. . . . But I cannot take my pen with my Heart overflowing and not give utterance to some of the abundance which is in it. Could you after a thousand fears and anxieties, long expectation and painfull suspences be satisfied with my telling you that I was well, that I wished you were with me, that my daughter sent her duty, that I had orderd some articles for you which I hoped would arrive &c. &c. — By Heaven if you could you have changed Hearts with some frozen Laplander or made a voyage to a region that has chilld every Drop of your Blood. — But I will restrain a pen already I fear too rash, nor shall it tell you how much I have sufferd from this appearance of — inattention."

The winter was harsh that year, and in December, 1778, Abigail wrote John: "How lonely are my days? How solitary are my nights? Secluded from all Society but my two Little Boys, and my domesticks, by the Mountains of snow which surround me I could almost fancy myself in Greenland."

Smallpox again cut through Braintree and the colony. Young Charles learned a Scottish song to cheer up his mother. Money was tight, and sometimes things got desperate. Abigail detailed the rising costs of food in a letter to John on March 20, 1779: "I blush whilst I give you a price current, . . . corn 25 Dollors . . . potatoes ten dollors per Bushel, Butter 12 shillings per pound, cheese 8, Sugar 12 shillings per pound, Molasses 12 Dollors per Gallon, Labour 6 and 8 Dollors a Day, a common Cow from 60 to 70 pound, and all English goods in proportion."

In France, John Quincy was attending Le Coeur's boarding school in Passy with Franklin's grandson Benjamin Bache. Abigail had admonished John Quincy in 1778 to "improve your understanding for acquiring usefull knowledge and virtue, such as will render you an ornament to society, an Honour to your Country, and a Blessing to your parents."

Early in May, 1779, John Adams fetched his son and

they sailed for Boston aboard the *Sensible*. Little was happening in Europe for Adams, and much was concerning him at home. It would be a short interlude. For three months Adams turned his intellectual attention to Braintree and Massachusetts concerns. On August 9, 1779, he was elected Braintree representative to the Massachusetts Constitutional Convention, where he soon became the actual drafter of the state constitution. With some minor changes, the constitution was adopted by the people in 1780 and remains in force today.

Meanwhile, on September 27, 1779, after "a great deal of disagreeable altercation and debate," John Adams was elected by Congress as minister plenipotentiary with instructions to negotiate treaties of peace and commerce with Great Britain. This time, Adams took John Thaxter as his private secretary and Francis Dana as secretary to the commission. Charles Adams, then nine, and John Quincy, twelve, went along. The five boarded the *Sensible*, which had brought John Adams and John Quincy home, and sailed on November 14, 1779, crossing the Atlantic in winter, putting in to Spain when their ship sprang a leak, and reaching Paris three months later after an arduous journey overland.

It was February, 1780, the beginning of a new decade. John Adams, New England farmer, lawyer, American statesman, would soon discover the rigors of international diplomacy.

Washington's army was pushed and battered, but always eluded the British and inflicted serious losses on them. In the north, in 1777, the British had returned to their original plan of advancing armies down the Champlain-Hudson and Mohawk valleys and dividing the colonies. George III and his ministers originally saw the problem in America as a simple one: apply major force and the rebellion would be quickly crushed. Strategically, driving a wedge between the New England colonies and those to the south of New York would be the means.

The American military position was weak. The colonies had no permanent army, and troops marched in or wandered off almost at will. Arsenals and a munitions industry were lacking, and the army continually went short of clothes and weapons. At best, it could only elude, attack and withdraw, pounce, bend and snap at the superior British forces. The American advantages lay in having a large number of veterans from the French and Indian War, in knowing the country, and in enjoying what Lord Cornwallis would soon call, "that damned American obstinacy."

Burgoyne, then, would lead an army southward from Canada. Howe would send units north along the Hudson toward Albany. The plan was perfect, but it never happened. Burgoyne's force of seventy-five hundred British regulars, Germans from Brunswick and Hesse, Canadians, Tories and Indians, swept over Fort Ticonderoga on July 6 and pushed on to Skenesboro the next day. Only General Philip Schuyler stood between the British and Albany.

But Burgoyne paused. Then he chose the more difficult overland route instead of going by water. "Gentleman Jack," moreover, would make no concessions to the American wilderness. He must have his plate service, his champagne and thirty wagons for his baggage. Baron von Riedesel, commander of the Brunswick mercenaries, was accompanied by his wife, whose diary tells of a series of lavish picnics that marked the army's advance. Short of horses and food, however, and slow-moving, Burgoyne sent a foraging party of 350 Germans with 300 Tories and Indians into the hostile woods toward what is now Vermont to seize supplies. John Stark's New Hampshire militia and Seth Warner's Green Mountain Boys marched out from Bennington and ambushed the slow-moving column, killing 207.

The Battle of Bennington brought a general turnout of militia in New England in support of the main body of American forces. Led by General Horatio Gates, the Americans had 11,000 men, including 2,700 Continentals, the most reliable American soldiers. On October 7, 1777, again short of food, the British made a reconnaissance in force to test the American left wing at Bemis Heights, near Saratoga. Contact touched off a wild, incoherent battle in which the British quickly lost 600 men. Benedict Arnold, who had been feuding with the jealous Gates, directed the American attack with masterful strokes of leadership, but was wounded leading the final charge. Gates, therefore, took the British surrender on October 17, when Burgoyne turned over his entire army of 5,000 to the Americans.

The victory, one of the most decisive battles in American history, had far-reaching consequences. The British returned to Canada from Lake Champlain and held only New York, Philadelphia, and Rhode Island in the north. Moreover, their army, considered the finest in the world, had been beaten, and the impact of that in England was profound. Most importantly, France recognized the infant nation, and moved toward war with England. Desperate battles and hardship lay ahead for the Americans, but after Saratoga the Revolution tilted in their favor.

France had been waiting and watching since 1763. In 1776, when Silas Deane had begun purchasing clothing, munitions and supplies through the bogus company, organized by Beaumarchais, the playwright, Franklin and Arthur Lee joined him to offer France a treaty of amity and commerce. After Saratoga, France agreed not only to a treaty of commerce, but also to one of alliance.

The French were enthusiastic about the American cause. The Declaration of Independence stirred them: Washington was the new Cincinnatus, and young Frenchmen, of whom Lafayette was among the first, rushed to join his command. Condorcet, charmed with reading about Connecticut, signed one of his tracts *Un Bourgeois de New-Haven*. Rousseau imagined the Indians to be true children of nature. Voltaire had taught the French to admire the society of Pennsylvania, with its religious freedom and good life, and had thus opened the way for a warm reception in France for Franklin. John Adams, in Paris in 1778, found this atmosphere heavy: he was revolted when at a meeting of the Academy of Sciences attended by Franklin and Voltaire, the members clamored for them to embrace, which they did, "kissing each others cheeks. . . . And the Cry immediately spread through the whole Kingdom and I suppose over all Europe. . . . How charming it was! Oh! it was enchanting to see Solon and Sophocles embracing!"

The intellectuals of France, however, did not reflect the caution of French rulers. A shrewd, practical statesman,

LE COMTE
DE VERGENNES.

THE COMTE DE VERGENNES.
ENGRAVING FROM THE
European Magazine, 1786

PORCELAIN OF LOUIS XVI
AND FRANKLIN TO COM-
MEMORATE THE SIGNING OF
THE TREATY OF ALLIANCE,
1778. BY NIDERVILLE,
1780–1785.

*Charles Gravier, comte de Vergennes, served as the
French foreign minister during John Adams's terms as
commissioner in Paris. Vergennes tried to thwart
Adams's efforts to negotiate with the English and Dutch.
He preferred to deal with Benjamin Franklin, who was
less impatient and more inclined to see things from the
French point of view. The porcelain of Franklin and
Louis XVI (right) commemorates the signing of
the Treaty of Alliance between the United States
and France.*

Charles Gravier, the comte de Vergennes, directed foreign affairs for the dim young Louis XVI. England was France's enemy, to be humbled. "Providence has marked this era," Vergennes wrote to the Spanish government in 1778, "for the humiliation of a proud and greedy power . . . glory and inestimable advantages will result for the two crowns" — for France and Spain, that is, and not England.

To this end, France from the first gave the United States munitions and supplies, and welcomed Yankee privateers into French ports. French manufacturers were also eager for the new American markets, formerly closed to them by the British Acts of Trade. "Always keep in mind," Vergennes wrote to the minister of finance after the war had ended, "that in separating the United States from Great Britain, it was above all their commerce which we wanted."

Burgoyne's surrender added much to this elaborate equation. Lord North, for the British, sought another effort at reconciliation with America as soon as he heard of the defeat at Saratoga. George III forbade it. Nevertheless, the king was willing to concede everything short of independence: a bill, which passed Parliament in February, 1778, appointed a peace commission with authority to halt taxation of the colonies, withdraw military forces, repeal all objectionable acts of Parliament, including the hated Coercive Acts and Acts of Trade — if America would remain loyal to the king.

But the British offer came too late. On February 6, 1778, eleven days before the conciliatory bills passed Parliament, Franklin and Vergennes signed treaties of alliance and trade. Vergennes, worried by Franklin's hints that the British offer might be acceptable to America, made a generous treaty: the United States gained much and gave little.

In June, 1778, Great Britain attacked French ships. Spain entered the fray as an ally of France in 1779, and proved useful to the American cause by opening New Orleans to rebel privateers and by capturing British bases in East Florida. The Netherlands, enjoying trade as a major neutral sea power, was pushed by England into the war in 1781. Catherine II of Russia formed the League of Armed Neutrality, which John Adams later dismissed as "a sublime bubble."

At the beginning of the decade, England found herself

In a fanciful scene, an admiring French lady teases Benjamin Franklin with her feather fan. John Adams, a bit envious, wrote: "On Dr. F. the Eyes of all Europe are fixed." Adams also complained of Franklin's "Love of Ease, and Dissipation," which the French found attractive.

FRANKLIN SURROUNDED BY THE LADIES AT COURT.
ENGRAVING BY W. O. GELLER, ABOUT 1830

increasingly engaged in a widening struggle. The shot fired at Concord had, by 1780, been heard around the world. There were naval engagements in the Atlantic, the Mediterranean, the Caribbean, the North Sea, the English Channel, and even the Indian Ocean.

John Adams had to make his way through the courts of Europe during this delicate time. The diplomatic role was difficult for him. He was quickly bored with inaction when he thought action was needed. His performance in Congress showed that he lacked the diplomat's finesse and patience. One report described him as having "quickness, pugnacity, want of tact, and naive egotism." Adams himself noted that, during his first mission to Paris, Sir John Temple had said of him that whatever else he may be "he is the most ungracious man I ever saw."

Back in Paris in 1780, after placing Charles and John Quincy in boarding school in Passy, John Adams began trying to get Vergennes's permission — he was instructed to work through the French government — to make his presence and purposes known both in France and in England. Vergennes had no wish to see the United States negotiate a commercial treaty with England when peace came. Further, he sought to control, however he could, the peace overtures as they were sounded. Although presented to Louis XVI on March 7, John Adams still suspected Vergennes of trying to delay him, and of attempting to get his instructions from Congress — which would be helpful to the French should negotiations with England begin — from the French minister in Philadelphia.

Insisting upon keeping himself busy, but with nothing to do, Adams wrote a series of articles about America, had them translated, and published them in a prominent French newspaper. Vergennes, always one to employ flattery, asked Adams to furnish him with whatever information about the United States might occur to him. Nothing could have pleased Adams more, since it fed both his abhorrence of idleness and his need to instruct. At a time when he should have been discreetly inactive — awaiting the chance to negotiate commerce and peace treaties with England — he was most blatantly industrious. He filed copious letters to Congress on every subject, and confided to his friend Elbridge Gerry: "I have written more to Congress, since my Arrival in Paris, than they ever received from Europe . . . since the Revolution." This was an obvious rub against Franklin, who was the only accredited American minister to the French court. Adams merely held commissions to negotiate at some future time, when negotiations might be possible.

Adams did fill letter book after letter book; he wrote Congress daily dispatches, and some days addressed as many as four letters to Samuel Huntington. Prevented by Vergennes from announcing his mission until the end of March, he wrote paragraphs and whole articles for whatever publication would print them. He now found Paris delightful and charming. "The Cookery and manner of living here . . . is more agreable to me, than you can imagine. The Manners of the People have an Affection in them that is very amiable. Their is such a Choice of elegant Entertainments in the theatric Way, of good Company and excellent Books, that nothing would be wanting to me in this Country but my family and Peace to my Country, to make me, one of the happyest of men."

His pen never rested. In May, 1780, he wrote Arthur Lee that "with nothing at all to do, I am as busy as ever I was in my life." In fact, a little too busy. He began writing Vergennes, tutoring the foreign minister in American fiscal matters. In July, he wrote a nine-page letter, urging France to increase her naval presence in American waters in order to prove her sincerity under the treaty of alliance. Near the close, he told Vergennes: "The United States of America are a great and powerful People, whatever European statesmen may think of them."

Vergennes replied with a long and contemptuous analysis of Adams's letter. But the New Englander could not be stopped. Ten days later, he wrote Vergennes again, pressing once more the naval question, and telling the foreign minister that he was "determined to omit no opportunity of communicating my sentiments to your Excellency, upon everything that appears to me to be of importance to the common cause."

Vergennes snapped back: "To avoid any more of the

kind, I think it my duty to inform you that, Mr. Franklin being the sole person who has letters of credence to the King from the United States, it is with him only that I ought and can treat of matters which concern them." He then forwarded the entire correspondence to Franklin, who, at the minister's behest, sent it to Congress with a note clucking over John Adams's lack of diplomacy. Congress understood Adams well, however, and its rebuke was mild. But the issue, among others, opened a feud between Adams and Franklin that was still simmering thirty years later, when Adams attacked Franklin's morals, abilities and even his patriotism while raking over the coals of Paris, 1780.

Adams was useless for the time being in Paris. Discomfited and perhaps bewildered by diplomacy under the unctuous Vergennes, he wisely made a trip in the summer of 1780 to the Netherlands as a private citizen, "to try," as Franklin reported to Congress, "whether something might not be done to render us less dependent on France." He took Charles and John Quincy with him, and in August placed them in the Latin School at Amsterdam.

About the same time, Congress appointed Adams as temporary replacement for Henry Laurens to negotiate a Dutch loan until Laurens, the duly appointed minister to the Netherlands, should arrive from the United States. Word reached Adams in September and he began holding meetings with Dutch statesmen and bankers. Laurens, however, was captured at sea and carted off to the Tower of London. With him the British found the text of a proposed treaty between the United States and the Netherlands; its publication in London caused an outcry — the Dutch were then still committed to the British by treaty — and British ships began attacking Dutch. Congress, having lost its first minister to the Netherlands, appointed Adams to negotiate a treaty of amity and commerce with the Dutch.

Adams's task was not easy. Embroiled with England, the Dutch felt that this was not the proper time to antagonize so near a rival for so distant an ally. Nevertheless he persevered. He drafted a memorial emphasizing the historical ties between the two nations and the advantages that would accrue from commercial relations.

THE KEIZERSGRACHT, AMSTERDAM. ENGRAVING BY
HUBERT PIETER SCHOUTEN, 1782

*Here are two views
of the street in
Amsterdam where
John Adams lived
from early 1781 to
early 1782. Adams
noted: "I have taken
an House on the
Keysers Gragt near the
Spiegel Straat." In the
drawing, his house is
the one with the twin
dormers.*

THE KEIZERSGRACHT, AMSTERDAM. FROM
"HET GRACHTENBOEK" BY CASPAR PHILLIPS, 1771

Vergennes, meanwhile, was plotting to get Adams recalled. He sent to Amsterdam for him, and at Versailles discussed with him a mediation proposal from the courts of Russia and Austria that, Adams believed, was a French ploy. The consultation convinced Adams that the French government was willing to sacrifice American independence for the exigencies of European diplomacy. Vergennes had better luck with the U.S. Congress, which turned around and appointed four other peace commissioners to join Adams — Franklin, Jefferson, Henry Laurens and John Jay. The four were also instructed that the commission — they and Adams — would be entirely under the advice and control of the court of France — Vergennes himself.

Adams, back in Holland, took the news badly. He immediately became ill with a "nervous Fever." He was alone, with only Thaxter to nurse him. Charles had become homesick, with his heart so set on going back to Braintree that John wrote Abigail: "[I]t would have broken it to have refused him." Charles sailed off, at the age of eleven, in August, 1781. But the ship had trouble with its captain and crew, and put into Spain. Charles wasn't heard from for four months; he finally sailed on the *Cicero* and arrived home in January. Abigail had written John in December: "Ah! how great has my anxiety been, what have I not sufferd since I heard my dear Charles was on Board and no intelligence to be procured of the vessel for 4 months after she sailed. Most people concluded that she was founderd at Sea, as she sailed before a violent Storm."

In July of 1781, John Quincy, just fourteen, had left his studies in Holland to travel as secretary to Francis Dana, who had been appointed minister to Russia. John Quincy remained at St. Petersburg until the late autumn of 1782. There, under private tutors, he studied German, and continued his Latin and Greek. He already spoke Dutch and French; in fact, his father had written that the lad wrote better in French than in English.

John Adams, ill and distressed by inactivity, was roused by victory. Combined French and American forces, and the French fleet, had bottled up Cornwallis's troops at Yorktown. Two British redoubts were taken on October 14, 1781. On October 19, Cornwallis surrendered his army: 7,247 soldiers and 840 seamen. The British handed over their swords and rifles, and marched out of Yorktown as their bands played an old English tune, "The World Turned Upside Down."

Adams, suddenly well and out of bed, pushed the Dutch to recognize the United States. In January, 1782, he made visits to eighteen Dutch cities. His efforts paid off. On April 19, seven years precisely after the battles of Lexington and Concord, the States General of the Netherlands recognized John Adams as the minister plenipotentiary from the United States. Adams began a round of ceremonial visits to the Dutch ministers and the diplomatic corps, including an audience with Willem V, prince of Orange. The next day, Adams proposed to the president of the States General that negotiations be opened for a treaty of amity and commerce between the Dutch and the United States. Such a treaty was finally signed on October 8.

Meanwhile, on June 11, Adams negotiated with a syndicate of Dutch banking houses a loan of $1,940,000, the first of four, which together reached $3.5 million. The loans propped up the languishing American credit and helped the government survive until Washington's new government could begin under the Constitution of 1787.

During this period, England put out feelers for peace once again. After Yorktown, Lord North, who had been threatening to resign every month since Saratoga (and once threatened thrice in a week), finally meant it. George III even drafted a message of abdication, but thought better of it, as sovereigns will, and called in Rockingham — whose earlier administration had repealed the Stamp Act — to form a government with Shelburne, Charles James Fox and other friends of America. Shelburne at once sent Richard Oswald to Paris to sound out Dr. Franklin.

At this juncture, in April of 1782, Franklin was the only one of the five commissioners in Paris. For two months, he and Oswald conferred sporadically until John Jay, the minister to Spain, could arrive from Madrid. (Adams was unable to leave the Netherlands till fall; Laurens was released from prison too late to take much part in negotiations; and Jefferson never succeeded in leaving America.)

Vergennes immediately began a series of machinations

HUIS TEN BOSCH, THE STADHOLDER'S RESIDENCE NEAR THE HAGUE. ENGRAVED BY IVAN BESOET, 1758

THE TRUCE CHAMBER IN THE HAGUE. ENGRAVING BY J. C. PHILIPS, 1738

JOHN ADAMS, MINISTER PLENIPOTENTIARY TO THE DUTCH REPUBLIC. ENGRAVING BY REINER VINKELES FROM THE DUTCH TRANSLATION OF ADAMS'S *Novanglus*, 1788

In 1782, John Adams, the American minister to the Netherlands, was received by Prince William V of Orange at the Huis Ten Bosch (upper left). Adams admired its black walnut floors and railings inlaid with mother-of-pearl. In the extravagant room (left) at The Hague, Adams and the Dutch signed the Treaty of Commerce. The Dutch liked Adams and made sympathetic portraits of him, like this engraving of 1785.

with the British over boundary lines and claims in North America. One proposal, according to Franklin, showed France's desire "to coop us up within the Alleghany Mountains." Both he and Jay saw that the first issue was to get the British to deal with them as representatives of an independent nation. Agreeing, after their fashion, the British finally instructed Richard Oswald "to treat . . . with any commissioners . . . vested with equal powers by . . . the Thirteen United States of America." Formal negotiations began at the end of September, 1782.

Adams, busy with Dutch loans in the Netherlands, moved slowly toward Paris. He deeply missed his family, and it didn't ease his loneliness when Abigail, growing restless after four years of separation, wrote: "Who shall give me back time? . . . How dearly have I paid for a titled husband! Should I wish you less wise, that I might enjoy more happiness? I cannot find that in my heart." And again she wrote: "I look back to the early days of our acquaintance, and Friendship, as to the days of Love and Innocence; and with an indiscribable pleasure I have seen near a score of years roll over our Heads, with an affection heightned and improved by time — nor have the dreary years of absence in the smallest degree effaced from my mind the Image of the dear untittled Man to whom I gave my Heart. I cannot sometimes refrain considering the Honours with which he is invested as badges of my unhappiness."

Adams arrived in Paris on October 26, and soon learned the news of the negotiations from Franklin and Jay. He entered in his diary that he was "between two as subtle Spirits, as any in this World, the one malicious, the other I think honest. I shall have a delicate, a nice, a critical Part to Act."

His first delicate act was to choose sides. The congressional instructions, as mentioned, called for the Americans to take no steps without consulting the French. Franklin, who had lived in Paris a long time, during which he had been flattered by French statesmen and Parisian ladies, was more inclined to obey the instructions. Jay, a descendant of French Huguenots, placed no faith in the Bourbons; he had watched the intrigues between France and Spain in the court of

Madrid. Jay strongly opposed allowing Vergennes to guide and limit American negotiations.

Adams joined Jay, and together they persuaded Franklin. Their decision to ignore Vergennes was a courageous one: the French minister was a powerful figure. To counter orders essentially written by him would require a stunning diplomatic success on their part.

The three Americans quickly sensed that the two British commissioners, Richard Oswald and Henry Strachey, were less able than they and willing to concede much more. Adams, writing in his diary, compared the situation of England and America to that of an eagle and a cat. The eagle swooped upon the cat, thinking it a hare. "In the Air the Cat seized him by the Neck with her Teeth and round the Body with her fore and hind Claws. The Eagle finding Herself scratched and pressed, bids the Cat let go and fall down. — No says the Cat: I wont let go and fall, you shall stoop and set me down." The British eagle, Adams and Jay noted, showed more inclination to stoop and set the American cat down at any cost than might have been expected, or hoped.

There were several basic questions. One, that of debts due British merchants and compensation due Loyalists, was raised, and Adams immediately pointed out that the question was really two. He suggested that a clause be inserted that Congress should recommend that the states "open their Courts of Justice" for the collection of just debts. Adams, the man of honor, felt that the American merchants should pay any debts contracted in good faith on both sides. Although the clause, in application, proved to be ineffective, at the time of the negotiation it brought in the British merchant class on the side of accepting the treaty — a point which the British negotiators readily understood.

On another point, Adams sought liberal terms for the rights of U.S. fishermen — most of them his fellow New Englanders — in the fisheries off the Newfoundland coast. Agreement on this point was in sight when an unexpected obstacle arose. "Mr. Stratchey," he wrote, "proposed to leave out the Word Right of Fishing and make it Liberty. Mr. Fitsherbert [added to the negotiations with the other two Englishmen] said the Word Right was an obnoxious Expression."

John Adams's anger surged, and he thundered at the British: "Gentlemen, is there or can there be a clearer Right? In former Treaties, that of Utrecht and that of Paris, France and England have claimed the Right and used the Word. When God Almighty made the Banks of Newfoundland at 300 Leagues Distance from the People of America and at 600 Leagues distance from those of France and England, did he not give as good a Right to the former as to the latter. If Heaven in the Creation gave a Right, it is ours at least as much as yours. If Occupation, Use, and Possession give Right, We have it as clearly as you. If War and Blood and Treasure give a Right, ours is as good as yours. We have been constantly fighting in Canada, Cape Breton and Nova Scotia for the Defense of this Fishery, and have expended beyond all Proportion more than you. If then the Right cannot be denied, Why should it not be acknowledged? and put out of Dispute? Why should We leave Room for illiterate Fishermen to wrangle and chicane?"

It was done. The rest of the treaty, involving questions of boundaries, navigation of the Mississippi, the Loyalists and other points, had largely been settled. Copies of the treaty were "signed, sealed and delivered, and We all went out to Passy to dine with Dr. Franklin."

During the negotiations, Adams was wined, dined and flattered by the French. At one dinner especially, on November 10, with the comte de Vergennes and madame la comtesse, a great fuss was made over him. He recorded much of it — to his later regret. The comtesse, "who gave me her hand with extraordinary Condescention . . . made me sit next to her on her right hand and was remarkably attentive to me the whole Time. The Comte who sat opposite was constantly calling out to me, to know what I would eat and to offer me petits Gateaux, Claret and Madeira &c. &c. — In short I was never treated with half the Respect at Versailles in my Life." Adams recorded that two gentlemen had told him that "I had shewn in Holland that the Americans understand Negotiation, as well as War."

Unfortunately, this section became part of Adams's so-called Peace Journal and fell into the hands of Congress, where it was read in 1783, much to the amusement and an-

After the signing of the preliminary treaty in Paris, Benjamin West started this painting, which was to include both the American and the British peace commissioners. He sketched the Americans: John Jay (standing, left), John Adams, Benjamin Franklin, Henry Laurens and William Temple Franklin, the secretary. The historic work remained unfinished because the British commissioners died before West could complete it.

DETAIL: AMERICAN COMMISSIONERS AT THE PRELIMINARY PEACE NEGOTIATIONS
WITH GREAT BRITAIN. OIL BY BENJAMIN WEST, ABOUT 1783

noyance of the members. Perhaps most damaging was Adams's quoting, in French, a dinner guest at the party who told him, "Monsieur vous etes le Washington de la Negotiation. —"

The treaty of alliance with France bound the United States not to sign any separate peace with Britain until it made peace with France. What Adams, Jay and Franklin (joined in the final days by Laurens) had signed was, in fact, a piece of paper embodying the terms of a treaty that could be signed as soon as France and England agreed to peace.

Once again, Vergennes played his hand with Congress. When the preliminary treaty between the United States and England was signed, Vergennes feared that having got all it wanted from England, the United States might try to gain more by turning on France. He bitterly wrote La Luzerne about the breach of faith on the part of the American envoys, but later countermanded his order to La Luzerne to protest to Congress. In fact, Vergennes and the British had already reached virtual agreement on a preliminary treaty of peace.

Before the British appointed David Hartley as their negotiator to work out definitive peace terms with the American commissioners, Adams found time lying heavy and declared himself to be "weary, disgusted, affronted and disappointed." He had reason to be. Not only were negotiations dragging, but also Robert R. Livingston, secretary for foreign affairs, sent, without congressional sanction, a rebuke — prompted by Vergennes — for acting without French approval. So convincing had Vergennes been that some in Congress wished to apologize to the French minister for the American envoys' success.

"I have been injured," Adams wrote, "and my Country has joined in the Injury. It has basely prostituted its own honour by sacrificing mine. But the Sacrifice of me for my Virtues, was not so servile, and intollerable as putting Us all under Guardianship. Congress surrendered their own Sovereignty into the Hands of a French Minister. Blush! blush! Ye guilty Records! blush and perish! It is Glory, to have broken such infamous orders." Adams spent the spring and early summer of 1783 working with his fellow commissioners and with the British in Paris on the Definitive Treaty of Peace.

Their British counterpart, David Hartley, proved weak, and negotiations from April until fall gained little because, as the commissioners wrote in September, Hartley's "zeal for systems friendly to [America] constantly exceeded his authority to concert and agree to them."

Stung by his Congress, bored by the listless negotiations in Paris, Adams decided again to visit the Netherlands in order to "turn the Speculations of the Dutch Merchants . . . towards America." Also, John Quincy, now fifteen, had come back from Russia to The Hague; his father had not seen him for two years. Like many sons, he had not been the best of letter writers. Abigail had complained to John: "Do you know I have not a line from him for a year and half. — Alass my dear I am much afflicted with a disorder call'd the *Heart-ach*, nor can any remedy be found in America."

On September 3, 1783, the British and Americans concluded their Definitive Treaty of Peace. Other treaties were signed the same day between England, France and Spain. In sum, these treaties divided North America among Spain, the British Empire and the United States. For all his machinations, Vergennes had been bested by the American commissioners. France got little out of the war except a few West Indies islands, a bankrupt treasury and the prospect of a new market in America. This prospect, the center of Vergennes's policy, never materialized.

After the Definitive Treaty was signed, John Adams promptly fell ill: "I had been some days unwell but soon fell down in a Fever. Sir James Jay, who was my Physician, gave me a vomit, &c. &c."

There was much on Adams's mind. He made his first trip to England shortly after his recovery, where he and John Quincy visited Parliament, toured the Queen's apartments, and traveled to Bath, where Adams hoped the hot mineral springs would help him as he thought the cold ones had in Connecticut. In London, the two met John Singleton Copley, whom Adams had known in America. Copley had left in 1774, and by 1783, at the age of forty-six, was a well-known artist. Since Adams was on the rise, Copley wanted to paint his portrait, which he did, and Adams paid Copley the "handsome sum" of 100 guineas for it.

Soon after sitting for Copley, Adams left for the Netherlands. The Dutch loan had been exhausted and without a new one, U.S. credit would founder. John and John Quincy crossed the North Sea in January, negotiating bad weather and conniving Dutch cart drivers, and arrived in time to obtain a second loan.

By early fall, Adams had written to Abigail to come to Europe with their daughter, either immediately or in the spring. But Nabby was in love with a young Harvard graduate, Royall Tyler; they were reluctant to be separated. Her father would hear none of that. On October 14, John Adams put his foot down and told Abigail to sail to Europe: "The Family affair which has been mentioned in several of your Letters, may be managed very well. The Lady comes to Europe with you. If the Parties preserve their Regard untill they meet again and continue to behave as they ought, they will be still young enough."

Abigail put the boys in school, and on June 20, 1784, she and Nabby sailed on the *Active* for Europe. Abigail, like John on his first voyage, soon had the sailors jumping to her orders, and as seasickness swept them, had the cabins scrubbed with vinegar. She wrote her sister Mary Cranch: "Our sickness continued for ten days, with some intermissions. We crawled upon deck whenever we were able; but it was so cold and damp, that we could not remain long upon it. And the confinement of the air below, the constant rolling of the vessel, and the nausea of the ship, which was much too tight, contributed to keep up our disease. The vessel is very deep loaded with oil and potash. The oil leaks, the potash smokes and ferments. All adds to the *flavor*."

Abigail and her daughter arrived in England in July, 1784, and after receiving news of her safe arrival, John wrote from the Netherlands: "Your Letter of the 23d has made me the happiest Man upon Earth. I am twenty Years younger than I was Yesterday."

Abigail and Nabby made an excursion to Copley's studio, and she wrote her sister Elizabeth Smith Shaw: "I have been to see a very Elegant picture of Mr. Adams which belongs to Mr. Copley, and was taken by him. It is a larg[e] full length picture. He is drawn with a Globe before him; the

Within a month after the Definitive Treaty of Peace was signed in Paris, John Adams rose from his sickbed and went to London. There he met an old American friend, John Singleton Copley, who began painting this lifesize portrait. Abigail admired the work, and wrote the next year: "The 2 most celebrated painters now in Britain are Americans Mr. Copley and Mr. West."

JOHN ADAMS. OIL BY JOHN SINGLETON COPLEY, 1783

Map of Europe in his hand and at a distance a female figure representing Innocence, and Peace. It is said to be an admirable likeness."

Although he had been ill, Adams appeared in the Copley painting to be in good health. Only a few years earlier he had written Abigail: "I never had so much Trouble in my Life, as here, yet I grow fat. The Climate and Soil agree with me — so do the Cookery and even the Manners of the People, of those of them at least that I converse with, Churlish Republican, as some of you, on your side the Water call me."

Adams was indeed growing fat. Much later, he was colorfully described by his grandson, Charles Francis Adams, as "not tall, scarcely exceeding middle height, but of a stout, well-knit frame, denoting vigor and long life, yet as he grew old, inclining more and more to corpulence. His head was large and round, with a wide forehead and expanded brows. His eye was mild and benignant, perhaps even humorous, when he was free from emotion, but when excited, it fully expressed the vehemence of the spirit that stirred within. His presence was grave and imposing, on serious occasions, but not unbending. He delighted in social conversation, in which he was sometimes tempted to what he called rhodomontade. . . . His anger, when thoroughly roused, was, for a time, extremely violent, but when it subsided, it left no trace of malevolence behind."

On August 7, 1784, the Adamses were reunited in London, and the next day set out for Paris. They settled at the Hôtel de Rouault in Auteuil. John Adams began more tedious rounds of negotiations for trade. Abigail and her daughter delighted in Paris and its social and theatrical life. She wrote constantly to her friends, and in one letter she confessed that the ballet at the opera in Paris at first "shocked me; the dresses and beauty of the performers were enchanting; but, no sooner did the dance commence, than I felt my delicacy wounded, and I was ashamed to be seen to look at them. Girls, clothed in the thinnest silk and gauze, with their petticoats short, springing two feet from the floor, poising themselves in the air, with their feet flying, and as perfectly showing their garters and drawers as though no petticoat had been worn, was a sight altogether new to me." Paris was not Boston. Abigail continued: "Shall I speak a truth, and say that repeatedly seeing these dances has worn off that disgust, which I at first felt, and that I see them now with pleasure?"

The fashions and elegance of Paris amused her. She wrote home to Mrs. Storer in Braintree that "the fashionable shape of the ladies here is to be very small at the bottom of the waist, and very large round the shoulders, — a wasp's, — pardon me, ladies, that I should make such a comparison, it is only in shape that I mean to resemble you to them. You and I, Madam, must despair of being in the mode."

While Abigail was enjoying herself, John was fretful. This was a period of dull politics and anxious waiting. Adams made little secret — to wife or diary — of wanting to be named America's first minister to Great Britain. One incident reveals, perhaps, the mood Adams was in during early 1785. Abigail wrote to Lucy Cranch on January 24, in a light mood, about the celebration of King's Day in France. It was the custom, which the Adamses enjoyed, to bake a large paste pie and put a bean in it. Whoever found the bean was king or queen. Nabby took the first slice, and found no bean. John Quincy carefully cut a larger slice and "bisected his paste with mathematical circumspection." Still no bean. Abigail declared that she had "no cravings for royalty," took a small slice, and found no bean. But John Adams, "who was all this time picking his chicken bone," seized the second half of the pie and slashed at it until he found the bean. "And thus," he announced, "are kingdoms obtained." But, Abigail wrote, "the servant who stood by and saw the havoc, declared solemnly that he could not retain the title, as the laws decreed it to chance, and not to force."

There was little force, and some chance, to what Adams won next. On February 24, 1785, he got his dream, but not the pleasure. The debate over his nomination had been acrimonious. He would not press for return of Negroes illegally taken by the British, said some congressmen. He would be soft on the issue of American debts, said others. But it was the reading of his "Peace Journal" — the laudations and preenings — that delayed Congress so long and slowed his nomination. Would someone with such vanity, asked congressmen, be trustworthy in so important a task?

It was not the last public airing of John Adams's vanity. But despite this humiliation, Adams could not refuse the post he so very much wanted. The French, including Vergennes, wished him well. In his diary Adams reported his conversation with a foreign ambassador who had just congratulated him: "You have been often in England. — Never but once in November and December 1783. — You have relations in England no doubt. — None at all. — None how can that be? You are of English Extraction? — Neither my Father or Mother, Grandfather or Grandmother, Great Grandfather or Great Grandmother nor any other Relation that I know of or care a farthing for have been in England these 150 Years. So that you see, I have not one drop of Blood in my Veins, but what is American. — Ay We have seen says he proofs enough of that. — This flattered me no doubt, and I was vain enough to be pleased with it."

Indeed he was pleased. In May, 1785, the Adamses prepared, with some trepidations, to depart for England.

4

Whiff for Whiff with His Excellency

[1785 – 1788]

*T*HE journey to England was almost mournful. Leaving Auteuil, the Adamses – without John Quincy, who had returned to America to attend Harvard – were surrounded by their weeping servants; Abigail left her pet bird with her Parisian chambermaid. John Adams's last meeting with Vergennes had been cordial; he reluctantly left the diplomatic corps in Paris. Both he and Abigail would especially miss their friend Thomas Jefferson, who had succeeded Franklin at the court of Versailles. It was a friendship forged ten years earlier in Philadelphia, and rich company not easily left. Slowly making his way with his wife and daughter toward the port of Calais and the uncertainties of England beyond, Adams read Jefferson's *Notes on the State of Virginia* as they crossed a French countryside that was "an heap of Ashes" from drought. He wrote his friend: "I am determined to be in a hurry about nothing from the Beginning to the End of this Adventure. It is best to give myself as well as others time to think."

Abigail, too, looked back fondly. She wrote Jefferson that "nobody ever leaves Paris but with a degree of tristeness. I own I was loth to leave my garden because I did not expect to find its place supplied. I was still more loth on account of the increasing pleasure and intimacy which a longer acquaintance with a respected Friend promised, to leave behind me the only person with whom my Companion could associate with perfect freedom, and unreserve: and whose place he had no reason to expect supplied in the Land to which he is destinied." And Jefferson wrote back to John Adams: "The departure of your family has left me in the dumps. My afternoons hang heavily on me. . . . P.S. Send me your address au plutot."

The Adamses reached London on May 26, 1785, and found the city full and noisy. Parliament was sitting, and the people were celebrating the king's birthday. The Adamses took two rooms and two chambers at the Bath Hotel in Piccadilly, which John described as "a vast concourse of carriages. It is too public and too noisy for pleasure." Abigail missed Auteuil. "I had lived so quietly in that calm retreat," she wrote, "that the Noise and bustle of this proud city almost turnd my Brain for the first two or three Days."

Their worries about the British and London, so recently a capital of enemies, proved nearly groundless. True, "the Tory venom has begun to spit itself forth in the public papers," as Abigail put it, and she reported to Jefferson that the "publick Advertiser" said of her husband: "An Ambassador from America! Good heavens what a sound! . . . tis hard to say which can excite indignation most, the insolence of those who appoint the Character, or the meanness of those who receive it."

But officially Adams was welcomed warmly and quickly. The family arrived in the afternoon, and that evening he wrote to the marquis of Carmarthen, the British foreign secretary, announcing his arrival. Lord Carmarthen wrote back the next morning, asking if Adams wished to see him at his house at one or his office at four that day. John Adams went at one, was "politely received," and was told that the king would meet with him the next Wednesday.

And so the historic meeting would take place: John Adams, so recently a rebel and traitor to the Crown, now minister from a sovereign state, would have an audience with George III, so recently an oppressor of Americans and the commander of forces against them. Adams composed a brief speech, and learned the rituals of court attendance. The meeting, dramatic in the abstract and carrying simple dignity, contained emotion for both men. In a letter to John Jay, secretary for foreign affairs, Adams told about the audience.

His carriage arrived at one on Wednesday, June 1, 1785, and took him to Carmarthen's office, and together the two men went to court by coach. As Adams waited in the antechamber at St. James's, while Carmarthen went to see the king, he had his first nervous moments. The ornate room was full of ministers of state, lords and bishops, "and all sorts of courtiers. . . . you may well suppose I was the focus of all eyes." They refused, however, to speak to him. Only the Swedish and Dutch ministers came over to him, and they engaged him in a "very agreeable conversation during the whole time," which drained off some of the tension.

Presently, Adams was summoned, and entered the king's chamber, where he was immediately announced and left alone with the king and Lord Carmarthen. The room was high and long, and as was the custom, Adams bowed once at the door, again about halfway down the room toward the king, and a third time before George III himself.

Adams spoke right away, finding his voice not as tight as he felt. He conveyed the wish of the American people for the king's "health and happiness, and for that of your royal family." He noted that the appointment of a minister from the United States was "an epoch in the history of England and of America." Then, with some emotion, Adams spoke of "restoring an entire esteem, confidence and affection, or, in better words, the old good nature and the old good humor between people, who, though separated by an ocean and under different governments, have the same language, a similar religion, and kindred blood."

The king listened carefully, "with dignity, but with an apparent emotion. Whether it was the nature of the interview, or whether it was my visible agitation, for I felt more than I did or could express, that touched him, I cannot say." Whatever it was, according to Adams, George III answered him "with more tremor than I had spoken with." As best he could, Adams reconstructed the king's words:

"The circumstances of this audience are so extraordinary, the language you have now held is so extremely proper, and the feelings you have discovered so justly adapted to the occasion, that I must say that I not only receive with pleasure the assurance of the friendly dispositions of the United States, but that I am very glad the choice has fallen upon you to be their minister. I wish you sir, to believe, and that it may be understood in America, that I have done nothing in the late contest but what I thought myself indispensably bound to do, by the duty which I owed to my people. I will be very frank with you. I was the last to consent to the separation; but the separation having been made, and having become inevitable, I have always said, as I say now, that I would be the first to meet the friendship of the United States as an independent power. The moment I see such sentiments and language as yours prevail, and a disposition to give to this country the preference, that moment I shall say, let the circumstances of language, religion and blood have their natural and full effect."

John Adams, of course, may have heard what he wanted to hear. Moved by the encounter, he may not have, as he himself admitted, "understood so perfectly, as to be confident of all his words or sense." But it was clear that the king warmed to the American. He continued the audience in a conversational manner, asking Adams if he had recently come from France and, when Adams replied that he had, laughing and stating: "There is an opinion among some people that you are not the most attached of all your countrymen to the manners of France."

This caught John Adams by surprise: "I thought it an indiscretion and a departure from the dignity." But he replied, affecting lightness: "That opinion, sir, is not mistaken; I must avow to your Majesty, I have no attachment but to my own country." George III replied — "quick as lightning," Adams wrote — "An honest man will never have any other."

The audience over, John Adams retreated, stepping backwards as etiquette demanded, toward the door, and bowing. As he left, the gentlemen-porters and underporters, "roaring out like thunder as I went along," called for his carriage. Reflecting upon his audience, he concluded that "I may expect from it a residence less painful than I once expected, as so marked an attention from the King will silence many grumblers; but we can infer nothing from all this concerning the success of my mission."

It was a wise disclaimer. For the Treaty of Paris was proving unsatisfactory to both England and the United States. Each party was refusing to fulfill its obligations. Debts, the treatment of Loyalists, and the presence of British troops on American soil remained as issues. (The resolution of boundary disputes would wait for the next generation.)

On June 17, 1785, John Adams began conferences with Lord Carmarthen in an attempt to adjust the major points of conflict between the United States and Great Britain. Adams's instructions from Congress called for his pressing the British to extend the time in which U.S. citizens could pay their debts to British creditors, to compensate for American slaves and other property carried away by the British, to evacuate the northern trading posts, and to liberalize trade between the two nations.

The difficulties for the United States during its first five years of peace centered on its loss of commerce, its paper money and depressed economy, and its social unrest. The commercial treaty negotiations, in which Adams, Franklin and Jefferson had played a part, had dragged on in Paris for more than a year before the Foreign Office in London cut them off. By a series of Orders in Council in 1783, the British had excluded American vessels from Canada and the British West Indies. Exclusion of American vessels from the West Indies and from England except for direct trade in American products threw almost all shipping within the British Empire into British bottoms. New England merchants and seamen particularly suffered, and trade turned in favor of the British. Indeed, the basic British plan was to shift the American trade to their advantage, and by 1789, the Board of Trade in London boasted that British exports to the United States had recovered their prewar dimensions.

The United States was weak, and efforts to retaliate were futile. If Boston, for example, closed its port to British goods, they would come in from New Hampshire or Rhode Island. There was no national power to bring sanctions against Britain. Independence, in fact, had merely transferred from England to the United States efforts to reconcile the issue of power between national unity and local rights. Thomas Paine's theory that all government was at best a necessary evil found acceptance in the American consciousness. Yet problems needed solving on a national level: taxation, regulation of commerce, the future of western lands, Indian affairs, paper money, military cooperation among the states, and, above all, the power of sanctions.

Under the Articles of Confederation, which governed the country after 1781, the states retained complete control over taxation and the regulation of commerce. The weakness of the Confederation was its dependence upon the goodwill of the states. In 1783, the foreign debt of the United States was more than $7.8 million; by 1789, the principal on foreign debts had reached about $12 million and the interest, $1.7 million. Robert Morris, the treasurer of the nation during the Revolution, was able to stave off bankruptcy only with the early loans that John Adams had secured from Dutch bankers. So hopeless were the financial affairs of the Confederation that Morris resigned, confessing that "it can no longer be a doubt . . . that our public credit is gone."

After the war, the finances of the states and the government fell into hopeless confusion. Demobilized troops sold at a sharp discount the scrip they had been given instead of pay. Hundreds of millions in paper money had been turned out by the central and state governments — $451.5 million at face value during the war alone — and most of it depreciated to utter worthlessness.

Because of a loss of trade, a growing depression, and an economy in a shambles, the United States government was a powerless bystander. It could make war and peace; send and receive ambassadors; regulate coinage, weights and measures; borrow money on credit; make treaties and alliances; raise an army and equip a navy. But it could not collect taxes, pay off debts, regulate commerce, or develop a system of enforcing its own laws. It could neither get British troops off its own soil nor protect its people from commercial exploitation;

nor could it force its citizens to honor their war debts or return confiscated property. In fact, states like Virginia, where war debts were heavy, actually passed laws blocking recovery of British debts despite the U.S. government's treaty agreement with England that called for their payment.*

For John Adams in London, therefore, the task was formidable. His country was weak, and the British were willing to delay working out points of contention in the hope that the new nation might founder. Adams wrote Carmarthen concerning the basic issues between them: trade, the British posts, debts, and the carrying off of slaves and other property. In late August of 1785, he met with William Pitt for further discussion. But Adams's efforts were fruitless, and on October 15, he wrote Secretary Jay that he could "obtain no Answer from the Ministry to any one demand, Proposal or Inquiry."

Five days later, Adams met with Carmarthen again, and they went over the familiar ground: continued British occupation of the western posts, trade regulations, slaves carried off during the war, American debts to British creditors. The secretary was cordial, but unresponsive, and Adams described the meeting as "useless." During another frustrating discussion between the two men in December, Adams offered a memorial, dated November 30, 1785, calling for withdrawal of British garrisons in the Northwest in accordance with Article 7 of the peace treaty. Carmarthen waited three months to reply, and then wrote Adams that the British retention of the posts in violation of Article 7 was no different from — and was counterbalanced by — the obstacles most American states had established blocking repayment of debts due British creditors.

As some historians have noted, the British had no intention of releasing their lucrative fur-trading and military posts on the American side of the Canadian border. On April 8, 1783, the British home minister sent a dispatch to the governor of Canada stating that the British posts would not be

* By 1789, with the new federal Constitution, a new judicial system opened the courts to British subjects seeking to recover prewar and wartime debts. The only impediment then was the courts' slow course. Further, by convention in 1802, the United States paid a lump sum to Great Britain in complete satisfaction of debts and interest.

DETAIL: THE COPLEY FAMILY. OIL BY JOHN SINGLETON COPLEY, 1777

evacuated "at least until we are enabled to secure the fur traders in the Interior Country." British garrisons in New York, for example, were to have been evacuated by December, 1783. But the seven military and fur-trading posts remained in British possession until 1796, largely because the British were unwilling to give up the commerce.

For the rest of his mission, John Adams would be unable to break the deadlock on these issues. They remained, in fact, unresolved until the Jay Treaty of 1795. The basic problem, as Adams understood, was the weakness of his young nation: lacking power under the Articles of Confederation, it was helpless against the restrictive British trade policy.

Adams never gave up hope of trying to get Carmarthen to act. But he was also realistic, and he turned his attention to his family, which was changing and growing around him, to his friends, his other commissions, and to the coming struggle inside his own country.

While diplomacy soured, the Adamses' social life sweetened. In fact, it became, like some large confection itself, almost more than the eye — or stomach — could retain. Abigail's fear that she might cut "an awkward figure" in sophisticated Europe after life in Puritan Braintree soon evaporated. Her first few days in London, while the city celebrated the king's birthday with a Handel music festival, were spent at concerts and in house hunting.

In June, 1785, after she had spent a fortnight looking, she found a house on Grosvenor Square, which the Adamses rented for twenty-one months at £160 a year. Abigail immediately had two rooms painted to receive their furniture from Paris and The Hague. She wrote her sister that Grosvenor Square "is one of the finest squares in London. The air is as pure as it can be so near a great city. It is but a small distance from Hyde Park, round which I sometimes walk, but oftener ride."

The Adamses had a tight budget; Congress, as noted, was not collecting much in the way of taxes, and money was scarce. In May John had written Thomas Jefferson in Paris that he couldn't bring in his wine stock without a heavy duty of six to eight shillings per bottle, which he could not afford.

He asked Jefferson not to ship any of the wine "except one Case of Madeira and Frontenac together."

On September 30, 1785, the entire London diplomatic corps of fifteen ministers, including Lord Carmarthen, dined with the Adamses at Grosvenor Square. Paying for the dinner was difficult. In a letter to one of her sisters, Abigail confessed that they had little to spend on entertainment, and invitation cards had to be sent out, as was the custom, ten days in advance. Fortunately, a Captain Hay arrived from the West Indies shortly before the dinner, and gave the Adamses a gift of a 114-pound turtle, which they hastily served the guests.

Abigail and John expanded their circle of English friends and diplomats from other nations. And Abigail and her daughter, then a pretty twenty-year-old, began to make the rounds of "ladies' routs" during the 1785–1786 social season. Abigail's letters to her friends and sisters in Massachusetts, who were in the middle of very hard times, made England sound like a different world indeed.

There were, she wrote them, two kinds of routs. The first was a daytime party given on the same day of the week, each week, for the five winter months, "it being quite out of fashion to be seen in London during the summer." Moreover, as she wrote Mrs. Cranch, "those persons who have not country-houses of their own, resort to the watering-places, as they are called, during the summer months, it being too vulgar . . . to remain in London."

The other kind of rout, far more frequent and conducted almost to the point of exhaustion, was an evening card party. "A lady sends to you for certain evenings, and the cards are always addressed in her own name, both to gentlemen and ladies. The rooms are all set open, and card-tables set in each room, the lady of the house receiving her company at the door of the drawing-room, where a set number of courtesies are given and received. . . . The visiter then proceeds into the room without appearing to notice any other person, and takes her seat at the card table. . . . At these parties, it is usual for each lady to play a rubber, as it is termed, when you must lose or win a few guineas. To give each a fair chance, the lady then rises and gives her seat to another set. It is no unusual thing to have your rooms so crowded that not more than half the company can sit at once, yet this is called *society and polite life*."

Abigail's Puritan heart did not enjoy cards and gambling. Of a winter evening at Madame de Pinto's, wife of the Portuguese minister, she wrote: "It being *Sunday* evening, I declined playing cards; indeed, I always get excused when I can. . . . Yet I must submit to a party or two of this kind."

The French ambassador held "a levee every Sunday evening, at which there are usually several hundred persons." On one occasion, "many very brilliant ladies of the first distinction were present. The dancing commenced about ten, and the rooms soon filled. The room which he [the French ambassador] had built for this purpose is large enough for five or six hundred persons. It is most elegantly decorated, hung with a gold tissue, ornamented with twelve brilliant cut lustres, each containing twenty-four candles. At one end there are two large arches; these were adorned with wreaths and bunches of artificial flowers upon the walls; in the alcoves were cornucopiae loaded with oranges, sweetmeats, &c. Coffee, tea, lemonade, orgeat, &c. were taken here by every person who chose to go for them. There were covered seats all round the room for those who did not choose to dance. In the other rooms, card-tables, and a large faro-table, were set; this is a new kind of game, which is much practised here."

Another time, she and John attended "a stupid rout" at the Swedish minister's with about two hundred people. "Three large rooms full of card-tables; the moment the ceremony of courtesying is past, the lady of the house asks you, 'Pray, what is your game; whist, cribbage or commerce?' And then the next thing is to hunt round the room for a set to make a party; and, as the company are coming and going from eight till two in the morning, you may suppose that she has enough to employ her from room to room. The lady and her daughter last night were almost fatigued to death, for they had been out the night before till morning, and were toiling at pleasure for seven hours, in which time they scarcely sat down."

At this party, Abigail could not beg off playing cards, and won four games. "But I never play when I can possibly avoid it, for I have not conquered the disagreeable feeling of

In both Paris and London, the Adamses enjoyed the theater
and the parks. Opera, however, interested Abigail and her
daughter, Nabby, more than it did John, who once remarked:
"The french Opera is an Entertainment, which is very
pleasing, for a few Times. . . . The Words are unintelligible,
and if they were not, they are said to be very insignificant."
Adams had no better luck with Italian opera, in which he
found "the Actors and Actresses very indifferent." It was
"a dull Entertainment to me." Abigail also loved the
concerts in London, and heard The Messiah with Nabby at
Westminster Abbey. They often walked from their house
on Grosvenor Square to watch the regal mounting of the
guard in St. James's Park.

GROSVENOR SQUARE, LONDON. AQUATINT BY ROBERT POLLARD, 1789

MOUNTING GUARD, ST. JAMES'S PARK. AQUATINT FROM
Microcosm of London, BY THOMAS ROWLANDSON, 1808

OPERA HOUSE, LONDON. AQUATINT FROM *Microcosm of London*, BY THOMAS ROWLANDSON, 1808

receiving money for play. But such a set of gamblers as the ladies here are! and such a life as they lead! Good Heavens! were reasonable beings made for this?"

There were other events — presentations to the queen, dinners, funerals of state, including that for the duke of Northumberland. London enjoyed a small but select colony of artists, who delighted in their acquaintance with the Adams family. Along with John Singleton Copley, there was Mather Brown, who had come to England from Massachusetts to study under Benjamin West. The Copleys were good friends of the Adamses, who greatly admired the portrait of John that Copley had painted after the Definitive Treaty. When the American minister gave "stag" dinners for the other diplomats in London, Abigail and her daughter often retreated to the Copleys' for the evening.

By 1785, Mather Brown had rented a house on Cavendish Square, and was very popular. When the Adamses first arrived in London, they had Mather Brown do their portraits, and were quite captivated by the experience. Nabby wrote her brother John Quincy: "A rage for Painting has taken Possession of the Whole family, one of our rooms has been occupied by a Gentleman of this profession, for near a fortnight, and we have the extreme felicity of looking at ourselves upon Canvass. The Paper yesterday had this paragraph . . . 'Copley and Brown are exerting their skill upon their illustrious Country Man Mr. Adams the American Ambassador.' *I expect it will be next that Mr. Brown is painter to the American Ambassador's family.* He was very sollicitous to have a likeness of Pappa, thinking it would be an advantage to him, and Pappa Consented. He has taken the best likeness I have yet seen of him, and you may suppose is very Proud, when so many have failed before him. Mamma has set for hers, and I followed the example. It is said he has taken an admirable likeness of my Ladyship, the Honble. Miss Adams you know. It is a very tasty picture I can assure you, whether a likeness or not. Pappa is much pleased with it, and says he has got my character, a Mixture of Drolery and Modesty. I wish we could have the other three yourself and Charles and Thomas. I think we should make a *respectable Group.* He has a good likeness of Mamma, too."

For John Adams, this was a time of frustrations, long walks, his other commissions and visits from friends. He admired the English farms, cows and meadows. During one of his "common Walks," he "carefully examined" large "heaps of Manure" and found them "composed of Straw, and dung from the Stables and Streets of London, mud, Clay, or Marl, dug out of the Ditch, along the Hedge, and Turf, Sward cutt up, with Spades, hoes, and shovels in the Road. This is laid in vast heaps to mix." Perhaps missing Braintree, Adams recalled his own manure heaps "upon my own Farm, of Horse Dung from Bracketts stable in Boston, Marsh Mud from the sea shore and Street Dust, from the Plain at the Foot of Pens Hill, in which is a Mixture of Marl." At a time when few satisfactions came his way, this reminiscence pleased him, and he noted in his diary that the English variety "may be good manure, but is not equal to mine."

Elsewhere, Adams and Jefferson still held appointments to negotiate treaties of amity and commerce with African and European states. Jefferson had been appointed minister to France — Franklin being recalled at his own request — and had arrived in Europe shortly after Abigail. He and Adams kept in close touch by letter during various negotiations, and when the ambassador from Tripoli arrived in London, Adams went by his residence to sound him out on terms that the two nations might accept. In a lighthearted letter to Jefferson — the tone of which Adams called "very inconsistent with the Dignity of your Character and mine, but the Ridicule of it [his visit with the ambassador] was real and the Drollery inevitable" — he described finding the ambassador, one Abdurrahman, at home, and being received. Two chairs were placed before the fire, and two members of the Tripoli legation stood at attention in the middle of the room during the meeting. The ambassador spoke only Italian and lingua franca — "in which," Adams wrote Jefferson, "you know I have Small Pretensions" — but they communicated well. The Tripolitan praised American tobacco, saying that it was milder than that of his country, and beckoned to the two aides, who brought large pipes already filled and lighted. The longer pipe was offered to Adams.

"I took the Pipe with great Complacency," he wrote,

ABIGAIL ADAMS. OIL BY MATHER BROWN, 1785

Mather Brown was a favorite with the
Adamses. In May, 1785, Abigail sat for her
portrait (left), and that year Brown also
painted Abigail Adams II and her husband,
William Stephens Smith (right). Nabby
wrote her brother John Quincy that her
portrait was "an admirable likeness of
my Ladyship . . . a very tasty picture I
can assure you."

TOP: ABIGAIL ADAMS II. OIL BY
MATHER BROWN, 1785

BOTTOM: COLONEL WILLIAM STEPHENS SMITH.
OIL BY MATHER BROWN, 1785

"placed the Bowl upon the Carpet, for the Stem was fit for a Walking Cane, and I believe more than two Yards in length, and Smoaked in awful Pomp, reciprocating Whiff for Whiff, with his Excellency, until Coffee was brought in."

Unfortunately, despite Adams's efforts with the long pipe, negotiations with the Barbary States didn't go well. Though Morocco signed a treaty in 1786, Algeria lagged. "Money and Fear," Vergennes had explained to Jefferson, "are the only two agents at Algiers." But the United States had neither the money to bribe with nor the power to cause fear.

In March, 1786, Adams suggested to Jefferson that he leave Paris and visit London to make a final effort to interest the British in a commercial treaty. The diplomatic negotiations failed, but the two friends enjoyed each other immensely. Jefferson, of course, was treated like a member of the Adams family. Abigail had written home to her sister that he was "one of the choice ones of the earth." At Adams's insistence, Jefferson sat for Mather Brown, whom he paid £10 for his portrait, which hung in the Adamses' house on Grosvenor Square.

Abigail also became very fond of Jefferson's eight-year-old daughter, Polly, who sailed alone in 1787 from America to join her father in Paris. Polly's ship docked in London, where Abigail met her and found the little girl unwilling to leave the ship's captain. But Abigail soon won her over, and when Jefferson, who was a widower, sent for Polly, Abigail wrote him: "I am really loth to part with her." The little girl went on to Paris heavily laden: Abigail had purchased for her (and was later reimbursed by Jefferson) a long list of items that included Irish-Holland frocks, white dimity for shirts, leather gloves, "a Brown Bever Hat and feathers," blue sash ribbons, "a comb and case, comb Brush, tooth Brush."

During Jefferson's visit in 1786, he and Adams had little to do, and so they made a leisurely tour of the British countryside. An early stop was Stratford-on-Avon, where they were shown a wooden chair said to be Shakespeare's. "We cutt off a Chip according to the Custom," Adams noted. Jefferson was an avid gardener, and carried his copy of Thomas Whately's *Observations on Modern Gardening* with him. Adams was more interested in the historic sites and the luxury of the country estates, although he entered notes in the margins of his own copy of Whately's book for each garden the two visited.

They had no fixed idea of how far they would travel or how long they would be gone. "We have seen Magnificence, Elegance and Taste enough to excite an Inclination to see more," Adams wrote Abigail from the village of Buckingham. "We conclude to go to Birmingham, perhaps to the Leasowes, and in that Case shall not have the Pleasure to see you, till Sunday or Monday." Jefferson paid for "ent[ertainmen]t" ten shillings and tenpence at High Wycombe, and for horses; Adams dutifully reimbursed Jefferson, which Jefferson noted in his Account Book.

Not all of life during those London years centered around John and Abigail. Their children, too, were growing older and more mature, and beginning lives of their own.

Nabby's romance with Royall Tyler failed to survive the separation of ocean and time. Perhaps her father had suspected this; in any event, Nabby had written to Royall, and they had exchanged miniature portraits. But by the spring of 1785, her letters were not being answered, and she wrote Tyler complaining of his neglect. Letters from her Aunt Mary Cranch gossiped that Tyler was reading her letters to his friends, and making fun of their engagement.

During this period, the London social scene was enlivened for Nabby by the presence of a young secretary of the American legation, Colonel William Stephens Smith. Smith had served with Washington at White Plains, Harlem Heights and Valley Forge, and under Lafayette in Virginia. He and Nabby spent much time together, and in the late summer, she wrote Royall Tyler, returning his few letters and his miniature, and requesting that he return hers to her uncle, Richard Cranch.

By the end of the year, Colonel Smith had composed a gallant letter to Mrs. Adams as a formal request for the hand of her daughter. The engagement was short, and the couple were married on June 12, 1786, by special license of the archbishop of Canterbury, at the legation on Grosvenor Square.

THOMAS JEFFERSON. OIL BY MATHER BROWN, 1786

Only the Copleys and a few American friends were present.

On April 2, 1787, John and Abigail Adams's first grand-child, William Steuben Smith, was born, and Adams wrote to C. W. F. Dumas that he now looked forward to "some Amusement." Abigail wrote Mrs. Warren: "I will not close this letter without informing you that I am a grand — O no! that would be confessing myself old, which would be quite unfashionable and vulgar — but true it is. I have a fine grand-son. I regret a little that it was not a daughter, for then I should have claimed the little one for the great one."

Meanwhile, John Quincy Adams was becoming more inde-pendent. Before his family had left Paris for London, John Quincy had had to make a major decision: he could go to England as secretary to his father or he could return to the United States and attend Harvard. The choice was his, al-though his parents — as parents will — took a hand in shaping it. As early as 1783, John Quincy's mother had written him from Braintree: "I have a desire that you might finish your education at our University, and I see no chance for it unless you return in the course of the year." And John Quincy's father had kept in touch with Harvard. In 1781, the univer-sity had awarded him an honorary LL.D. In London, he had found himself among the largest Harvard community outside of Boston, many of whom had been Loyalist exiles.

Although it was natural for John Quincy to consider Harvard, the prospect did not elate him. He had gathered much from his experiences in Europe. By the age of seven-teen, he had been private secretary to the minister to Russia in St. Petersburg, and to his father in Paris. He had traveled widely, often on his own, and had lived in several of the major European cities. He knew Latin and Greek, and he spoke French, Dutch and German.

He had also met and knew many of the leading men of the day. Some of them appeared in his diary, begun on November 12, 1779, with his departure from home for Europe, which carried his father's admonitions: don't waste time; always write in a clear hand. John Quincy obeyed both instructions, and kept his diary almost without interruption from 1795 to 1845. On its early pages appear the names Ver-

Thomas Jefferson visited John and Abigail Adams in London during the spring of 1786. Jefferson, probably at Adams's insistence, sat for this portrait by Mather Brown—and paid Brown £10 for the painting. It has remained in the Adams family ever since.

gennes, Franklin, Pitt. Jefferson exerted the strongest influence, and John Quincy soon wrote, "Mr. Jefferson is a man of universal learning," and later, "Spent the evening with Mr. Jefferson whom I love to be with."

John Quincy also delighted in Paris, the soirées and the diplomatic dinners he was sometimes invited to attend. He often went to Lafayette's, who gave a dinner every Monday evening for American diplomats and friends. He shared Abigail's delight in the French theater, and later in his life confessed, half-seriously, that "the first woman I ever loved was an actress . . . who performed at the Bois de Boulogne near Passy. . . . She remains upon my memory as the most lovely and delightful actress that I ever saw; but I have not seen her since I was fourteen. She was then about the same age."

Amid the glitter of Paris, the thought of the rigors of Harvard was hardly enticing. After all, what could compete with a gossamer actress flittering in the Bois de Boulogne? But Harvard was something he knew he must do. He would not end up like Benjamin Franklin's grandson, William Temple Franklin, who had (like John Quincy) come to Paris as a boy and attended the same schools. But now, as a young man about Paris, Franklin did little else than attend parties and lead a cat about the city on a ribbon. Harvard, "that darling childe of New England Puritanism," would be a struggle, with its narrow and difficult curriculum followed by the "dry and tedious study of the law." The temptation was to stay in Europe, but John Quincy's ambition pushed him homeward.

In languages and literature John Quincy was admirably prepared to enter Harvard with advanced standing. From Paris John Adams wrote to Benjamin Waterhouse, "If you were to examine him in English and French Poetry, I know not where you would find anybody his Superiour." The classics had always been part of the young man's reading, and would continue to be so as long as he lived; he and his father would exchange reflections upon classical writers when John Adams was in retirement in Quincy. But John Quincy's knowledge of mathematics was deficient. He needed tutoring. "In the Course of the last Year, instead of playing Cards like the fashionable world, I have spent my Evenings with him," John Adams wrote. They struggled with geometry, trigonometry, conic sections and differential calculus; the elder Adams concluded that "he is as yet but a Smatterer like his Father."

In the fall of 1784, John Adams wrote to President Joseph Willard of Harvard asking that John Quincy be admitted, and Willard replied in December that the young man could join whichever class an examination showed him qualified to enter. It was arranged that John Quincy would prepare for his advanced standing examination at the home of Aunt Elizabeth (Abigail's sister) and Uncle John Shaw in Haverhill.

It was done. John Quincy left Auteuil for America on May 12, 1785, and docked in New York on July 17. He missed his parents and sister. The family house in Braintree looked "gloomy and sad," and John Quincy again wrote in a rich and melancholy mood to his sister: "When I shall see you and my ever dear and honored parents again, alas, alas, I know not. The ocean is again between us! The interests of a nation keep you on that side, and the duty of an individual keep me on this. But the hope that some day will come when we shall all meet again together, still cheers and encourages me; although it is like trees in the dusk, which seem lengthening as you go."

By October, John Quincy was settled at the Shaws' and beginning his preparations for Harvard. He wrote Nabby again, a little overwhelmed by the work to be covered: "I am told I have much more to do than I had any idea of. . . . In the Greek I have to go from the beginning to learn the grammar, which is by no means an agreeable task; to study the New Testament nearly or quite through, between three or four books in Xenophon's Cyropaedia, and five or six books in Homer's Iliad. In Latin I have but little else to go through but Horace, part of which I have already done. In English, I have to study Watts' Logic, Locke on the Human Understanding, and something in Astronomy."

In March of 1786, John Quincy was admitted to Harvard as a junior. He wrote Nabby that during the previous fall and winter he had not left the Shaw house (and his books) for more than four hours a week. Once in college, however, he did take some time off for reading and "taking lessons on the flute, for you must know we are all turning musicians."

His father crowed a bit from Europe: "Give me leave to congratulate you on your Admission into the seat of the Muses, our dear Alma Mater, where I hope you will find a Pleasure and Improvements equal to your Expectations. You are now among Magistrates and Ministers, Legislators and Heroes, Ambassadors and Generals, I mean among Persons who will live to Act in all these Characters. . . . You are breathing now in the Atmosphere of Science and Litterature, the floating Particles of which will mix with your whole Mass of Blood and Juices. Every Visit you make to the Chamber or study of a Schollar, you learn something."

But not all Harvard scholars so easily impressed John Quincy. He wrote of the Greek tutor, a Mr. Jennison, who at twenty-four years of age was "very far from being possessed of those qualities which I should suppose necessary for a tutor here. He is so ignorant in Greek, that he displays it sometimes in correcting a scholar that is right, and other times suffering the most absurd constructions to pass unnoticed."

Adams was a serious student who soon learned, as he wrote his father on May 21, 1786, that "a person who wishes to make any figure as a scholar at this University, must not spend much time either in visiting or being visited." He stuck to his studies, including the flute. Indeed, his tutor was so disturbed by John Quincy's practicing that he sent a fresh-man upstairs with orders for quiet. Later on, when John Quincy was forty-two, he would note: "I was always of a studious turn and addicted to books beyond bounds of moderation, yet my acquirements in literature and science have been all superficial, and I never attained a profound knowledge of anything."

On July 16, 1787, he graduated from Harvard as a member of the newly founded Phi Beta Kappa society. Then he studied law for three years under Theophilus Parsons of Newburyport. He continued reading the classics and history, and learned shorthand by Biron's system. Parsons was a "deep and attractive man" who enjoyed literature as much as law. One day, after cutting off a quid of tobacco, while rocking in the chair in his office, he told his students: "Lord Bacon observes that 'reading makes a full man, conversation a ready man, and writing a correct man.' Now, gentlemen, I would have you full, ready, and correct."

After his first month of study, Adams read a quotation from Blackstone that troubled him: "It is a principle of *universal law* that the natural-born subject of one prince, cannot by any act of his own, no, not by swearing allegiance to another, put off or discharge his natural allegiance to the former: for this natural allegiance was intrinsic and primitive, and antecedent to the other, and cannot be divested without the concurrent act of that prince to whom it was first due." Adams took this to Parsons, for it seemed to him, so recently a witness to the American Revolution, that a man could not be forced to serve and assist his sovereign. "If it is read *common law* instead of universal law," Parsons replied, "the assertion would be just; but in my opinion every man has a right by the law of nature to put off his natural allegiance, for good cause."

Here was a theme that would echo in John Quincy Adams's life: the basic conflict between complete allegiance versus the assertion of expatriation and choice. It was the heart of the coming differences between British and American principles, and would be the focus of the issue of impressment.

While John Quincy Adams studied law, his brothers Charles and Thomas Boylston were attending Harvard. They seldom wrote their mother (or father) in London, and Abigail Adams complained to Mary Cranch in 1787: "Those dear lads do not write so often as I wish them to do, because they have nothing more to say than that they are well; not considering how important that intelligence is to an affectionate parent."

Like most mothers, Abigail suspected more than she knew. John Quincy's life was not all books and innocent fluting. His diary is stuffed with notations about social events in Newburyport, and late-night drinking at the young men's social club. There were all-night serenades of young ladies; dinners, dances, sailing parties in summer; sleigh rides in winter, which prompted a later observation reminiscent of his father's on bundling. "The art of making love," John Quincy

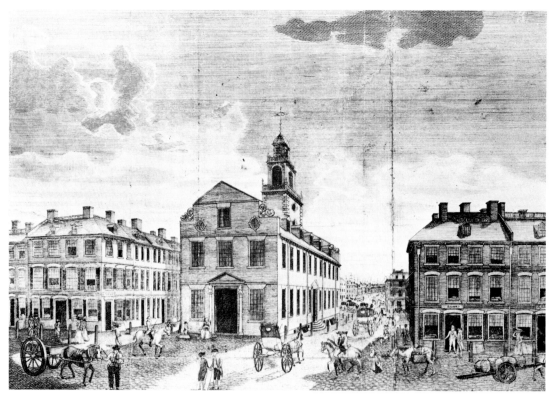

A SOUTH WEST VIEW OF THE STATE HOUSE IN BOSTON. ENGRAVING
BY SAMUEL HILL FOR THE MASSACHUSETTS, MAGAZINE, 1793

CHARLES ADAMS. OIL ON IVORY,
UNKNOWN ARTIST, 1795

THOMAS BOYLSTON ADAMS.
OIL ON IVORY BY PARKER, 1795

wrote in his late sixties, "muffled up in furs, in the open air, with the thermometer at Zero, is a Yankee invention, which requires a Yankee poet to describe."

John Quincy held his own in sporting the young ladies of Newburyport, but he was not always enticed by the offerings. The education of American girls disappointed him: "Miss Sally Jenkins . . . is of the middling female size and has a fine form. . . . She conversed not much, and indeed in the state of female education there are few young ladies who talk and yet preserve our admiration." Like his father he was attracted by intelligent and well-spoken — perhaps outspoken — women.

Toward the end of his stay, however, John Quincy Adams discovered someone different: Mary Frazier, daughter of a patriot selectman, Moses Frazier. He wrote to James Bridge on September 5, 1790: "You may know (though it is known to very few) that all my hopes of future happiness in this life, center in the possession of that girl." Adams was then twenty-two, and Mary Frazier, sixteen. Both realized that he could not support a family, and so did her parents. Therefore, for "prudential and family reasons" they broke off their attachment, ending the relationship. But John Quincy could not entirely extinguish the embers. These "troubles of the heart" were "deep and distressing" he wrote his son Charles Francis on March 15, 1828. And, clearly, they were never to die completely. At the age of twenty-three, John Quincy Adams, a broken-hearted but perhaps wiser young lawyer, opened his first law office in Boston, far enough from Newburyport and its temptations.

While John Adams and Thomas Jefferson were suffering the frustrations of European politics, the nation they left had won the war, but was in danger of losing the peace. In the ten years since the Declaration, political America was shifting noticeably. The Revolution, perhaps unwittingly, released progressive forces that brought some social progress. And while it would be wrong to describe the American Revolution as a social revolution, like those later in France and Russia, it was a catalytic force in American society.

Of the 3,250,000 people in the United States at the close

of the Revolution, about one third were not free. These included 600,000 black slaves, 300,000 indentured servants and 50,000 convicts, who, despite laws against their entry, were smuggled in. The remainder included American debtors and vagrants sold into involuntary labor by court order; and youthful apprentices let out by their parents to journeymen or master workers.

While one million people in this new nation had neither freedom nor political voice, another million or so — women — had limited legal standing. If married, they could neither hold property nor will it, nor could they sit on juries or sue. They were often denied education and employment. And although women accidentally were given the right to vote in several of the early state constitutions, that too was gradually taken from them.

By the time Adams and Jefferson were seeking treaties of amity and commerce for their young country, fewer than 700,000 free adult American men — the voters and law-makers — existed in the United States. Tens of thousands, however, held no land — thus excluding them under some state laws from voting — and moved toward the shifting frontiers of Vermont and Maine, the Mohawk Valley of New York, the Monongahela of Pennsylvania, the wilderness of Kentucky and Tennessee. "The Americans," Governor Dunmore of Virginia had written during the 1770's, "acquire no attachment to Place. But wandering about seems engrafted in their Nature; and it is a weakness incident to it, that they should ever imagine the Lands farther off, are Still better than those upon which they are already Settled."

In all, at the close of the Revolution, many Americans could not meet the property, religious or other qualifications to vote. Further, the men of property and money who ran their communities and governed their states were not always well educated. In Virginia in the 1780's, for example, less than one third of the men making deeds or serving on juries could sign their names — and these men were the most prominent in their communities.

Several forces began working in the United States after the Revolutionary War, and affected rapidly changing social patterns, an increasing depression, and a weak Confederation.

For one, land was being sold for a few cents an acre. Almost anyone could afford fifty acres, or a forty-shilling freehold, which would entitle him to vote. This brought a growing number of Americans into the political process, and in some of the northern states, where representation was reapportioned according to population, the backcountry for the first time swung some weight.

Still another was westward expansion. While the original thirteen colonies adjusted themselves into independence, new commonwealths were created in Vermont and the trans-Appalachian country. Settlers pushed into the Northwest Territory, and toward the Mississippi. One of the major delays in the signing of the Articles of Confederation was the conflict over who would control these western lands; states like Virginia wanted to use the land to pay off war debts and reward soldiers. Before Jefferson left for Europe, he had been appointed by Congress to chair two committees, one of which devised a plan that became the Ordinance of 1784, for ultimate self-government of the West, which would be divided into ten states eventually admitted on an equal basis with the original thirteen. The Land Ordinance of 1785 provided for surveying lands and for the division of land into townships six miles square — thirty-six sections of 640 acres in each township. Most important, four sections would be set aside for the U.S. government, and one for public schools. Speculation and private land companies soon forced Congress into taking action again on the western lands, and in July, 1787, Congress passed the Northwest Ordinance, which bridged the gap between wilderness and statehood with a system of limited self-government.

These enlightened provisions laid the foundation for American territorial expansion and development. But they did more than that: for the first time, men could apply new democratic principles to their lives. Sturdy and independent citizens hewed new territories out of the wilderness, escaped foreign entanglements, and voted themselves into the United States.

At the end of the war, traditional markets were lost, largely due to British restrictions on trade. Indebtedness increased. Soon, debtors began pressuring state legislatures to postpone collection of debts and to pass "tender acts" that would provide cheap money and make legal tender of produce at fixed values. This stunned gentlemen of property. James Madison later wrote that this radical movement within the states, which threatened the propertied people, "contributed more to that uneasiness which produced the Constitution, and prepared the public mind for a general reform" than any of the specific weaknesses of the Articles of Confederation.

The economic depression hit bottom by 1786. Seven states continued printing paper money. North Carolina purchased tobacco from its farmers at twice the specie value. In Charleston, young radicals of the Hint Club paid rice planters with sections of rope. Rhode Island loaned large amounts of paper money to landowners, and forced the stuff on other people. In Massachusetts, the farmers suffered greatly, and their plans often went ignored by their legislature. Farm produce glutted the market, partly as a result of the stoppage of West Indian trade. Taxes were heavy, the courts were filled with suits for debts, and the cost of seeking — not to mention getting — justice was exorbitant.

During the summer of 1786, conventions of Massachusetts farmers and townspeople demanded reform from the state administration. No relief came, and the oppressive process of taking cattle and land in payment for debts continued. Farmers, facing debtors prison and loss of family property, rebelled; the wonder is that more didn't follow.

In the fall, mobs of farmers under Daniel Shays (a former Revolutionary War captain and himself a farmer), Luke Day, Job Shattuck and others began trying to prevent the county courts from sitting. It was a pathetic gesture but one the people of Massachusetts had used with success in the 1770's: if the courts couldn't sit, and pass judgment on the debts, the farmers could work and perhaps repay what they owed. John Hancock had retired as governor, and in his place was James Bowdoin, a firm-minded merchant, who ordered the mobs dispersed. Shays and his farmers quickly became rebels.

Attempts to capture the government arsenal at Springfield were dispersed with grapeshot. Loyal militia, financed by contributions from local merchants, arrived from the eastern counties; college boys, the sons of the upper classes, formed a cavalry regiment. Shays's rebels scattered, and were hunted in the hills of Massachusetts. Later, after the rebellion had been crushed, the state called for a general amnesty, and the legislature considered the grievances that had caused it.

Still, Shays's Rebellion had taken place in the seat of revolution. Abigail Adams and her friends back in Braintree voiced their deep concern over Shays's action. Some conservatives in America even turned toward monarchy.

Shays's Rebellion, the economic depression and other disturbing events raised the specter of disorder and disintegration — and possible foreign intervention — in America. Men of property and education felt threatened by the possibility of disunion. These were the men who would assume leadership in the coming constitutional movement. But the common man would also lose his liberty and the chance for economic betterment by disunion. And, most important, the common man had much to gain by a stronger nation.

John Adams, on final diplomatic business at The Hague, felt the distant tremors of Shays's Rebellion and the upheaval in America. He had brought Abigail with him, to see the land of his early diplomatic triumphs, and they toured the Dutch countryside: Delft, Leyden, Haarlem, Amsterdam. Abigail wrote enthusiastically about the neat little country of dikes and canals, brick houses and streets. "It is very unusual to see a single square of glass broken, or a brick out of place, even in the meanest house. They paint every piece of wood within and without their houses . . . [even] their milk pails are painted within and without, and so are their horse-carts."

In Utrecht, John Adams happened to see the new magistrates of that city sworn in — a result of constitutional reform at the hands of the Patriot party. He was deeply moved. "In no Instance, of ancient or modern History," he wrote Jefferson, "have the People ever asserted more unequivocally their own inherent and unalienable Sovereignty." Adams felt that the Dutch Patriots were tangible evidence of the American Revolution in Europe, and conversations with Dutch friends and his own reflections on what was happening in the Netherlands stirred him. Further, news of "the Seditious Meetings in Massachusetts" that led to Shays's Rebellion caused him to worry for the future of his own nation.

Returning to London from the Netherlands, Adams began the reading for his three-volume treatise, *A Defence of the Constitutions of Government of the United States of America,* perhaps his most important piece of writing.

In the United States, meanwhile, men were gathering to write a constitution, and to shape a new form of government. This would be a revolution itself, but peaceful and lasting. Almost at the same moment, Abigail wrote of her son, John Quincy Adams:

"I have never once regretted the resolution he took of quitting Europe, and placing himself upon the theatre of his own country; where, if his life is spared, I presume he will neither be an idle nor useless spectator. Heaven grant, that he may not have more distressing scenes before him, and a gloomier stage to tread, than those on which his father has acted for twelve years past. But the curtain rises before him, and . . . Sedition hisses, Treason roars, Rebellion gnashes her teeth, Mercy suspends the justly merited blow, but Justice strikes the guilty victim."

5

The Throw of a Die

[1788–1796]

*B*Y 1788, John Adams's work in England ·had reached a stalemate, and with the exception of trips to the Netherlands to secure loans for the United States, there was little for him to do. He was determined to return home. He had asked Congress to accept his resignation, but its letters of recall and praise got bungled and caused him some embarrassment abroad. Finally, as he was leaving London by coach for the ship, the letters arrived. Congress thanked him for his "patriotism, perseverance, integrity, and diligence."

The Smiths sailed on April 5, on the *Tyne* packet, for New York. The Adamses, diplomatic business cleared, sailed on the *Lucretia* on April 20, for Boston.

The America to which John Adams returned was very different from the one he had left. Philadelphia, with a population of forty thousand, was the metropolis of the nation. New York, with thirty thousand, was Philadelphia's postwar rival, and until 1789 it was the nation's capital. As in Philadelphia, large numbers of Loyalists remained in New York after the war. Newcomers like John Jacob Astor, who arrived from Germany in 1783, developed the city's business. Brilliant young lawyers appeared: Aaron Burr, a grandson of Jonathan Edwards; and Alexander Hamilton, an illegitimate West Indian of English descent who in 1780 had married a daughter of General Philip Schuyler, thus gaining the support (if not the respect) of New York's powerful Dutch aristocracy.

Boston, on the other hand, had lost much. Loyalist capitalists had deserted the town for England and Canada during the war. Diminution of the West Indian trade hurt both Boston and the state of Massachusetts.

There were, of course, other American towns, and they were beginning to grow and thrive. Charleston, South Carolina, was the chief city of the South and, according to some travelers of the time, the most aristocratic city in the Union. Baltimore, too, was busy, and new capitals — Augusta, Georgia; Columbia, South Carolina; Richmond, Virginia — were springing up inland as settlers pushed toward the West.

At the time the first volume of Adams's *A Defence of the Constitutions of Government of the United States* appeared, a convention was meeting in Philadelphia. A year earlier, when Shays's Rebellion was at its height, James Madison had led the Virginia legislature to propose a convention of the states to adopt a uniform system of regulating the navigation of rivers. Representatives of five states met at Annapolis, Maryland, in September, 1786. Among the delegates were Madison and Alexander Hamilton, who soon persuaded the representatives that the issue was too broad and important to be taken up by so small a group. On February 21, 1787, the Congress of the Confederation invited all the states to send delegates to Philadelphia on May 14, "for the sole and express purpose of revising the Articles of Confederation." In effect, the first American government had failed; it would be replaced — peacefully — with a strong central government and one established by popularly elected ratifying conventions.

What took place has been widely discussed. A new government needed building on the old foundations that would be strong, but not imperial; that would include — and be agreeable to — the people; that would seek, once again, balance between order and liberty. The convention in Philadelphia was without precedent. There, the nation's most notable leaders — with the exception of John Jay, Patrick Henry, Thomas Jefferson and Samuel and John Adams, who were overseas or otherwise unable to attend — gathered as a self-constituted party. No war, no tyranny moved them this time, only the basic understanding that they needed a better way of governing themselves. They wrote and helped ratify a constitution for a new federal state that would replace the existing government; they brought that federal state into being without violence, purges, exiles, assassination or war. The theory of government in the Declaration of Independence was given form in the Constitution, which made it possible to abolish, or create, government without revolution and by peaceful means. These men in Philadelphia in 1787 sought and achieved with the pen what others elsewhere had failed — and would soon fail again — to gain with the sword.

The temper of this assembly has been portrayed as realistic and objective. Its members worked sixteen hours a day nearly continuously for four months. What emerged was called the Federal Constitution, and it created an organism called the Federal Government.

The new Constitution brought the states together, enforcing common laws and requiring state officeholders to pledge their support of it "by oath or affirmation." It gave the states territorial integrity, a republican form of government and protection against invasion or domestic violence — a response to Shays's Rebellion. It provided for a peaceful means of enforcing federal law. It absorbed all of the old powers under the Confederation and added a limited taxing power, various civil laws, regulation of foreign and interstate commerce, and a judicial power that could act directly upon individual citizens. It established a senate and a house of representatives, and the election of a president and a vice-president — and defined the powers and limitations of each.

James Madison, James Wilson and others played a strong role in framing the Constitution, but John Adams's imprint was on it too. In its distributing powers among the legislative, executive and judiciary, the federal Constitution reflected closely the Massachusetts state constitution of which Adams was the chief architect. It also contained echoes of his

Defence essay, which, though much misunderstood and remembered later as an attempt to favor monarchy, actually examined the workings of the British constitution and advocated a republican form of government.

Congress submitted the federal Constitution not to the state legislatures but to specially elected state conventions in an effort to give the document wide acceptance, and also stipulated that the Constitution, unlike the Confederation, would go into effect when nine of the thirteen states ratified it. Passage, however, seemed doubtful when they adjourned in September, 1787.

The Federalists — as the supporters of the Constitution called themselves — could count on merchants and seaport towns, public creditors and speculators in the western lands, officers of the Revolutionary army, farmers with surpluses and easy access to markets, and most of the press for support. They could — and would — appeal to popular fears: law and order versus anarchy. Still, there was widespread opposition among people who were suspicious of central government. Massachusetts, for example, put up a tough struggle against the Constitution. The state convention, when it met in Boston, contained an anti-Federalist majority. Agrarian discontent still held power in the state, and insurgents, including some of Shays's officers, were in the audience. Amos Singletary, a delegate, groused about "these lawyers, and men of learning, and moneyed men, that talk so finely, and gloss over matters so smoothly, to make us, poor illiterate people, swallow down the pill, expect to get into Congress themselves; they expect to be the managers of this Constitution, and get all the power and all the money into their own hands, and then they will swallow up all us little folks . . .; yes, just as the whale swallowed up Jonah!"

The Federalists flattered and wooed the doubtful folk from the rural districts, and after heated arguments, the Constitution passed in Massachusetts — but by only 19 votes out of 355. Maryland followed, then South Carolina. By May, 1788, eight states had ratified, but neither New York nor Virginia, the key states to any union, had done so. In June, New Hampshire came in as the ninth state and the new government could begin.

When John and Abigail Adams sailed into Boston harbor aboard the *Lucretia* on June 17, 1788, amid the boom of cannon on Castle William and "huzzas" of greeting from "several thousand people," their nation stood on the very edge of change. The federal Constitution, with its system of popular sovereignty, was about to be ratified by New Hampshire. The nation could now grow. Commerce could flourish: the Acts of Trade and Navigation no longer suppressed it. But now began political intrigue. How would the new government be run, and by whom?

At the time Adams was leaving Europe, his friend Thomas Jefferson wrote this candid appraisal of him and sent it to James Madison: "He is vain, irritable and a bad calculator of the force and probable effect of the motives which govern men. This is all the ill which can possibly be said of him. He is as disinterested as the being which made him: he is profound in his views: and accurate in his judgment except where knowledge of the world is necessary to form a judgment. He is so amiable, that I pronounce you will love him if ever you become acquainted with him. He would be, as he was, a great man in Congress."

But Adams would not serve in the old Congress, although he was elected to it in 1788, almost as he landed in Boston. Instead, he wisely retreated to his home and farm, where he could measure this emerging nation and its people. While in London, he had purchased an old colonial dwelling built in the early eighteenth century by Major Leonard Vassal. Instead of politics, Adams once again thought of leisure: his books, his farm. He announced his "unchangeable determination" to refuse public office, and stayed in Braintree unpacking his books, getting his new house organized, looking after his fields.

But two events of lasting significance took place in 1789: the inauguration of the national government under the new Constitution, and the beginning of the French Revolution. And John Adams would be caught up in both of them.

Old political alignments were shifting at the time the Constitution was ratified. But where, and how deeply? Adams recognized that many of the old patriots of '76 were gone; in their places had come Federalists and (soon enough) anti-Federalists, a boisterous lot of politicians without equal in the courts of Europe. There would be a new Congress, and a president and vice-president to lead the nation. The only man being considered for president was George Washington, a Virginian. The second position, for "balance," might fall to a New Englander. John Hancock was a possibility; so was Samuel Adams. But only John Adams had the prestige and the support to make him the logical choice, and Alexander Hamilton, the leader of the Federalists, reluctantly agreed to the endorsement of Adams as the Federalist candidate.

A young and ambitious framer of the Constitution, Hamilton put his trust in the privileged class. He sought close collaboration between the United States and England, and wanted a powerful central government. He would have preferred a more pliant vice-president, but he was also wise enough to know he couldn't — and shouldn't — alienate the New England Federalists. Though Hamilton supported Adams, he was determined to whittle down Adams's electoral vote.

The electoral procedure during this period was cumbersome. Candidates didn't campaign, but stood aloof from the process. The person receiving the largest number of votes — from electors selected in each state — became president, while the one receiving the next largest became vice-president. This first election — marked by delays, bungling — was also marked by slick intrigue.

Hamilton, who had set himself up as kingmaker and was seeking power behind the throne, knew that Washington would win the presidency. But he was concerned over John Adams's popularity, and to keep the race from being close, instructed his Federalist henchmen outside New York State to vote for Washington but to scatter their votes for the second candidate. His reasons, stated in a letter to Theodore Sedgwick, were that Adams and Richard Henry Lee might form a "Cabal" and embarrass Washington. In letters to James Monroe and James Wilson, a Philadelphia lawyer, Hamilton expressed his concern that Adams would gain too many votes and end up president because some ill-disposed electors might refuse to vote for Washington. "Under this impression," he wrote, "I have proposed to friends in Connecticut to throw away two [votes] to others in Jersey to throw away an equal number & I submit it to you whether it will not be well to lose three or four in Pensylvania."

As it turned out, Washington was elected unanimously, as everyone knew he would be, and in spite of Hamilton's machinations, Adams received more votes than any of the other candidates — 34 out of 69. Although stung by his failure to win a majority, Adams decided to accept the vice-presidency. He left Braintree on April 13, 1789, and rode at the head of a procession of forty carriages, including a military escort, to New York. But he soon discovered, as others have since, that the vice-presidency was not the job he imagined. "My country has in its wisdom," he wrote Abigail with some sarcasm, "contrived for me the most insignificant office that ever the invention of man contrived or his imagination conceived."

A debater, Adams was reduced by the vice-presidency to silence. Worse, neither Adams nor the members of the Senate, over which he presided, regarded one another very highly. Adams's duties were not clearly defined under the Constitution, and the presidency of the Senate had been given to the vice-president to provide him with a dignified position. Adams enjoyed lecturing the senators, as he would a class of unruly pupils in Worcester, reminding them of his superior knowledge of parliamentary procedures and "etiquette."

According to several senators, his major concern in the first session of Congress was the proper protocol to be followed. After living in Europe, Adams felt that titles and dignities should be used to impress on the people the importance of the men they elected. In his first communication between the Senate and the House, he proposed that the speaker of the House be addressed as "Honorable," and was hooted down.

He next worried the Senate about how it should address the president when he came to speak. Should there be one chair for him, or two? Adams was relentless in his efforts to adorn the presidential office with "dignity and splendor." Since England had a throne, he told the senators, they could do no less than have a seat "with a canopy" for the president. And he would need a title. The Senate spent days debating

Edward Savage painted several portraits of the Washingtons, one of which was described by William Dunlap, the art historian, as "an execrable thing." The pictures here, done at John Adams's request, were sent to the Adamses and hung in the dining room of the Old House in Quincy. The bill was pasted on the back of one of the portraits (it is still there), noting payment of "46 2/3 dollars" by Adams.

GEORGE AND MARTHA WASHINGTON.
OILS BY EDWARD SAVAGE, 1790

what to call Washington when he appeared before them: His Electoral Highness was a favorite. The specially selected Committee on Titles offered: "His Highness the President of the United States of America and Protector of the Rights of the Same."

Adams so approved of such efforts that when one senator dared to propose dispensing with all titles, the vice-president quickly reminded him that he, Adams, had witnessed the impressive ceremonies at Versailles and the court of St. James's. "What will the common people of foreign countries, what will the sailors and soldiers say: 'George Washington, President of the United States?' They will dispise him *to all eternity*."

When Washington did appear to address the Senate, the reception came off in a grand manner, although, said Adams later, not "with all the propriety that was proper." Washington appeared embarrassed by the fuss, and the republican senators became agitated when Adams reminded Washington that "the eyes of the world were upon him" and thanked Washington for "his most gracious speech" — words identical to those used in addressing the king of England.

The senators, for their part, did not take John Adams too seriously. His short, fat figure lecturing them on the proper etiquette soon won him their sobriquet of "His Rotundity." If Adams failed in his efforts to teach Old World public manners to the Senate, he fared even worse in the House. The congressmen laughed at him outright. Senator Maclay of Pennsylvania, who kept a diary of Adams's puffings during the Congress, noted that when Adams appeared before the House, the representatives of America's common man spent their time deliberately misbehaving and "in lampooning him before his face, and in communicating the abortion of their Muses, and embryo witlings around the room."

As president of the Senate, Adams was simply meant to preside, leaving debate to the senators and voting only to break ties — an exercise he performed no less than twenty times, almost always on the Federalist side. But he could not keep still: he lectured, expounded, reminisced, much to the annoyance of the senators, who thought him the usurper of their prerogatives. His *Defence* had been misconstrued as favoring a monarchy, and some of his tie-breaking votes — giving the president power to remove presidential appointees from office, aiding Hamilton's fiscal measures — only reinforced the misinterpretation. He also tended to favor New England on tariff matters, and when he broke a tie in favor of strengthening the presidency, he was, some said, preparing for his own ascendancy. Such actions frustrated quite a few senators, and as Senator Maclay protested: "Ye Gods, with what indignation do I review the late attempt of some creatures among us to revive the vile machinery [of imperial power]! O Adams, Adams, what a wretch thou art!"

Outside of politics, life in New York was pleasant enough. The Adamses rented a house at Richmond Hill, on Staten Island, and Abigail wrote her friends in Braintree: "In front of the house, the noble Hudson rolls his majestic waves. . . . Beyond the Hudson rises to our view the fertile country of the Jerseys, covered with a golden harvest, and pouring forth plenty like the cornucopia of Ceres. On the right hand, an extensive plain presents us with a view of fields covered with verdure, and pastures full of cattle."

The town honored Congress and celebrated holidays with fireworks. There were dinners with the president and his lady, presidential "levees" that aroused republican ire, and perhaps best of all in the Adamses' view, whole days spent resting at Richmond Hill.

Adams was called upon to consult with President Washington, but the president allowed few men to have strong influence. Adams wrote Silvanus Bourn that "he seeks information from all quarters, and judges more independently than any man I ever knew." Hamilton was secretary of the treasury; Edmund Randolph, attorney-general; Henry Knox of Massachusetts, secretary of war. Six months after the election, Thomas Jefferson, who had sent Adams his "cordial homage" upon news of Adams's election to the vice-presidency, was selected as secretary of state, and the two were reunited in New York.

With each new program and debate in Washington's administration, the nation's factions became more apparent. Hamilton's fiscal proposals aroused the Congress because they

The morning was bright and clear on April 30, 1789, when George Washington stepped onto the balcony of Federal Hall (right) overlooking Wall Street in New York to take the oath of office. John Adams was vice-president, and he and Abigail rented a house (below) on Richmond Hill, now Staten Island, that overlooked the harbor and farmlands.

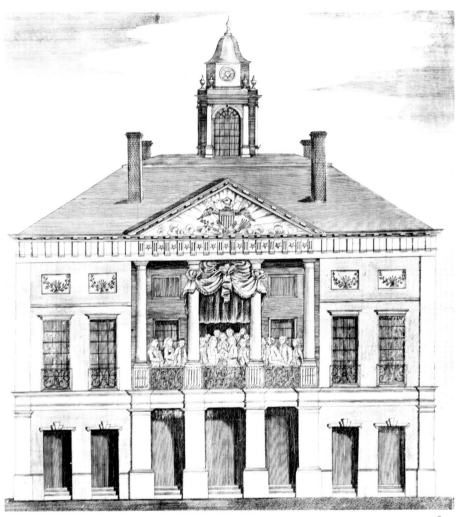

FEDERAL HALL, NEW YORK. ENGRAVING BY AMOS DOOLITTLE AFTER A DRAWING BY PETER LACOUR, 1789

THE ADAMSES' RICHMOND HILL HOUSE.
ENGRAVING AFTER AN ILLUSTRATION
IN "NEW YORK MAGAZINE," 1790

tended to favor the moneyed interests over the common people. Few Americans equaled Hamilton, only thirty-two at the time of his appointment, in administrative genius. And few matched him in favoring the old families, the merchant-shipowners, the public creditors, and financiers — the Federalists who backed the Constitution — with the power of his office. But while he might swing his weight in mercantile-shipping-financial states, like Massachusetts, he had little power among the planting-slaveholding Americans, like those in Virginia. The great mass of the American people was untouched directly by Hamilton's economic concepts, and yet wary of them.

When Thomas Jefferson took office in March, 1790, Hamilton's fiscal policy was well under way, and government circles were ringing with his praises. Hamilton wanted the federal government to assume Confederation and state debts at face value, a measure that met with favor in the North. Jefferson approved of the payment of domestic and foreign debts at par, but did not approve of government assumption of state debts in principle. Yet, as he later wrote, he saw "the necessity of yielding to the cries of the creditors in certain parts of the Union for the sake of union; and to save us from the greatest of all calamities, the total extinction of our credit in Europe."

According to Jefferson's own account, he and Hamilton entered into a bargain. Jefferson wanted the federal capital to be in the South; Hamilton wanted the government to assume state debts. Jefferson agreed to induce his fellow Virginians to vote for assumption if Hamilton would round up New Englanders to back transferring the capital from New York to Philadelphia for ten years while a new capital was built along the Potomac. And so it was agreed. But when Hamilton pressed for a national bank, Jefferson opposed it as unconstitutional. The two began a falling-out that, in many ways, symbolized the split taking place in the country.

Political battle lines demarking positions for the coming decade — battle lines that in some ways still persist — were being drawn fast. With the new Constitution, Americans had challenged their own future. They now would see whether a federal and republican government was workable on such a scale. The Constitution had neither tradition nor political support. Now, in this last decade of the eighteenth century, it would be tested and threatened by sectional self-interests, ideological differences, social and territorial growth, and war.

During this period, the French people revolted. Most Americans greeted the news as an affirmation of their own struggle for liberty, and regarded the French Revolution as an extension of their own. U.S. citizens formed democratic societies like the Liberty Boys of 1776; when the European monarchs invaded France, Americans celebrated their defeat at the hands of French citizen armies. John Adams had reservations about the revolt, and in 1790, disquieted by a French pamphlet advising America to modify its own Constitution, Adams began writing a series of essays, *Discourses on Davila*, which appeared in thirty-two installments in the *Gazette of the United States. Davila*, which Adams later called a "dull, heavy volume," was theoretical and academic, calling upon a formidable array of sources from Epictetus and Plato to the marquis de Condorcet. In it, Adams sought to prove the statement that the only possible remedy for revolution was to create a well-balanced government, and to remind America that security and peace depended upon maintaining a system of checks and balances within the three branches of the government.

Davila did not attack the American Constitution or offer any amendments to it. But it was received as ominous — given the times — and tended to underscore Adams's dissatisfaction with the Constitution. It was known publicly that he favored increasing the powers of the presidency. Actually his opinion was that these powers should be made greater — or less: "The limitations upon them in the cases of war, treaties, and appointments of office, and especially the limitation on the president's independence as a branch of the legislative, will be the destruction of this constitution, and involve us in anarchy, if not amended."

Adams's views conflicted with the idols of the day: equality and the French Revolution. Anti-Federalist editors attacked him on *Davila*, although perhaps few had read all thirty-two installments; he was denounced as a monarchist, an opponent of the common man, a champion of aristocratic mummery and show. In an attempt to defend himself, he wrote in 1790 to his friend Dr. Benjamin Rush: "I am a mortal and irreconcilable enemy to monarchy. I am no friend to *hereditary limited* monarchy in America. This I know can never be admitted without an hereditary Senate to control it, and an hereditary nobility or Senate in America I know to be unattainable and impracticable. I should scarcely be for it, if it were. Do not, therefore, my friend, misunderstand me and misrepresent me to posterity."

Even the Federalists backed away in mock horror. Hamilton, no theoretician, gave Adams little support. But the issue was just being joined. While *Davila* was appearing, copies of Thomas Paine's *The Rights of Man* reached America in early 1791. As a reply to Edmund Burke's hostile *Reflections on the French Revolution*, Paine had compared the contemporary French revolution with the American one, and criticized the British constitution as the bulwark of reactionary government that opposed the great revolutionary movements — first in America and now in France.

Paine's writings had attracted Jefferson when they were both in France, and Jefferson had borrowed a copy of *The Rights of Man* to read. He returned it with a note expressing pleasure that it was to be printed and appear in America: "Something is at length to be publicly said against the political heresies which have sprung up among us," Jefferson wrote Paine. "I have no doubt our citizens will rally a second time round the standards of 'Common Sense.' "

Such an endorsement was too tempting not to use, even in those days, and the printer, thinking perhaps that it would help sales, included Jefferson's note as the preface of the book. When *The Rights of Man* landed in America, as an antidote against "the political heresies which have sprung up among us," Adams was furious — and hurt. It was clear, as Jefferson later admitted to James Madison, that by "heresies" he had meant Adams's *Davila*.

A basic argument about government within the Washington administration was fast becoming public. With Adams and Hamilton almost daily avowing their admiration for the British constitution, British finance and British society, Jefferson and Madison saw that it was the Federalist objective to make the United States a mere copy of the mother country rather than the great social experiment Jefferson envisioned. It was his repulsion with these ideas, as much as his attraction to France, that made Jefferson oppose the Adams-Hamilton viewpoint.

Instead of direct and open debate, these men chose the forums of their time: books, essays in the press, letters. But their exchanges were as fundamental and vital as any ever held, for they shaped and directed and interpreted the new Constitution, and began moving the young government toward positions of policy in both foreign and domestic matters.

As Jefferson's preface to *The Rights of Man* was stirring the Americans, including their angry vice-president, a series of rebuttals, signed PUBLICOLA, appeared in a Boston newspaper, the *Columbian Centinel*. The writer condemned both Jefferson and Paine, but the real motive of PUBLICOLA was to defend John Adams, and there was some suspicion that the writer was Adams himself. But the printer of the *Centinel* denied it categorically, and in fact the author was John Quincy Adams, then a young Boston lawyer, arguing his father's doctrine.

Jefferson tried to heal the wound opening between him and Adams. He wrote, explaining how the preface got into Paine's book, and added: "That you and I differ in our ideas of the best form of government is well known to us both: but we have differed as friends should do, respecting the purity of each other's motives, and confining our difference of opinion to private conversation. And I can declare with truth in the presence of the almighty that nothing was further from my intention or expectation than to have had either my own or your name brought before the public on this occasion." Jefferson, covering over his direct and public attack on Adams, said that some people had suggested that he was AGRICOLA or BRUTUS — both rebutters of PUBLICOLA's articles — and added, "I never did in my life, either by myself or by any other, have a sentence of mine inserted in a newspaper without putting my name to it; and I believe I never shall."

Adams wrote back, upbraiding Jefferson for allowing his name to be used by Paine, and scorning the "misconduct of the person, who committed this breach of your confidence," for he "has sown the Seeds of more evils, than he can ever attone for." Adams's feelings were deeply injured. He went on to say that Jefferson's preface had been looked upon by others as "a direct and open personal attack upon me, by countenancing the false interpretation of my Writings as favouring the Introduction of hereditary Monarchy and Aristocracy into this Country. The Question every where was, What Heresies are intended by the Secretary of State?" Adams complained that he was getting "Whirlwinds of tempestuous Abuse" for his writings, by those who hadn't "taken the pains to read them." He also claimed that he "neither wrote nor corrected Publicola. The Writer in the Composition of his Pieces followed his own Judgment, Information and discretion, without any assistance from me."

Although Jefferson sought to end the argument, it was just beginning. For one thing, it accentuated distrust between Hamilton and Adams. For another, *Davila* was a political mistake. The French Revolution had become an American domestic issue, and by attacking it Adams had, in the eyes of the Jeffersonians, attacked his own revolution and system of government. In fact, the views of both men were not as far apart — as later letters and diaries would show — as popular discussion and publication made them seem. The press argued that those Americans who did not endorse the French Revolution were "the well-born, the first class, of high birth and good families" and none other.

Adams was roughed up by the press as favoring "the progressive administration of [the government] into monarchy." He was pilloried as being among those men who proposed "the principles of monarchy and aristocracy, in opposition to the republican principles of the Union, and the republican spirit of the people," to quote the *National Gazette.* The emblem of these people, the newspaper went on, should be a "Leech clinging to the bowels of an old soldier," and their title should be "their Fulnesses."

The invective increased as the second national election approached. Washington, his popularity still intact, would be reelected president. But the vice-presidential candidates included George Clinton of New York, John Jay, Thomas Mifflin, James Madison, and John Adams. The *New York*

When the government moved from New York to Philadelphia, the Adamses were not pleased. But they soon found the new capital—here seen from Congress Hall along Chestnut Street —a place of "politeness and civility." The ladies of Philadelphia, Abigail Adams wrote, were "well-educated, well-bred and well-dressed."

DETAIL: CONGRESS HALL IN PHILADELPHIA. COLORED LINE ENGRAVING BY WILLIAM BIRCH, 1800

Journal, listing these candidates, pointedly asked its readers to look out for those "who have endeavored to prepare . . . the people of America for a King and nobility."

Amid plots and counterplots, Adams withdrew to Braintree. The political attacks and turmoil were depressing to a man who so enjoyed the purity of debate and intellectual exchange. Both he and Abigail had been ill (Adams suffered from pyorrhea and sore eyes). The move to Philadelphia from New York during the first administration had been difficult. The Adamses' house, on Bush Hill, was cold and damp; during the winter they consumed forty cords of wood in their fireplaces in four months. Abigail longed for the climate of New England where the "people do not grow old half so fast." In Philadelphia, "two thirds of the year here, we must freeze or melt."

Thomas Boylston Adams, who was studying law in Philadelphia (after graduating from Harvard), was "very ill and almost helpless with the rheumatism" during that first Philadelphia winter. Prices were almost double those of New York, and the Schuylkill River didn't match the beauty of the Hudson. Still, there were invitations to teas and cards "in the European style." During the first winter, the Adamses attended receptions and countless official dinners, and went to the theater with President Washington, who never missed a new performance. "I should spend a very dissipated winter," wrote Abigail, "if I were to accept of one half the invitations I receive, particularly to the routs, or tea and cards. . . . I have been to one assembly. The dancing was very good; the company of the best kind. The President and Madam, the Vice-President and Madam, Ministers of States, and their Madams, &c.; but the room despicable; the etiquette, — it was difficult to say where it was to be found. Indeed, it was not New York; but you must not report this from me."

There were some good moments, too. Abigail and John found the Philadelphians people of "politeness and civility. The ladies here are well-educated, well-bred, and well-dressed. There is much more society than in New York." And they both enjoyed visits with their grandson John, Abigail Adams Smith's second child, who could make his grandfather do just about anything for him, and did. Abigail

Adams wrote of one visit: "As to John, we grow every day fonder of him. He has spent an hour this afternoon in driving his grandpapa round the room with a willow stick."

The anti-Federalists had coalesced into a party organization under the name Republicans. Although both parties, Federalists and Republicans, backed George Washington, they split over the other candidates. By March 1, the states had chosen: Washington was reelected unanimously; Adams received 77 votes, Clinton 50, Jefferson 4 and Aaron Burr 1. John Adams was again vice-president.

The revolution in France was fast becoming a major issue in American politics. American domestic issues remained unsolved while attention focused on the French people's struggle against the monarchical coalition.

The execution of Louis XVI and the Reign of Terror were sobering for Americans. Events grew worse on the Continent, and the news increasingly shocking. Then France declared war on England and the Netherlands — an act that took America by surprise. A land war was one thing; but a maritime war would interfere with American shipment of goods and with duties on goods imported from England to America on English ships.

Worse, according to the Treaty of 1778, the United States was bound to guarantee "forever against all other powers" protection of French possessions in the New World. But to war with France against England would destroy American commerce, wipe out American revenue, and "cut up credit by the roots," as Alexander Hamilton put it.

France never invoked the treaty. For one thing, American neutrality was more vital to France than American military support, which would be meager. American ships could export goods and materials to France under the flag of neutrality, and France could feed her army and outfit her navy — if the British would recognize American neutrality and the right that free (neutral) ships make free goods.

The arrival of Edmond Charles Genêt, the new French minister plenipotentiary, forced the issue of whether the United States would recognize the new French government and whether it would remain neutral.

For Washington, the French Revolution had created the

most difficult crisis of his administrations, and it taught a lesson that would linger in American politics. Hamilton, opponent of the French Revolution, argued that the Treaty of 1778 was invalid since the king had been executed, and that America should proclaim her neutrality and reject Genêt. Jefferson, although he considered the French cause "the most sacred cause that ever man was engaged in," agreed that war should be avoided. Washington's advisors, including Jefferson, counseled for neutrality. On April 22, 1793, Washington issued his famous proclamation that it was "the disposition of the United States" to "pursue a conduct friendly and impartial toward the belligerent powers" and that American citizens "aiding or abetting hostilities" would be prosecuted in the federal courts.

It was a wise choice, and an unpopular decision. Jacobin clubs had sprung up in the United States, and American citizens sporting tricolored cockades paraded around village greens, including the square in Philadelphia. Washington decided to recognize Genêt as minister of the French Republic, and told Genêt, who was also outfitting privateers and enlisting Americans for the French Revolution, to halt his violations of American neutrality. But Genêt persisted, and went over the head of the president to the American people. In August, 1793, Washington demanded his recall.

The British, meanwhile, were seizing American ships in the West Indies, taking their cargoes and imprisoning their crews. French privateers were being armed in American ports and were setting out to capture British vessels; in one case, that of the *Little Sarah*, a British ship was taken to Philadelphia and refitted on orders from Genêt.

Without a fleet to protect her merchantships, or even her own ports, the United States was vulnerable to British aggression and French intrigue. In the House, representatives made fiery speeches against the British violations at sea and unwarranted retention of posts along the northern borders. John Adams gloomily predicted that "it will require all the address, all the temper, and all the firmness of congress and the States, to keep this people out of the war."

When the British minister Lord Grenville announced to the American minister in London at the end of December,

1793, that the British government was planning to hold the northwest posts indefinitely, the war cries rose. This, plus the British seizures in the Caribbean, brought pressure from the trading community, the backbone of Hamilton's party. In April, 1794, Washington appointed John Jay envoy extraordinary to the court of St. James's to seek British recognition of American neutral rights and a commercial treaty. Jay's appointment, unfortunately, was a weak one for the United States; he was too susceptible to flattery and much too pro-British. "Mr. Jay's weak side," Lord Grenville was advised, "is Mr. Jay."

John Adams watched these events from the Senate. He never believed in the ultimate wisdom of the people, for *vox populi* was "sometimes the voice of Mahomet, of Caesar, of Catiline, the Pope, and the Devil." From his unique seat, Adams was not allowed a voice in the international matters that interested him and concerned his nation, and he was "as in a prison, to see nothing done, hear nothing said, and to say and do nothing." He was, he vowed, "wearied to death with *ennui.*"

Thomas Jefferson had retired from Washington's administration on December 31, 1793, and lived in uninterrupted seclusion in Monticello for three years, "out of the hearing of the Din of Politicks and the Rumours of War," as Adams enviously described it. They exchanged cordial letters that expressed their opposition to war and their mutual "love of rural peace."

As he observed proceedings in the Senate, Adams tallied up his blessings. He was, he wrote, thankful for "good parents, an excellent wife, and promising children; tolerable health upon the whole and competent fortune." His children were a special pleasure. Nabby Smith was living with her husband and children in New York. Charles Adams, after some misconduct at Harvard, had settled down, also in New York, and lived for a while with the parents of William Stephens Smith, his brother-in-law. He fell in love with Sarah (Sally) Smith, and married her in August, 1795 — although his parents disapproved because they thought Charles was too young.

On May 29, 1794, after a vacancy had come up, President Washington had nominated John Quincy Adams minister to the Netherlands, a post once held by his father. The next day, John Adams had the rare pleasure of watching the Senate confirm the nomination of his son. Here was the splendid start, "in the cabinet or the field," that John and Abigail had hoped for their firstborn. John Quincy's writings had caught President Washington's attention — some had been shown to him by the boy's proud father. Under the name MARCELLUS, John Quincy had warned Americans in the *Columbian Centinel* against privateering under the flag of another nation at war, and the next two installments, written after Washington's proclamation against Genêt and the French, extolled "impartial and unequivocal neutrality." Under another pen name, COLUMBUS, John Quincy also defended Washington's right to dismiss foreign ministers under the Constitution, and warned: "Of all the dangers which encompass the liberties of a republican State, the intrusion of a foreign influence into the administration of their affairs, is the most alarming."

John Adams immediately began readying John Quincy for his new post. He directed his son to learn more of international law and diplomacy; observe the views and motions of belligerent powers; attend to his dress and person — "no man is more attentive to these things than the President, neat at least and handsome."

John Quincy should continue to write, but (his father warned him from experience) he should be cautious in what he wrote. In a letter to his son, John Adams set forth a primer on diplomacy, and advised: "You must make yourself master of all our disputes with England, Spain, France, &c. You must study the lines and boundaries of the United States. You will have to watch the English Ambassador and all the Anglomani[ac]s. . . . It is a serious trust that is about to be committed to you. I hope you will reflect upon it with due attention, collect yourself, let no little weakness escape you, and devote yourself to the service of your Country, and may the blessing of Heaven attend you. So prays your affectionate father, John Adams."

John Quincy, well armed with his father's advice, left his growing Boston law practice and sailed on September 15,

1794, for Europe, taking along his younger brother Thomas Boylston as his private secretary. On their way to The Hague, they passed through London to deliver dispatches to John Jay and Thomas Pinckney during the negotiations with Lord Grenville. For almost two weeks the Adams brothers "whirled round in the fling of London." John Quincy confided to his diary: "There is something so fascinating in the women I meet in this Country that it is not well for me. I am obliged immediately to leave it."

There would be time for women and whirling. The Hague was the least significant of the five United States diplomatic posts overseas: France, England, Spain, Portugal and the Netherlands. Adams's salary, $4,500 a year, did not leave much to spend, but he was single and his instructions from Secretary of State Randolph were only to tend to the treasury loans borrowed by his father, and keep a watchful eye on European affairs. John Adams had told his son: "You will see Europe at the most interesting period of its history."

He was right. The Hague was an excellent place to watch the French Revolution sweep the Continent. The army of the French republic slowly shifted from a force of liberation and ideology to an army of occupation as it overran more and more territory. John Quincy saw this, and reported it in letters to the United States.

In London, Jay's negotiations had not gone well with the clever and brilliant Grenville. The American press watched him, and when it learned that he had kissed the queen's hand, accused him of having "prostrated at the feet of majesty the sovereignty of the people." Abuse was heaped upon Jay. John Adams wasn't ignored either: when an effigy of Jay was pilloried in Philadelphia, the *New York Journal* reported that "hung from the neck by a hemp string was a copy of the 'Defence of the Constitutions.'"

Jay's treaty was, in fact, a British diplomatic triumph. The United States gave much and gained little in its effort to avoid war. After a long series of closed sessions, the Senate ratified the treaty by 20 to 10, barely gaining the necessary two-thirds majority vote. Details of the treaty were leaked by the pro-French Philadelphia newspaper *Aurora*, and its editor, Benjamin Franklin Bache (the grandson of Benjamin Franklin

LOUISA CATHERINE ADAMS. OIL ASCRIBED TO EDWARD SAVAGE, ABOUT 1801

JOHN QUINCY ADAMS. OIL BY JOHN SINGLETON COPLEY, 1796

who had been at school with John Quincy Adams in Passy), traveled to the major cities of the East to distribute copies and stir up protest. Mob outbreaks spread from South Carolina to Kentucky, and even Alexander Hamilton was stoned as he spoke in favor of the treaty in New York.

To be sure of implementing the treaty, Washington needed the signed and ratified work ready for the next session of Congress, scheduled for December, 1795. This would assure him that legislation would be enacted executing the provisions of the treaty; it would eliminate any pretext by England for not delivering the frontier posts by June 1, 1796. With Jay back in the United States, and Pinckney off in Spain, Washington called upon John Quincy Adams to go to London and complete the exchange of ratifications and other diplomatic matters necessary to seeing the treaty to completion.

It was a delicate and complicated task for the young envoy. His father wrote him on September 29, 1795: "If I have heard a true whisper you have a part to act concerning the treaty. Be of good courage and good cheer. It will not hurt you finally, though it may raise a popular clamour. *Publicola* knows what a popular clamour is." And in December, impatient for word on the treaty negotiations and his son, Adams wrote again (a little pessimistically): "I hope you have not flinched."

Abigail was more encouraging, and added this fist-in-the-air challenge: "You are called to take part in this important business. You have put your hand to the plow, and I know you too well to believe or even wish you to look back or shrink from your duty however arduous or dangerous the task assigned to you. You will prove yourself the genuine scion of the stock from which you spring."

But John Quincy Adams wasn't so sure of himself. He confided to his diary: "This business is unpleasant and unpromising, but I have no election."

In London, John Quincy won his first diplomatic round with George Hammond, undersecretary of foreign affairs. But he was shredded by Lord Grenville, who had for years commanded the entire diplomatic corps of the British Empire with brilliance and polish. Adams felt ill at ease, clumsy, and bitter. He wrote home on December 29, 1795: "I have been accustomed all my life to plain dealing and candor, and am not sufficiently versed in the art of political swindling to be prepared for negotiating with an European Minister of State. In other words, besides numerous other deficiencies of which on this occasion I am strongly sensible, I have not the *experience* which the proper performance of the duty would require."

An early failure diplomatically, John Quincy won victories socially. There were the usual rounds of levees and dinners, and above all else, there was romance. Now twenty-eight, his career well begun, John Quincy frequently visited the home of the American consul and friend of the Adams family, Joshua Johnson. The Johnsons had seven daughters, and at first the eldest, Nancy, caught John Quincy's eye. But it was Louisa Catherine, the second daughter, a quiet girl of twenty, who won his heart. They were quickly engaged.

But almost immediately John Quincy's duties called him back to The Hague. There he was delighted to learn that on April 30, 1796, the House of Representatives had passed appropriations giving effect to the Jay Treaty. Delivery of the frontier posts took place that summer. The danger of war with England was, for the moment, ended.

While Britain was being weakened by war, America was being strengthened by peace. Trade was growing, the nation was expanding. Its neutral policy was returning benefits. But hostility was in the air between the two continents. John Quincy wrote his father from London on March 20, 1796: "Between the United States and Great Britain no *cordiality* can exist. I do not think it is on our part to be desired. But peace may, and I hope will, continue, notwithstanding all the conspiracies that may be formed against it in America and in Europe." Less than a year earlier, on May 22, 1795, John Quincy, repeating his theme of America's need for neutrality, had written John Adams: "above all I wish that we may never have occasion for any political connections in Europe."

It was a theme reaching favor in America. John Quincy's letters from Europe were passed along by his father to George Washington. The president, in acknowledging four of them received in 1795, wrote to John Adams: "They contain a great deal of interesting matter, and No. 9 [that of May 22, 1795, above] discloses much important information and political insight. Mr. J. Adams, your son must not think of retiring from the walk of life he is in."

There were echoes of John Quincy's letters in Washington's Farewell Address; but the speech also repeated what Americans of 1796 were concluding: that they must guard against foreign intrigues; they must have no political connections with foreign nations; they must watch for foreign meddling in domestic affairs and its danger to national unity. That Adams and Washington thought alike was not surprising. Washington said as much a few days after his Farewell Address when he and John Adams were going over a new batch of John Quincy's letters: "Things appear to me exactly as they do to your son."

The election period 1796–1797 was marked by injury and scurrilousness. The Republicans accepted Jefferson and Burr; the Federalists selected John Adams and Pinckney. Adams was accused of plotting against the Republic, of having no confidence in elective government. The *Aurora* of November 11, 1796, further accused him of agreeing "with the jealous enemies of our Constitution abroad that a Monarchical Constitution is not only better than a Federal Constitution, but that a Mixed Monarchy is the best of all possible governments." His *Defence of the Constitutions* and *Discourses on Davila* were gone over line by line, and used to support the pro-monarchy theme. And there was concern that Adams's pro-British feelings would lead to war with France.

Jefferson was also abused. He was called a rank atheist, a coward who had fled before Tarleton's cavalry during the Revolutionary War, a philosopher concerned with the anatomy and "odiferous glands" of the Negroes, as appeared in *Notes on Virginia*.

While the acrimonious debates raged, Jefferson and Adams remained aloof. They did not participate in the election; no platform was issued by either candidate; there were no speeches, no promises, no appearances. Jefferson remained at Monticello content with his farming and nail manufacturing, on horseback most of the day, experimenting with potatoes as a large-scale substitute for Indian corn for feeding his animals.

At home in Quincy (formerly Braintree), John Adams rose at four on some mornings to enjoy "the Charm of earliest Birds." He had a new barn built, "very stately and strong," and concluded in August, 1796: "Of all the Summers of my Life, this has been the freest from Care, Anxiety and Vexation for me. The Sickness of Mrs. A. excepted. My Health has been better, the Season fruitful, my farm was conducted. Alas! what may happen to reverse all this? But it is folly to anticipate evils, and madness to create imaginary ones."

John Adams lingered in Quincy, improving his farm, until cold weather set in. On November 23, 1796, he left for Philadelphia, pausing for a day with Abigail Adams Smith and her husband in East Chester, and with Charles Adams in New York. He arrived in Philadelphia on December 2, and Congress opened three days later. The city was in a fervor of presidential politics as the voting of the presidential electors in the sixteen states (Vermont, Kentucky and Tennessee had been added since 1791) began.

Adams, in his letters, appeared calm; perhaps the long term on his farm, a sort of gathering time for himself, had helped. A year earlier he had written to Abigail: "I am weary of the game, yet I don't know how I could live out of it. I don't love slight, neglect, contempt, disgrace, nor insult, more than others." In December, 1796, he wrote his wife: "John Adams must be an intrepid to encounter the open assaults of France, and the secret plots of England, in concert with all his treacherous friends and open enemies in his own country. Yet I assure you, he never felt more serene in his life." He wrote John Quincy on December 5: "I look upon the Event as the throw of a Die, a mere Chance, a miserable, meagre Tryumph to either Party."

The intrigues continued as the election drew to a close. Hamilton, believing he couldn't control Adams, worked to defeat him with an elaborate scheme of shifting votes to Pinckney. As Hamilton explained later, when he had publicly broken with Adams, the "plan would have given Mr. Pinckney a somewhat better chance than Mr. Adams; nor shall it be concealed that an issue favorable to the former would not have been disagreeable to me; as indeed I declared at the time in the circle of my confidential friends. My position was that if chance should decide in favor of Mr. Pinckney, it probably would not be a misfortune; since he to every essential qualification for the office added a temper far more discreet and conciliatory than that of Mr. Adams."

By the eighth of February, the tellers had readied the votes, and the ballots of the electors were opened. John Adams had 71, Thomas Jefferson 68, Pinckney 59, Aaron Burr 30, and Samuel Adams 11.

John Adams announced the results of the balloting to the Senate. He was "President by three votes," as he himself declared — a margin his enemies were to remind him of during the next four years.

6

President by Three Votes

[1797–1801]

THE die is cast," John Adams wrote Abigail the day after he was elected, "and you must prepare yourself for honorable trials."

To Adams now fell Washington's foreign policy and the task of preserving American neutrality during the rupture with France. But the France of early March, 1797, just before his inauguration, was far different from the France of 1794. Danton and Robespierre, friends of the United States, had been guillotined. France was being run by the Directory, a five-man executive that had quickly abandoned the republican idealism of 1792 to invade and terrorize Europe. The Directory regarded Jay's treaty with England as evidence of an Anglo-American alliance, and the American government appeared to reinforce this view when it ordered French privateers out of American ports and failed to protest British seizure of ships carrying food to France. James Monroe, too sympathetic to the French, had been recalled by Washington in 1796. In reaction to these measures and in the hope of

MILLIONS FOR OUR DEFENCE NOT A CENT FOR TR... BUT...

NEW HAMPSHIRE	VERMONT	MASSACHUSETTS	CONNECTICUT	RHODE ISL...
INDEPENDENCE MDCCL XXV	INDEPENDENCE & LIBERTY	ENCE PETIT PLAC... SERVIATE QUIETEM	QUI TRANSTULIT SUSTINET	IN GOD WE...
...Senators 4 Representatives	2 Senators 2 Representatives	2 Senators 15 Representatives	2 Senators 7 Representatives	2 Senators 2 Repres...
...858 Inhabitants	106.923 Inhabitants	422.845 Inhabitants	251.002 Inhabitants	69.122 Inhabitant...

NEW YORK				PENSYLVAN...
EXCELSIOR FRUSTRA				VIRTU LIBERTY & INDEP...
...Senators 11 Representatives				2 Senators 14 Repres...
...170 Inhabitants				602.365 Inhabitants

NEW JERSEY				MARYLAN...
INDEPENDENCE MDCCLXXVI				INDEPENDENCE MDCC...
...Senators 5 Representatives				2 Senators 9 Repres...
...114 Inhabitants				300.635 Inhabitant...

DELAWARE				VIRGINI...
INDEPENDENCE MDCCLXXVI				INDEPENDENCE MDCC...
...nators 1 Representatives				2 Senators 23 Repres...
...273 Inhabitants				878.959 Inhabitant...

JOHN ADAMS President of the United States

NORTH CAROLINA	SOUTH CAROLINA	GEORGIA	TENNESSEE	KENTUCK...
INDEPENDENCE MDCCLXXVI	ANIMIS OPIBUSQUE PARATI	PRO MORIS MAG... QUA FECIT	FREE... ENJOYMENT	...ACCOMPLIS... PRE...
...nators 11 Representatives	2 Senators 9 Representatives	2 Senators 3 Representatives	2 Senators Representatives	2 Senators 4 Repres...
...003 Inhabitants	345.591 Inhabitants	162.686 Inhabitants	97.678 Inhabitants	229.955 Inhabitant...

A New DISPLAY of the UNITED STATE...

New Haven, Engraved & Sold wholesale by Amos Doolittle, August 1st 1799.

cutting off all American trade with England, French corsairs began seizing American merchant ships in blatant violation of American neutrality rights. By June, 1797, President Adams knew that more than three hundred American ships had been captured by the French.

Adams made few changes in the government when he came into office. He kept Washington's cabinet of Charles Lee, attorney general; Timothy Pickering, secretary of state; Oliver Wolcott, secretary of the treasury; and James McHenry, secretary of war. This was Adams's original mistake in administration, and a fundamental error from which others would arise. The last three men were devoted to Alexander Hamilton, who from his law office in New York City intended to run the national government.

Thomas Jefferson, of course, was vice-president, and although he and Adams remained cool to one another, Adams was in fact closer politically to him than to Hamilton. Adams was sharply aware of events in France and elsewhere on the Continent, for he had the benefit of John Quincy's keen perceptions.

For his inauguration, Adams became more republican and discarded the sword he sometimes wore while presiding over the Senate. He appeared in a simple light-gray suit, without jeweled buckles or buttons, and even refused to allow, said the newspaper *Aurora* in its account, "the marshall and other officers to walk in procession before his carriage." The House of Representatives was filled with spectators and officials as Washington left office and Adams entered. They came, the new president wrote in his diary, because "the sight of the sun setting full orbed, and another rising, though less splendid, was a novelty. . . . There was more weeping than there has ever been at the representation of any tragedy."

The weeks before and immediately after the inauguration had been a trying time for Adams. Expenses in Philadelphia were high. "The plenty of paper has unsettled every thing," he wrote. "Nothing has a price. Every one asks and every one cheats as much as he can." Even George Washington was selling his furniture (some of which Adams bought) and a pair of horses, one nine and the other ten years old — they brought $1,000 — before he left for Mount Vernon.

On February 4, 1797, Adams's diary recorded: "House rent at twenty-seven hundred dollars a year, fifteen hundred dollars for a carriage, one thousand for one pair of horses, all the glasses, ornaments, kitchen furniture, the best chairs, settees, plateaus, &c., all to purchase, all the china, delft or wedgewood, glass and crockery of every sort to purchase, and not a farthing probably will the House of Representatives allow, though the Senate have voted a small addition. All the linen besides. I shall not pretend to keep more than one pair of horses for a carriage, and one for a saddle. Secretaries, servants, wood, charities which are demanded as rights, and the million dittoes present such a prospect as is enough to disgust any one. Yet not one word must we say."

The newspapers had begun attacking him before the inauguration, and he found that he detested the machinations of politicians. "Jealousies and rivalries have been my theme, and checks and balances as their antidotes till I am ashamed to repeat the words; but they never stared me in the face in such horrid forms as at present." After a visit to President and Mrs. Washington to say goodbye, Adams wrote: "I believe that I envied him more than he did me, and with reason."

To add to his discomfort, Adams was again without his family. Abigail had returned to Quincy for her health. By March, he was in a steady grump. The President's House wasn't ready, he wrote her. "The weather is bad. I have a great cold. The news is not pleasant, and I have no society but statesmen. Mr. Jefferson has been here and is gone off to-day for Virginia. He is as he was. . . . I must go to you or you must come to me. I cannot live without you till October." Two days earlier he had written of his farm: "I hope Billings will sow the barley and grass seed well. What will become of my meadow cornfield I know not." He concluded: "Oh! my poor meadow and wall, &c., &c., &c."

None of his family attended his inauguration. He wrote wistfully: "It would have given me great pleasure to have had some of my family present at my inauguration, which was the most affecting and overpowering scene I ever acted in. I was very unwell, had no sleep the night before, and really did not know but I should have fainted in presence of all the world. I was in great doubt whether to say any thing or not besides repeating the oath."

What John Adams did say struck a theme of his administration. His address called for unity and an end to internal dissension. Adams recognized the growing pressure of foreign affairs and said he favored "an inflexible determination to maintain peace and inviolable faith with all nations, and that system of neutrality and impartiality among the belligerent powers of Europe which has been adopted by the government, and so solemnly sanctioned by both Houses of Congress." But, he added, he also felt "a personal esteem for the French nation, formed in a residence of seven years, chiefly among them, and a sincere desire to preserve the friendship which has been so much for the honor and integrity of the people of America."

Relations with France, Adams understood, would be the first and perhaps major problem of his administration. After Monroe's recall, the Directory had refused to receive his successor, Charles C. Pinckney, or even allow him to remain in French territory. This break in relations stirred war cries in the Federalist press. Republican newspapers defended France and Philadelphia celebrated French victories on the Continent. Hamilton, meanwhile, quietly began anticipating war.

John Adams sought to steer a course between France and England, and between the two dominant parties in America. He would not submit to further indignities, but he would also seek neutrality. He resolved to find a mission that "by its dignity should satisfy France, and by its selection from the three great divisions of the continent, should satisfy all parts of the United States."

Clearly, Adams's role was as delicate at home as it was difficult abroad. A special session of Congress was called for May 15, 1797. His speech to Congress on that day offered peace and threatened war. He detailed "the wound" that recent events had "inflicted in the American breast." He described French attempts to "produce divisions fatal to our peace" among the American people, and declared that he was ready "to institute a fresh attempt at negotiation." That was the olive branch.

For his stick, Adams called upon Congress to support a series of defense measures: a strong navy to protect American commerce against the abuses of foreign nations; an increase in the regular artillery and cavalry; and new laws for "organizing, arming, and disciplining the militia, to render that natural and safe defense of the country efficacious."

To carry out the first part, Adams proposed a three-man peace commission to France. Pinckney, at The Hague, was reappointed a special envoy; John Marshall of Virginia and Elbridge Gerry of Massachusetts, an old friend of Adams's, were appointed to join him. The selection of Gerry, a Republican, made when another appointee declined to serve, did not sit well with the Federalists. But Adams insisted that one member of the mission come from the opposition party, even though his cabinet grumbled. In letters to Gerry urging him to serve, Adams stated his determination to reach agreement with the French.

He authorized the commission "to terminate our differences in such manner as without referring to the merits of our complaints and pretensions, might be best calculated to produce mutual satisfaction and good understanding." William Vans Murray was appointed minister to The Hague, replacing John Quincy Adams (who had accepted a new post) in a move that would later prove useful and important. The American envoys set off immediately for the Netherlands, where they joined Pinckney.

Almost the entire first year of John Adams's administration passed without word from the three American commissioners. In the meantime, party cleavage became deeper. When Congress adjourned on July 10, 1797, Adams retired to Quincy for a gloomy summer, during which he felt that "a torpor, a despondency has seized all men in America as well as Europe."

For one thing, Monroe had returned to Philadelphia that spring and had taken up his fight. He accused Secretary of State Pickering of treating him unjustly and asked for a fair hearing and the "blessings of an honest fame." He got neither, nor was he able to get a satisfactory explanation for his sudden recall. In anger, Monroe turned over all his correspondence with Pickering to the Republican newspapers, where it was played up with righteous indignation.

Although John Adams stayed out of the Monroe affair, his hand was upon Senator William Blount of North Carolina and Tennessee. Blount was implicated in a wild scheme to incite the Creek and Cherokee Indians to aid the British in conquering Spanish West Florida. He was brought, with Adams's approval, before the House, and impeachment proceedings were begun, but they ended when the Senate expelled Blount on July 8, 1797, as guilty of "a high misdemeanor, entirely inconsistent with his public trust and duty as a Senator."

Further, the newspapers continued to attack Adams and his administration. There were no libel laws or other restrictions on the papers of the day, and most of them were journals of opinion first, and records of fact or news second. In 1790, Benjamin Franklin Bache, nicknamed "Lightning-Rod Junior," had founded the *General Advertiser*, later well known around the Adams household by its popular name, *Aurora*. Bache, as mentioned in the previous chapter, used his newspaper to campaign against Jay's treaty, with great success, and the *Aurora* became widely quoted. Bache called John Adams "The Duke of Braintree," and more than once Abigail spoke of "Baches lies and abuse" and despaired of Bache as he "opend his batterys of abuse and scurility" against her husband.

There were, of course, other newspapers. PETER PORCU-PINE was the pen name of William Cobbett, an Englishman who lived in the United States between 1792 and 1800 and from 1817 to 1819 as a political refugee. On March 4, 1797, he started up *Porcupine's Gazette & Daily Advertiser*, an advocate of alliance with England and of war against France. *Porcupine's* strongest words, however, were saved for the Republicans. Abigail sometimes mailed to Quincy issues of John Fenno's *Gazette of the United States*, which was founded in New York City in 1789, and moved to Philadelphia in 1790 with the federal government. Fenno's *Gazette* was supported financially by prominent Federalists, including Hamilton.

Like all presidential families, the Adamses soon came

under the wrath of the newspapers of their day. Almost every move that Adams or his administration made was criticized. In Philadelphia, the *Aurora*, only three months after Adams's inauguration, called in its June 19 issue for all patriots of America to "come forward in a manly tone of remonstrance to induce Mr. Adams to resign the helm to safer hands before it be too late to retrieve our deranged affairs." In Boston, the *Independent Chronicle and Universal Advertiser* took out after Adams so outspokenly that Abigail wrote her sister: "I think impudent as Bache is the Chronical has more of the true spirit of Satan."

Between attacks on her husband's decisions regarding France and John Quincy's affairs, Abigail quickly had enough of the free press: "What bold and dareing lies these wretches are capable of. Yet when calld upon for proof, they have not a word to offer. The wretch who is supposed to have written this [article] for the Aurora is a Hireling Scotchman. . . . The mischief of these publications arises from their circulating amongst persons and in places where no inquiry is made into facts."

Such personal and public ridicule hit John and Abigail Adams at a vulnerable time. For while John Quincy and Thomas Boylston Adams were developing their careers satisfactorily, Abigail Adams Smith and Charles Adams were struggling in their private lives.

On the way from Boston to Philadelphia in the spring of 1797, Abigail stopped off in New York to visit her daughter. On May 5, she wrote one of her sisters that Nabby "grows very fleshy" and was troubled with domestic problems. Colonel Smith was frequently away for long periods of time, and would neither tell his wife where he was going nor get in touch with her while he was gone. His extravagances and long, silent absences from home displeased the Adamses greatly, as did his speculation in western land that he had begun in 1788. During this visit, Abigail found Nabby's marital difficulties so upsetting that they "took from me all appetite to food, and depresst my spirits, before too low. The Col[onel] gone a journey, I knew not where, I could not converse with her. I saw her Heart too full. Such is the folly and madness of speculation and extravagance. To her no blame is due." Like other grandmothers, Abigail sometimes took care of her grandchildren, William Steuben Smith and John Adams Smith, to give Nabby time to herself.

Abigail also visited her son Charles, who lived on Beaver Street in New York City with his wife, Sarah Smith Adams, and the first of their two daughters, Susanna Boylston. "Charles lives prettily but frugally," was all Abigail wrote in 1797. But Charles had long found life painful; he was the homesick lad whose journey alone at the age of eleven from the Netherlands to Massachusetts, back to his mother, had been imperiled at sea and who had been put into port in Spain and "lost" to his parents for almost four months. In 1797, his mother must have seen, but did not mention, the early stages of depression and alcoholism that were already starting to consume this young man.

In all, it was a sad spring for the Adamses. John Adams's mother died on April 21. Abigail, who described herself as "grown grey with years," suffered from attacks of fever and rheumatism that sometimes confined her to bed and home for a week at a time. She found the trip southward to Philadelphia physically (as well as emotionally) exhausting. Still, during her early weeks as first lady, Abigail spent long days greeting the ladies and gentlemen of her husband's government.

Meanwhile, John Quincy had been spending many hours in "literary idleness" in The Hague. He had finished Gibbon, Adam Smith's *Wealth of Nations* ("A book to be reread and studied and meditated on"), Milton's *Paradise Lost,* Hume and Rousseau, and Luzac's difficult *Richesse de la Hollande.* He had learned to read Italian, and took up Ariosto's *Orlando Furioso.* And he had read Caesar again, and Terence, Tasso and Tacitus.

He was worried that others were getting ahead of him in law in Boston, and that he might have to return to the United States and practice in the South to make a living. His father counseled against it: "I am still delighted with your Facts, your Opinions, your Principles, and your Feelings. I believe them just. I do not approve of your projects of quitting the diplomatic career at present; much less of your thought of settling in the Southern States."

In July, 1797, he appointed John Quincy minister pleni-potentiary to the new American legation in Prussia. He had wisely consulted George Washington about John Quincy's new post, and Washington had replied: "If my wishes should be of any avail, they should go to you in a *strong hope*, that you will not withhold merited promotion from Mr. Jn°. Adams because he is your son. . . . Mr. Adams is the most valuable public character we have abroad . . . there remains no doubt in my mind that he will prove himself to be the ablest, of all our diplomatic corps."

This certainly wasn't the opinion of the anti-Federalists. Benjamin Bache wrote in the *Aurora* that "George Washington had never appointed to any station in government, even the most distant of his relations." Bache saw the nomination as proof that the president and his family were seeking profit from public office. For the next year, he hammered at this theme, and claimed at one point that John and John Quincy Adams would make more than $100,000 from government service, an obvious exaggeration. Still, by the spring of 1798, the issue of just how much John Quincy and his father drew from government salaries was taken up by the House and newspapers like the *Independent Chronicle* and the *Columbian Centinel* of Boston. Abigail mailed her sister a copy of John Fenno's *Gazette* and wrote angrily: "Bache has the malice & falshood of Satin, and his vile partner the Chronical is equally as bad. . . . An abused and insulted publick cannot tolerate them much longer. In short they are so criminal that they ought to be Presented by the grand jurors."

John Quincy's marriage to Louisa Catherine Johnson did not ease the outcry of the opposition press. Privately, both Abigail and John themselves had worried about the engagement. Abigail had wondered about "Maria" — Mary Frazier — and had written John Quincy about her. Were there lingering doubts? "As you tell me the enthusiasm of youth has subsided," she wrote her son, "I presume that reason and judgment have taken its place." Abigail worried that the girl was too English — her mother was English and her father an American. "I would hope for the love I bear my country that the Siren is at least *half-blood*."

John Adams had not been any more enthusiastic. "I

wished in my heart it might have been in America. But I have not a word to say. You are now of age to judge for yourself; and whether you return [to England] and choose her or whether you choose elsewhere, your deliberate choice will be mine."

To Americans, and especially the Republicans, Louisa Catherine Johnson was an Englishwoman. The opposition newspapers examined the event for signs of dark life, and the *Independent Chronicle* of Boston noted gleefully: "Young John Adams's negotiations have terminated in a marriage treaty with an English lady, the daughter of one Mr. Johnson, on Tower-Hill. It is a happy circumstance that he had made no other Treaty."

John Quincy and Louisa were married in London on July 26, 1797. His salary had doubled, to $9,000, with his promotion, and he was entitled to a supplement for "outfit" of one year's pay — $4,500, his old salary. John Quincy could at last afford to support a wife from his salary and savings, which were his only source of income throughout his public service.

The Senate, growling over the establishment of a new American legation at Berlin, took three months to debate John Quincy's new assignment. The younger Adamses enjoyed a leisurely honeymoon in England. Finally, on October 18, they left London with Thomas Boylston Adams, and spent eight stormy days reaching Hamburg, where they rested a week, and then traveled another five days by stage over bad roads to Berlin. Louisa became ill with a fever; during the next three years she was sick and despondent much of the time. The young woman, although spunky, never enjoyed the courts of Europe. She wrote her mother-in-law that after their arrival in Berlin: "we have not been permitted to spend an evening at home, which is so extreemly unpleasent to me, that I am obliged to pretend sickness, to avoid it. The King and Queen are both young, and I think the Queen one of the most beautiful women I ever saw. She is now pregnant with her fourth child, and is but 21 years old. She goes into company, and dances from 6 in the Evening untill 6 in the morning, notwithstanding her situation. The Courts are twice a week, one of which is a Ball & the other a card party. The

Etiquet and usage of the Court, require all Ministers & their Ladies to attend, so that I am obliged to make one in this *Elegant Mob*. On every Monday Evening I am obliged to pay my respects to the Princess Henry, a Great Aunt of the Kings, where I am necessitated to sit 2 or 3 hours at whist. Once a fortnight we are obligated to visit Prince Ferdinand, who is Great Uncle to the King. The Princess is an old Lady who has been very Handsome. She is remarkable kind to me, and has interested herself very much about my Health. Her sister, some years Younger than herself, is the most Elegant woman I ever beheld. She has been pleasd to take such a fancy to me, as to make me sit down with her, at her work table, and talks whole evenings with me. I was invited to a Ball the other Evening, and she undertook to find me partners. . . . Yet after all this, my dear Mamma, I do not think I am calculated for a Court."

Even so, Abigail concluded to her sister in 1797, John Quincy "is very happy and I doubt not will remain so, for the Young Lady has much sweetness of Temper and seems to Love *as she ought*."

One purpose of John Quincy's mission to Berlin was to obtain a new treaty with Prussia. For two years, he and his Prussian counterparts worked slowly but cooperatively. Archives in Berlin show that John Quincy wrote and rewrote memorials and treaty drafts in their entirety three times; he was a patient, straightforward and conciliatory diplomat. His work resulted in a treaty, signed on July 11, 1799, his thirty-second birthday. Although it deliberately omitted a doctrine then very much under discussion in the capitals of England, France and America — that of free ships, free goods -- the treaty did include all other points stressed in his instructions from the secretary of state.

The treaty signed, John Quincy continued his other mission: being his father's observer of events in Europe. John Adams had written his son in June, 1797: "You have wisely taken all of Europe for your theatre, and I hope you will continue to do as you have done. Send us all the information you can collect. I wish you to continue the practice of writing freely to me, and cautiously to the office of State."

It was a perceptive warning.

CONGRESSIONAL PUGILISTS, CONGRESS HALL IN PHILADELPHIA, FEBRUARY 15, 1798.
CARTOON, ARTIST UNKNOWN, 1798

America's relations with Europe split the U.S. Congress, the political parties and the people. Fights broke out in the Congress, and in one (above), Federalist Roger Griswold attacked Republican Matthew Lyon with a cane. Lyon defended himself with firetongs. He was less successful against the Sedition Act, and went to jail in 1798. That same year, the XYZ Affair turned the American people against France. Three French agents attempted to extract from the American envoys (right) a bribe of $250,000 and a loan of $10 million as the price for opening negotiations with Talleyrand, the French foreign minister.

DETAIL OF A CONTEMPORARY CARTOON OF THE XYZ AFFAIR

The American peace commission arrived in Paris on October 7, 1797, at an unfortunate moment. The Directors had pulled off a coup d'etat against the French peace party, and Talleyrand was the French foreign minister. He engaged the commissioners in some fast bargaining.

On the eighth of October, Pinckney, Gerry and Marshall had a short audience with him, but he refused to discuss any issues of substance with them. A few days later, they received a visit from three mysterious emissaries of the French minister, who sought to play on their fears and solicit bribes. Recognition of the American commission would be forthcoming, they said, only if Talleyrand received a gift of $250,000 and a loan of $10 million. Marshall argued: "Our case is different from that of the minor nations of Europe. They were unable to maintain their independence, and did not expect to do so. America is a great, and so far as concerns her self-defense, a powerful nation."

But Talleyrand was playing with the Americans. Marshall and Pinckney soon quit Paris; only Gerry lingered, his pro-French emotions getting the best of him.

Adams's envoys filed their dispatches, which did not reach the president until March 4, 1798. Their reports referred to the French emissaries as X, Y, and Z, and as Adams read the dispatches, and the significance of the French rejection and bribe attempts unfolded, he knew he faced war. Adams moved cautiously, first sounding out his cabinet, and on March 16 sent to the Senate and House a brief message apprising Congress that he could "perceive no ground of expectation that the objects of their mission can be accomplished on terms compatible with the safety, honor, or the essential interests of the nation." He concluded that the country should push ahead with its defense.

When the Congress asked Adams for the correspondence, and the "X, Y, Z dispatches" were made public, the uproar was loud and warlike.* The president vowed to Con-

*The American outcry against the French demand for bribes did not consider the record. In 1784, Adams wrote from London to Jefferson in Paris that the Barbary Coast pirates might be bought off. In 1786, a treaty was concluded with Morocco calling for annual payment of American tribute. On April 10, 1792, President Washington submitted to the Senate a treaty under which $40,000 would be paid

When President John Adams called for millions for defense, American shipyards got busy. This line engraving shows the Southwark shipyard in Philadelphia with the Swedish Church in the background. Workers carry timbers to carpenters as the frigate Philadelphia *takes form. Wealthy merchants, whose vessels were being harassed at sea by the French and British, supported the shipbuilding, and although the Treaty of 1801 temporarily settled differences, the skill gained in shipbuilding and the ships themselves served the nation well in 1812.*

DETAIL: PREPARATION FOR WAR TO DEFEND COMMERCE. COLORED LINE ENGRAVING BY WILLIAM BIRCH, 1800

gress: "I will never send another Minister to France without assurance that he will be received, respected, and honored, as the representative of a great, free, powerful, and independent nation."

The Republicans were shocked by this evidence of French hostility. "Trimmers dropt off from the party like windfalls from an apple tree in September," wrote Fisher Ames. While Jefferson remained quiet, the Federalists were noisily jubilant. Songs were written, bonfires lighted. President Adams was toasted and supported. Harvard undergraduates, wildly excited by the XYZ Affair, sent their most prominent alumnus a copy of a patriotic address signed by almost every one of them. The toast of the day became: "Millions for defence, but not one cent for tribute."

Congress gladly passed the measures Adams requested. A Navy Department, separate from the War Department, was established, and a fleet authorized. A "provisional army" of 10,000 men with three-year enlistments was approved; money was appropriated for artillery and the militia reorganized under federal supervision. The frigates *Constitution, Constellation* and *United States* were outfitted, and by the end of 1798, the United States had fourteen men-of-war at sea. The French treaties of 1778 were officially abrogated, as well as the consular convention of 1788.

The Federalists delighted in the increased national unity and new legislation. They saw an opportunity for increased political strength, and in the congressional elections of 1798–1799 they won a strong majority in both houses.

Then, having gained political power, the Federalists proceeded to abuse it. Few people understood John Adams during these four years. James Madison wrote Jefferson: "You know the temper of Mr. A. better than I do, but I have always conceived it to be rather a ticklish one." Indeed it was, and one of the things John Adams found most pestering were the Republican taunts, both in Congress and in the press, that he and his family had to endure. Albert Gallatin, a Swiss who had become a Republican leader in Congress in 1797, sneered at Abigail Adams as "Her Majesty," and reminded her hus-

---

to the pirates of Algiers. President Adams continued the policy of paying blackmail to the pirates of the Mediterranean.

band that he was "President by three votes." Adams was also offended by Irishmen who openly carried on their anti-British struggle in America, and by French intellectuals in the United States whom he (often correctly) suspected of engaging in espionage. Nor could he ignore the continuing barbs from Bache and his *Aurora*. Abigail, a strong influence on her husband, sounded an alarm in a letter to her sister: "In any other Country Bache & all his papers would have been seazd and ought to be here, but congress are dilly dallying about passing a Bill enabling the President to seize suspisious persons, and their papers."

Amid the power and hysteria of a quasi-war and the fear of foreigners and opponents, the U.S. Congress stopped dilly-dallying and passed the Naturalization, Alien and Sedition acts. The Naturalization Act of 1798 extended from five to fourteen years the time "necessary for an alien to reside here before he can be admitted a citizen." Two Alien acts gave to the president (and took from the states) the power to expel foreigners from the United States both in time of war and of peace.

But it was the Sedition Act that provided an excellent rallying point for the scattered Republican forces. It contained two parts; one proclaimed a fine not exceeding $5,000 and imprisonment not exceeding five years for anyone who "threatened any person holding an office under the government." The second part stated that "any libellous attack by writing, printing, publishing or speaking" against the president or members of Congress "with the intent to defame" or to bring them "into contempt or disrepute" was punishable by a fine not to exceed $2,000 or imprisonment not to exceed two years.

It was this law that was vigorously enforced by the Federalists, who savored a distaste for opposition and considered Republicans little better than anarchists. Seventeen newspapermen and officeholders — including Benjamin Bache — were indicted, and ten convicted. Bache would have gone to jail, but he died of yellow fever before being sentenced. Thomas Cooper got six months for supporting the Republicans. James Callender, who for several years had ridiculed John Adams, was arrested in Richmond, Virginia, for publication of his pamphlet *The Prospect before us*, imprisoned and fined — but not silenced.

There is evidence that President Adams encouraged the prosecution of at least two of the men. In a letter to the *Boston Patriot* ten years later, he tried to defend the Alien and Sedition acts as coming from Hamilton: "Such was the influence of Mr. Hamilton in Congress, that, without any recommendation from the President, they passed a bill to raise an army, not a large one, indeed, but enough to overturn the then Federal Government. Nor did I adopt this idea of an alien or sedition law. I recommended no such thing in my speech. Congress, however, adopted both these measures." But President Adams signed these bills into law. Of the Alien and Sedition acts he said: "I knew there was need enough of both, and therefore I consented to them. But as they were then considered as war measures, and intended altogether against the advocates of the French and peace with France, I was apprehensive that a hurricane of clamor would be raised against them, as in truth there was, even more fierce and violent than I had anticipated."

The Republicans protested loudly, and viewed the Sedition Act as, in James Madison's words, "a monster that must forever disgrace its parents." Madison and Jefferson viewed the acts as a naked play for power and control that must be answered. In the atmosphere of persecution, two startling protests erupted from the state legislatures: the Resolves of Virginia, drafted by Madison, and the Resolves of Kentucky, written by Jefferson. These Resolves developed the first "states-rights" interpretation of the Constitution. Kentucky declared that when Congress blatantly transcended its powers, as in the Sedition Act, each state "has an equal right to judge for itself, as well of infractions as of the mode and measure of redress." Kentucky called on other states to concur in declaring the acts void and to unite "in requesting their appeal." Virginia, declaring the acts unconstitutional, spoke of "interposing" the state authority between persecuted citizens and their government. The Resolves clearly expressed the alarm of the people at the "Federalist reign of terror."

In the spring and early summer of 1798, John Adams had shown a bellicose spirit. He had welcomed the calls of young

Whatever John Adams's popularity elsewhere in the country, Bostonians celebrated his birthday. Mounted troops passed in review on Boston Common during a birthday ceremony in front of the new State House.

DETAIL: THE BOSTON TROOPS AS REVIEWED ON PRESIDENT ADAMS'S BIRTHDAY. FROM A COLORED ENGRAVING BY SIDNEY L. SMITH, REENGRAVED AFTER A LOST ORIGINAL, 1903

Americans pledging themselves to the defense of their country, and he replied to those in Boston: "To arms! . . . my young friends, to arms!" And to the young men of New York he had written, "Beware of contaminating your country with the foul abominations of the French Revolution." In a letter to the Massachusetts legislature he denounced French imperialism "aiming at dominion such as never has before prevailed in Europe."

But by late summer he had cooled. He felt no strong urge to arms. "One thing I know," he wrote McHenry, "that regiments are costly articles everywhere, and more so in this country than any other under the sun. If this nation see a great army to maintain, without an enemy to fight, there may arise an enthusiasm that seems to be little foreseen. At present there is no more prospect of seeing a French army here, than there is in Heaven."

Nonetheless, an army had to be put together, and President Adams busied himself with it. George Washington would be commander in chief. But he was in poor health, and it was clear that the second in command would actually control the army in fact if not in spirit. Hamilton was a major power behind the Adams administration: he controlled senators, representatives and three members — Wolcott, Pickering and McHenry — of the cabinet. Hamilton wanted the number-two spot, inspector general, but Adams refused to appoint him. A quarrel began between Washington, Hamilton, Knox, McHenry, Wolcott, Pickering and Adams over filling the command positions, and continued all summer, generating no fewer than thirteen lengthy documents. It finally ended on October 13, when Adams gave in and nominated Hamilton.

Hamilton did not propose to stop with armed neutrality. He already had grand plans to lead an American army overland against West Florida, Louisiana, and New Orleans — even pushing on to Mexico. At the same time the British fleet would blockade the mouth of the Mississippi River.

But while Hamilton planned for war, Adams searched for peace. Publicly, the president remained bellicose. His speech before Congress on December 8, 1798, contained none of his private concerns of the fall, when just a week after

Hamilton was appointed second in command of the army he had written to Secretary Pickering: "To keep open the channels of negotiation, it is [my] intention to nominate a minister to the French republic, who may be ready to embark for France, as soon as he, or the President, shall receive from the Directory satisfactory assurances that he shall be received and entitled to all the prerogatives and privileges of the general laws of nations."

Before Congress, however, Adams waved the stick. He denounced as "an unequivocal act of war" the Directory's decree declaring neutral ships a prize if they carried any cargo of British origin, and he saw no indication from the French that "ought to change or relax our measures of defence," rather, "to extend and invigorate them is our true policy. . . .

"Whether we negotiate with her [France] or not, vigorous preparations for war will be alike indispensible. These alone will give us an equal treaty, and insure its observeance."

Still, the president said, he sought peace: "It is peace that we have uniformly and perseveringly cultivated; and harmony between us and France may be restored at her option. But to send another minister without more determinate assurances that he would be received, would be an act of humiliation to which the United States ought not to submit. It must, therefore, be left to France, if she is indeed desirous of accommodation, to take the requisite steps."

The president was, in fact, bidding for time, and directing an appeal to Talleyrand. Earlier in 1798, Vice-President Jefferson had gone to lengths to warn France and her minister to the United States that France's policy could push his country into the arms of the British. It was a convincing argument, and one that Talleyrand, annoyed that the XYZ dispatches had exposed his venality to the amused courts of Europe, had reached himself. The French had begun using every available channel to communicate peaceful intentions; French seamen were ordered to respect American ships and West Indian seizures were halted.

During the summer of 1798, while at Quincy, John Adams had begun to receive from William Vans Murray in The Hague an account of his conversations with the secretary of the French legation there, Monsieur Pichon. This might explain Adams's cooling ardor for war, for Murray's dispatches showed that Talleyrand, although wily, was aware that it was in France's best interest to come to an understanding with America. Talleyrand communicated through Pichon to Murray that he hoped the United States would send to Paris for discussions "a plenipotentiary favorably known in France."

Murray sent John Quincy Adams copies of the correspondence, and John Quincy wrote his father directly that he thought Talleyrand and the French government were willing to negotiate, probably to prevent the United States from forming a bond with Great Britain. John Quincy filed Dispatch No. 137, on October 6, 1798, to Pickering and the president, urging him to empower the "spirited and prudent" Murray to enter into preliminary discussions at The Hague with an authorized French representative. But John Adams wanted more, and said so. He demanded that Talleyrand through Pichon inform Murray that any American sent must be recognized and welcomed by France; there would be no more French rebuffs and American embarrassments.

By December, 1798, while Adams waved his stick before Congress, he awaited Talleyrand's correspondence from Europe, to be delivered by Thomas Boylston. The president was impatient; he had much on his mind, including his wife's declining health. When Thomas Boylston's packet finally arrived, Adams had what he needed. Talleyrand wrote that "any plenipotentiary sent by the government of the United States to France, to put an end to the difficulties which remain between the two countries would be undoubtedly received with the attentions suitable to the envoy of a free, independent and powerful nation."

On February 18, John Adams made the most courageous — and politically fatal — act of his public life. He sent to the Congress, along with a copy of Talleyrand's letter, his proposal for renewed negotiations with France, and nominated William Vans Murray minister plenipotentiary of the United States to France to begin talks.

His bold move took Congress — and the Federalists — by surprise. Two months earlier, he had sounded bellicose.

Now he wanted peace negotiations – the third such attempt – after deliberate French rebuffs and open attacks on American warships. Even as he addressed Congress, the House was discussing a bill "encouraging the capture of French armed vessels by armed ships or vessels owned by citizens of the United States." It was defeated two days later. The Senate, shocked, sent a five-man committee, headed by Theodore Sedgwick, to ask the president to withdraw his nomination. But the resolute little New Englander knew he was right. He told them: "I have, on mature reflection, made up my mind, and I will neither withdraw nor modify the nomination."

In an instant, Hamilton's plans for military glory in the South and Mexico were dashed. The war effort ground to a halt, for the Hamiltonians were trapped: they couldn't oppose peace for war. In a rearguard action, they demanded that Adams add two Federalist colleagues to Murray's commission, and the president chose Chief Justice Oliver Ellsworth and Patrick Henry, who was ill and was later replaced by Governor William R. Davie of North Carolina.

What had happened? For one thing, the Hamiltonians never understood the basic, independent nature of this president who, although opposed to Jefferson's belief in the common man, was equally opposed to plutocracy or militarism. Adams was a political philosopher, not a party man. He could not pass up a final chance for peace simply because his party clamored for war. Either he was a deliberate martyr to peace or an astute politician. In any event, his unexpected shift separated him further from his cabinet and widened the split in the Federalist Party. John Adams might have formed a new and independent party, but he couldn't or wouldn't rally to himself those "friends of the country" who sought, as he did, "tranquillity upon just and honorable terms."

He instructed Davie and Ellsworth to "make immediate preparations for embarking." Although he had little confidence in the outcome of their mission, he was determined "to delay nothing, to omit nothing." As soon as he could, Adams went home to Quincy and Abigail. He had written her in February: "Your sickness last summer, fall, and winter, has been to me the severest trial I ever endured. Not that I am at this moment without other trials enough for one man." He entrusted the peace mission to his cabinet, and departed from Philadelphia.

President Adams was certain he could run his government from his home. "Here at Quincy," he wrote a friend, he could conduct his work "as readily as I could do at Philadelphia. The Secretaries of State, Treasury, War, Navy, and the Attorney-General, transmit me daily by the post all the business of consequence." He entertained the illusion that "nothing is done without my advice and direction."

But Pickering and the other Federalists in Adams's cabinet worked to delay the peace mission. Pickering had slowed the transmission of Adams's instructions to Murray, who did not learn of the new envoys until May 5, 1799. Talleyrand's letter to Murray was received a week later; it expressed, as Adams had demanded, the Directory's pleasure at the nomination of the special American envoys, and assured that they would be properly received. The French were seeking peace.

But the American government, unknown to President Adams in Quincy, was stalling for a chance at war. Throughout the summer, Pickering balked. Adams's friends wrote the president and urged him, for the good of the country, to return to Trenton (the cabinet had fled there to escape the yellow fever in Philadelphia). On August 26, Pickering received news of another coup d'etat in Paris, and his proposal to suspend the mission, now out in the open, took on new meaning.

News from the Continent heartened the Hamiltonians. Great Britain had raised a second coalition of Russia, Austria, Portugal, Sardinia, Naples and the Ottoman Empire against France. A British expedition had landed in the Netherlands; the Dutch fleet had surrendered. Austrian forces were driving the French from Switzerland and the Rhineland, and the Austro-Russian army was pushing them from northern Italy. Hamilton, among others, thought that momentarily Louis XVIII would be restored to the throne.

After further delay, John Adams finally left Quincy for Trenton, reaching there October 10. Hamilton arrived in the city at the same time, "by an accident," he said. According to one account, the president looked unwell and "more fit for a chamber and bed of sickness than for much labour of the head or hands."

For three days, Adams held conferences, discussing paragraph by paragraph the instructions to the American envoys. The Federalists, led by Hamilton, pushed to halt the mission. They wrote Washington that many citizens viewed the effort as "fraught with irreparable mischief." But Adams persisted, and ordered Ellsworth and Davie to sail on the frigate *United States*, lying at Rhode Island, by November 1, or sooner.

The Federalists had been fatally hurt. To their dismay, John Adams had not acted as head of their party, or as a toady to Hamilton. He was a national president, with all his faults, who felt no obligation either to party or politicians, but to his country. He had constantly sought peace and accommodation throughout his career; he had always been a man of law over mob rule. Had not that been one of the reasons for his defense of Captain Preston after the Boston Massacre? In his speech before Congress on December 3, 1799, Adams called for "maintaining our just rights" while approving only of a "system of national defence, commensurate with our resources and the situation of our country."

Hamilton's faction, sapped of its power, now lost its prestige. The death of George Washington on December 14 deeply saddened the country and weakened the people's trust in the Federalists, whom they felt he had restrained. Adams made clear his opposition to appointing Hamilton commander in chief. Hamilton would have neither his war nor his command.

In France, meanwhile, Napoleon had returned from Egypt, and began leading his countrymen to victory after victory. The American envoys were greeted by Talleyrand and Napoleon, who were anxious to encourage them; Washington's recent death gave the French an opportunity to touch American sensitivities. Napoleon ordered the pennons of France's victorious armies draped with crepe for ten days. Negotiations, however, dragged for more than seven months. Napoleon scaled the Alps and broke the back of the Second Coalition with a brilliant victory at Marengo on June 14, 1800. In the end, fearing an entangling alliance, the Americans brought home a mere commercial convention. Still, peace was achieved.

BRAINTREE. OIL BY E. MALCOM, 1798

John Adams bought the Old House (above) in Braintree shortly after he and Abigail returned to the United States from Europe. Abigail, perhaps spoiled by the large mansions of Europe, was disappointed in its size. "In height and breadth," she said, "it feels like a wren's house." This painting of the Old House was made in 1798, when Adams was president and before the large extensions were built behind the house. The painting of Alice Mason (right), one of the oldest in America, was finished in 1670 and was eventually inherited by Abigail Adams.

ALICE MASON. OIL BY AN UNKNOWN ARTIST, 1670

News of the treaty signaled the end for the Federalist Party. But the breakup had been occurring steadily ever since Adams had insisted upon sending the peace mission. For as John Quincy had written to Murray, his father had acted "not as a man of a party, but as the man of the whole nation."

The Federalists argued that Adams had suddenly switched sides. Oliver Wolcott, puzzled, wrote in December, 1799, to Fisher Ames: "The President's mind is in a state which renders it difficult to determine what prudence and duty require from those about him. He considers Col. Pickering, Mr. McHenry, and myself as his enemies; his resentments against General Hamilton are excessive; he declares his belief of the existence of a British faction in the United States."

Both Ames and Wolcott thought John Adams had shown too much "respect for the voice of the people." In fact, on entering his last year of public service, Adams had seized an initiative that had eluded him in other situations. His best work had come in the forums of law, at the Continental Congresses, and in the Netherlands: at times when he could work directly — and not through others — to bring about the will of his political philosophy. As president, he had trusted too much in his cabinet which, in every sense, had betrayed him. In December McHenry worried "whether the President will think it expedient to dismiss any, or how many of us."

By early February, 1800, the split was open, and the end in sight. The *Aurora* called attention to the schism in the Federalist camp: "The President's party" consisted of "the New England party, the Connecticut illuminati, the office-hunting party," while the Hamiltonians were "the old Tory, or refugee party, the Army and Navy, the profit-hunting party, the funding, banking and loan party, the British agency and, finally, the monarchists and anti-Gallican party."

Beginning in May, Adams peeled apart the Federalist hold on his government. It was too late. He asked McHenry to see him, and during their discussion, lost his temper; a sharp argument and an unpleasant scene erupted. McHenry resigned. On May 10, Adams informed Pickering that he had "the opportunity of resigning, if he chose." Pickering, however, had planned to stay in office, and didn't have enough money to leave. He flatly refused, and Adams told him he was "hereby discharged from any further service as Secretary of State."

Now Hamilton swung into action. A letter from him attacking Adams found its way during 1800 into a pamphlet called *The Public Conduct and Character of John Adams, Esq., President of the United States.* This letter, published in the *Aurora* and the *New London Bee*, was a final, public airing of the Federalist split. Hamilton wrote that Adams "does not possess the talents adapted to the *administration* of government and that there are great and intrinsic defects in his character, which unfit him for the office of chief magistrate." Hamilton accused Adams of being vain and jealous, and of humiliating the nation with peace ministers to France.

The Republicans made much of this in 1800, an election year. But Adams refused to acknowledge Hamilton's outburst while he was in office, and did not officially reply until 1809, when he published eighteen letters of rebuttal. Still, on December 3, as the election was clearly moving away from him, John Adams wrote a remarkably charitable letter about Hamilton's attack: "This last pamphlet I regret more on account of its author than on my own, because I am confident it will do him more harm than me. I am not his enemy, and never was. I have not adored him, like his idolaters, and have had great cause to disapprove of some of his politics. He has talents, if he would correct himself, which might be useful. There is more burnish, however, on the outside, than sterling silver in the substance."

Yet the Hamilton attack stung John Adams deeply. As late as 1813, Adams, in a letter to Thomas Jefferson, referred to Hamilton as "a bastard Bratt of a Scotch Pedlar."

At the beginning of the new century, the government left Philadelphia for the District of Columbia on the Potomac River. In May, the government's records, furniture from the President's House, files and documents began moving by ship and wagon from Philadelphia to Washington; the moving continued throughout the year and into 1801.

Toward the end of May, President Adams rode a

"Chariot and four" from Philadelphia to see how the new and permanent capital looked. On June 3, he entered the city and was greeted by a party of Marines, and escorted to the Union Tavern in "George Town on the Potomac." Later that day he crossed the Rock Creek Bridge at K Street, stopping to check on the progress of the new President's House. There was an inspection of the unfinished Capitol, seventeen toasts at McLaughlin's City Tavern in Georgetown, and dinner with the parents of Louisa Catherine, John Quincy's wife. Before he left Washington on the fifteenth, John Adams wrote to Abigail: "I like the Seat of Government very well and shall sleep, or lie awake next Winter in the Presidents house." He would have cause enough to do both.

For the last two years, Abigail's health had not improved. The journey between Quincy and Washington would be extremely difficult, "with five hundred and fifty or six hundred miles to ride through the mud." Her health concerned John and Abigail both; she recounted her symptoms and suggested remedies. "You complain of always having a share of Rhumatism," she wrote one of her sisters. "That is just my case. I have it floting about, sometimes in my head, Breast, Stomack &c. but if I can keep of[f] fever I can Parry it so as not to be confined. Dr. [Benjamin] Rush is for calling it Gout, but I will not believe a word of all that, for Rhumatism I have had ever since I was a Child. When I feel any thing like fever, nitre in powder of about 6 Grains with a 6 part of a Grain of tarter Emetic & a 6 part of a Grain of Calomil in each taking 3 powders in a day, generally relieves me."

On October 15, 1800, Adams left Quincy for his last journey into government service, to Washington. He reached the new capital alone — Abigail was just recovering from another attack of her persistent "intermitting fever" and would follow him later. Adams was the first president to sleep in the President's House, and on November 2, he wrote Abigail that "the building is in a state to be habitable, and now we wish for your company." Then he closed with the famous sentence: "I pray heaven to bestow the best blessings on this house, and on all that shall hereafter inhabit it. May none but honest and wise men ever rule under this roof!"

Abigail set out from Quincy, and with a brief (but

tragic) stop in New York, continued to Washington, where she arrived on November 16. She lost her way in the woods south of Baltimore, "holding down & breaking bows of trees which we could not pass, untill we met a solitary black fellow with a horse and cart" who directed them toward the capital. "You find nothing but a Forest & woods on the way, for 16 and 18 miles not a village. Here and there a thatchd cottage without a single pane of glass, inhabited by Blacks."

The tragic news Abigail carried was of Charles Adams, "laid upon a Bed of sickness, destitute of a home. The kindness of a friend afforded him an assylum. A distressing cough, an affection of the liver and a dropsy will soon terminate a Life." She carried this "melancholy report" to her husband. Charles Adams died of cirrhosis on December 1, at the age of thirty, leaving a wife and two young daughters. "His constitution was so shaken," his mother wrote, "that his disease was rapid, and through the last period of his Life dreadfully painfull and distressing. . . . His mind at times was much deranged thro his sufferings." In the President's House, John Adams mourned "the melancholy death of a once beloved son."

Their surroundings in Washington did little to relieve the gloom. Abigail found Georgetown "the very dirtyest Hole I ever saw for a place of any trade, or respectability of inhabitants. It is only one mile from me but a quagmire after every rain."

The President's House was enormous, far larger than anything John or Abigail had ever lived in. "This House is twice as large as our meeting House [in Quincy]. I believe the great Hall is as Bigg. I am sure tis twice as long. Cut your coat according to your Cloth. But this House is built for ages to come." Still, the unfinished house wasn't comfortable to live in. Abigail wrote: "I had much rather live in the house at Philadelphia. Not one room or chamber is finished of the whole. It is habitable by fires in every part, thirteen of which we are obliged to keep daily, or sleep in wet & damp places."

Only six rooms of the house were ready. The weather was chilly, and there was no wood: "Surrounded by forests, can you believe that wood is not to be had, because people cannot be found to cut and cart it. . . . [The steward] has

In 1800, when the capital was moved from Philadelphia to Washington, D.C. the new Capitol building (right) was unfinished and without its famous dome. Congressmen lived in jerry-built boardinghouse and the President's House was still under construction. Congressman and president alike rode over dusty (or muddy) tracks to reach Georgetown (below), then bucolic and isolated.

GEORGETOWN AND FEDERAL CITY. AQUATINT BY T. CARTWRIGHT AFTER GEORGE BECK, 1800

had recourse to coals; but we cannot get grates made and set. We have, indeed, come into *a new country*."

Then there was the problem of laundry. "The great, unfinished audience room [the present East Room] I make a drying-room of, to hang up the clothes in. The principal stairs are not up, and will not be this winter."

By the middle of December, John Adams knew he would not be reelected. The Republicans were supporting Jefferson for president and Aaron Burr for vice-president. The Federalists put forth Adams and Charles C. Pinckney of the XYZ mission, but their hearts weren't in it. Hamilton's faction, seeking revenge against Adams for making peace, vowed to swing votes to Pinckney and bring him in as president. In the voting, Adams received 65 electoral votes to Jefferson's 73; Jefferson and Burr, in the unusual voting of the day, were tied.

Not until 1804 would the Twelfth Amendment to the Constitution remove the possibility of a tie between two candidates on the same ticket. In 1801, however, the House of Representatives, voting by states, had to choose between Jefferson and Burr. The party division was so close that it took thirty-six ballots and five days to break the deadlock. On February 17, 1801, Jefferson was president by a majority of two states.

Election analysts argue that with a change of 250 votes in New York City, Adams would have beaten Jefferson, 71 to 61, in the national election of November, 1800. The Republicans won the presidency, these historians suggest, because they manipulated the methods of selecting electors in Virginia and Pennsylvania, and had enjoyed the skill of Aaron Burr's ward-heeling in New York City in the election of the legislature in May.

It was in the House of Representatives that the Federalist collapse appeared most sharply. The Federalists had enjoyed a majority: 73 to 33 Republicans. After the elections, the tally was reversed: 68 Republicans to 38 Federalists. The Senate, overwhelmingly Federalist before the elections, became Republican by a small majority. The Federalists went out of power in every branch of the government except one, the judiciary — and the exception would soon prove important.

Adams saw "nothing wonderful" in Jefferson's victory. And of Aaron Burr, the new vice-president, he said: "All the old patriots, all the splendid talents, the long experience, both of federalists and antifederalists, must be subjected to the humiliation of seeing this dexterous gentleman rise, like a balloon, filled with inflammable air, over their heads."

One of John Adams's last recommendations was the reorganization of the national judiciary system, which passed Congress on January 20, 1801. With the resignation of Ellsworth to serve as one of the envoys to France, there was also vacant the office of chief justice of the Supreme Court. Adams appointed his new secretary of state, John Marshall, as chief justice. In his last days in office, Adams succumbed to his feelings of fear and misgiving concerning the victory of the Jeffersonians, and began packing the judiciary with Federalists. The appointments, for the most part, were for life, so Adams knew he was strengthening the check and control that this branch of government would exercise on the next.

He also recalled John Quincy from his post in Berlin, and wrote Abigail, who had left the capital on February 13, about tidying up his affairs. "The burden upon me in nominating judges and consuls and other officers, in delivering over the furniture, in the ordinary business at the close of a session, and in preparing for my journey of five hundred miles through the mire, is and will be very heavy. . . . My anxiety for you is a very distressing addition to all my other labors. . . . I sleep the better for having the shutters open, and all goes on well. I pray God to bless and preserve you." The letter closed with mention of one of his final official duties: "I gave a feast to-day to Indian kings and aristocrats."

The judicial appointments opened old wounds between Adams and Jefferson. Between 1796 and 1801, no letters had passed between the two men: the breach ran deep, and appeared to be largely on Adams's side and of his making. Until nine o'clock the night before Jefferson's inauguration, John Adams was still making judicial nominations to the Senate, which approved them without debate. It was a bitter act against Jefferson, who wrote in 1804 to Abigail Adams: "I can say with truth that one act of Mr. Adams's life, and one only, ever gave me a moment's personal displeasure. I did consider his last appointments to office as personally unkind. They were from among my most ardent political enemies, from whom no faithful cooperation could ever be expected, and laid me under the embarras[s]ment of acting thro' men whose views were to defeat mine, or to encounter the odium of putting others in their places. . . . If my respect for him did not permit me to ascribe the whole blame to the influence of others, it left something for friendship to forgive, and after brooding over it for some little time, and not always resisting the expression of it, I forgave it cordially, and returned to the same state of esteem and respect for him which had so long subsisted."

Early in the morning of March 4, while the capital slept, John Adams called for his coach. He left Washington, deliberately avoiding Jefferson's inauguration, and only later wrote that he had been too upset by "the funeral of a son, who was once the delight of my eyes, and a darling of my heart, cutt off in the flower of his days," to remain in the capital. It was a poor excuse since Charles had died and been buried three months earlier. Adams may have wished to make a deliberate snub; or, as one historian has suggested, he may have left the capital because he had to vacate the White House and there was no other place for him to stay in crowded Washington.

Whatever, after twenty-six years of public service, John Adams went home. It took him just twelve days to reach Quincy, "having trotted the bogs five hundred miles." He left the nation, he felt, in good shape, with "its coffers full, and the fair prospects of a peace with all the world smiling in its face, its commerce flourishing, its navy glorious, its agriculture uncommonly productive and lucrative."

It was, perhaps, an optimistic appraisal. But John Adams had reason to feel satisfied. At home, in his barnyard, he found a hundred loads of seaweed, a boon for his fields, and he thought he had made a good exchange "of honors and virtues for manure." Whatever else might happen, John Adams knew that at last he would be left to enjoy his beloved fields and farm.

7

You Must Risque All

[1801 – 1815]

*O*N the morning of August 5, 1809, John Quincy Adams, his wife, Louisa Catherine, and their youngest son, Charles Francis, aged two, left their home at the corner of Boylston and Nassau streets in Boston, and drove by carriage over the Charles River Bridge to William Gray's wharf in Charlestown. There, the sailing ship *Horace* awaited them.

Adams had been appointed the first American minister to Russia. The post meant a long and possibly final separation from his aging parents, who had been "deeply affected" by his going. He and Louisa had also left their two oldest sons behind — a parting that especially troubled her — to live with relatives; Thomas Boylston Adams would look after their education. In all, John Quincy wrote in his diary, it was a "painful" leave-taking. But this assignment was — for him — an enticing opportunity, and the post would soon be a vital one for the United States. His work in Russia, he confided, might prove to be "the most important of any that I have ever in the course of my life been engaged in."

And so, precisely as the Boston and Charlestown bells were ringing one o'clock, with the Adamses and their entourage safely aboard, the *Horace* cast off for St. Petersburg and the awaiting conflicts of Europe.

As much as John Quincy wished to reenter the perils of international diplomacy, Louisa wished to remain at home. She was unprepared for her husband's acceptance of President Madison's offer. "Stun[n]ed," she considered the assignment a "most terrible and tedious voyage." Neither did she look forward, once again, to "the meanness of an American Ministers position at a European Court."

Louisa's years with John Quincy were often times of trial. He was a short and intense man, stern and severe in temperament and outlook: "more a natural force . . . than a mere human being." Louisa was a dark-eyed, delicately featured woman, one who was fortunate in keeping her beauty into middle age. But she was a gentle person, who had been teased as a child. Since she had lived her early years in Nantes, where her father was a merchant and an agent for the state of Maryland, she was partial to the French way of doing things, and by the time the Johnsons moved to London, her schoolmates thought her aloof and foreign, and nicknamed her "Miss Proud." But she managed to grow up, with her parents' encouragement, to be a spontaneous and open young woman, lively and independent.

John Quincy, in contrast, was an icy New Englander. He was thought to "welcome deprivations of peasure, even serious misfortunes, as means of improving his own character." Whatever real emotions he had he buried in his diary, where he wrote of intense hatreds and loves, and humor and sorrow — and kept a list of his enemies. From it we learn that the Russian Princess Woldemar Galitzin was "venerable by the length and thickness of her beard," and that "Mr. Jefferson tells large stories." The diary reveals a man pushing himself intellectually, reading and rereading great literature. Even when he was president he rose at four or five, built his own fire, read his Bible, worked a full day, and lamented the social events of the evening that interfered with his work. He exercised with the same intensity: daily horseback rides; summer swims against the tide. In St. Petersburg, he would stride along the quay measuring his steps, and discovered that as a man five feet seven inches tall, "by experiments frequently reported . . . my ordinary pace is two feet six inches and eighty-eight one-hundredths of an inch . . . and . . . in my ordinary pace I walk one hundred and twenty steps to the minute." He fretted over such details. He was driven to achieve and to be perfect. Unfortunately, what he demanded of himself, he demanded of those close to him. All too often they found his expectations impossible to meet.

Louisa Adams was more of a free spirit, who in her youth had explored the excitement of her own impulses. Strains in the marriage between this tightly controlled man and this open woman were inevitable. Years later, Louisa told her son, Charles Francis, when he became engaged, that the Adams men were "peculiarly harsh and severe" with their women. "There seems to exist [in them] no sympathy, no tenderness for the weakness of the sex or for that incapacity of occasional exertion which is a part of their nature." With characteristic restraint, John Quincy wrote this evaluation of his marriage in 1811: "Our union has not been without its trials, nor invariably without dissensions between us. There are many differences of sentiment, of tastes, and of opinions in regard to domestic economy, and to the education of children, between us. There are natural frailties of temper in both of us; both being quick and irascible, and mine being sometimes harsh. But she has always been a faithful and affectionate wife, and a careful, tender, indulgent, and watchful mother to our children, all of whom she nursed herself. I have found in this connection from decisive experience the superior happiness of the marriage state over that of celibacy, and a full conviction that my lot in marriage has been highly favored."

Louisa found her marriage a severe test after the freedom of her childhood. Throughout her fifty years with John Quincy, she never completely recovered from a sense of shame and guilt at her father's financial collapse in 1797, which, she felt, tainted her and her marriage. Her father's money problems gave the appearance of his having lured John Quincy, a promising young man, into marriage with his penniless daughter and then fleeing to the United States to escape his European creditors. Humiliated, Louisa sank into a depression that was followed by a physical illness — a pattern that repeated itself throughout her life.

Her depression and guilt were added to by the Adamses themselves. John Adams, while president, took a political risk and in 1800 appointed Louisa's father superintendent of the Stamp Office in the Department of the Treasury. On the strength of his generosity, a train of Johnsons, all of them Louisa's relatives, bothered members of the Adams family for loans of money, education funds, employment and other favors and support over the years.

The four years that Louisa and John Quincy spent in Berlin — her first time away from home — were the most difficult of her early years. She suffered several miscarriages and repeated illnesses that brought with them the "still greater torment" of having her husband impatiently standing about in "helpless solitude." Their first son, George Washington Adams, was born on April 12, 1801, in Berlin, a little more than a year after Washington's death. The birth was a difficult one for Louisa, but a proud moment for John Quincy. According to one account, John Quincy wrote his brother Thomas Boylston: "I was not induced merely by the public character of that great and good man to show his memory this token of respect. President Washington was, next to my own father, the man upon earth to whom I was indebted for the greatest personal obligations. I knew not whether upon rigorous philosophical principles it be wise to give a great and venerable name to such a lottery-ticket as a new-born infant — but my logical scruples have in this case been overpowered by my instinctive sentiments." The boy would find his famous name a heavy burden to bear.

While Louisa suffered in Berlin, John Quincy cultivated Prussian leaders and became a correct and pleasant diplomat. He studied German several hours a day and, to perfect himself, completed a poetic translation of Wieland's *Oberon*. He and Louisa did find time to enjoy the galleries of Dresden and to travel to Bohemia, Saxony and Silesia.

With her husband's recall, Louisa began to dread the inevitable first meeting with the Adamses in Quincy. She felt

As one of the American peace commissioners, John Quincy Adams helped negotiate the Treaty of Ghent ending the War
of 1812. This portrait of Adams (right),
wearing formal diplomatic dress, was
painted at Ghent in 1815. In his hand he
holds a scroll which reads: "Pacification of
Ghent, December 24, 1815." Over his left
shoulder are the tall gothic spires of the
town, one with a dragon at its pinnacle.
The 1815 portrait of Adams was later used
for the rendering of the signing of the
Treaty of Ghent (below).

JOHN QUINCY ADAMS. OIL BY
PIETER VAN HUFFEL, 1815

THE SIGNING OF THE TREATY OF GHENT. OIL BY SIR AMEDEE FORESTIER, 1914

inferior to this formidable family, and put off the encounter. When they landed, John Quincy headed for New England; Louisa went to Washington, D.C., to visit her parents.

John and Abigail Adams had retired in 1801 to Quincy, and Abigail's health continued to be a problem. She had written during the winter of 1801: "I cannot say that I have enjoy'd so much health this winter as the last. I am very frequently shut up, tho but for a few days at a time; I fancy we have too much damp here for Rhumatick Constitutions, but my constitution appears to have sufferd severely from the Ague and fever, and to be much broken by repeated attacks of an intermitting kind. I patch up, but it is hard work."

Practically all of Abigail Adams's remaining life would be spent at Quincy, where the years would pass as tranquilly "as that bald old fellow, called Time," would allow. She sometimes rose at five, and could be seen skimming the milk or padding about the house with her pet dog Juno. To her son, she wrote: "You will find your father in his fields, attending to his haymakers, and your mother busily occupied in the domestic concerns of her family."

It was this "family," in its specific personalities, that troubled Louisa. After visiting her parents — she extended her stay as long as she properly could — she headed northward in late November. She was sick in Philadelphia, where Dr. Benjamin Rush treated her, and again in New York, where Abigail Adams Smith took her in. When she finally reached Quincy, she found the social climate bleak and the Adams family terribly stiff. Such was the press of Adams relatives wanting to see her that she felt utterly overwhelmed. As she later wrote in her autobiographical sketch, "Adventures of a Nobody": "Had I step[p]ed into Noah's Ark I do not think I could have been more utterly astonished. Even the Church, its forms, the snuffling through the nose, the Singers, the dressing and the dinner hour were all novelties to me. . . . Do what I would there was a conviction on the parts of others that I could not *suit*. . . . I was literally and without knowing it a *fine* Lady." Particularly did Louisa feel unacceptable to her mother-in-law, whom she described as "the equal of every occasion in life."

Indeed, Abigail Adams found Louisa wanting. In letters

to Thomas Boylston and to her husband, she deplored Louisa's precarious health and questioned her ability to please John Quincy. But John Adams immediately took a liking to Louisa and she to him. She may have found him a warm refuge from the cold side of the Adams family, or a replacement for her own father, who had died in 1802. Whatever the reason, their fondness for each other found expression in their letters, and as late as 1839, Louisa wrote glowingly of John Adams: "Among all the great characters that it has been my lot to meet . . . I have never met with a mind of such varied powers, such acute discrimination, and which if I may use the expression, was so intrinsically *sound*; with a memory so fertile, so clear, and so perspicuous. Every thing in his mind was rich, racy and true." In 1824, John Adams wrote a friend that his son's marriage to Louisa Johnson was "the most important event" in John Quincy's life.

As Louisa and John Quincy settled into life in Boston, where he tried to resume his law practice, they faced several problems. For one, John Quincy's financial position was uncertain. His "Waste Book and Journal," which he had begun on New Year's Day in 1802, listed property valued at $43,702.54. Included were two houses in Boston, worth $5,000 and $6,000; $11,000 in eight-percent U.S. stocks; and a library worth $5,000. There was also $9,000 in uncollectable debts. But Adams, while overseas, had suffered setbacks: he had entrusted much of his savings to a friend to be invested in Boston real estate, and the money had drained away from mismanagement. In addition, between $6,000 and $10,000 had been squandered by his brother Charles. Later, both John Quincy and his father suffered serious financial calamity when the London banking house of Bird, Savage & Bird failed. The Adamses had money tied up in the firm, and it took several years — long after John Quincy had to sell his real estate and borrow against his own credit — before they were paid in full.

His tenuous financial position, and his distaste for the practice of law, caused John Quincy Adams some anxiety. Like his father, he needed time for reflection and took long walks in solitude. In his diary on January 28, 1802, he wrote: "Walked in the mall just before night. I feel strong temptation and have great provocation to plunge into political controversy. I hope to preserve myself from it by the considerations which have led me to the resolution of renouncing. A politician in this country must be the man of a party. I would fain be the man of my whole country."

John Quincy's first attempts at politics held small reward. Although elected to the state senate in April, 1802, "on the Federal list," he was defeated in his bid to gain a seat in the U.S. House of Representatives from his Boston district in November, 1802. He lost to William Eustis by 59 votes out of 3,739 cost. In a classical politician's lament, he said: "I had a majority of votes in Boston; but two or three neighboring towns annexed to the Congressional district and a rainy day lost me the election."

Better opportunities would come, but they would test this "man of my whole country." Although his independence was already well known, the Federalists selected him for a vacant U.S. Senate seat on February 8, 1803, taking him over Timothy Pickering, the fifty-eight-year-old former secretary of state who had been dismissed from office by John Quincy's father three years earlier. Only thirty-five, John Quincy Adams became U.S. senator from Massachusetts. But Pickering was not done for yet, and got himself chosen to fill another vacancy, thus putting the two wings of the Federalist Party of Massachusetts into the U.S. Senate at the same time.

The Federalists, in selecting John Quincy, had picked a maverick. As early as October 8, 1802, he had written to Rufus King that the Federalist Party was "completely and irrevocably abandoned and rejected by the popular voice. It never can and never will be revived. The experiment, such as it was, has failed, and to attempt its restoration would be as absurd as to undertake the resurrection of a carcase seven years in its grave."

Adams was correct in his assessment of the Federalists. They had gone out of power in 1801, and would never again win a national election. They had seen the republic through its early difficult moments, but they had also erred in their well-known conviction that the people were unfit to govern themselves. Swept from power by Republicans who, at the time, were more popular and trusted, they shriveled to clusters of embittered men, like the Essex Junto — a term that John Hancock had applied to Federalists in Essex County, Massachusetts, during the Revolutionary War, and that Thomas Jefferson gave to his abrasive New England opponents: Theophilus Parsons (John Quincy's law teacher), Senator Timothy Pickering, Fisher Ames, to name a few. But as John Quincy would soon learn, while the old dogs might not bite as hard, they could still bark loudly.

At that time any party embracing "the people" of the United States had time and space on its side. Between 1800 and 1810 Americans multiplied by twenty-five percent, to a population of 7,250,000. This number of people — only 2,000,000 of them were adults — had to expand, occupy and govern 880,000 square miles of land, which doubled with the Louisiana Purchase. They elected Thomas Jefferson and, in 1808, James Madison to preside over their "seedling democracy," which was, as the nineteenth century unfolded, just putting down firm roots.

Only one American out of twenty-five lived in the cities — that is, about 200,000 people. Most towns had volunteer fire departments, and Philadelphia even had public sewage and water systems by 1801. But garbage often went uncollected and stood in piles, which mixed with dust and dung in dry spells to raise a tangy odor. Washington was a swampy little village of small houses and dirt streets that turned to mud during rainfalls. Even by 1803, the Capitol could hardly contain the members of Congress, and most congressmen lived in shared rooms in "shabby boarding houses without privacy."

Outside the few cities, the American farmer still got low yields on his land, and crop rotation was seldom practiced. The iron-covered plowshare was just starting to be widely used, and corn, wheat and rye were fast becoming cash crops from Massachusetts to the Middle States. Cotton was growing up to be king in the South. Almost twenty-five percent of all laborers toiled in the textile industry. By working from sunup to sundown, a man could earn in 1815 between 80 cents (in rural areas) to $1.50 (in the cities) a day — and that might feed a family of six for three days.

Commerce, and the ceaseless push westward, brought a continuing need for roads. Crossing the Appalachians meant increased isolation from people and protection. Rivers and streams were major barriers: bridges anywhere were few. The cost of shipping goods was high and subject to the whim of the toll collector. Wagoners might pay ten cents a mile on toll roads; a ferryman might collect twenty-five cents for a wagon, or a hogshead. Nine dollars would ship a ton of produce from Europe, a journey of more than four thousand miles, but it would cost another nine dollars to move the same ton just thirty miles inland.

The country, isolated and vast, contained regional and economic interests remote from one another, separated by distance and outlook. To the varied interest groups of New England, the West, the South, the coastal regions, slavery was becoming an increasingly important concern. During the Jefferson and Madison administrations, as cotton production grew in the South, the market value of a top field hand doubled, from $400 to $800. Slavery was opposed by both presidents as well as by other southerners. The Constitution banned the importation of slaves after 1808.

Jefferson, a man of intelligence and peace, took over from John Adams a government in superb order. He appointed James Madison his secretary of state and Albert Gallatin, secretary of the treasury. Gallatin and Jefferson regarded the national debt as a mortgage, to be paid off quickly. They cut the army to $1.9 million, half the Federalist budget, and reduced its numbers to 3,350 officers and men. The navy budget dropped from $3.5 million to $1 million. Jefferson trimmed the U.S. legations at The Hague and Berlin.

Despite these cuts, Jefferson's first brilliant achievements came in war and diplomacy. He dispatched the American navy — a three-frigate coastal outfit that had the charming tradition of shifting commanding officers with each sailing season — to the coast of North Africa, some five thousand miles from home, to deal with the Barbary States, which had preyed upon U.S. shipping.

While the U.S. Navy was working the Barbary coast, Jefferson was also keeping an eye on Louisiana. The Mississippi River was vital to commerce in the American West, and as more Americans pushed westward, the importance of the river increased. Inhabitants of the Ohio Valley were annually transshipping a million dollars worth of produce to New Orleans. Pinckney's Treaty of 1795 had guaranteed to U.S. citizens the right of deposit of their goods in the city of New Orleans, but in 1802, when the king of Spain withdrew this right, U.S. citizens became alarmed.

Although western congressmen, and Federalists seeking to undermine Jefferson, offered resolutions for the occupation of New Orleans, the president waited. He calculated that Napoleon's interest in America and in the Mississippi Valley, which had been taken by treaty from Spain, would diminish as the prospects of war between England and France increased. And when Jefferson heard that Napoleon might finance a renewed war with England — by selling New Orleans and the Floridas to the United States — he immediately sent James Monroe to France as minister plenipotentiary to assist Robert R. Livingston with negotiations. On April 11, 1803, when Livingston, who had already begun parleying, approached Talleyrand with the usual offer for New Orleans, the French foreign minister reportedly asked: "What will you give for the whole of Louisiana?"

An agreement was reached so quickly that Monroe arrived in Paris only in time to help with the final papers. The price was $6 million and the terms were easy: in six-percent U.S. bonds redeemed at $3 million a year starting in 1818; the United States also assumed payment of claims its citizens held against France for past spoliation of commerce. Napoleon sold the bonds to London bankers for the cash he needed to equip an army against England.

No one was sure what the boundaries of the new purchase might be; only the Spanish government could document that — and their definition would remain for the future. Livingston and Monroe studied the boundaries and finally agreed, unilaterally, that at one end of the vast purchase the United States owned sand and marshland lying south of 31 degrees and running from New Orleans to the Perdido River, the present western boundary of Florida. It included 50,000 new citizens and some 150,000 Indians.

Jefferson, who had never been west of Monticello by more than fifty miles, encouraged exploration of the western

BOTANICAL SPECIMENS COLLECTED
BY LEWIS AND CLARK

CALIFORNIA CONDOR FROM LEWIS'S JOURNAL

part of the territory. The expedition of Meriwether Lewis and William Clark (1804–1806) went to the Pacific and back by the Missouri and Columbia rivers at a total cost of $22,393.51. Dr. Benjamin Rush, who treated the Adamses, provided for the health of the expedition with a helpful list of rules that included: "10. Lying down when fatigued." Only one man died during the entire trip.

In the fall of 1803, the question of the Louisiana Purchase was being hotly debated in Washington. Senator John Quincy Adams and his family arrived too late for him to vote on the Louisiana treaties during the special session called by the president. Their overland journey from Quincy had been arduous: Louisa had given birth on July 4, 1803, to their second son, John Adams II, and the trip especially exhausted and troubled her.

Adams immediately plunged into the controversy. The New England Federalists, led by the Essex Junto, vehemently opposed the Purchase. Fisher Ames proclaimed that "the acquiring of territory with money is mean and despicable." Adams, on the other hand, supported the Constitution and the Union, and if buying Louisiana kept Napoleon out of the Mississippi Valley and opened the West to commerce, well and good.

Adams made proposals to the Congress about the Purchase, voted for the financial measures to complete the acquisition, supported the purchase of the territory, and even joined a Republican celebration banquet. He had, much to the notice and chagrin of the Federalists, become a nationalist in outlook and interest, and in 1804 his father wrote him in support: "I do not disapprove of your conduct in the business of Louisiana. I think you have been right, though I know it will become a very unpopular subject in the Northern States."

The Federalists and the Essex Junto labeled John Quincy undependable and erratic. "Like a Kite without a Tail," complained the Boston banker Stephen Higginson, "he will be violent and constant in his attempts to rise . . . and will pitch on one side and the other, as the popular Currents may happen to strike, without soaring to his intended point. His views are ambitious, even to the Chair of State." And another wrote to Timothy Pickering, "Curse on the stripling, how he apes his sire." The *Worcester Aegis* proclaimed in its December 4, 1803, issue: "The Hon. John Quincy Adams will certainly be denounced and excommunicated by his party. On the leading questions in the Senate he has acted and voted with the friends of the Administration."

Senator Adams found Washington politics as swampy as the land, and he frequently returned to Quincy for chats with his father (and mother), and relief from the heat of the capital. In 1803, he bought from his father the original Penn's Hill farm, and began enjoying his summers there between the two old houses. Abigail kept a maternal eye on John Quincy, nursing his colds and illnesses by letters filled with home remedies for diet and exercise. She told him to "unbend in company" and relax. "You must not let the mind wear so much upon the body," she scolded. "You eat too little and study too much."

She also told him how to dress for the Senate. "Now I hope you never appear in the Senate with a beard two days old, or otherwise make what is called a shabby appearance. Seriously I think a man's usefulness in society depends much upon his personal appearance. I do not wish a Senator to dress like a beau, but I want him to conform so far to the fashion, as not to incur the character of singularity, nor give occasion to the world to ask what kind of mother he had or to charge upon a wife negligence and inattention when she is guiltless. The neatest man, observed a Lady the other day, wants his wife to pull up his coller, and mind that his coat is brush'd."

Life in the U.S. Senate was not all neat dress and hard work. Although two years remained of his term as senator, and Louisa sometimes went horseback riding together, or he swam in the Potomac. Washington was a dull town; what little amusement there was came from dinners and other social events. The Adamses entertained and dined out. In 1806, one guest was Thomas Moore, a melancholy versemaker of the day who is best remembered for "The Last Rose of Summer." Louisa recalled: "I heard him sing many of his Songs and two or three Evenings sang with him. He said that I sang delightfully but I wanted *Soul*."

Dinners with President Jefferson were filled with politics and fun, and John Quincy enjoyed them as he had during his boyhood in Paris. Jefferson could indeed tell "large stories." He teased the senator by claiming to have learned Spanish in nineteen days during a voyage to Europe. And he declared that during his winters in Paris the temperature reached 20 degrees below zero Fahrenheit and remained so for six weeks without relief. Adams was appropriately skeptical.

Despite his friendship with the president, Adams worried about his own career in politics. As the Federalists continued attacking his positions on various issues, he wrote, on the last day of 1804, "My political prospects have been daily declining." Then, in 1805, Harvard University offered him the first Boylston professorship of rhetoric and oratory. He accepted it and excitedly began planning seven years of scholarly work. Although two years remained of his term as senator, Adams anticipated leaving the arena. As he wrote to Louisa a few months later: "The term of my public service will soon be at an end, and in the present condition of politics in this state, as well as almost all the rest, there is no danger that when my time expires I shall have the opportunity to continue in public life." He would bid, as his father had, "Farewell [to] Politicks." Looking to the future he purchased a house in Boston for $15,000. He knew that to be reelected in 1809 he would need to win the endorsement of the Federalist Party by playing Federalist politics and compromising his beliefs. This he refused to do. Furthermore, his break with the Federalists and the Essex Junto over Louisiana was soon intensified by the increasing hostilities between England and the United States. While the Federalists sought closer relations with England, Adams remained firm in his devotion to the Union. Like his father, he would be always a man not of party, but of the whole nation.

When Jefferson took office for his second term in 1805, elected by an overwhelming majority, Napoleon was entrenched on the Continent and Britain was in control of the seas. Each side sought to starve or strangle the other by blockade. In attempting to keep the United States neutral, Jefferson found himself dealing with two antagonists at once.

Until 1807, his primary problem came from British sea power. Severe treatment in the Royal Navy caused a high degree of desertion, and British seamen were constantly jumping over to the American merchant marine and navy. The British determined to take them back, and as early as 1803, New York harbor was blockaded by British ships seeking to halt and impress seamen from American ships. At sea, and even along the American coast, when a shorthanded British man-of-war stopped an American ship, lads were taken for service in the Royal Navy at the whim of the British boarding party. With the renewal of war in Europe, impressment off the American coast increased. The total number has been hard to come by, but one study indicates that between 1793 and 1811, some 9,991 Americans were impressed.

Impressment was only the most obvious issue. At the same time, as American trade was thriving, the question of neutral rights arose again. American tonnage tripled between 1790 and 1810; its value for the twelve years from 1800 to 1812 would not be equaled again during the century. New York and New England together put to sea almost half as much tonnage as all of Great Britain. To do this, America had 65,000 seamen; its shipbuilders yearly constructed 70,000 tons of shipping.

Neutral trade was highly lucrative, and the British admiralty soon began denouncing American ships that landed French colonial produce in the United States, largely from the West Indies, reloaded it to escape customs duties, and hauled it to European ports that were under Napoleon's rule. Reexporting in the maritime United States quadrupled, and the British courts tried to stop it by arguing that the voyage was continuous and not broken by its pause on some American dock, that the Americans were really moving enemy property between enemy ports.

Negotiations with the British over this matter foundered, and impressment was marked by outrage after outrage. Vice-Admiral George C. Berkeley, who commanded the Royal Navy in American waters, was bothered by the continuing desertions from his forces. He ordered HMS *Leopard* into action, and on June 22, 1807, the *Leopard* began tracking the USS *Chesapeake* out of Norfolk Roads, Virginia. The *Leopard* signaled "Dispatches" and the commander of the *Chesapeake* came about, believing that the British wanted him to take on mail for Europe, a courtesy shared by the two navies during these years. But the British sent over a boarding party that carried orders from Admiral Berkeley to seach for deserters. The American commander refused to allow the search, the British boarding party was recalled, and eight minutes later the *Leopard* boomed three full broadsides into the *Chesapeake*. The American ship, its deck littered with stores and its guns unmounted, took a ripping: twenty-one Americans were injured. Splintered, she struck her colors and limped back to port.

The American outrage was immediate; anger spread throughout the country, and newspaper editors called for war. Congress might have given the president war in 1807 — and war at that time might have been more popular and successful than in 1812 — but Jefferson remained calm. He instructed James Monroe, the American minister in London, to demand apologies and reparations, and ordered British warships out of American waters. But British commanders contested the weaker U.S. Navy by anchoring in Chesapeake Bay, impressing sailors within U.S. harbors, and cannonading the Maine coast. In October, Congress appropriated $4 million for gunboats, forts, weapons, and eight regular regiments, and ordered the three U.S. frigates into port for arming.

Instead of attacking the British, Jefferson and the Congress embargoed America. In April, 1806, Congress had passed the Non-Importation Act, and when Jefferson in December, 1807, asked for an embargo act, Congress passed that, too. These acts prohibited all exports from the United States, they forbade American vessels to clear for foreign ports, and they refused entry to certain British manufactures. For fourteen months, all American ships not already abroad, or that could not escape, lay up in port.

During these events, John Quincy Adams joined other senators in protest against British impressment. He prepared resolutions declaring that captures of cargoes and vessels by England were an "unprovoked aggression" and a violation of American neutrality, and called upon President Jefferson to "demand and insist upon" restoration and indemnity. Further, Adams was the only Federalist in Congress to vote for non-importation.

These positions by the Massachusetts senator again

angered the New England Federalists, who preferred things as they were — even impressment — rather than a break with England. When the *Leopard–Chesapeake* affair occurred, Adams proposed that the Federalists express their displeasure in a town meeting in Boston. But they hesitated, and when the Republican citizens of that city held a mass meeting with neighboring towns, John Quincy joined them. His split with the Federalists was complete. As he himself wrote in 1820: "The really important period of my life began with the British attack upon our *Chesapeake* frigate, in the Summer of 1807."

As a man experienced in diplomacy and foreign affairs, Adams soon found himself in the center of a growing national controversy. But he was without a party and was watched suspiciously by the Republicans in Washington. He and Madison, the Republican secretary of state, agreed on most issues, and their respect for one another, and their friendship, grew. It was a fortunate connection: Madison would soon be president. Still, in 1807, adrift between parties, John Quincy wrote once again: "My political prospects are declining, and as my term of service draws near its close, I am constantly approaching to the certainty of being restored to the situation of a private citizen."

The Essex Junto and the arch-Federalists in New England saw the embargo as treacherous, and they grumbled about secession in 1808 and 1809. The embargo had little impact on Great Britain except to hurt some English workingmen by raising farm prices. In effect, it gave England a gift of monopoly over world oceanic trade. There was little impact on France either. Napoleon, vowing that "he would have no neutrals," issued his Bayonne Decree of April 17, 1808, arguing that American ships appearing in European ports would henceforth be considered as having arrived from British ports. American ships now had to dodge both French and British interceptors.

In America, however, the embargo had severe effect. Many American farm prices dropped, especially that of cotton. Mortgages were foreclosed, and speculators held commodities for the juiciest price fluctuations. Recorded exports dropped 80 percent in 1808.

"OH! THIS CURSED OGRABME." CARTOON BY ALEXANDER ANDERSON, 1813

Handbills jabbed with blunt humor at early-nineteenth-century issues. Readers understood the bitten smuggler's protest, "Ograbme," when they read it backwards. At right, William Pitt helps himself to a large cut of the Americas while Napoleon slices up Europe.

GERMAN CARTOON ABOUT ENGLISH-FRENCH RELATIONS, 1805

Little wonder, then, that the New England Federalists attacked John Quincy Adams. Their region, so dependent upon maritime commerce, was especially hurt. The Essex Junto quickly renewed correspondence with their English contacts, and a British agent, John Henry, traveled throughout New England in 1809 talking publicly of neutrality — and in private of secession.

John Adams supported his son's actions, advising him "steadily to pursue the course you are in, with moderation and caution, however, because I think it the path of justice." When the Federalists howled at his son, John Adams wrote: "Parton has denounced you as No Federalist, and I wish he would denounce me in the same manner, for I have long since renounced, abdicated, and disclaimed the Name and Character and Attributes of that Sect, as it now appears."

Without warning, but with ample reason, the Federalists dumped John Quincy from office. The Massachusetts legislature met at the end of May, 1808, and voted 248 to 213, to replace him with James Lloyd, Jr., in the U.S. Senate. This was six months before the vote normally would have been taken, and the rebuke was further accompanied by instructions to the Massachusetts senators in Washington to vote for repeal of the embargo. Adams noted in his diary that the vote in the legislature was done with the purpose "of specially marking me." He resigned from the Senate on June 8, 1808, and his fearful premonitions about politics appeared to be coming true.

Adams returned to Boston to practice law (his Harvard appointment had ended). By way of rebuttal, he published in early 1809 in the *Boston Patriot* a searing analysis of Fisher Ames's political philosophy. Jefferson left office that same year a hounded and disappointed man. He had pursued a bloodless solution for war, and ended up without peace. The embargo, as President Madison soon learned, was a failure, which left hard choices: submission to further British maritime wishes, persuasion that French decrees no longer mattered — or war.

Between 1807 and 1812, the French seized more American ships than the British did. The British continued grabbing American sailors, including former British subjects, and defended their right to do so with the argument that birth was undeniable and carried perpetual obligation to serve the Crown. Adams argued that expatriation was a natural right — a point he had learned while studying under the Federalist Theophilus Parsons. But there would be no debating this issue any longer. As George III sank deeper into permanent illness (he would die on January 29, 1820), the British foreign ministry became more intractable and indolent, refusing to change or reexamine any policy.

On March 6, 1809, Adams was in Washington to argue the case *Fletcher* v. *Peck* before the Supreme Court. At breakfast, word came that President Madison wanted to see him. When Adams reached the President's House, he found Madison in a hurry: would Adams accept the post of minister plenipotentiary to Russia? Madison already had his name on a list to be submitted in half an hour to Congress. Adams wrote in his diary, "I could see no sufficient reason for refusing the nomination."

The Senate delayed confirmation — debating the expediency of the post — until June, when Napoleonic rumblings in Europe made the contact with Russia attractive. Adams was confirmed, 19 to 7; all five Federalist senators, and two Republicans, opposed him.

At sea, aboard the *Horace*, Adams had time to pursue a regular schedule. He read his Bible, sometimes as many as fifteen chapters a day; he walked the deck and at noon took a bearing with a quadrant. Afterwards, he would "read or write in the cabin until two. Dine. After dinner read or write again; occasionally visiting the deck for a walk until seven in the evening. Sup. Read or play at cards till eleven or twelve, when we all retire to bed. There is much time for study and for meditation at sea."

There was time, too, to look back over the turbulent last few years. In a letter to a friend, former Senator William Plumer, who planned to write a history of the United States, Adams suggested: "I hope, that the *moral* of your history will be the indissoluble union of the North American continent."

The Adamses arrived in St. Petersburg on October 23, 1809. They entered Russia during the colorful and dramatic time of Tsar Alexander I—the exact period of Tolstoy's *War and Peace*. Alexander, a warm and congenial man, had gained the throne in 1801 and was to hold it for twenty-five years. When John Quincy was formally presented to him on November 5, the tsar was just past thirty and Adams was forty-two. Besides their meetings at official functions, the two became acquainted informally through their common pleasure in walking. In St. Petersburg, Adams kept up his early-morning routine of reading the Bible (in both French and German) and writing, and then went out for a constitutional, usually to the local foundry. He and the tsar met frequently and conversed in French. The tsar confessed that he sometimes did not recognize the bald-headed Adams outdoors without his wig. On one occasion, he spoke with "good humor" about Adams's financial problems. The court at St. Petersburg was the most lavish in Europe, and the American minister's low salary created for Adams "temptations to excess" that amounted "almost to compulsion." The Adamses had to house and feed twenty-one servants, plus their wives and children. "I have baker's, milkman's, butcher's, greenman's, poulterer's, fishmonger's, and grocer's bills to pay monthly, besides purchases of tea, coffee, sugar, wax and tallow candles. The firewood is, luckily, included as part of my rent." Adams was offered money by other diplomats and special-interest seekers in St. Petersburg, and he found it "difficult to resist the opportunities this presented . . . but I am determined to do it." He felt it important to live within his income, however frugal his life might be made, and found this rule "the first and most important principle of private economy." He rejected these temptations, and hoped "for firmness of character to withstand them in future."

Adams and the tsar found their walks and chats leading to a trustful friendship, which spilled over to include the Russian foreign minister, Count Nicholas Rumyantsev. Although they rarely discussed official business, their relationship opened the door to peace when events in Europe and the United States turned toward war.

By 1812, France's continental system was choking Russia's economy, and Napoleon's soldiers were about to march. Some 500,000 French troops were massed along the Russian border; Tsar Alexander could mobilize only 200,000 men, and counted (correctly, as it turned out) on distance, time and climate for his victory. On March 19, 1812, Adams watched Russian regiments marching out of St. Petersburg as he walked off his 120 steps a minute. He met the tsar, who confided somberly: "And so it is, after all, that war is coming which I have done so much to avoid — everything. I have done everything to prevent this struggle. . . . but thus it ends."

The French occupied Moscow during the fall of 1812, but the tsar's troops stiffened, and on October 27, Moscow was retaken; the cannon in St. Petersburg boomed out the joyful news. Napoleon's forces began their fatal winter retreat across Russia's vastness.

Meanwhile, the United States and England were also at war. To Madison war had seemed the only honorable alternative if American neutral rights were to be protected. Ironically, Britain had yielded to American pressure and repealed its Orders in Council just a few days before the unknowing American government declared war. On the same day the St. Petersburg cannon carried good news, Adams learned of the British capture of Fort Detroit; the news from home was bad. The American army had fewer than twenty-four regiments, and the British were pushing them around at will. By spring, Adams heard of defeat in Canada. At sea, the United States put out its three "superfrigates," which were larger and more heavily armed than their British counterparts, thirteen lesser vessels and 185 privateers. Battles raged along the coast and as far away as West Africa and Brazil. The USS *Constitution* sank the frigate HMS *Java*, and Adams entered in his diary: "further disasters by land, and successes upon the sea."

At this time, Adams's diplomacy in Russia paid off. The situation was delicate: Russia, fighting the French, remained close to England, which was at war with America. But Tsar Alexander, through his foreign minister, Count Rumyantsev, offered to mediate between the United States and England — an offer made, in part, because of his closeness to John Quincy Adams. President Madison, watching Napoleon's disasters in the field (which strengthened Britain's hand) and faced with losses at home, eagerly accepted. Albert Gallatin and James A. Bayard were quickly dispatched to Russia to join Adams and be ready for negotiations — a fact Adams learned from the American newspaper *National Intelligencer*.

The door to peace was opening — slowly. Gallatin and Bayard arrived in St. Petersburg in July, 1813, and waited. Meanwhile, Lord Castlereagh, the British foreign secretary, twice rejected Russia's offer to mediate, and the tsar, perhaps absorbed with battles on the German front or embarrassed at his failure, did not inform the Americans of the rejections until January, 1814. Bayard and Gallatin, hoping to do better on their own, left for Amsterdam, where they learned that President Madison had accepted Lord Castlereagh's proposal for direct negotiations, and had appointed a new peace commission.

By April 1, 1814, the news that he had been appointed one of the commissioners reached Adams in St. Petersburg. He regarded the mission as one of major import: "On the providence of God alone is my reliance. . . . The welfare of my family and country, with the interests of humanity, are staked upon the event. To Heaven alone it must be committed." Leaving his wife and son in St. Petersburg, he set out at once for Ghent in Flanders (now Belgium).

He and most of the American delegation arrived there in late June. The five men represented the various sectional interests in the United States at that time: Albert Gallatin, secretary of the treasury; James Bayard, a Federalist from Delaware; Henry Clay, of Kentucky, who was Speaker of the House of Representatives; and Jonathan Russell, the youngest delegate and the first American ambassador to Sweden. The five waited, not a little impatiently, almost six weeks for the British to arrive. Gallatin soon proved to be the leader of the group. Clay probably preferred to be in Kentucky smoking cigars, swigging bourbon, and playing poker. Adams, whose regime and constitution drove him to rise early and write by candlelight, stayed aloof. He dined alone at one, the others dined together at four. He also remained unsullied: "They sit after dinner and drink bad wine and smoke cigars, which neither suits my habits nor my health, and absorbs time which I cannot spare. I find it impossible, even with the most rigorous economy of time, to do half the writing that I ought."

The British commissioners, when they finally appeared for the first meeting on August 8, 1814, were a cut below the Americans in diplomatic ability: Admiral Lord Gambier, described by Bayard as "wellbred, affable and amiable"; Dr. William Adams, an admiralty lawyer; and the "quick-tempered, fidgety" Henry Goulburn, a member of Parliament. The British first-string team was back in London, preoccupied with the opening of the peace conference in Vienna that would settle the European situation. Napoleon's defeat had removed England's enemy on the Continent, and regiments of her crack troops were sailing for the United States, where the war was going very well indeed for the British. Time was on their side, and to Lord Castlereagh and the government in London, negotiations at Vienna were the focus, Ghent the periphery.

From the beginning, the British at Ghent took a hard line and made extreme demands. They insisted on an Indian buffer territory north of the Ohio River, abandonment of U.S. rights to the Atlantic fisheries off Newfoundland and Labrador, and revision of the boundary line between British Canada and the United States that would give Canada access to the upper Mississippi. The reasons for the War of 1812 — impressment of seamen, blockades, freedom of the sea for neutral ships — they completely ignored.

John Quincy Adams, an experienced diplomatist, thought negotiations would break off at this point. But Clay the cardplayer and the others thought the British might be bluffing. The Americans, cautiously but firmly, held their ground. And the British, slowly but surely, shifted theirs. The negotiations soon took the form of memorandums exchanged between the two sides, and time dragged, for the British sent everything back to London for consideration.

With little to do — meetings were held in the afternoons, communiqués were exchanged slowly during the fall — the Americans turned to what appeared to Adams to be a frivolous social life. Clay gave card parties in his room, which was unfortunately near Adams's: "Just before rising, I hear Mr. Clay's company retiring from his chamber." And: "There was another card-party in Mr. Clay's chamber last night, and I heard Mr. Bentzon retiring from it after I had risen this morning." Adams, however, wasn't so stiff that he couldn't find time to attend a large tea and card party. The affair "became a ball," and he played whist with some ladies. He also confessed: "I danced part of a Boulangère."

The American commissioners knew that the British were stalling for time and with good reason. News from the United States was encouraging to the British but disheartening to the Americans. The British were marching across the eastern seaboard. That August, they had taken Washington, D.C., driving Madison and his administration out and burning the President's House and the Capitol. The Virginia militia had folded in the field. At Baltimore, on August 25 and 26, the Marylanders had stood firm, however, and a naval bombardment of Fort McHenry inspired scores of Americans including a young lyricist named Francis Scott Key. In the late fall, a British expeditionary force sailed from Jamaica for New Orleans, with the intention of seizing control of the Mississippi River. After an initial engagement just before Christmas, they were defeated on New Year's Day by troops under General Andrew Jackson. Meanwhile, the Essex Junto was meeting with delegates from the New England states at the Hartford Convention, where there was open talk of secession.

The formal exchanges between the British and the Americans at Ghent seemed to go nowhere. There were at least six, and John Quincy Adams cared for none of them: "We received this day [October 22] the fifth note from the British Plenipotentiaries. It has the same dilatory and insidious character as their preceding notes, but is shorter."

At one point the British wanted to settle things on the basis of where the opposing armies stood at that time, which would have required the Americans to surrender eastern Maine and other United States territory. Adams vigorously opposed this ploy. The British also wanted navigation rights to the Mississippi River, and became stubborn over the offshore fisheries question. But where Adams was willing to grant the right of navigation on the Mississippi, his opponent Clay was "earnest in defence of it." And where Adams was firm about American fishing rights, Clay was "willing to leave the matter of the fisheries as a nest-egg for another war, but to make the peace without saying anything about it. . . . Mr. Clay considers this fishery as an object of trifling amount." Adams went on to note: "Mr. Clay is losing his temper and growing peevish and fractious. I, too, must not forget to keep a constant guard upon my temper." But his guard was not good enough, and explosions between Adams and Clay often had to be settled by Gallatin.

Despite their differences, the Americans decided in November, 1814, to put together a strong treaty. They wrote and argued and rewrote for ten days — and it was rejected. But rather than despair, they agreed to follow Clay, the Kentucky poker player, and try a bluff. Clay "was for playing *brag* [poker] with the British Plenipotentiaries; they had been playing *brag* with us throughout the whole negotiation; he thought it was time for us to begin to play *brag* with them. He asked me if I knew how to play *brag*. I had forgotton how. He said the art of it was to beat your adversary by holding your hand, with a solemn and confident phiz, and outbragging him."

So the Americans held their hands, and stood firm on the negotiations. In the end, the United States was able to keep the territory she had held before the war began, and gained peace. Since England was exhausted by the long war on two continents, Lord Castlereagh was understandably unwilling to break off negotiations over territory in North America and was worried over events at Vienna. He sent word to his commissioners to put together their agreements and sign the treaty. At last hostilities ended — although the Battle of New Orleans would be fought in January, 1815, before word of the peace reached the United States. The terms of the treaty called for return to prewar boundaries. Decisions on the fisheries and the navigation of the Mississippi were postponed. Four boundary commissions were set up to determine the line between Canada and the United States. But if the *brag* worked at all, it did so in the sense that the five Americans resisted British efforts to carve into the territory of their country by changing frontiers or establishing Indian barrier states in the Midwest. The Treaty of Ghent kept the West open, and made expansion to the Pacific Ocean possible.

On Christmas Eve, 1814, the envoys signed the peace. In

In August, 1814, British forces
shelled and fired Washington, D.C.
This British rendering shows the
attackers' cannon (at A) above the
American fleet (D), which is sinking in smoke and flame. The Senate
(L), the Treasury (M), the President's House (K) and the docks are
are all on fire. The Patent Office
was spared only after its American
superintendent protested (below).
When the British reached Baltimore and Fort McHenry (below,
bottom) they met stubborn resistance. In this engraving by an
eyewitness, the American flag still
waves above the bombardment of
the fort, seen from Federal Hill,
Baltimore.

CAPTURE OF THE CITY OF WASHINGTON. COLORED
ENGRAVING FROM RAPIN'S "HISTORY OF ENGLAND," 1815

A VIEW OF THE BOMBARDMENT OF FORT MCHENRY.
AQUATINT BY JOHN BOWER, 1814

THE TAKING OF THE CITY OF WASHINGTON
IN AMERICA. BRITISH ENGRAVING, 1814

his diary that night, Adams added: "I cannot close the record of this day without an humble offering to God for the conclusion to which it has pleased him to bring the negotiations for peace at this place, and a fervent prayer that its result may be propitious to the welfare, the best interests and the union of my country."

The Treaty of Ghent was quickly ratified in London, but by the time it reached Washington, the British had been thrown back at New Orleans, their commander killed in Andrew Jackson's victory on January 1, 1815. By the middle of February, Congress ratified the treaty and President Madison proclaimed peace.

As for the commissioners, Gallatin went to Paris as minister plenipotentiary. Adams was seeking a new assignment. Bayard, asked to take the post in Russia, declined because of failing health (he died in August). Clay returned to the United States, and as Speaker of the House continued his arguments with Adams. Russell returned to Sweden; he, too, would soon become Adams's antagonist.

His duty done, Adams went to Paris to await final word of ratification by the Congress. On January 20, 1815, he wrote Louisa, who had remained in St. Petersburg: "I . . . now invite you to break up altogether our establishment at St. Petersburg, to dispose of all the furniture which you do not incline to keep, to have all the rest packed up carefully, and left in the charge of Mr. Harris to be sent next summer either to London or to Boston, and to come with Charles to me at Paris, where I shall be impatiently waiting for you."

Louisa Adams was stunned. It was winter in Russia. How would she manage? "I know not what to do about the selling of the goods and I fear I shall be much imposed upon." But she would do as she was told. Her life in Russia had been hard and lonely. She had given birth to a daughter, who had lived only a year. The baby had been buried in St. Petersburg and would now be left behind in Russia's "inhospitable clime."

Having followed her instructions as best she could, she engaged two coaches. At five o'clock in the evening of February 12, 1815, she and her seven-year-old son Charles Francis set out across the winter wastelands of Russia and eastern Europe for Paris. At first, they traveled by carriage on runners instead of wheels, for the snow. Louisa's French maid, Madame Babet, rode with them. Behind, in a *kibitka*, followed two menservants, who were armed.

Their food froze solid in the cold winter weather; "even the Madeira wine had become solid ice." The carriage sank so deeply into the snow on occasion that local people had to be summoned to dig it out with pickaxes and shovels. They got lost at night beyond Mitau, and "jolted over hills, through swamps and holes, and into valleys into which no carriage had surely ever passed before." Through it all, Charles Francis "lay sweetly sleeping on his little bed in the front of the carriage." To cross the frozen Vistula into Poland, they hired men to walk ahead of the carriage and horses with poles to test the ice, and although they reached the other side safely "the ice had given way on the border, and it required a violent effort in the horses to prevent the coach from upsetting on the bank."

In Poland, they could travel in wheeled carriages, and once the fore wheel of Louisa's carriage "fell to pieces." The only help was from a "dirty, ugly and ill-natured" woman and "two or three very surly, ill-looking men" near "a hovel, consisting of two rooms and a blacksmith's shop." They would fix the carriage wheel, they said, but — as at all repair shops — it would take time. Louisa reluctantly took one of the two rooms in the hovel and brought in Charles Francis's bed; she ordered one servant to sleep in the carriage to guard it, and the other to post himself outside her door. Through the night, "my woman and I sat up, neither of us feeling very secure." The next morning the wheel was ready, and although "clumsy and not painted," it worked well enough for them to proceed to Berlin.

It had been fourteen years since Louisa had been in Berlin, "and youth seemed again to be decked with rosy smiles and glad anticipation." The city appeared "much as I had left it . . . excepting the manners and dress of the people. All the nationality of the costume had disappeared, and French was almost universally spoken." Still, Louisa noted with pleasure, "the beautiful Linden Strasse, the fine Brandenburg gates, the bridges, the palaces, all spoke of the former times; but yet it was cold and flat and dull, and there was a foreign air about it

RETURN OF BONAPARTE, MARCH 20, 1815. ENGRAVED BY COUCHE FILS

which dampened the pleasure I felt in revisiting the scenes of my youth."

The royal family greeted her warmly. Countess Pauline de Neale "flew to meet" her. "The Princess Ferdinand invited me to dine and the Princess Louisa [Radziwill] invited me to pass every evening at her palace. . . . My friends greeted me with the most unaffected warmth and my reception was that of a separated and beloved sister."

In her account, Louisa recalled an unusual event that occurred in St. Petersburg just before she left. She had called upon the Countess Colombe to "take tea" and found with her a Russian lady, the Countess Apraxin, "a fat, coarse woman" who had arrived uninvited several days earlier. Because Louisa was going on a journey, Countess Apraxin insisted on reading her fortune. Louisa agreed, drew "a Queen" from a pack of cards, and was told, first, that she was glad to be leaving St. Petersburg (embarrassingly true); then that she would soon see her loved ones, and that "when I had achieved about half of my journey I should be much alarmed by a great change in the political world, in consequence of some extraordinary movement of a great character, which would produce utter consternation and set all Europe into violent commotion; that this circumstance which I should hear of on the road would necessitate a change in my plan, cause me great inconvenience, and render my journey very difficult, but that after all I should find my husband well, and that we should have a joyous meeting after so long an absence."

After five days in Berlin, her journey half over, Louisa started for Paris. Heading toward Frankfurt, she passed the horrible battlefields: "We entered on a wide extended plain, over which, as far as the eye could reach, were scattered remnants of boots, clothes, and hats or caps, with an immense quantity of bones bleaching in all directions in a field which appeared to have been newly ploughed. My heart throbbed and I felt a sensation of deadly sickness with a fear that I should faint, guessing where I was, when the postilions pointed to a board indicating that this was the famous battle where the Bavarians had turned upon Napoleon, and 10,000 men were left upon the ensanguined plain. Conceive my horror at the loathing sight of such a butchery! My spirit

While John Quincy Adams was in Paris, and Louisa Catherine Adams (and her son Charles Francis, age seven) were crossing the wintry landscape of eastern Europe, Napoleon returned triumphantly to France. His enemies mobilized their troops, and the countryside became dangerous to travelers. On March 20, 1815, at the Tuileries in Paris, Napoleon's soldiers lifted him to their shoulders in celebration (left).

sank within me and I asked, Lord, what is man that he should thus destroy?"

Outside Frankfurt, Louisa began hearing the first rumors — at Eisenach and then at Hanau — that Napoleon had returned from Elba to France. The Countess Apraxin's prophecy was coming true. German soldiers began gathering along the road, and the countryside was in turmoil. At Frankfurt, her two menservants, fearful of having to join the French army, refused to continue to Paris. Louisa engaged a "Prussian lad of fourteen," who fortunately "proved very smart and active." They hurried toward Paris — from Strassburg, where she was warned against going on; to Nancy, where "the square was full of [French] troops, who were mustering to make preparations for joining the Emperor"; to Château-Thierry and Epernay.

"We had gone about a mile and a half when we suddenly found ourselves in the midst of the Imperial Guards, who were on their way to meet the Emperor. The first notice I had of my danger was hearing the most horrid curses and dreadful language from a number of women, who appeared to be following the troops. Madame Babet was as pale as death and trembled excessively. Presently I heard these wretches cry out: 'Tear them out of the carriage, they are Russians, take them out, kill them.' At this moment a party of the soldiers seized hold of the horses and turned their guns against the drivers. I sat in agony of apprehension, but had presence of mind enough to take out my passports. A general officer, with his staff, consisting of four or five, immediately rode up to the carriage and addressed me. I presented my passports and he called out that I was an American lady going to meet her husband in Paris, at which the soldiers shouted 'Vive les Américains' — and desired that I should cry 'Vive Napoléon!' which I did, waving my handkerchief; they repeated their first cry, adding 'ils sont nos amis.' A number of soldiers were ordered to march before the horses, and if we attempted to push on out of a walk, the order was to fire on us directly. The General and his suite rode on each side of the carriage. He told me my situation was a very precarious one; the army was totally undisciplined, that they would not obey a single order; that I must appear perfectly easy and unconcerned;

and whenever they shouted I must repeat the 'Vives.' That when we arrived at the post house he would use his influence with the lady of the house to admit me to pass the night, and advised that the next morning I should delay my departure until the troops had all passed, and then take a circuitous route to Paris; as the whole army would be in motion to greet the Emperor. . . .

"He complimented me on the manner of my speaking French, and said that my perfect knowledge of the language would contribute much to my safety, as no one would believe me to be a foreigner. My poor boy seemed to be absolutely petrified, and sat by my side like a marble statue. God in His great mercy seemed to give me strength in this trying emergency; for excepting a heightened and glowing color in my cheeks there was no evidence of fear or trepidation; yet my heart might have been heard to beat, as its convulsive throbbings heaved against my side. In this way we journeyed; the soldiers presenting their bayonets at my people with loud and brutal threats every half hour. The road [was] lined on each side for miles with intoxicated men, rife for every species of villainy, shouting and vociferating: 'A bas Louis dix huit! vive Napoléon!' "

At night, they reached the post house the general had mentioned, and he asked the "lady of the house" to admit Madame Adams and her son and maid. The woman refused. After some arguing, she agreed on the condition that they not show a light in their room. The Russian-made coach was concealed, and the three travelers retired. But sleep was difficult. Soldiers stomped about the inn "all night, drinking and swearing, and making the most uproarious noises." The innkeeper's wife joked with them to prevent them from discovering her guests.

"Charles had fallen asleep, but Madame Babet . . . appeared to have lost her senses. She clasped her hands continually while the tears rolled down her cheeks, crying out that the Revolution was begun again, and that this was only the beginning of the renewal of its horrors. During my stay in my chamber, these ferocious creatures had attacked the poor boy who was in my service with a bayonet, and forced him to burn his Prussian military cap, and it was with great difficulty his life was saved by the dexterity of the hostess. Until five o'clock in the morning it was utterly impossible to feel a moment of ease or safety. After that time the doors were barred, and although stragglers frequently roared for admission and thundered at the door, no notice was taken, and we at last obtained some repose."

Following an "excellent breakfast," Louisa and her entourage departed for Sens and Meaux, where she heard tales of the "atrocities of the Cossacks," and saw the graves of "six of the most beautiful young girls of the place, who had fallen victims to the murderous horrors of savage and desolating war, with all its detestable concomitants. They were laid side by side." Then came the dark and forbidding forest of Bondy, then a delay to repair a broken rear wheel, and finally they reached the gates of Paris "in perfect safety." At eleven o'clock on March 23, 1815, they arrived at the Hôtel du Nord on the rue de Richelieu. "My husband was perfectly astonished at my adventure," she wrote, "as everything was quiet in Paris, and he had never realized the consequences of the general panic in any other place."

On May 7, Adams received word of his next post: he would follow once again his father's footsteps as minister plenipotentiary to Great Britain. In London, the Adamses (with Charles Francis) met their two oldest sons and settled into their third diplomatic post.

The two years at the court of St. James's covered little new ground. A commercial convention — with Clay and Gallatin joining him in the negotiations — was signed in July. And Adams insisted upon a diplomatic nicety called the alternat, whereby a nation's name and that of its sovereign appear first in the title, preamble, text and signature of its copies of any treaty signed with another nation — a recognition the United States had not previously enjoyed.

Domestically, the years in England were among the most pleasant for the Adamses. Louisa found a charming little country house in Ealing, eight miles from Hyde Park Corner — about a two-hour carriage ride away. They could also stay overnight in the legation's chancery in London after social functions. Louisa enjoyed the theater and concerts with her husband and sons, but ventured into town rarely for court functions or an occasional visit with friends. Adams frequently attended diplomatic dinners alone. He put on weight and soon became the plump shape of his later portraits. He pushed his sons' education, particularly that of George Washington Adams, who got special tutoring for Harvard. George was already "a nervous, overgrown boy of unsteady health"; his brothers, John Adams II and Charles Francis, were more outgoing and eager.

While the boys studied the stars with their father, and took strolls in the English countryside with both their parents, they were missed deeply by their grandparents back in Quincy. The Big House, which had echoed with the noise of George and John II for five years, was terribly quiet. The old gentleman, who loved having his children and grandchildren about, wrote:

"Oh, how I want John to divert me and George to assist me! I can scarcely get a book from my Office without him. Charles is a little Jewell too! How delighted I should be to have them all about me. Yet they would devour all my Strawberries, Raspberries, Cherries, Currents, Plumbs, Peaches, Pears and Apples. And what is worse, they would get into my Bedchamber and disarrange all the Papers on my Writing Table."

How the old man would love that. But there was more to his feelings than the fondness of a grandfather. John Adams knew the diplomatic frustrations his son was facing — he, too, had faced them at first hand in London. He wrote, in effect, for John Quincy to come home: "A man should be in his own country." And when the new president-elect, James Monroe, selected John Quincy to be his secretary of state, John Adams urged his son "to accept it without hesitation and share the fortunes of your country whatever they may be. You are now approaching fifty years of age. In my opinion you must return to it, or renounce it forever. I am well aware of the critical situation you will be in. I know you have not the command of your feelings, nor the immutable taciturnity of Franklin and Washington. But you must risque all."

Risk he would. John Quincy Adams accepted the appointment, and in June, 1817, he and his family sailed for home.

8

Our Proper Domain
[1815 – 1825]

*I*MMEDIATELY after sunrise on August 6, 1817, in view of the new lighthouse on Sandy Hook outside New York harbor, John Quincy Adams paced the deck of the *Washington:* "The morning was fine," he later recorded in his diary, "the sun rose clear, and Venus was visible more than a quarter of an hour after she had risen; air and water both at 67." So ended fifty days at sea, and at one that afternoon, John Quincy and his family landed in New York. He was glad to be back, but apprehensive about the future.

His parents awaited his arrival in Quincy with bubbling enthusiasm. "Yesterday," his father wrote him the day after he landed, "was one of the most uniformly happy days of my whole life. A thousand occasions exalted the delight . . . a succession of warm showers all day; my threshers, my gardiners, and my farmers all behaved better than usual, and altogether kept me in a kind of trance of delight the whole day. Kiss all the dear creatures for me. Wife, George, John and Charles. I hope to embrace them all here in a few days. God Almighty bless you all. So prays John Adams."

The younger Adams family took a sailing packet, the *Fame*, to Providence, where John Quincy hired a special stage to take them directly to Quincy. After several days on the road, they sped over Penn's Hill on the turnpike from Milton, raising dust on the hot August morning, and were spotted by Louisa Smith, one of Abigail Adams's nieces, who sounded the welcome. The senior Adamses rushed to the stage. Young John was the first to jump out, followed by George, crying "Grandmother! Grandmother!" Louisa Adams, looking tan and fit, embraced her in-laws, and then John Quincy Adams kissed them. He later wrote rather stiffly: "I had the inexpressible happiness of finding my dear and venerable father and mother in perfect health." Only Charles Francis Adams, ten years old that very day, held back "half frightened." He had been away the full eight years, and hardly knew his grandparents.

Soon, aunts and uncles, nephews and nieces filled the Old House. The neighbors flocked in. Everyone gathered around, eating and drinking and celebrating. They grabbed the boys and took their height measurements, marking them off on the doorjamb: Charles, measured first because it was his birthday, was four feet four inches; John, four feet nine and a half inches; George, five feet seven and a half inches — already half an inch taller than his father. During these pleasant weeks before Washington, John Quincy touched a few old favorite spots in Boston, swam again at Black's Wharf in Quincy, and measured the growth of the area he once had known so well. He also visited friends in Quincy, Cambridge and Boston, and enjoyed a pleasurable "dissipation."

Much had happened to the family during John Quincy's eight-year absence. In 1813, his sister Abigail Adams Smith, after twenty-seven years of unhappy marriage, died of breast cancer. His mother, at the age of seventy-two, was content with her home and family, and his father, almost eighty-two, was blissfully happy with the farm. Moreover, during the years 1809–1812, the bitter rivalry between John Adams and Thomas Jefferson had been healed, largely through the work of Dr. Benjamin Rush, a mutual friend of the two former presidents. Dr. Rush had tried everything to bring the stubborn Adams back into communication with the more willing Jefferson. He even told Adams about a dream, possibly apocryphal, in which the two men resumed their correspondence and continued it until they "sunk into the grave nearly at the same time." Adams had written back to Rush that the dream cheered him, but "it is not History. It may be Prophecy." Indeed it was.

By 1812, Adams and Jefferson were writing to each other again, and arguing, and enjoying it. Jefferson had left the presidency deeply in debt and was still saddened by the early death of his daughter Polly in childbirth. The two men had much to share. They discussed scientific and religious questions. They exchanged historical information about Virginia and Massachusetts. By the summer of 1813, despite the salting of some old wounds, their friendship was firmly reestablished. But the man who had brought them together, Dr. Benjamin Rush, died in April of that year. Adams and Jefferson mourned the loss of their old friend, and took account of the surviving signers of the Declaration of Independence. Besides themselves, only eight remained.

The Old House was in turmoil, and the rooms, Abigail complained goodnaturedly, were "covered with trunkes Bookes and papers." In John Quincy's room there were "no less than Eighteen large packages, addrest to all the Governours in the United States." The packages contained inquiries about weights and measures — a complicated subject that Congress had asked the new secretary of state to look into, and which John Quincy had already begun to do with the customary Adams vigor. For the next four years he would work on it in his spare time, often getting up at three or four o'clock to write. The work, printed in 1821 under the title *Report on Weights and Measures*, is a neglected classic. Even John Adams could not read it all, though he praised it as a "mass of historical, philosophical, chemical, metaphysical, and political knowledge."

In September, 1817, leaving their two oldest sons behind in Quincy to be educated, John Quincy and Louisa Adams set out for Washington. After six steamboats and six stages, they arrived in the capital on the twentieth, the day John Quincy had promised President Monroe he would be there. Washington was still a rough little village, although at least the damage done by the British had been repaired. The President's House had been restored in 1814 and, Adams noted, "is now for the first time again habitable." Not everyone thought as much of the town: a Massachusetts representative called it "a miserable desert" and complained that "the first appearance of this seat of the national government has produced in me nothing but absolute loathing and disgust."

The Adamses rented a house on the northeast corner of $4\frac{1}{2}$ and F streets, N.E., for $650 a year. The house was about a mile from the Capitol and a mile and a quarter from the old State Department building. In April, 1820, they bought a house on F Street, with a ballroom that Louisa soon came to love. John Quincy's salary as secretary of state was $3,500 a year, which Congress generously boosted to $6,000 in 1819. But his family expenses for the first year in Washington totaled more than $11,000, and would exceed his income by at least $4,000 every year of his eight in office. Fortunately, Thomas Boylston Adams had wisely invested his brother's money, and by the time the Adamses reached Washington, John Quincy was worth $100,000, which he squirreled away in bank stock paying six percent interest a year. He would live off this, and his meager salary, during his public service.

As secretary of state, John Quincy soon discovered — as his father had discovered during Franklin's peace commission in Paris — that not everyone was as meticulous a worker as he. The public business was in disarray, and Adams set about straightening it out. Dispatches and letters, inherited from the previous incumbent, lay about his desk. Important letters had been misplaced. The translation of the Swedish Treaty of 1816 couldn't be found anywhere, nor could other papers concerning Sweden. Adams immediately had an index prepared of all diplomatic correspondence, and settled into the business.

And what was the business? At that time, the secretary of state read all the dispatches from ministers and consuls abroad, as well as the notes from foreign representatives in Washington. He wrote replies in his own hand, although (his mother reported) Louisa copied, as she had done in the past, "all his private letters into his Letter Books to save his hand and Eyes, his Eyes being very weak, and his right hand . . . much upon the tremble like his Fathers." He oversaw a wide variety of administrative functions in the capital, from superintending the census to managing the custody, printing and distribution of all congressional acts and resolutions. He also attended regular cabinet meetings.

In addition to Adams, Monroe's cabinet contained Benjamin Crowninshield of Massachusetts, a lazy and unambitious man who served as secretary of the navy (later replaced by Smith Thompson of New York and, in 1823, by Samuel Southard of New Jersey); and William Wirt of Maryland, the attorney general. These two men, Crowninshield and Wirt, were holdovers from the Madison administration, kept by inertia. Another Madison holdover was William H. Crawford of Georgia, secretary of the treasury, who was too powerful to oust. Crawford was a huge and handsome man, but a bit coarse. One of the upland Georgia planters, he had killed another Georgian in a duel and, in turn, had had his wrist shattered by a pistol ball in a second duel. Clearly, he was not someone the quiet Monroe would treat carelessly. Finally, there was John C. Calhoun of South Carolina, secretary of war, the belligerent young man of the cabinet.

At best, these men barely tolerated one another, and relations among them were often strained. The reason was political ambition. In 1818, John Quincy Adams exclaimed: "This Government is indeed assuming daily more and more a character of cabal, and preparation, not for the next Presidential election, but for the one after — that is, working and counterworking, with many of the worst features of elective monarchies."

With only one party, the Republican, the next presidential campaign (after Monroe's second term) would be decided by personalities, and three of the leading contenders with the most national exposure were in Monroe's cabinet: Adams, Calhoun and Crawford. Almost from the start of the president's first term, a campaign to determine his successor began.

A fourth candidate, Henry Clay, used the Speaker's position as the platform for his candidacy, and lost no time in raising his voice in growing opposition to Monroe and Adams.

The election of 1824 appeared as a simple footrace in this detail from an etching. John Quincy Adams leads with his bald head while Andrew Jackson veers off the track, cane in hand. The finish line offered an elevated throne and a fat money bag on a pole.

DETAIL: A FOOT RACE. CARTOON BY DAVID CLAYPOOLE JOHNSTON, 1824

Clay had opposed Adams's appointment as secretary of state; he had sought the position for himself, knowing it had become a traditional steppingstone to the presidency. Rebuked, Clay settled into the Speaker's position determined to make noise and seize any chance to play kingmaker.

To Adams, the cabinet meetings were "a new scene and new views of the political world. Here is a play of passions, opinions, and characters different in many respects from those in which I have been accustomed heretofore to move." He was soon characterizing those around him. Of Monroe he wrote: "There is slowness, want of decision, and a spirit of procrastination in the President." Of Crawford: He was "a worm preying upon the vitals of the Administration within its own body." Of Clay (no favorite of Adams's): "He has more than once won and lost an affluent fortune at the gaming-table [at one point more than $8,000]. . . . Clay is essentially a gamester, and, with a vigorous intellect, an ardent spirit, a handsome elocution, though with a mind very defective in elementary knowledge, and a very undigested system of ethics, he has all the qualities which belong to that class of human characters."

For these men, and all Americans, this was a time of nationalism, marked by unity in the nation, a balance between order and liberty, and a sense of growth. The continent was opening to the plow. The western rivers were being conquered: in 1817, a steamboat churned from New Orleans against the flow of the Mississippi and Ohio rivers to Cincinnati; within two years, sixty such stern-wheelers would be hauling goods between the Gulf of Mexico and the Midwest. There was the feeling also in 1817, with the peace of Ghent, that the nation's dangers had passed. Americans were optimistic, and when President Monroe, a Virginian, toured New England, he received a strong welcome. In Boston, the capital of Federalism, the *Columbian Centinel* cheered his visit as an "Era of Good Feelings."

The Treaty of Ghent had assured the United States of her independence. Now it fell to John Quincy Adams, as secretary of state, to negotiate other treaties and define a U.S. foreign policy that would solidify that independence. During the next eight years, Adams would deal with the Spanish and

British over Florida and the northwest boundaries. He would formulate a policy of nonintervention and noncolonialization that would create the backbone of the Monroe Doctrine, which in turn would shape American foreign policy for the remainder of the century. He would prove to be a nationalist at a time when nationalism in the United States was a driving force; he was a continentalist when the opportunity came to expand. In brief, John Quincy Adams would affirm that the nation extended from the Atlantic to the Pacific, and would expand its sphere of influence and strength as well.

In 1818, Adams had to deal with two nations whose interests in the United States at that moment focused on opposite ends of the continent: Spain and England. The issues with Spain carried with them overtones of war and European involvement in the Americas. The Spanish empire in the New World was fast unraveling. Since 1810, revolution and civil war had been flaring from Mexico to South America, and the Spanish were diverting troops from their Florida possessions to fight against insurgents in her South American colonies.

Spain had few American sympathizers, largely because she had sided with England during the War of 1812, and because, by the Pinckney Treaty of 1795, she was supposed to maintain troops in her Florida forts to keep the Indians and fugitive slaves at peace. By 1818, her diversion of troops from the Floridas to South America encouraged the Seminole Indians to cross the border into Georgia on raiding parties. Skirmishes between them and frontiersmen culminated on November 30, 1817, when Seminole Indians jumped an American ship sliding along the slow-moving Apalachicola River, and killed thirty-four soldiers, seven women and four children. This shocking attack was publicized as further proof that the Spanish couldn't (or wouldn't) control the Indians in their Florida colonies.

American nationalism ranged the frontier, and a flamboyant and — as it happened — undisciplined General Andrew Jackson was its personification. As the attacks increased, Calhoun and Monroe gave Jackson orders to repress them; he could pursue the Indians into Spanish territory if necessary, but he must respect Spanish authority. Jackson wrote President Monroe suggesting that the "whole of East Florida be seized and held as indemnity for the outrages of Spain upon the property of our Citizens." Monroe did nothing to check Jackson's enthusiasm.

While Jackson was preparing his men for action, Adams was engaged with the Spanish on another front. The question of the Florida and western boundaries of the Louisiana Purchase had been left unsettled by Thomas Jefferson and his Republican diplomats. As a senator, Adams had opposed Jefferson's Florida policy as too weak. He thought the scope of the Purchase was clear enough, and the boundaries broad and inclusive. After the Treaty of Ghent at the end of 1814, Monroe, then secretary of state, had tried to settle the boundary questions by proposing to Spain that the Colorado River, which runs through what is now the middle of Texas, or even the Sabine River (the western boundary of the present state of Louisiana), be designated the southwestern boundary of the Purchase if Spain would cede the Floridas. The Spanish in those heady days, however, argued that they would gladly cede the Floridas if the United States would set the western boundary at the Mississippi River — that is, return one half of the United States to Spain. Negotiations ground to a halt.

At the beginning of 1818, Adams, as secretary of state, resumed the negotiations with Spain, conferring with Don Luis de Onís y Gonzales, the Spanish minister in Washington. Adams knew the Florida question well, and he also knew that time was on his side. As the war in South America intensified, Spain's control of the Floridas would weaken further. In addition, in December of 1817, President Monroe had announced his intention of sending troops to occupy the Spanish port city of Galveston on the Gulf of Mexico. Pirates based there had been preying on U.S. shipping and the Spanish had been unable to stop them. He had also sent troops to Amelia Island off the northeast coast of East Florida. Adams told Onís: "If we don't come to an early conclusion of the Florida negotiations, Spain won't have the possession of Florida to give us."

Adams's knowledge of the West was more inaccurate than the current maps. At one time he referred to the region as "a wilderness, the geography of which is unknown." But if he was fuzzy about western geography, he was sharply clear on one point. The Louisiana Purchase extended to the Pacific Ocean. He and Monroe had agreed on this early in 1818, when they moved the boundary back from the Colorado River to the Arkansas River, and at its source "thence due West to the Pacific." Adams sought first to remove all Spanish claims to the Pacific Northwest; then he could work on unseating the British and the Russians. Negotiations with Spain, however, soon froze along the old boundary-line dispute, and neither side appeared willing to give an inch.

While Adams and Onís were negotiating, Andrew Jackson undertook a little foreign-policy maneuver of his own in the Floridas. His letter of January 6, 1818, to Monroe had not been answered, and he construed silence as official approval. With a force of three thousand men, he cut through the Floridas in April and May, shattering Indian resistance and capturing the Spanish forts at St. Marks, Pensacola and St. Augustine. During the campaign, Jackson's forces detained two British citizens: an elderly Scottish trader named Alexander Arbuthnot, and a young adventurer named Captain Robert C. Ambrister. A court-martial was quickly put together at St. Marks, and Arbuthnot was charged with espionage and inciting the Indians. He denied the charges, with a stout defense, but was found guilty and sentenced to be hanged. Ambrister was charged with leading the Indians in war, and he admitted it, throwing himself on the mercy of the court. As a military man, he was sentenced to be shot, rather than hanged.

Jackson, without checking with Washington and without any backing from the United States government, ordered the sentences carried out. The reverberations of the Jackson Seminole campaign and the trials of Arbuthnot and Ambrister echoed from the Floridas to the capitals of Spain, England and the United States.

In Washington, Jackson's dispatches on his actions against the Seminoles made lively reading. When the cabinet met on July 15, 1818, everyone but Adams was for disavowing Jackson. Crawford wanted to embarrass President Monroe for political reasons and ruin his bid for a second term. Calhoun, an ardent nationalist who surely in private approved of Jackson's moves, called publicly for a court-martial on the grounds that the general had disobeyed the secretary of war's orders not to invade St. Augustine, and had been motivated by speculation in Florida land deals. Henry Clay, from his position in the House, attacked the Monroe administration and Jackson for invading the Floridas without the consent of Congress — a violation, he claimed, of the Constitution.

Only Adams supported Jackson. Monroe, slow to make decisions and a willing listener to strong argument, heard Adams argue at length that Jackson had violated no instructions, that his military action could be justified on the grounds that it was defensive — that is, in response to Indian attacks brought about by Spanish military laxity. If anyone erred in Florida, Adams stated, it had been the Spanish, who could not control their own colony.

At first, Adams contended that the United States should keep Pensacola until Spain made some guarantee of restraining the Indians. But it was finally agreed that Adams would tell Onís that the forts would be surrendered, but that General Jackson would not be censured for capturing them.

Although Onís loudly protested to Adams about the "outrage" of Jackson's campaign and insisted upon "lawful punishment" for his "flagrant" violation of orders, he already knew that Spain was willing to concede much on this issue. With rebellion breaking out anew in South America, Spain feared that the United States might recognize these insurgent peoples' bid for independence. Jackson's sweep had proved to officials in Madrid that the Floridas were indefensible; they would cede the Floridas, but only for a western boundary that would leave Texas for Spain, and for a pledge from the United States not to recognize any of the newly emerging South American nations.

Until the Florida forts were returned, Onís and the Spanish government slowed the negotiations. Hyde de Neuville, the French minister to the United States, offered to mediate, and contact was continued through the French. De Neuville feared that a breach between Spain and the United States might favor Britain and perhaps increase the British fleet and influence in the Caribbean.

Meanwhile, between November 7 and 28, 1818, Adams

composed his instructions to the American minister in Madrid, George W. Erving — a dispatch that soon became famous among American state letters. In it, Adams replied to Onís's insistence that Jackson be dismissed and punished. He cleared Jackson of all blame and scored both the weakness of the Spanish commanders in the Floridas and the cunning and treachery of Arbuthnot and Ambrister, who, Adams claimed, had been engaged in "a creeping and insidious war, both against Spain and the United States . . . to plunder Spain of her province, and to spread massacre and devastation along the borders of the United States." General Jackson had merely chased "a defeated savage enemy beyond the Spanish Florida line" — a "necessary" pursuit of great innocence when compared to the British Colonel Nicholls's "shameful invasion" of Florida during the War of 1812. Had Spain protested then? "If a whisper of expostulation was ever wafted from Madrid to London," Adams wrote, "it was not . . . energetic enough to transpire beyond the walls of the palaces from which it issued, and to which it was borne."

Adams, of course, was not only rattling the Spanish, but also challenging the British. But though the British public clamored for revenge after the executions of Ambrister and Arbuthnot, and as Lord Castlereagh later said, "war might have been produced by holding up a finger," the British government did nothing. Indeed, Castlereagh argued in 1819 that Ambrister and Arbuthnot had been "engaged in unauthorized practises of such a description as to have deprived them of any claim on their own Government."

The impact of this in Europe was profound. Spain immediately realized that she would have no European assistance in the Americas. And British silence, particularly in the face of public outcry, impressed the European powers with the independence and power of the United States.

During this period in London, Albert Gallatin and Richard Rush, acting under Adams's instructions, reached an agreement with the British that resulted in the Convention of 1818, signed on October 20. It was important for several reasons. Although the convention said nothing about impressment of seamen and the question of indemnity for American slaves carried off during the War of 1812, it did renew

United States fishing privileges off the coasts of Newfound-land and Labrador, and the commercial convention of 1815. Perhaps most importantly — given the current negotiations between Adams and Onís — the convention defined the American-Canadian border along the 49th parallel from Lake of the Woods to the crest of the Rocky Mountains. No boundary for the region west of the Rockies was fixed, but the two nations agreed that the Oregon country would be jointly occupied for ten years. This part of the convention, then, fixed at last the northern boundary of the Louisiana Purchase.

In January, 1819, Spain settled the western boundaries of the Purchase. At Adams's suggestion, both parties waited until February 22, Washington's birthday, to sign the Transcontinental Treaty. For $5 million, Spain ceded all her lands east of the Mississippi and surrendered her rights to the Oregon country. In addition, the boundary between the United States and Mexico was determined (which excluded all of present-day Texas). On the day of the signing, Adams wrote in his diary that this was "the most important day of my life." His nationalism burst forth: "The acquisition of the Floridas has long been an object of earnest desire to this country. The acknowledgement of a definite line of boundary to the South Seas [Pacific Ocean] forms a great epoch in our history. The first proposal of it in this negotiation was my own."

But Adams's self-congratulatory vanity was soon to evaporate. Although the treaty opened up the United States from the Atlantic to the Pacific — as the original Louisiana Purchase had implied — it contained two flaws. Spain probably would have ceded Texas as well as the Floridas, but neither Monroe nor Adams pressed the issue. Further, Article VIII allowed land grants made in the Floridas before January 24, 1818, to remain valid. The Spanish king had awarded grants to three court favorites, and although the U.S. minister in Madrid had warned Adams of this treaty provision in a letter, Adams had overlooked it. Henry Clay, however, had not. He gleefully pointed out to President Monroe (and the American public) that their secretary of state had been fooled. By the stipulation of Adams's own treaty, most of East Florida was owned by three Spaniards.

Adams was embarrassed, and President Monroe had to repair the damage of his secretary's oversight. He instructed Erving in Madrid to insist that King Ferdinand VII renounce the grants. But the king refused, and for two years further negotiation went on. Finally, a change in the Spanish government and a threat by the United States to seize the Floridas and Texas brought a renunciation of the land grants and ratification in October, 1820. The Senate had to ratify the treaty again, and did so the following February.

Adams was deeply pleased at the signing. The treaty, however flawed, was a major achievement by a single American diplomat. It also reflected his unique thinking at this time: that the United States had a right to expand to its continental coastlines. In conjunction with the Convention of 1818 with England, it assured the Oregon country for America. Other nations must now consider, Adams told the cabinet in 1819, "our proper domain to be the continent of North America."

If this was indeed an "era of good feelings," it was also a period of economic disaster. The American economy was going through another periodic upset: the panic of 1819. But as debt and hard times set in — they would last until 1824 — yet another issue was rising that would have a far more damaging effect upon the tranquillity of the Union: slavery.

By 1815, upland or staple cotton, which had previously been grown only in Georgia and South Carolina, was being cultivated in the new states of Alabama, Mississippi and Louisiana. The cotton was hardy and cheap to grow; the number of acres planted with it doubled within five years, and by 1825 would double again.

Upland cotton and the cotton gin brought with them planters and slaves. And as the amount of cotton and the number of slaves increased, so did fear in the planters of emancipation by congressional fiat. The defense of slavery was soon interwoven with the issue of states' rights, and when Illinois entered the Union in 1818, pro- and antislavery forces struggled over her state constitution, which finally made her a free-soil state. But the issue was raised, and with it another question: Could Congress place conditions upon the admission of the states?

In Missouri the issue would reach high tension. In 1810,

Missouri had three thousand slaves; by 1820, she had ten thousand. After Louisiana, Missouri would be the first state formed out of the Louisiana Purchase — and the first after the treaty with Spain was ratified. If slavery were excluded from Missouri, other states formed on the western side of the Mississippi River, it was argued, would also come in on the same basis. (The fact that Missouri would probably not be a cotton-growing state — her southern soils were unfavorable — did not deter the slaveholding states from the issue.) The proslavery plan was to get Missouri admitted as a slave state. Since slaveholding states were in a minority in Congress, this would assure that her legislature would elect proslavery senators, and the free-soil/slave-state balance would be preserved.

The debate in Congress was heated. John Quincy Adams visited the Senate on February 11, 1820, and heard speeches on the Missouri Compromise. "By what fatality does it happen that all the most eloquent orators of the body are on its slavish side?" he wrote. "There is a great mass of cool judgment and plain sense on the side of freedom and humanity, but the ardent spirits and passions are on the side of oppression." Adams strongly opposed slavery, calling it "the great and foul stain upon the North American Union."

Missouri was admitted as a slave state without qualification. Maine, which was detaching itself from Massachusetts, was admitted as a free state, making twelve of each in the nation and the Congress. The question of slavery was at rest for a while. Adams saw its import, and wrote: "I take it for granted that the present question is a mere preamble — a title-page to a great, tragic volume."

Congress was not the only political forum in Washington. The presidential campaign of 1824 was well under way, and every social event contained some overtone of politics. The intensity of Washington social life increased, and along with it the activity of Washington wives. Louisa Adams paid all the obligatory social calls upon the wives of other public officials in Washington, a duty considered by many to be a serious one. In 1818, while her husband was negotiating with the Spanish and the British, Louisa Adams was in delicate negotiations herself over an "etiquette war." The ladies in

Washington, led by Mrs. Monroe, had "taken offence at her not paying them the first visit." The issue touched upon the fundamental Washington question of who — cabinet wives or the wives of senators and congressmen — should make the initial social call at the opening of Congress. Washington even then was a demanding social town, and feelings ran high. Some thought the wives of lower-ranking officials should make the first call; others, that the wives of the higher-ranking should do so. In December, 1819, the question was discussed by the president's cabinet, and state papers were written about it. The issue was not as frivolous as it might appear. There was much presidential campaigning going on during Monroe's terms, and Louisa Adams, and presumably her husband, considered that wives who made first calls were hustling future votes for their husbands.

Adams noted in his diary that "Mrs. Monroe neither pays nor returns any visits." Louisa Adams negotiated her own position: she decided that she would return all visits from the wives of congressmen, but would not visit first. Adams, calling himself a noncandidate, nonetheless allowed his wife to throw open their home every Tuesday evening during the social season "without reference to pretensions to form." To Adams's astonishment — and future political benefit — the wine and company were so agreeable that few prominent Washingtonians stayed away.

Not everyone, however, thought the Adamses' "watering place" the most fun in town. Senator Elijah H. Mills arrived late and left early one night, after a bow to Louisa and a cup of tea and some ice cream. He concluded: "a more unsocial and dissonant party I have seldom been in, even in this wilderness of a city." Still, he returned two days later for dinner, and "passed the time very pleasantly." He found Louisa Adams "on the whole, a very pleasant and agreeable woman; but the Secretary has no talent to entertain a mixed company, either by conversation or manners."

John Quincy was aware of his social shortcomings and commented on them in his diary: "I am a man of reserved, cold, austere, and forbidding manners; my political adversaries say, a gloomy misanthropist, and my personal enemies, an unsocial savage. With a knowledge of the actual defect in my character, I have not the pliability to reform it." Still, his friends urged him "to mingle more in society" and to make himself "more extensively known." But he found social gatherings boring. "My wife had a large tea-party this evening," he wrote, "but as there was scarcely any music, and no other occupation, it was dull."

He was not very good at Washington chitchat or conversation. "I never knew how to make, to control, or to change it. I am by nature a silent animal, and my dear mother's constant lesson in childhood, that children in company should be seen and not heard, confirmed me irrevocably in what I now deem a bad habit."

It was Louisa who balanced the meagerness of his sociability, and who made the rounds, sometimes spending whole afternoons bouncing along the dirt streets to look up the wives of diplomats or congressmen who had left their cards. One day she made eleven social calls and covered an area six miles square. All of it was done for the advancement of her husband's career.

The Adamses' entertainments were enlivened by the presence of their three sons, who visited during the holidays from school and Harvard. John Quincy had tried to give them an education broad and rich in the classics, like his own, and to push them toward public service. He expected much from them but they continually disappointed him. Only George showed early signs of brilliance, and that was badly flawed. His grandfather wrote John Quincy that "George is a treasure of diamonds. He has genius equal to anything; but like all other genius requires the most delicate management to keep it from running into eccentricities." George was a gentle young man who preferred art and music, like his mother, to the politics and law his father demanded that he study. Adams had no "delicate management" in him toward this strange son.

Toward the others, he was also stern. He preached. He demanded that they rise early, keep a diary, be punctual and temperate and attend church. He scolded, regulated, berated — and detailed their life schedules from sunrise to sundown. He seemed unable to relax and enjoy his children. On Christmas Day, 1820, for instance, he read Pope's *Messiah* to them,

During John Quincy Adams's second term as secretary of state, Washington was a rural and unfinished place. This is the view of F Street at Fifteenth as it appeared from the home of the Baron Hyde de Neuville, the French minister to the United States.

THE CORNER OF F AND FIFTEENTH STREETS, WASHINGTON, D.C. WATERCOLOR BY THE BARONESS HYDE DE NEUVILLE, 1817

JOHN QUINCY ADAMS. OIL BY THOMAS SULLY, 1825

and was keenly disappointed by their reaction. "Not one of them, excepting George, appeared to take the slightest interest in it; nor is there one of them who has any relish for literature." On another occasion he admonished George to stop reading the easy Greek Testament, and to stop shirking hard study. Another time, Louisa intercepted an especially bitter letter from her husband in which he scolded George for participating in a student riot at Harvard.

John, a member of the "notoriously rowdy" Harvard class of 1823, excelled more at sports than scholarship. When his father learned that John stood only forty-fifth in a class of eighty-five students, he refused to allow him to come home for the Christmas holidays: "I could feel nothing but sorrow and shame in your presence until you should not only have commenced but made large progress in redeeming yourself from that disgraceful standing." After this lashing, John's standing rose to twenty-fourth, still not good enough for his father. John Quincy told the lad that he would not attend his Harvard graduation unless the boy stood fifth or better. He never got the chance: John Adams II was among forty-three students expelled during the student rebellion just before commencement.

Of the three sons, Charles Francis alone would turn out well. "A thinking boy," his grandmother called him, a Harvard graduate (1825), he would progress unlike the others and be "much surer in the end." Although he tried hardest to please, he, too, never felt that he had ever won his father's full approval.

When not reading or writing, Adams enjoyed walking, horseback riding and swimming. He thought the climate of Washington, especially in summer, unhealthy and he swam in the Potomac to keep cool and in shape. On hot summer days he swam to "the bridge against the tide, and returned with it." The British minister in Washington (among others) often reported finding the secretary of state floating down the Potomac in black swimming cap and green goggles for his eyes — and nothing else.

Whenever he could, Adams went home to Quincy, but it was not as often as he or his parents would have liked. Returning to Washington after one visit in 1818, he was shocked to learn of his mother's death from typhoid fever on Wednesday, October 28, 1818. "While she lived, whenever I returned to the paternal roof I felt as if the joys and charms of childhood returned to make me happy. All was kindness and affection, at once silent and active as the movement of the orbs of heaven. One of the links that connected me with the former ages is no more."

His father's health was also failing. In August, 1823, John Quincy went home and observed: "Within the last two years since I had seen him, his eyesight has grown dim, and his limbs stiff and feeble. He is bowed with age, and scarcely can walk across a room without assistance." His father sat that fall for his portrait by Gilbert Stuart, and in that same year Charles Bird King painted George Washington Adams and John Adams II. In 1821, he had painted Louisa Adams. Her portrait reveals something of the Washington social scene and her spirit. She was shown with a harp, and in her left hand was a volume of music open to Thomas Moore's song "Oh Say Not That Woman's Heart Can Be Bought."

Louisa Catherine Adams sat for this portrait by Charles Bird King in 1824. At least one member of the family thought she was "overdressed."

In the seven years after the Treaty of Ghent, the entire American continental area, from Mexico to Cape Horn, was freed from European control. Revolutions had swept the Spanish colonies, and they looked to the United States for recognition and protection from Spanish and other European interference.

In Europe, a Holy Alliance had been formed in 1815 by Tsar Alexander I, who had gathered Russia, Prussia and Austria together as "members of the same Christian nation" that believed and acted upon "the sublime truths which the Holy Religion of our Savior teaches." Lord Castlereagh regarded this as "sublime nonsense." But he still watched carefully as the Holy Alliance and, later, the Quadruple Alliance, which included Great Britain, planned military action against Spain and economic intrusion in the New World colonies.

Castlereagh, and later George Canning, were not sympathetic to the new republics in South America, and yet they sought Latin American commerce and struggled to prevent any extension of Spanish or French influence into the New World. Reconciliation among the European powers failed at

LOUISA CATHERINE ADAMS. OIL BY CHARLES BIRD KING, ABOUT 1824

Aix-la-Chapelle in 1818, and England irrevocably split from the rest of the Quadruple Alliance. Tsar Alexander invited his old friend John Quincy Adams to join the Alliance, and Adams's reply set a theme that was to be repeated in the Monroe Doctrine four years later: "For the repose of Europe as well as of America, the European and American political systems should be kept as separate and distinct from each other as possible."

Both Monroe and Adams remained cautious, and on March 8, 1822, Monroe wrote a brief message to Congress asking recognition of the United Provinces of the Río de la Plata, Colombia, Chile, Peru, and Mexico. Congress approved, and appropriated $100,000 for ministers and legations.

Adams, in supporting the plan, was reacting to a number of forces. He considered turbulence in Latin America as undermining these new republics. Recognition might decrease that turbulence. He was also reacting to Henry Clay's loud and public support of the insurgents.

Adams addressed the House of Representatives in 1821 with a warning to the Holy Alliance not to involve itself in South America. "From the moral and physical nature of man," Adams later wrote, "*colonial establishments cannot fulfil the great objects of government in the just purpose of civil society*." There could be no intervention in foreign wars, "even wars for freedom," since that changed "the very foundations of our government from *liberty* to *power*." In 1821, when the Quadruple Alliance threatened South America with intervention, Tsar Alexander issued an imperial ukase extending Alaska to the 51st parallel, well within the Oregon country, and closing the waters from there to the Bering Strait to foreign commerce. The tsar was warned that further colonization of the Americas by Europe had ended. John Quincy Adams told the Russian minister in Washington "that we should contest the right of Russia to *any* territorial establishment on this continent, and that we should assume distinctly the principle that the American continents are no longer subjects for *any* new European colonial establishments."

Adams's nonintervention and noncolonization principles were now clearly before the powers of Europe. They were further defined by the resulting convention with Russia, in which the tsar gave up his *mare clausum* (closed sea) and accepted as his nation's boundary with the United States the line 54°40'. For Adams, the issue was not simply Russian or other European presence, but the larger one of future relations between the Old World and the New. In reaction to these pressures, Adams supported Monroe's recognition of the South American republics. Formal recognition was extended in 1822, and diplomatic relations established.

Castlereagh, in seeking a balance of power on the Continent, failed to attain his objective. Overworked and overwrought, his emotional stability wavering, he slit his throat in August of 1822, and died. His great rival, George Canning, took over as foreign secretary in London. In November, 1822, the Quadruple Alliance (now France, Austria, Russia and Prussia) agreed to restore the Spanish king, Ferdinand VII, to power; France would do the heavy work on the ground, and she invaded Spain. The British feared that France would follow with a Franco-Spanish intervention in South America, a fear increased by the welcome in Madrid for the French move. Canning sought a pledge from the French barring the acquisition of any territory in Spanish America. France refused. Canning next turned to America, and Adams.

The obvious move — one even urged by *The Times* of London — was for Canning to follow Adams's lead and call for independence in Latin America. George IV opposed such a plan; yet Canning could not sit by and let Adams and the United States reap commercial advantages from recognition of the South American republics. Instead, he proposed, through Richard Rush, the American minister in London, that the two nations make a joint Anglo-American protest against intervention in the New World. Rush, wisely, remained cool to Canning's richly phrased overtures, and referred the matter back to the secretary of state and the president.

John Quincy Adams was suspicious of Canning's motives and came out strongly against the proposal. What revealed Canning's hand, Adams determined, was his request that both nations pledge not to acquire any part of Spanish America — a pledge designed to keep the United States away from Cuba rather than the British out of the New World. Besides, Adams reasoned, the United States as the military ally of England made little sense: the British navy was supreme in the Atlantic and was quite capable, by itself, of keeping France and Spain at home. Adams felt that the time was right for the United States to assert his policy of nonintervention and noncolonization. He thought a formal statement would enable the United States to make a stand against the Holy Alliance apart from England. "I remarked," he wrote, "that the communications recently received from the Russian Minister . . . afforded, as I thought, a very suitable and convenient opportunity for us to take our stand against the Holy Alliance, and at the same time to decline the overture of Great Britain."

At the November 7, 1823, cabinet meeting, Monroe and the other officers appeared to agree, and Adams worked at keeping them in line. Calhoun, for one, was for following Canning; Monroe vacillated between doing nothing and carrying war against the Holy Alliance by aiding the Greeks, whose struggle for independence had captured the enthusiasm of a wide number of Americans. After this cabinet meeting, Adams wrote of the Canning proposal: "It would be more candid, as well as more dignified, to avow our principles explicitly to Russia and France, than to come in as a cock-boat in the wake of the British man-of-war."

Monroe began working on his annual message to Congress. His first draft contained a sharp rebuke to the French for invading Spain, and a long, glowing paean to the Greeks. But Adams cautioned and advised him: "I spoke to him again, urging him to abstain from everything in his message which the Holy Allies could make a pretext for construing into aggression upon them. If the Holy Alliance were determined to make up an issue with us, it was our policy to meet, and not to make it. . . . The ground that I wish to take is that of earnest remonstrance against the interference of the European powers by force with South America, but to disclaim all interference on our part with Europe; to make an American cause, and adhere inflexibly to that."

Adams wrote a draft for Monroe, but the cabinet rejected much of it as too shrill and warlike. Instead, they took,

Adams complained, "the cream of my paper," to be skimmed off for the speech. The cream was good enough, for Monroe's message, delivered on December 2, 1823, in the president's concise and formal language, contained the points on noncolonization and nonintervention that Adams had made. Its major themes were four:

> "The American continents, by the free and independent condition which they have assumed and maintain, are henceforth not to be considered as subjects for future colonization by any European powers."
>
> "The political system of the allied powers is essentially different . . . from that of America. . . . We should consider any attempt on their part to extend their system to any portion of this hemisphere as dangerous to our peace and safety."
>
> "With the existing colonies or dependencies of any European power we have not interfered and shall not interfere."
>
> "In the wars of the European powers in matters relating to themselves we have never taken any part, nor does it comport with our policy so to do."

Political maneuvers disguised as social events occurred all the time in Washington during these years, and on January 8, 1824, John Quincy and Louisa Adams gave a huge and glorious ball for General Andrew Jackson in their house on F Street. The pretext was to celebrate the ninth anniversary of the Battle of New Orleans, and the ball was the best of the Washington social season. Jackson, a recently elected senator, was being pushed as presidential material by his supporters, and he owed Adams some political back-rubbing for Adams's defense in the cabinet of his Florida campaign. The two might make agreeable running partners — Adams seeing himself as president, of course — and the ball immediately took on political overtones.

Newspaper coverage started several days beforehand, and the morning of the event, John Agg, "a literary light of the period," wrote five stanzas of doggerel for the *Washington Republican* in which were listed some of the guests expected at the Adamses' that evening. The second stanza went:

> *Wend you with the world to-night?*
> *Sixty gray, and giddy twenty,*
> *Flirts that court, and prudes that slight*
> *Stale coquettes and spinsters plenty.*
> *Mrs. Sullivan is there,*
> *With all the charms that nature lent her;*
> *Gay M'Kim, with city air;*
> *And winning Gales, and Vandeventer;*
> *Forsyth, with her group of graces;*
> *Both the Crowninshields, in blue;*
> *The Pierces with their heavenly faces,*
> *And eyes like suns that dazzle through;*
> *Belles and matrons, maids and madams,*
> *All are gone to Mrs. Adams'.*

In January, 1824, the Adamses gave a large ball honoring Andrew Jackson on the ninth anniversary of his victory at New Orleans. This imaginary engraving, done in 1871, shows Andrew Jackson (center) hand on belt, and the Adamses (far right). Louisa, in profile, carries a fan and wears a turban, the style for married ladies of that time.

About five hundred invitations went out, and indeed, nearly a thousand guests did show up at Mrs. Adams's. Fortunately, John Quincy wisely had had pillars installed in the lower floors of the house for additional support. The family also wove garlands of flowers and leaves for decorations, and military emblems were chalked on the ballroom floor according to the master plan Louisa Adams had drawn up.

Just about everyone in Washington social circles was there — except President and Mrs. Monroe, who did not want to seem to be favoring any particular candidate, and whose custom it was not to visit private homes. Jackson arrived at eight — the city was illuminated for him, with bonfires and fireworks — and ducked out later to attend another ball. "In fact," wrote *Harper's Bazar* in 1871, "every body who was any body was there . . . and this, be it known, was when *shoddy* was not — society was unmixed, and every one knew who was who, and was free to act accordingly."

There was dancing on the first floor, and a supper table on the third. When the table opened at nine-thirty, the guests rushed in to find "natural and candied fruits, pies, sweetmeats, tongues, games, etc., prepared in French style, and arranged with most exquisite taste."

"The dancing continued till near one in the morning,"

BALL GIVEN BY MRS. JOHN QUINCY ADAMS IN WASHINGTON, JANUARY 8, 1824. PHOTOENGRAVING FROM "HARPER'S BAZAR, MARCH 18, 1871"

Adams wrote in his diary. "The crowd was great and the house could scarcely contain the company."

Louisa Adams, *Harper's Bazar* reported, "without being a beauty . . . was a very attractive woman," and she and her guests danced the popular Spanish quadrille, and the waltz, which was newly introduced. She wore "a *suit* of *steel*. The dress was composed of steel llama; her ornaments for head, throat, and arms were all of cut steel, producing a dazzling effect. General Jackson was her devoted attendant during the evening, and caused much comment by such assiduous attentions." His manner was what Washingtonians of later years called "smiling for the Presidency."

Jackson, of course, wasn't the only one "smiling" in 1824. There were, at the start of the year, five candidates — Adams, Clay, Calhoun, Crawford and Jackson. Crawford, an early front-runner, took ill. Doctors mistreated his disease, bleeding and blistering him until he was occasionally blind and bedridden, and out of the presidential race although still popular among his supporters. All the candidates were avowed Republicans, and all took about the same position on every topic. Calhoun dropped out in March, and ran for vice-president. John Quincy Adams stood on his record as secretary of state, and Henry Clay offered his American System. Jackson, with obscure political views, knew that his military achievements appealed to the common man.

The contest featured loud accusations and short tempers. By 1824, Adams reported that "the Presidential canvassing proceeds with increasing heat." In Quincy, John Adams cheered his boy on, and wrote fondly to Thomas Jefferson at Monticello about "our John." At one point John Adams told Jefferson, perhaps recalling John Quincy's closeness to the Virginian, "He appeared to be almost as much your boy as mine."

In the election of 1824, the popular vote went: Jackson, 153,544; Adams, 108,740; Clay, 47,136; and Crawford, 46,618. Jackson had 99 electoral votes; Adams, 84 (consisting of 51 from New England; 26 of New York's 36; 1 of Delaware's 2; 3 of Maryland's 11; 2 of Louisiana's 5; and 1 of Illinois's 6); Crawford, 41; and Clay, 37.

Since no candidate had a majority, the verdict now lay

with the House of Representatives, whose members would choose among Jackson, Adams and Crawford, with each state casting one vote. Clay, in his own words, was transformed as Speaker of the House from "a candidate before the people, into an elector for the people." He had become a kingmaker, and began working the parties and banquets, the boarding-houses of Washington.

Clay and Adams, after some arranging, met privately in the evening of January 9, 1825. There is much debate about what was said and agreed upon, but Adams wrote in his diary only that he and Clay discussed politics and that Clay spoke "with the utmost freedom of men and things." There may have been an "understanding" about the voting in the House, but Clay would have considered any bargaining naive, and Adams would have thought it sinful.

Whatever was agreed upon, votes were delivered. On January 23, Clay publicly began lining up his troops. Adams wrote in his diary: "There is at this moment a very high state of excitement in the House. Mr. Clay and the majority of the Ohio and Kentucky delegations having yesterday unequivocally avowed their determination to vote for me." On January 28, the *Columbian Observer* of Philadelphia accused the two men of a deal for the delivery of these votes.

The burden of the election, with all its wheeling and dealing, fell in one cold moment upon Stephen Van Rensselaer of New York, "a kindly, upright, simple old Federalist gentleman." Toward the end, it was widely believed that Van Rensselaer was wavering between Jackson and Crawford. New York's delegation in the House was split, 17 to 17. By some accounts, Van Rensselaer's mind had been made up to vote against John Quincy Adams "not five minutes before the vote was taken." Martin Van Buren, in his autobiography, gives this colorful account of Van Rensselaer's decision and choice: "He took his seat fully resolved to vote for Mr. Crawford, but before the box reached him, he dropped his head upon the edge of his desk and made a brief appeal to his Maker for his guidance in the matter — a practise he frequently observed on great emergencies — and when he removed his hand from his eyes he saw on the floor directly below him a ticket bearing the name John Quincy Adams.

This occurrence, at a moment of great excitement and anxiety, he was led to regard as an answer to his appeal, and taking up the ticket he put it in the box."

The first ballot, with Van Rensselaer's help, was significant. Adams received the vote of 13 states; Jackson, 7; and Crawford, 4. On February 9, John Quincy Adams, president-elect, wrote in his diary: "May the blessing of God rest upon the event of this day!"

One longtime antagonist, John Randolph, saw things a little differently: "It was impossible to win the game, gentlemen," he said. "The cards were packed." If they were, what remained was to play out the hand. Two days after his election, John Quincy Adams went to President Monroe and told him that Henry Clay would be his choice for the new secretary of state. It was an important move, for every president since John Adams had first served as secretary of state. Monroe may have wanted to see De Witt Clinton as secretary, but he remained polite, and quiet, to the end.

From this moment on, Henry Clay would spend his life refuting the accusation that "bargain and corruption" had won for him the State Department post. Cries of bargain and corruption echoed in Washington — and would persist — as John Quincy Adams, the sixth president of the United States, went by carriage weary and dark-eyed after two sleepless nights to his inauguration.

9

The Great Object of My Life Has Failed

[1825–1829]

*A*LMOST from the beginning, John Quincy Adams's four years as president were filled with political blunder, miscalculations and personal sadness. The sixth president, the second member of his family to attain the office, sought to unite his squabbling nation and mold it to his personal vision.

In his inaugural address, President Adams asked his countrymen to make the sacrifice "of discarding every remnant of rancor against each other, of embracing as countrymen and friends." But America was already splitting into self-interested sections. To unite this fractious country would take a man sensitive to its many voices, who could woo and jolly the disparate men and regions. But Adams was a humorless and stern New Englander who preferred to lecture, not coax. To move the nation toward his vision required majority support. But Adams was rumored to have gained his office by "bargain and corruption," not by popular acclaim.

He thought – he hoped – that the American people would rise above party politics and sectionalism for the betterment of their nation. He was wrong, and what was worse, he was, as always, stubborn.

On November 25, 1825, he spent an hour and a half reading aloud to his restless cabinet a draft of his first annual message to Congress, to be given in December. The message contained the details of his plan for the massive internal development and improvement of America. He recommended the founding of a national university, the financing of scientific explorations, the establishment of a uniform standard of weights and measures, the building of astronomical observatories, the creation of a department of the interior, the reform of patent laws and the undertaking of a large-scale development program, including canals and highways.

From today's perspective, none of the proposals appears unusual. But in 1825, large numbers of Americans strictly interpreted the Constitution, and strongly opposed federal intrusion into their lives. The speech contained something that offended every special-interest group in the country.

In some ways, Adams could not have picked a better initial audience than his cabinet, for rather than being filled with his supporters it represented almost all of the principal factions and bickerings of the nation. There was Samuel L. Southard of New Jersey, secretary of the navy and John C. Calhoun's friend; James Barbour of Virginia, secretary of war and a friend of the slowly dying but still popular William H. Crawford; William Wirt, retained as attorney general. Southard, Barbour and Wirt heard the draft and disliked it. Even Henry Clay, secretary of state, whose American System proposed similar internal projects and growth, opposed the new executive department, the changing of patent laws and the national university. He "approved of the general principles" but "scrupled a great part of the details." Only Richard Rush of Pennsylvania, recalled from London to be secretary of the treasury, liked "near the whole."

President Adams felt compelled to present his ideas and ignored the opinions of his cabinet. On December 6, 1825, he went before the Congress and delivered his first annual message. With it, he ended any influence he might have had over that body, and lost his already precarious popularity with his fellow countrymen. His speech did not consider the fears and desires of the American people; indeed, he himself was out of touch with them. It failed to take account of political realities and offended opinion widely held in that day. Its tone seemed threatening and superior.

Adams called the government's refusal to use all its power for the benefit of the people a "treachery to the most sacred of trusts." But many Americans in 1825 saw a far more sacred trust: the reduction of the government's power, not its expansion. Adams jabbed at Congress for its "indolence" and "palsy" before its constituents — a poor method of seeking congressional support in the face of the suspicion with which his victory was regarded. Moreover, in his argument for America's development he cited the example of "the nations of Europe and their rulers," an echo of his father, who had been labeled a monarchist by some of the men who were still serving in the Congress.

In this one speech, President Adams had succeeded in arousing not only the animosity of his countrymen, but also the cries that "All Adamses are monarchists."

The American people did not share Adams's views of their nation, nor his desire to increase the role of the central government. They accused him of seeking power for himself and greeted his ideas with mockery: his unfortunate term for the national observatories — "those light-houses of the skies" — became a national joke. "I fell," Adams wrote much later, "and with me fell, I fear never to rise again in my day, the system of internal improvement by means of national energies. The great object of my life . . . has failed."

Concern for the power of the central government was not lessened when Adams proposed that revenue from the sale of the public lands be used for his internal improvements. Since this would raise the price of those lands, Adams was accused of seeking to restrain the westward flow of the American people, of holding them in the East as a labor pool for eastern industrialists. This opinion was not diminished when in 1827 Secretary Rush called the American pioneer a "consumer of capital and a drain on the labor market." Thus, the western pioneering states joined in opposition to the president and his "perilous experiment."

Almost from the outset of Adams's administration, the

Jackson, Calhoun and Crawford factions turned against him and Clay. Vice-President Calhoun went over to Andrew Jackson's camp as early as 1826. After the elections of that year, a new party began to emerge from the old Republican Party: the Democratic Republican Party, or the Democratic Party, whose supporters later simply called it "The Democracy."

President Adams sent former supporters to this new party in droves. For one thing, he refused to gather power by patronage, nor would he dismiss opponents from government service. (He removed only twelve men from office during his four years.) John McLean of Ohio, an outspoken Adams opponent, was retained as postmaster general, where he dispensed valuable patronage to Adams's enemies. The customs-house officers in Philadelphia and Charleston — the customs were a grand political plum in those days — were hostile to the president and appointed hostile subordinates. But Adams told Clay he would remove "no officer for merely preferring another candidate for the Presidentcy." He wrote in his diary: "I will not dismiss, or drop from the Executive offices, able and faithful political opponents to provide for my own partisans."

By 1826, Congress was in fine voice against the president, and nowhere was the tone more strident than in the Senate. When Adams nominated two delegates to an abortive congress in Panama, the Senate challenged his right to do so. Martin Van Buren of New York proposed two seemingly tame resolutions asking the president whether all documents by him on the Panama mission could be made public, and if so, which ones. Adams could have made a brief and courteous reply. Instead, he resorted not to conciliation but haughty resentment.

Adams's reply aroused the frail body and tormented mind of Senator John Randolph of Virginia, who sometimes spoke from the Senate floor with a bottle of his favorite porter close at hand, but employed a tongue corrosive in its sarcasm. He had long opposed the Adamses, and called them "the American House of Stuarts." He particularly disliked John Quincy Adams. "The cub," Randolph had once said, "is a greater bear than the old one."

He took up the Senate's cry with a rambling and disconnected speech on March 30 that began, "Our name is Legion." Haunted by drink and poor health, he poured his shrill invective on Clay and Adams. He described the secretary of state as "this being, so brilliant and yet so corrupt, which, like a rotten mackerel by moonlight, shines and stinks and stinks and shines." With dark insinuation verging on madness, he declared that the invitations to the congress in Panama had been forged or doctored by Clay. Recalling *Tom Jones*, he spoke of the association of Clay and Adams as "the coalition of Blifil and Black George — by the combination, unheard of till then, of the puritan with the blackleg." No senator called the Virginian to order; neither did Vice-President Calhoun, presiding over the Senate, raise his voice. Clay immediately challenged Randolph to a duel, according to the custom of the time.*

The Clay–Randolph duel, held in Virginia, was bizarre. Both parties were so flustered that they blazed away after the first count and hit nothing. When the next count was made, Randolph stood calmly while Clay, a poor shot, fired, ripping the senator's long flannel coat at the hip. Randolph, the southern gentleman, fired into the air, and marched toward Clay with hand extended: "You owe me a coat, Mr. Clay," he said. The secretary of state grasped his hand and replied: "I am glad the debt is no greater." Everyone returned to Washington in high spirits.

Meanwhile, President Adams, writing as PATRICK HENRY in the *National Journal*, took aim at Vice-President Calhoun for not silencing Randolph in the Senate. He accused Calhoun of being "the residuary legatee of General Jackson's pretensions to the Presidency." Calhoun, writing as ONSLOW in the *Intelligencer*, argued that while the Constitution made him a member of the Senate it did not give him authority to call a senator to order for language used during a debate. Adams replied, and the debate in the newspapers revealed to

* Dueling was in its prime during Adams's presidency, and he strongly disapproved of it. Gentlemen who were insulted demanded apologies or the opportunity for revenge upon a field of honor, as in the famous Burr–Hamilton duel of 1804. Even major officials dueled: Lord Castlereagh, William Pitt, George Canning, the duke of Wellington.

the American public and foreign diplomats the widening schism between members of the Adams administration.

Adams never spoke or wrote publicly of Randolph, but in his diary he noted his "besotted violence" and "drunken speeches" in the Senate, and he characterized him as "the image . . . of a great man stamped upon base metal."

Randolph knew how to prick Adams's sensitive tissues, and no comment pierced as deep as the accusation that Adams's presidency was doomed to failure. "I have borne some humble part in putting down the dynasty of John the First," Randolph announced, "and by the Grace of God, I hope to aid in putting down the dynasty of John the Second." He had some help — much of it from Adams himself.

Since the War of 1812, the United States had sought improved trading rights with the British colonies in the West Indies. But while the British in their own view had been conciliatory, the Americans had replied by crippling the slave-trade convention and with the protective tariff of 1824. Where diplomacy and tact might have altered the outcome, the Americans — and John Quincy Adams — had remained, the British thought, brusque and stubborn.

Adams sent Gallatin off to London to seek a balance between the British and the American trading interests. Gallatin was instructed to accept what the British had asked for in 1824, when Adams was secretary of state. It was too late. Gallatin got off his ship in England to read of a new Order in Council that blocked trade by the United States with all British colonies except those in North America, and imposed a heavy duty on that trade.

The outcries in America were loud. Opposition newspapers attacked the Adams administration for indirection and weakness. "Heaven grant," said the *Richmond Enquirer*, "it may be drawing to a close." Martin Van Buren in the Senate was sure the administration was doing just that, and declared smugly: "You may rest assured that Mr. Adams' re-election is out of the question."

Congress abandoned Adams to the British, and under the Act of 1823, the president issued a proclamation closing American ports to British ships sailing from British colonies in the Western Hemisphere. This left Gallatin and the negotiations in London as the only hope of settlement. But the Orders in Council were proving popular among the British people, who were suffering a depression, and the government refused to cancel them. Gallatin left London, beaten. For John Quincy Adams, Van Buren's prediction proved correct: the loss of the West Indies trade in 1826 and his failure to regain it helped to end his administration.

Adams's third annual message to Congress was composed "in such agony of mind . . . that I am ashamed of it, and am almost afraid to read it to my confidential advisors." It was a sad commentary, but there was little to report except defeat and frustration. Abroad and at home, the Adams administration commanded little respect.

In 1827, Adams also had to face growing rebellion in the remote sections of the nation. In one case, the cotton farmers of Georgia wanted rich bottom land that belonged to Creek and Cherokee Indians, land the federal government in Jefferson's day had promised to obtain for the Georgians. When he took office, Adams had found on his desk the Treaty of Indian Spring, which agreed to an exchange of 4,700,000 acres of Georgia cotton land for equal acreage west of the Mississippi and $400,000. It had been signed, it was claimed, by the "Chiefs of the Creek Nation, in Council assembled." President Adams approved it, even though a United States Indian agent, Colonel John Crowell, rushed to Washington and exposed the treaty as a fraud. Tired of federal delay, Georgia had gone ahead and obtained the lands by gaining the agreement of a few minor chiefs.

This treaty was replaced by another, the Treaty of Washington, in which the Indians ceded all lands in Georgia except those west of the Chattahoochee River. But the governor of Georgia and the state legislature argued that a treaty once proclaimed was law, and sought to return to the old Indian Spring agreement. The governor claimed that the new treaty was a violation of states' rights. "Georgia," he told the president, "is sovereign on her own soil." Through a letter to the governor from Secretary of War Barbour, Adams hinted at sending in U.S. troops. The Georgian put his militia on alert and vowed to attack any federal troops. Adams had to yield because he lacked political support for his treaty. In yet a third treaty, the Creeks and Cherokees lost their land in Georgia and faced a long march to the West, over the "Trail of Tears," on which many of them died. Georgia's stance, moreover, encouraged Alabama and Mississippi to take a strong states' rights position against Indians within their borders.

The issue troubled Adams long afterwards, and in a letter in 1837 he wrote: "We have done more harm to the Indians since our Revolution than had ever been done to them by the French and English nations before. . . . These are crying sins for which we are answerable before a higher jurisdiction."

States' rights defenders, victorious in Georgia, quickly tested President Adams over another instrument of national policy: the protective tariff. The elections of 1826 gave — for the first time in U.S. history — a large majority in Congress against the administration.

The West held new power, and was growing at a phenomenal rate. Between 1820 and 1830, the population of Ohio increased 60 percent; that of Indiana, 58 percent; of Illinois, 170 percent; of Missouri, 125 percent. In the northeast and New England, capital was shifting into industry, especially into textiles. The economy was thriving again after the panic and depression of 1819–1821. The tariff of 1824 had pleased the Midwest and New England. On the other hand, the agricultural South, which sold cotton to England and bought manufactured goods cheaply from abroad, saw the tariff as opposing her interests. States' rights proponents — "Southern boll-weevils in the growth of nationalism" — argued that the Constitution did not specifically grant the federal government the power to pass a protective tariff.

Adams was well aware of the entangling briar patch of states' rights, slavery and the tariff. He let Rush, his secretary of the treasury, extol tariffs. He remained publicly silent. But the tariff issue burst onto the national scene by late 1827; conventions were held and lobbyists besieged the Capitol.

Andrew Jackson's supporters saw the tariff as a means of separating President Adams from his protectionist constituents. By putting together an unreasonable tariff, they could get protectionists to vote against it. Should it pass, Adams would have to sign it, and alienate the South, or veto it, and

When the Creek and Cherokee Indians were banished from Georgia and most of the Southeast, they marched along the "Trail of Tears" into Oklahoma Territory. They made peace with their new neighbors, the Plains Indians, during this seventeen-tribe council to promote friendship, held during the summer of 1843 in Tahlequah, Oklahoma.

DETAIL: TRIBAL COUNCIL AT TAHLEQUAH, OKLAHOMA 1843. OIL BY JOHN MIX STANLEY

anger the protectionist Middle and New England states. This was a politicians' tariff, designed, said Senator Randolph, for "the manufacture of a President of the United States" — Andrew Jackson.

Senators loaded the bill with "abominations": high duties on anything any senator wanted protected. One commented: "Its enemies spiced it with whatever they thought would render it distasteful; its friends took it, drugged as it was."

The Tariff of Abominations passed narrowly, and President Adams, knowing he couldn't win, signed it. In his last annual message before Congress, in December, 1828, he referred to the tariff publicly for the first time and placed the blame for its passage squarely on the members of Congress.

His placing of the blame had little effect; the damage was done. In the South, the price of cotton had dropped from a high in June, 1825, of 29.2 cents a pound to 12 cents in 1826 and to 8.8 cents in 1827. At a large antitariff rally in Columbia, South Carolina, Thomas Cooper raised an ominous cry: "Is it worth our while to continue this Union of States, where the North demands to be our masters and we are required to be their tributaries?"

Dark times were coming for the nation, and for John Quincy Adams. Life in the President's House, first occupied by his father and mother, was "gloomy" and was marred by personal loneliness, family squabbles, illness, hypochondria and deep sadness.

There were, of course, pleasant moments: dinners with old friends like Lafayette, who paid his farewell visit to the United States in 1824–1825, and Henry Clay, who enjoyed rehashing old controversies or chewing over current politics. These especially delighted Charles Francis Adams. Just as his father had done in Paris at Jefferson's house, he listened in. And there were weddings and new babies, levees and "drawing-rooms." But from its beginning to its end, John Quincy Adams's presidency was tainted with argument, dissension, strife, and sometimes danger, and even death.

Sixteen months after taking office, on July 4, 1826, Adams was listening in the Capitol to patriotic speeches. It was the fiftieth anniversary of the signing of the Declaration of Independence, and unknown to the president his father lay dying in Quincy while Jefferson was near death in Virginia.

John Adams, ninety-one years old, knew it was the Fourth: "It is a great day. It is a good day!" he said. He had already sent a toast to the townspeople of Quincy: "Independence forever!" Resting quietly, he spoke to members of his family, and in the afternoon, about one o'clock, his granddaughter Susan B. Clark saw his lips moving and heard him say: "Jefferson still survives." These were his last words. Although he remained alert enough to recognize his favorite grandson, George Washington Adams, John Adams could no longer speak. At six o'clock, he slipped quietly into death.

Only five hours earlier — at one o'clock, just as Adams spoke his last words — Thomas Jefferson, the author of the Declaration of Independence, died at Monticello.

The deaths of the two old men who had been colleagues in Philadelphia that hot July, then political rivals, presidents, and — in the end — friends once again, seemed beyond mere coincidence. When John Quincy Adams learned of the events and circumstances he would write: "The time, the manner, the coincidence . . . are visible and palpable marks of Divine favor."

Not until the ninth of July did Adams hear of his father's death. His grief was deep. He had lost a friend and advisor, perhaps the only other human being who understood his loneliness and isolation as president.

As he arrived in Quincy, Adams, then fifty-nine, felt that his life, too, was drawing to its close. His father had left him an option to buy ninety-three acres of land and the house "where for near forty years he [had] resided and where I have passed many of the happiest days of my life." He could not abandon it. "I shall," he wrote in his diary, "within two or three years, if indulged with life and health, need a place of retirement. Where else should I go? This will be a safe and pleasant retreat, where I may pursue literary occupations as long and as much as I can take pleasure in them."

He accepted the option, then headed back to Washington with the "anxious and consoling hope" of returning for good in three years. It would be, as it turned out, a long and trying three years.

ABOVE: MEMORIAL WREATH PRESENTED TO
MRS. JOHN QUINCY ADAMS.
NEEDLEWORK BY SCHOOLGIRLS, 1826

MEMORIAL WREATH TO JOHN ADAMS
AND THOMAS JEFFERSON. NEEDLEWORK,
DATE AND MAKER UNKNOWN

In the capital, the President's House, now beginning to be called the White House, stood about a mile from the Capitol on the dusty road to Georgetown, and looked in 1826 much as it does today, except that the north portico had not yet been built and the large shade trees were yet to be planted. The house was surrounded by low sheds and stables for eight horses, a small dairy and other farm uses. It had an unobstructed view into the open countryside west of Sixteenth Street and had been built to overlook the Potomac River. From its south porch, beyond the formal garden, meadowland swept several hundred yards to the river. Cows and sheep grazed there. From the east, Tiber Creek flowed across Fifteenth Street to the Potomac, forming islands and finally a shallow estuary.

The White House had no plumbing and no running water, but the Adamses somehow made themselves comfortable. The house was filled with family and relatives — most of them Louisa Adams's. Three orphaned children of her sister, Nancy Hellen — Mary Catherine, Johnson and Thomas J. Hellen — became permanent residents. They caused John Quincy Adams almost as much trouble as his own sons. Thomas went to Exeter and then to Harvard for two years — all paid for by John Quincy Adams. But Thomas disliked the rigors of Harvard and dropped out, popping up at the White House, where, without a job or education, he was a constant headache. Johnson, the older brother, enjoyed life at the White House for three years before he ran away — taking one of the family housemaids with him.

As difficult as the boys were, Mary Catherine caused her aunt and uncle — not to mention her masculine cousins — even more anxiety. She had lived with the Adamses since 1817. Each of the Adams boys found Mary Hellen, who was short and round and flirtatious, a very enticing young thing indeed. In his diary, Charles Francis called her "one of the most capricious women that were ever formed in a capricious race." But while Charles may have fallen first, it was George Washington Adams who fell hardest and thought he had won Mary's fickle and tempting heart. In the summer of 1823, he approached his grave father, who had very firm ideas about when a young man should marry, to ask his consent to an engagement. George assured his father that the engagement would be long, at least until he was established as a lawyer, "perhaps four or five years." John Quincy Adams set forth conditions and gave his reluctant consent.

In pursuing his studies, first at Harvard, then in Daniel Webster's law office in Boston, George was in Washington relatively little. He was admitted to the Massachusetts bar in 1824, and won a seat in the state legislature in 1826. In these years he unfortunately proved to be an indifferent letter writer and an inattentive suitor.

Meanwhile, Charles Francis graduated from Harvard, returned to Washington to study law under his father, and then went back to Boston to follow George into Daniel Webster's office. In 1829, at the age of twenty-two, Charles was admitted to the Massachusetts bar. During visits to Washington, he had found Mary still a tease despite her engagement to George. "She has some alluring ways which are apt to make every man forget himself," he confided to his diary. "George . . . would be in a perfect fever and sickness if he was to imagine that she had encouraged me in the least."

When the Adamses moved into the White House, Mary and her brothers moved in, too. She soon discovered that John Adams II was very much on hand. Thrown out of Harvard with most of his class in 1823, John had little to do until 1825, when he became his father's private secretary after the election. Before long, Charles Francis was writing anxiously: "Mary has been behaving unworthily to George. . . . My Mother is half inclined to the marriage and half opposed, my Father tacitly opposed. . . . I am sorry for John, who, I understand, is the victim of her arts."

But John was a willing victim. He and Mary saw each other daily. He was handsome and carried an air of "affected mystery" about him that was both alluring and repelling. John stole the lady, and sometime before 1827, Mary broke her engagement to George. A sensitive and romantic man, George was shattered.

Although the Adamses frowned on the romance, a wedding date was set. On February 25, 1828, a handful of guests attended the wedding of John and Mary in the Blue Room of the White House. Neither Charles nor George was present.

Despite his misgivings, President Adams enjoyed the ceremony and danced "a Virginia reel with great spirit." At the end of the day, he wrote in his diary: "The company retired about midnight. May the blessing of God almighty rest upon this union." For her part, the mother of the groom reported to Charles: "I am not much in a humour to write. I shall therefore only announce to you the fact that the wedding is over, that Madame is cool easy and indifferent as ever and that John looks already as if he had all the cares in the world upon his shoulders and my heart tells me that there is much to fear."

But there was little peace in the White House yet for President Adams. The "cool" bride and her nervous groom honeymooned at home and enjoyed a large formal reception for them in the Yellow Room, and several dinners. Louisa was "quite unwell" through most of it: "Dr. Huntt was with her three times in the day." Mary and John stayed on at the White House, and their first baby, Mary Louisa Adams, was born there on December 2, 1828. Less than two years later, Georgiana Frances Adams was born in Quincy.

To enliven slow evenings at the White House, Louisa Adams and her sons, and sometimes other relatives, played the pianoforte and the harp, a popular instrument at that time. Mrs. Adams could not only play both, but she also wrote verse, much of it reflecting her early meetings in Washington with Thomas Moore, "the sentimental favorite of the day." She wrote original dramatic pieces; one was titled, "The Wag, or Just from College: A Farce in three Acts." Another, reflecting American sympathy for Greek independence, was called "The Captives of Scio of the Liberal Americans: A Melo-Drame." She made several copies of these plays, and the Adams family undoubtedly acted in them during evenings in the White House.

The president and Mrs. Adams stayed home a great deal. They continued the rule begun during Monroe's administration of not accepting invitations to go out, and preferred to entertain at home. They could do so impressively, if they wished. A young sculptor, recently graduated from Harvard, where dinners were not the equal of those at the White House, attended a typical Adams party: "I dined yesterday at the President's. The party consisted of about twenty members of Congress and twenty gentlemen from different parts of the country. . . . The furniture was in the gout Français. An enormous gilt waiter, with many vases, temples, and female figures in different attitudes holding candles, gave light to the whole table. We sat down at six o'clock, and had every variety of fish, flesh and fowl. I cannot pronounce on the canvasbacks, for they had been boned and cut in slices. I took them for cake. We had macaroni! Every drinkable under the sun — porter, cider, claret, sherry, Burgundy, champagne, Tokay, and the choicest madeira that ever passed my larynx. We came away about ten."

To company that interested him, John Quincy Adams could be "eloquent," rising above all others. But the slow-witted and mundane he bore with silence. When Gulian C. Verplanck dined at the White House, he came away certain that the president "himself is very dull and his neighbors at table when he gives formal dinners have a hard time of it."

The Adamses also held New Year's drawing rooms or receptions that lasted from noon until three o'clock and were sometimes attended by several thousand guests. Their fortnightly levees were a social event in Washington; anyone could attend, and invitations were sought by friend and foe alike. One major incident began at a White House reception on April 2, 1828. That evening, Russell Jarvis, a reporter for the *United States Telegraph* and a partner of Duff Green, the *Telegraph*'s editor and a "fiery opposition journalist," attended. Jarvis's barbs had rankled the Adamses, and would continue to do so, but he brazenly entered the levee with his wife, her parents and two other ladies.

After being presented to Mrs. Adams, and received cordially, they walked into the East Room. There, John Adams II was talking with the Reverend Caleb Stetson, who turned to admire the entering ladies and asked John who one of them was. Adams replied in a loud voice heard by everyone in the room: "That is the wife of one Russell Jarvis. *There* is a man who, if he had any idea of propriety in the conduct of a gentleman, ought not to show his face in this house."

The insult was clearly heard by Jarvis, who politely left with his wife and friends. He mulled over the incident for a few days; then he and Green saw an opportunity to strike at the president by challenging his son to a duel. It was known that the president opposed dueling, but if John ignored a challenge, many parts of the country would call him a coward. Jarvis wrote John Adams II demanding an explanation. But young Adams refused to answer the letter. Jarvis then planned to accost Adams, as prescribed by the dueling code, to personally insult him and provoke a challenge.

Jarvis lay in wait for him at the Capitol, and on April 15, jumped him in the Rotunda as he was carrying messages from his father to the Congress. He yanked Adams's nose — an approved provocation — and slapped his face. Ribald rumors of the day said that he also spun Adams around and delivered several kicks to his backside.

Jarvis's attack did not provoke a duel, as planned. Instead, President Adams sent to the Congress — after Clay had carefully measured its mood — a message that his private secretary had been "waylaid and assaulted" in the Rotunda by a "person," and that Congress should consider legislation that would secure the official avenues of exchange between White House and Capitol and prevent such disorders.

Newspapers around the country took sides, and the capital was in tumult. The *National Journal*, an Adams paper, called the "assault within the Capitol" an "outrage." But the *Telegraph*, protecting one of its own, considered "the pulling of the Prince's nose" a "signal chastisement" of the "Royal puppy."

Congress held an investigation, at which both antagonists appeared and were cross-examined. The public outcry was quieted. But although the scuffle in the Rotunda passed slowly from the public mind, the practice of dueling did not. Attempts to censure Russell Jarvis failed, and Mrs. Adams long held that the nose pulling had ruined her son's career.

Louisa Adams was a troubled woman during these later years in Washington. She still suffered from long periods of poor health and depression. After 1826, she no longer traveled to Quincy with her husband. She withdrew more and more into the White House, becoming at times almost a recluse, grieving at other times that she was a political liability to her husband. His relentless ambition to be president, spurred by his parents, had made him distant and restrained; she hated the social duties, the politics and the abrasions that came with public office. Where he was anxious, vigilant and strict with their sons, she was inclined to be easygoing and never pressured them to earn higher grades or honors. He could scour the White House with his temper; so could she. Where he was irascible, she fought with razor sarcasm.

In 1828, John Quincy Adams must have felt that life itself was unraveling. His ambition to be president had turned to bitter political trial, and his career and family seemed to be coming apart at the same time. He tried to hold himself together, as his father might have, with self-discipline and self-determination. He busied himself with the details of his office. He read Plutarch, Cicero, Milton and, as always, his Bible. Every night, as was his lifelong habit, he said the child's prayer taught to him by his mother: "Now I lay me down to sleep. . . ." He increased the pace of his walks, and reduced the time it took him to go from the White House to the Capitol and back from an hour and fifteen minutes to sixty minutes. He was fond of the early morning, when he could listen to the various birdcalls, and sometimes rode horseback twelve miles or more into the rural countryside. He took a keen interest in the vegetable garden at the White House, and in the trees and shrubs planted around Washington — he noted which had been hurt by storms or insects. He collected acorns, nuts, seeds, vines and shoots for transplanting.

He also loved to swim, and thought it good for his health. Before sunrise, during the hot months, he often strode down Seventeenth Street to a point of land not far from the present site of the Washington Monument, where the Tiber and Potomac flowed together. There, an old sycamore and a large rock made an ideal place in which to peel off his clothes and dive in. Although few Washingtonians were out at this hour, a few did catch the president swimming in the buff. There appears to be no proof, however, that Anne Royall, a persistent journalist, sat on President Adams's clothes early one summer's morning until he promised to give her an interview. Thurlow Weed of New York was one of those who spotted him and gave this account: "[I saw] a gentleman in nankeen pantaloons and a blue pea jacket, walking rapidly

When John Quincy Adams was president, the White House was a short distance from Tiber Creek, which flowed south of the mansion. Not far away, the Tiber joined the Potomac, and there Adams liked to peel off his clothes and swim— near this spot in the engraving.

THE PRESIDENT'S HOUSE FROM THE RIVER. FROM AN ENGRAVING, ABOUT 1830

from the White House towards the river. This was John Quincy Adams, President of the United States. I moved off to a respectful distance. The President began to disrobe before he reached a tree on the brink of the river, where he deposited his clothes, and then plunged in head first and struck out fifteen or twenty rods, swimming rapidly and turning occasionally upon his back, seeming as much at ease in that element as upon terra firma. Coming out, he rubbed himself thoroughly with napkins, which he had brought for the purpose in his hand. The sun had not yet risen when he had dressed himself and was returning to the presidential mansion."

But even this enjoyment was tinged with danger and warning. One summer, the president, John Adams II and a servant set out to cross the Potomac — John Adams II swimming, the others in a leaky small canoe. The president had removed only some of his clothes; the servant, Antoine, was naked. The canoe began taking water and was overturned almost in midriver. The president struck out for shore, but the long sleeves of his shirt "filled with water and hung like two fifty-six pound weights upon my arms." He later wrote that "while struggling for life and gasping for breath, [I] had ample leisure time to reflect upon my own indiscretion." He made the far bank, where John joined him; Antoine easily swam in, and after dressing himself with what clothes had been left behind, walked into town for a carriage. They got home almost six hours late, and found that no one had missed them.

By 1828, after the opposition had taken control of Congress, his prospects were depressingly clear: he would be the second one-term president in the nation's history. His father had been the first. Adams discovered new aches; he was nervous. Pains cramped his right side, sometimes endangering him while he swam. Indigestion and catarrh kept him awake at night. He was dejected, and recoiled at the "toil and distemper" of his office. He felt "a sluggish carelessness of life, an imaginary wish that it were terminated" — the identical symptoms his son George was complaining of in Boston. He wrote that "my eyes complain of inflammation, and my heart is sick."

His state of mind caused him to see portents in common-place events. A chronometer stopped functioning, and he thought of the old moral "Lean not on friendship, nor on time." The election a foregone conclusion, he wrote on January 1, 1829: "The year begins in gloom. My wife had a sleepless and painful night. The dawn was over-cast, and, as I began to write, my shaded lamp went out, self-extinguished." Was it an omen? Adams considered, and reflected that "it was only for lack of oil, [but] the notice of so trivial an incident may serve but to mark the present temper of my mind."

By the presidential elections of 1828, the population of the nation had increased further, and the qualifications for voting had become less severe in a number of states; the electorate had changed so much that Martin Van Buren, who was running for the governorship of New York, was advised to make "justices, constables & all the minor active men in the towns familiar with your name" — sound advice that reflected the new forces in national politics.

In that year Americans had legitimate grievances. They wanted to abolish imprisonment for debt — in Massachusetts a blind man who owed six dollars could be jailed, and in Rhode Island a woman could go to prison for a debt of sixty-eight cents. They wanted lien laws passed that would prevent employers from declaring themselves bankrupt — as many of them did — to avoid payment of wages. A lien might at least get a worker part of what he was owed.

Americans in 1828 sought better opportunities; they engaged in what might be called the politics of aspiration. Free tax-supported education, a major issue, meant much; in New York State alone some twenty-four thousand children between the ages of five and fifteen did not go to school, partly because their parents, unable to pay tuition, would not take a pauper's oath. Children worked from sunup to sundown in the factories of the cities and in the fields of America. Education promised relief from such labor and the opportunity to get ahead.

Workingmen were organizing. Boston carpenters had gone on strike in 1825. Philadelphia journeymen carpenters had struck in 1827, and that same year the Mechanics' Union of Trade Associations was organized. In 1828, laborers held their Workingmen's Party Convention. The common man was demanding that he share in democracy and that his voice be heard. He looked upon John Quincy Adams and his national improvement scheme as favoring "aristocracy" and the moneyed elite. He agreed with the *Mechanics Free Press* that the tariff (which stuck to Adams like a tar baby) was "most prone to reduce the wages of workmen," and he had been hurt by Adams's West Indian trade policy. Andrew Jackson was his man, a symbol of the changes taking place. It was an image Jackson enjoyed, and one his friends had been cultivating since 1825 at fish fries and militia musters around the nation.

The campaign of 1828, then, turned not on issues but on personalities. Adams was called a monarchist, gourmandizer and spendthrift. A billiard table and chess set were offered as proof of his using public money to enhance the "President's Palace" with "gaming tables and gambling furniture." He was accused of being a procurer while in St. Petersburg and of obtaining a young American girl for the enjoyment of Tsar Alexander I. He was accused also of being an intellectual, and Jackson of being a "ruffian," gambler, duelist, and drunkard. The campaign was between "John Quincy Adams who can write" and "Andrew Jackson who can fight."

Jackson was accused of a lot more. John Binns, editor of the *Philadelphia Democratic Press*, printed a handbill attacking Jackson as the murderer of six militiamen during the War of 1812. This became known as the Coffin Handbill. Worse, as early as 1825 there had been whisperings that Jackson was an adulterer. The *Cincinnati Gazette* claimed that Jackson had knowingly lived in adultery with Rachel Jackson, and the story was quickly picked up by the *Washington National Journal* — a paper that supported Adams. The president might have stopped the slanderous reports there, but he did not.*

On this issue, Jackson was the one who behaved like a

This detail from a political cartoon of 1829 spoofs the Adams-Jackson presidential campaign. The Adams turtle, its neck labeled Quincy, tugs a rope attached to a Jackson crocodile (not seen) that is busily chewing up militiamen.

---

* In fact, Rachel Jackson was a divorcee. She and Jackson had been married about two years before discovering that the legislative act supposedly granting her divorce had only awarded her a preliminary decree. They immediately remarried, but the rumor spread, and stung.

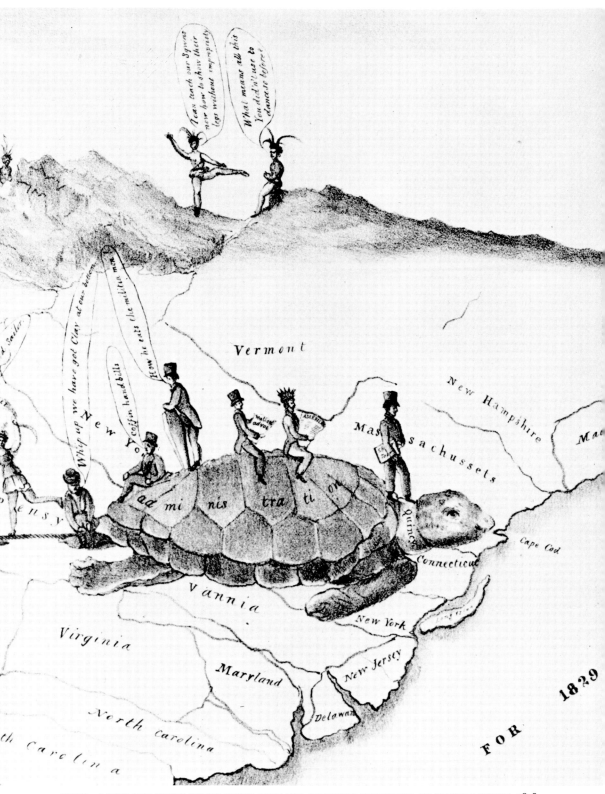

DETAIL: A NEW MAP OF THE UNITED STATES WITH THE ADDITIONAL TERRITORIES. BY ANTHOLY IMBERT, 1828

gentleman. When Duff Green sought to balance the attack by creating in his *Telegraph* a fabricated issue over alleged premarital relations between the Adamses, Jackson quickly crushed the effort. "I never war against females," said the general, "and it is only the base and the cowardly that do."

Rachel Jackson was dragged into the glare of the publicity. A short, swarthy woman with the manners of the frontier, she enjoyed her evening pipe. Jackson deeply loved her and had fought a duel because her honor had been questioned. Now he watched helplessly as the attacks fell upon her. Her health had been poor and now failed quickly. "I had rather be a door-keeper in the house of God," she told him, "than to live in that palace in Washington." She got her wish.

Jackson swamped Adams, 647,276 to 508,604; he took 178 electoral votes to Adams's 83. But the victory was hollow: The month following the election, Rachel Jackson died, and her husband was certain that the campaign abuse from Adams's "friends" had killed her. He refused to make the customary call upon the outgoing president.

Adams, for his part, refused to attend Jackson's inauguration. Adams viewed himself as rejected by the people, who had mocked and flouted his plans and dreams. He and Clay saw "threats of disunion from the South, and the graspings after all the public lands." In defeat, he wrote: "The sun of my political life sets in the deepest gloom." And then added: "But that of my country shines unclouded."

On March 3, 1829, he and his family moved out of the White House to another home on Meridian Hill, outside the capital. Washington was filled with Jackson's noisy supporters, who were a loud and coarse lot. The general had some eleven thousand jobs to dispense as patronage, and the seekers packed the inns and boardinghouses of Washington, Georgetown and even Alexandria. They were "a hungry and unmanageable mob," and whenever Jackson appeared, although he was still in mourning, they gave him thunderous cheers. Gadsby's Hotel, where Jackson stayed before the inauguration, was besieged. On March 4, after the ceremony at the Capitol, the Jackson mob followed their new president down Pennsylvania Avenue to the White House. Bursting into the rooms, they soon began turning that austere mansion of aristocratic presidents into a place of the people. "Orange punch by barrels full was made," Henry Clay later reported, "but as the waiters opened the door to bring it out, a rush would be made, the glasses broken, pails of liquor upset, and the most painful confusion prevailed. . . . Wines and ice-creams could not be brought out to the ladies, and tubs of punch were taken from the lower story into the garden, to lead off the crowd from the rooms. On such an occasion it was certainly difficult to keep any thing like order, and it was mortifying to see men, with boots heavy with mud, standing on the damask satin chairs, from their eagerness to get a sight of the President."

On that same day, far from the thundering crowds, John Quincy Adams took his routine exercise. He was alone, a solitary figure riding horseback down Meridian Hill toward the city, along F Street, where he had once lived, to the Rockville Turnpike, and then back by way of College Hill. An embittered man, he was certainly aware of the distant noise and excitement. As he rode near the old post office, he was overtaken by a man named Dulaney, who stopped him and asked "whether I could inform him how he could see John Quincy Adams." It was a question the lonely and un-recognized Adams, too removed from the people, might have asked himself.

On April 8, 1829, Louisa Adams wrote her son George "to beg . . . that you will . . . come on here to escort your father and myself on our way home. You know that we are neither of us famous travelers and your assistance for me will be absolutely necessary."

But George was buckling under the Adamses' pressure. He had been the gentle child, left at the age of eight (with his brother John) under the care of aunts and uncles and strong-willed grandparents while his mother and father went on the long diplomatic mission to Russia. It was George who had loved and lost Mary Catherine Hellen; who had become a lawyer as his father had wished but who wanted to write poetic literature. And it was George, whose every waking thought was haunted by his father, who had been dreaming during his freshman year at Harvard of his love for a girl when his father entered the dream and admonished: "Remember, George, who you are and what you are doing." How could he forget? His father wrote him weekly letters, telling him how to work, when to play; he detailed George's time from rising to bed, and exhorted the young man to shape himself into the traditional Adams mold: "My sons have not only their own honor but that of two preceding generations to sustain." It was a heavy burden.

In 1826, George was a member of the Massachusetts bar and the state legislature; he had been entrusted with handling his father's personal financial affairs in Boston. His star appeared to be in the ascendance. But he suffered from swings of mood — from ecstasy to depression — and he was, said one brother, "indolent." George could not be as meticulous a lawyer as his father wanted. He was careless and late with statements and work details. His financial accounts got tangled, and in 1827 he began neglecting his law practice. He drank, cavorted, stayed out late, and rejected the rigid self-discipline his father sought to impose. Like his mother, George Adams never measured up.

In the summer of 1827, George became ill with abscesses and fever, and his mother overcame her own illnesses, real or imagined, and rushed to Boston to nurse him back to being, as she put it, "the same old exaggerated conceited timid enthusiastic negligent cold and eccentric being that he has been since he was born." Louisa wrote John Quincy in Washington that their son was nervous and run-down and "constantly acting like one divested of understanding."

John Quincy Adams was, as he had always been, alternately harsh and soft. He chastised George for his weakness and snarled about the tangled business affairs, but he covered his son's debts. In another letter he suggested the usual Adams panaceas: stay busy, exercise, be temperate, attend church, read and keep a diary. He insisted that George send him samples of his diary for evaluation. Later in the summer, he even managed to visit George in Boston and wrote his wife that "George's health is as it was, and is likely to be — depending entirely upon himself. He is to me dutiful and affectionate, and wants nothing but a firm purpose to be all that I could wish."

While John Quincy
Adams was secretary of
state and president, his
family had their portraits
done from life. George
Washington Adams (top)
was painted in 1823, when
he was twenty-two and in
Washington after his
graduation from Harvard.
John Adams II was about
the same age, and also in
Washington. The portraits
are thought to be by
Charles Bird King, whose
studio at 1333 F Street
was close to the Adams
residence. King is known
to have painted John
Quincy and Louisa
Catherine Adams, her
sister, and Charles Francis
Adams as well.

TOP: GEORGE WASHINGTON ADAMS.
OIL ASCRIBED TO CHARLES BIRD KING,
1820-1825

BOTTOM: JOHN ADAMS II. OIL ASCRIBED
TO CHARLES BIRD KING, 1820-1825

By 1829, when George was asked to travel to Washington to meet his mother and father, he was slipping fast. But even his brother Charles Francis interpreted his illness in typical Adams fashion. "He wants bracing and enlivening," Charles wrote to his mother. "His entire seclusion from society . . . and his want of occupation produce a listlessness peculiarly oppressive. He complains of dejection, low spirits, and inability to occupy himself, and this acts upon reflections of a melancholy kind in regard to Father and himself." Two days before he left for Washington, he appeared to Charles to be "very much disarranged."

On April 29, George set out for Providence, where he boarded the steamer *Benjamin Franklin* for New York City. He complained of a headache in the evening, and told shipboard acquaintances that he heard voices and suspected that his fellow passengers were conspiring against him. About three o'clock in the morning, he demanded that the captain stop the ship and let him off. He jumped or fell overboard, and drowned off Long Island; his hat was found near the ship's stern and his body was recovered near City Island two weeks later.

Charles was greatly upset, and the sudden death struck "with double vehemence. I wrote a few lines to my father, and I bent my soul in humble and fervent prayer that God would soften the stroke upon my poor afflicted parents." John Quincy Adams replied that "we are in great distress" and assured Charles that "your mother and myself, relying on him who chastiseth in Mercy, still look for consolation in the affectionate kindness of our remaining Sons."

Charles could not recover as quickly as his parents. He tried reading Clarendon, but that did not help. "My thoughts rest upon the horrible circumstances, and the singular indifference with which he was observed in his extravagance. Poor fellow, he complained to Dr. Welsh before he went, but I never suspected alienation of mind or he should never have gone. I went to his room and examined his papers. They display nothing but pain, mental agitation about his future prospects which he had been much indulged in, but no despair."

But Charles also found in George's papers what he had already suspected: that there was another side to his brother hidden from the family. George had seduced a chambermaid of Dr. Welsh's, Eliza Dolph, and the girl had given birth to an illegitimate child. The story soon became more complex. On May 28, Miles Farmer, a superintendent of some houses in Boston, approached Charles Francis in an attempt at blackmail. Farmer said that in January a Dr. David Humphreys Storer, perhaps at George Adams's request, had asked Farmer to take Eliza Dolph and her child, then about eight weeks old, into his family and "to restore the mother to her friends and society again." Farmer claimed that George Adams continued coming around to see Eliza, and his attentions aroused the tenants' suspicions and threatened Farmer's job. Farmer claimed that George had promised him $100 and protection should his employer ask questions. George's death, however, had deprived Farmer of the money and the protection, and he hoped that Charles and the Adamses might pay him off. "I was a little shocked by what he told me," Charles wrote.

Charles refused to be blackmailed. Eliza, he wrote Farmer, "must work for herself," although "she shall be in no worse situation than she was before this occurrence, so far as demands upon the money she may earn will go." In fact, she returned to work as a domestic shortly thereafter. As for the child, "I will make some provision probably similar to what it would be entitled [to] by law." The name and sex of the child were never mentioned in the Adamses' writings.

Farmer, it turned out, owed George Adams "a considerable debt," which Charles told him would not be pressed. But Farmer threatened him with "a public statement." Charles stood fast: "Whatever I might be disposed to do as Charity . . . I certainly will be *forced* to do nothing. You are welcome to all the benefit a disclosure will give you."

Farmer was determined to blackmail someone, and he next tried Dr. Storer. The conflict reached the Massachusetts courts, and in March, 1831, three referees awarded Farmer $200 damages. But Farmer thought he should have gotten more. He published his story in a forty-four-page pamphlet that attacked both Dr. Storer and the Adams family and caused scandalous talk in New England. As for the doctor, Charles thought him as culpable as Farmer and refused to deal with him. When the doctor submitted a bill against George's estate, Charles rejected it since it did not detail the number of visits made to Eliza. Dr. Storer finally did collect $37 for his services to the chambermaid.

In July, when Charles was coping with Farmer and Dr. Storer, he wrote of his brother's affairs: "There is much to tease and perplex one in this business and the more I progress the more I feel it. Poor fellow, he had wound himself nearly up in his own web."

Louisa Adams took the death of her first son very hard — with illness, prostrations, deep depression and doubts about her own sanity. In September, she and John Quincy were to travel to Massachusetts to attend the wedding of Charles to Abigail Brooks of Medford. But George's death was still so distressing that Louisa only got as far as New York City, where Charles met her. At the hotel, he found his mother in deepest mourning, "altered, more than I expected and unwell." Charles had unwisely booked his parents on the *Benjamin Franklin* to Boston — the same steamer that George Adams had taken. Shortly after midnight, Charles found his mother "lying under one of those violent attacks which she is subject to with all the family and servants up and trying to assist her in her distress." A doctor arrived two hours later, and "relieved her of the coldness about the breast of which she complained . . . so dreadfully." The next day, although calm, she was "unable to move at all." She later returned to Washington, and missed Charles's wedding.

"To her dying day," wrote Lyman Butterfield, former editor-in-chief of *The Adams Papers*, "Louisa Catherine Adams continued to believe, rationally or irrationally, that her son George was a sacrifice to the political ambitions of the Adams family, particularly those of her husband."

John Quincy Adams traveled alone to Quincy in 1829, where he took stock of his fields and barns. He planned a memorial to his parents. He brought home the body of his oldest son, that "lottery ticket" of a lad, and reburied it in Quincy. He began organizing his library, and surveyed the land inherited from his father. He took measure. John Quincy Adams, sixty-two years old, was embittered, alone, beaten and saddened — and he had no way of knowing that the most important work of his life lay ahead of him.

10

No!

[1830–1848]

*A*T home, in the summer of 1830, John Quincy Adams gathered strength from the simple patterns of his life, which sustained him as they had sustained his father, and gave him pleasure.

Every morning, he rose by five. He read as many as fifteen sections of Cicero's orations, and three chapters of his Bible (the New Testament that summer), before breakfast. Cicero contributed the tone for oratory. The Bible offered him comfort and direction at his age, "a guide through the darksome journey of life." In a sense, Adams was preparing for two events: his return to politics and his death.

After breakfast, he often gardened, digging vigorously with spade and hoe, or making "barren observations upon vegetation." Like his father, he was proud of his vegetables, his fruit trees, his New England berries. Behind the garden, he had constructed a chicken house, and he attempted that summer to get his black Norman hens to produce eggs. They proved to be as stubborn as any Adams.

He also went swimming, usually from Daniel Greenleaf's

wharf with John Adams II and Charles, and the old man could sometimes be seen bobbing in the cold seawater with a white nightcap protecting his bald head from the summer sun. The garden digging, the swimming, the hikes across the salt marshes made John Quincy Adams feel more mortal than ever. He tired easily. The catarrh in his lungs persisted and weakened him with coughing spells every morning. He felt the aches of lumbago and rheumatism. He reflected on his age — he was sixty-three that summer — and planted, along with the fruits and vegetables of his garden, acorns and walnuts that would grow into tall trees above the Adamses of future generations.

The rest of his day varied little. The family — Louisa, Mary Hellen Adams, his sons and granddaughters — ate dinner at two. In hot weather — and the summer of '30 was dry, sunny and very hot — Adams took a nap until five o'clock teatime. In the cool of evening, he might ride around the village on horseback or enjoy a New England clambake or "chowder dinner" along the shore with friends. If not, the dinner bell always rang promptly at nine, followed by an evening of writing or conversation before bed at eleven.

In all, his retirement appeared to be shaping up much as his father's had been: banishment to New England, then work on his fields, books and writings. He enjoyed a splendid library, his farm, his father's diaries and letters (which needed organizing). After long years of bitter politics, he was not likely to return to Washington.

In September, 1830, however, a movement was already under way to send Adams back to Congress as a representative. He was soon approached by the National Republicans from the Plymouth District and sounded out. The *Hingham Gazette* suggested his name for the election, and two readers supported the proposal. Adams played coy, as he always had in elections, and told his supporters that his acceptance would have to wait until the people acted.

Most of the opposition came from his family. Louisa Adams said that only "mortification and agony" would come from her husband's "insatiable passion" for public office. She had welcomed leaving Washington and what she called the "Bull Bait" of politics. Charles Francis felt that his father had devoted enough time and energy to public service, and not enough to his family. He wanted to work with his father on his grandfather's papers by editing and writing a biography that would voice the family's defense against political attack and firmly ground its reputation. During October he tried to dissuade his father from running. "I regret the decision on his account; I regret it upon my own. To neither of us can it prove beneficial to be always struggling before the public without rest or intermission."

The old warrior couldn't resist the call, and the election went off without complication or disappointment on November 1. He won a seat in the U.S. House of Representatives and defeated two opponents by a large majority — taking almost three fourths of the votes cast. It marked the first time in his entire public career that he would assume office as the result of popular election. He was elated: "I am a member-elect of the Twenty-second Congress," he wrote in his diary. "My election as President of the United States was not half so gratifying to my inmost soul. No election or appointment conferred upon me ever gave me so much pleasure." At that time, no member of the House had such varied experience and familiarity with government; Adams had spent more than forty years close to the political history of the nation. He saw his election as a call to duty — and he would return for eight successive Congresses. "For myself," he wrote to Charles Adams, "taught in the school of Cicero, I shall say, *'Defendi respublicam adolescens; non deseram senex.'* — 'I will not desert in my old age the Republic that I defended in my youth.' "

As a member of the House for seventeen years (less ten days), John Quincy Adams had his hand once again upon the destiny of the nation. He served as chairman of a special House committee that created the Smithsonian Institution. He battled three presidents — Jackson, Van Buren and Polk — and gave Jackson fits by opposing him over the Bank of the United States and arguing against his treatment of the Indians and his "Second Seminole War"; yet he backed him eloquently in his quarrels with France and South Carolina.

But of all his actions and of all the committees on which

he served, none attracted his interest more than those that touched upon slavery. This was the coming issue of mid-century America: the Union and the slave. John Quincy Adams, who as a boy had watched the Union battle for its freedom, would now as an old man battle the threats to its survival.

For a time, the coming struggle was anticipated in the debates over protective tariffs, especially in South Carolina. There, the protective tariff was seen as the force behind the rising costs of slave labor and the falling price of cotton. Arguments, similar to the Virginia and Kentucky Resolves of 1798, called for the state to interpose its authority and seek nullification.

As Adams saw it, nullification meant secession. When Robert Y. Hayne of South Carolina and Daniel Webster of Massachusetts debated in the Senate, setting forth the two issues of states' rights and nullification versus, as Webster said, "Liberty and Union, now and forever, one and inseparable," Adams wrote: "The two doctrines are now before the nation. The existence of the Union depends, I fully believe, upon this question."

In Quincy during the summer of 1831, Adams got an opportunity to speak on this issue at the Fourth of July cele-bration. He carefully wrote and rewrote his speech, and ar-duously rehearsed its delivery. To an audience that overflowed the new stone meetinghouse, he traced the meaning of the Declaration of Independence, that "social compact" between the individual citizen and his government, and said, "To this compact, union was as vital as freedom or independence." The doctrine of nullification, Adams continued, "never has been delegated to any one State, or to any partial combination of States," and any attempt at nullification was nothing "more nor less than treason, skulking under the shelter of despotism."

If that wasn't enough to bring the southern members of the House to a boil, Adams then rallied the New Englanders with a powerful cry. He looked out over the crowd in Quincy that Fourth and knew that many of them would re-member his father's last toast on this day five years ago: "Independence Forever!" He wished them years of prosperity and freedom, and vowed that his last words would be: "Independence and Union Forever!" A printing of two thousand copies of his speech soon took his rallying cry to the nation.

By the end of October, John Quincy and Louisa Adams began their trip back to Washington, and their stops in New York and Philadelphia were affectionate encounters with old friends. Charles Francis still thought his father wrong to re-enter national politics. But John Quincy Adams brushed aside his son's objections: "I must fulfill my Destiny."

His first appointment, as chairman of the House Committee on Manufactures, took him only indirectly into the issue of South Carolina's nullification stand. But he cleverly used his standing in the House and his reputation to engage himself in the growing debate. He listened with irritation to debate on the new tariff bill. "Our slaves," he heard Augustus Smith Clayton of Georgia say, "sail the Northern ships and run the Northern spindles. . . . *Our slaves are our machinery*, and we have as good a right to profit by them as do the Northern men to profit by the machinery they employ."

Slaves are machinery? Adams's anger rose. He accused the southerners of already enjoying protection of "Southern machinery" under the U.S. Constitution. The federal army protected the people of the South against domestic violence, whether from Indians or slaves — a most necessary provision, Adams went on, since "that 'machinery' sometimes exerts a self-moving power." Adams had touched a slowly opening wound. In 1831, Nat Turner led a slave rebellion in Virginia that had killed fifty-seven whites, including eighteen women and twenty-four children, and across the South the slave owners had risen in retaliation and had appealed to the United States for protection. "My constituents," Adams continued, "possess as much right to say to the people of the South, 'We will not submit to the protection of your interests,' as the people of the South have the right to address such language to them."

"The member from Massachusetts," shouted William Drayton of South Carolina, "has thrown a firebrand into the Hall."

"It is not I who have thrown the 'firebrand,'" Adams

later responded. "The Nullification Ordinance is the fire-brand."

Hardly a day passed without Adams's voice being heard from the House floor. Every member, even those who constantly opposed him, looked to his ability and prestige. None could debate better, or control more facts, or use parliamentary rules to greater advantage. Adams was a learned parliamentarian. When the House was near anarchy in 1839, he would, on the motion of a member from South Carolina, take the chair and control the House until a Speaker was elected. Adams worked hard. He showed up every day despite rheumatism and the perils of age. Only the worst illnesses, and those rarely, kept him from his desk on the floor, and he stayed sometimes long after midnight.

During the summer of 1833, in Quincy, John Quincy Adams wrote in his diary that "all is discouraging and gloomy." He felt that the "Tide" of life was turning against him. In September, however, his flagging spirits got a boost. Charles Francis and Abigail Brooks Adams, who had been married in 1829 and who already had a daughter, now produced a baby boy, "a stout little fellow," said his father. They named him John Quincy Adams II, and his grandfather was ecstatic. It was the first boy of the fourth generation; the family name would be continued. His diary on September 30 reads: "There is no Passion more deeply seated in my bosom than the longing for posterity worthily to support my own and my father's name. . . . For this I have done my part. My sons must do theirs. There is now one Son of the next Generation, and my hopes revive."

The grandfather need not have worried, for Charles and Abigail would have three more sons: Charles Francis Adams Jr., in 1835; Henry Adams, in 1838; and Brooks Adams, in 1848. They also had a second daughter, Mary, in 1846. Charles and Abby were warm and loving parents. They fussed over "little Louisa" and worried through her teething. Charles devoted whole days "to quiet and my children."

Like his father and grandfather, Charles drove himself; he had the Adams self-discipline and need for self-improvement. He regarded "the turning point of most men's lives" to

Charles Francis Adams was just twenty when he sat for this portrait by Charles Bird King. Adams thought the artist had "not made a good picture" and Louisa Adams, his mother, asked King for more sittings. He obliged, but the additional effort still did not satisfy the Adamses. Abigail Brooks Adams, Charles's wife, sat for this portrait, thought to be by William West, about 1840.

TOP: CHARLES FRANCIS ADAMS. OIL BY CHARLES BIRD KING, 1827

BOTTOM: ABIGAIL BROOKS ADAMS. OIL BY WILLIAM E. WEST, ABOUT 1840, PREVIOUSLY ASCRIBED TO CHARLES BIRD KING, 1829

be the age of twenty-seven. His father had launched his career at twenty-seven, and "Cicero made his defence of Roscius [at that age]. . . . This was the age at which Demosthenes entered upon the public business. . . . I have long been impressed with the idea that if I made no reputation at all at this age, I should never make any." His inner tension would soon bring him to harsh words with his father.

Charles's brother, John Adams II, had been struggling in Washington to save his father's finances. George Johnson, a relative of Louisa Adams's, had lost money in a grist mill, and just before the bank foreclosed, John Quincy Adams had pumped much of his savings into the business. Adams had hoped it might provide some income for his retirement. In the late 1820's, John took over the management of the mill, but it began losing money quickly. Lack of grain, drought, then a drop in demand hurt, and by 1833 John was overworked. He began drinking heavily; he suffered from fevers, stiff joints and limbs, loss of memory. His father wrote: "My dear Son has been in a declining and drooping state of health more than three years."

In October, 1834, news arrived from Washington that John was gravely ill. John Quincy Adams set out immediately for the capital, and arrived there only four hours before John died. "I went to his bedside twice," he wrote, "and saw and heard him; he had no consciousness of any thing on Earth." He wrote of his lost son: "A more honest soul, or more tender heart never breathed on the face of this earth."

The death brought to the surface underlying tensions and anger within the Adams family. Both Louisa and Charles, during the next months, accused John Quincy of having sacrificed his children to his political ambition. Father and son had sharp discussions about the family and finances. After one argument, Charles wrote that his father's "nerves [were] so shaken that he could not control his feelings at all." Whatever was said between them, Charles left Washington abruptly: "My father and I parted coldly and silently."

Almost from his first session in Congress, John Quincy Adams had presented petitions to the House on slavery. By 1834, the toughest struggle of his second career had begun. To halt public debate on slavery, proslavery factions in the House were already at work attempting to suppress the right of any citizen, association or state legislature to petition the government.

Adams recognized, as did others, that social movements are often carried on a wave of religious fervor. Corps of abolitionists, organized by Theodore D. Weld, swept the New England states with the moral outcry of abolition. Societies sprang up pledging their members to abolition; William Lloyd Garrison was a founder of the New England Anti-Slavery Society and later of the American Anti-Slavery Society. At one time there may have been as many as two thousand groups in the North with two hundred thousand members.

If the northern abolitionists saw slavery as anti-Christian, the southern slave owners saw the abolitionists as a threat to their profitable trade, peace and safety. While abolitionists were attacking slavery from the safety of northern pulpits, southerners in Virginia put down the Nat Turner rebellion. In the slaveholding states laws were passed with strict penalties for anyone inciting slaves to rebellion, and Georgia put up a reward for the delivery of Garrison. Laws were demanded to prevent the mailing of abolitionist literature — such as Garrison's radical *Liberator* — or antislavery speeches into southern states.

Abolitionist petitions to Congress against slavery prodded the southerners and their northern supporters into action. In May, 1836, Henry Laurens Pinckney of South Carolina brought in three resolutions from his House committee. The first stated that Congress had no constitutional power to interfere with slavery in any state. The second said that Congress ought not interfere with slavery in the District of Columbia. But the third was more basic: "all petitions, memorials, resolutions, propositions, or papers, relating in any way, or to any extent whatsoever, to the subject of slavery or the abolition of slavery, shall, without being either printed or referred, be laid on the table, and that no further action whatever shall be had thereon."

Pinckney and his supporters wanted all discussion of slavery in the House stopped. He wanted to halt — gag —

The idyllic scenes of a cotton plantation (right), thought to be in Louisiana, showed little of the harsh conditions of American black slaves. The abolitionist sought to overcome such ignorance with emotional pleas, like this page (left) from an antislavery book published in Philadelphia. The leaping slave girl exclaimed: "—but I did not want to go, and I jump'd out of the window.—"

DESPERATE SLAVE JUMPING FROM A WINDOW. ENGRAVING FROM AN ANTISLAVERY BOOK, PHILADELPHIA, 1817

DETAIL: COTTON PLANTATION. OIL BY CHARLES GIROUX ABOUT 1860

free speech and the right to petition that elected body. The resolutions were clearly a violation of the Constitution, but the Speaker, James K. Polk, a Tennessee slaveholder, shut off any argument against them. When Adams rose to protest, the Speaker and members of the House blocked him.

During a lull in the voting, John Quincy Adams did get to the House floor and, although the question then before the members concerned relief rations to Georgia and Alabama refugees from the Seminole wars, Adams brilliantly turned to the broader issue of the war powers of Congress and slavery. He warned that the desire of some to conquer Mexico and take Texas was really wrapped in the issue of slavery, and that the administration, and its coterie of southern slaveholders and northern Democrats, were leading the country into an aggressive war at the bottom of which was the issue of slavery. Would France and England, which opposed slavery, stand idly by?

Adams saw, as few did in those days, the long-term danger to the Union. "Mr. Chairman, are you ready for all these wars? A Mexican War? A war with Great Britain, if not with France? A general Indian war? A servile war? And, as an inevitable consequence of them all, a civil war? . . . From the instant that your slaveholding states become the theatre of war, civil, servile, or foreign, from that instant the war powers of Congress extend to interference with the institution of slavery in every way by which it can be interfered with."

But Adams's warning persuaded few of his opponents in the House. The next day, they voted on the last two of Pinckney's resolutions. The clerk of the House called the roll on the third question — that of silencing all discussion of slavery in the House — and John Quincy Adams's name was first. The old man rose and shouted above the opposition: "I hold the resolution to be in direct violation of the Constitution of the United States, of the rules of this House, and of the rights of my constituents." Again, he went unheeded. The rule passed, 117 to 68.

Pinckney's third resolution became known as the notorious Gag Rule, which the House slaveholders and northern supporters renewed regularly in increasingly strict form.

Adams battled them for eight years, but from 1836 to 1840, the Gag Rule was repassed at each session of Congress; after 1840, it became a standing rule of procedure, known as the Twenty-first Rule.

Antislavery petitions still came in to Adams and other members of Congress. In the years 1837 and 1838 alone, the American Anti-Slavery Society by itself sent to the House 196,720 petitions opposing slavery and another 32,000 against the Gag Rule. But under this rule, not one petition was accepted. American abolitionists were silenced in the halls of Congress.

Adams looked for any opening through which to sneak petitions before the House. He strongly believed in the right of the people to petition their government, and the obligation of their representatives to present those petitions. He opposed the vote on the rule at the beginning of each new session. In January, 1837, before the House had renewed the Gag Rule for that session, Adams quickly presented three petitions calling for the abolition of slavery in the District of Columbia. One was signed by 150 women from Dorchester, Massachusetts; the second, by 228 women in South Weymouth; and the third by townsmen in Dover. On a Monday, the regular petition day for the House, Adams moved that the petition from the "pure and virtuous citizens" of Dorchester, who were asking for "the greatest improvement that can possibly be effected in the condition of the human race — the total abolition of slavery on earth," be read. Adams appealed to the chivalrous southerners to hear the pleas of these women. But the House voted to table their petition. Adams then presented the South Weymouth petition. Over rising objections and outcries, he began reading: " '. . . impressed with the sinfulness of slavery, and keenly aggrieved by its existence in a part of our Country over which —' "

"A point of order!" Pinckney was on his feet. "Has the gentleman from Massachusetts a right under the rule, to read the petition?"

Speaker of the House Polk said that Adams had "a right to make a statement of the contents" of the petition.

"It is a privilege I shall exercise," Adams said, "until I am deprived of it by some positive act."

"You have a right to make a brief statement of the contents of the petition," the Speaker warned him.

"I am doing so, sir," Adams replied.

"Not in the opinion of the Chair," Polk continued.

Adams pressed on: ". . . 'keenly aggrieved by its existence in a part of our Country over which Congress possesses exclusive jurisdiction in all cases whatever —' "

"Order! Order!" The shouts echoed in the House.

". . . 'Do most earnestly petition your honorable body —' "

"Mr. Speaker," John Chambers of Kentucky shouted. "Mr. Speaker, I rise to a point of order."

Adams was reading faster now. ". . . 'immediately to abolish slavery in the District of Columbia —' "

"Mr. Speaker!" Chambers was screaming. "A call to order!"

Polk leaned over and called to Adams: "Take your seat."

As he slowly eased into his chair, Adams's voice continued over the din: ". . . 'and to declare every human being free who sets foot upon its soil.' "*

The obnoxious document was instantly tabled by the House. Adams rose once more to inform the members that the good ladies of Massachusetts had vowed to renew their petition every year "in the holy cause of human freedom." Within nine days, the Gag Rule was renewed for the remainder of that session of Congress.

Petitions of all kinds tumbled into Adams's office in the House. He carefully listed each of them — he did his own clerical work — and sought to present them to the House for discussion. The House was often stormy for days after one of his presentations, but Adams seemed to thrive on the adversity. He enjoyed his signal talent for needling his opponents to the point of exasperation. The slaveholders and northern supporters regarded him as incendiary and dangerous. Calhoun called him a "mischievous, bad old man."

Adams was not an abolitionist; abolitionists attacked him as well as the slaveholders. But he saw, as few men did, that denial of the freedom and right to discuss openly any public

Even though, in 1709, a slave market had flourished on Wall Street in New York, antislavery groups were active in the city by the mid-1800's. Here, the cover of a pamphlet from the American Anti-Slavery Society (one of many such organizations) protests slavery and the hypocrisy of northern states toward runaway slaves.

* Samuel F. Bemis, *John Quincy Adams and the Union* (New York, 1956), pp. 341–342.

"THE AMERICAN ANTI-SLAVERY ALMANAC," 1840

—VOL. I. NO. 5.—

THE
AMERICAN
ANTI-SLAVERY
ALMANAC,

FOR

1840,

BEING BISSEXTILE OR LEAP-YEAR, AND THE 64TH OF AMERICAN
INDEPENDENCE.   CALCULATED FOR NEW YORK; ADAPTED
TO THE NORTHERN AND MIDDLE STATES.

NORTHERN HOSPITALITY—NEW YORK NINE MONTHS' LAW.

The slave steps out of the slave-state, and his chains fall.   A free state, with another chain, stands ready to re-enslave him.

———

Thus saith the Lord, Deliver him that is spoiled out of the hands of the oppressor.

———

NEW YORK:
PUBLISHED BY THE AMERICAN ANTI-SLAVERY SOCIETY,
NO. 143 NASSAU STREET.

question threatened one of the basic premises on which the republic was founded, and the continuance of the Union. He willingly became a channel for petitions and the outspoken opponent of the Gag Rule, largely because he saw the rights of *all* Americans under threat.

Southern House leaders wanted to discipline Adams, and even expel him. But he quickly showed himself superior to them in using parliamentary rules to hold his position and put his opponents in the wrong. In another test of the Gag Rule, on February 6, 1837, he presented a large stack of petitions, and tucked among them was one from "nine ladies of Fredericksburg, Virginia," calling for the "prohibition" of slave trading in the District of Columbia. Adams began to sit down, but then took a piece of paper from his desk that, he told the Speaker, appeared to be a petition but was signed with scrawls and marks, "purporting to come from slaves."

The House was in an uproar. Was Adams suggesting that *slaves* had a right to petition Congress? "I object!" bellowed Joab Lawler of Alabama. "I want it to appear on the Journal that I objected!" Charles Eaton Haynes of Georgia also protested, and Waddy Thompson of South Carolina accused Adams of inciting slaves to rebellion and called for his indictment. There were shouts that Adams was a pawn of "incendiary fanatics," that he was offending the South, that he was threatening the Union. "Expel him! Expel him!" someone shouted. Another called for a resolution of censure.

While the debate raged, John Mercer Patton of Virginia, who claimed that he had been brought up in Fredericksburg, sidled up to the stack of petitions that Adams had presented (Adams held the slave petition himself), and examined the one from the "ladies" of that city. He loudly announced that he "would state in his place, and on his responsibility, that the name of no *lady* was attached to that paper." All of them were free Negroes or mulattoes, he said. He even recognized one name, that of a lady of "infamous" reputation.

Adams stepped into the battle. He reminded the House members that he had merely asked the Speaker a parliamentary question on the second — slave — petition: Was the petition in order? He had neither presented the petition nor said that it was, in fact, from slaves. He then announced that the petition was indeed from slaves — twenty-two of them — but *against* abolition!

Another uproar began, and then cooler heads took over. Three resolutions were quickly presented, two of which called any petitions from slaves to the House disrespectful to the "feelings" of the House and the "rights" of southern states, and "unfriendly" to the Union; and stated that slaves did not have the right to make such petitions. The third resolution exonerated Adams, but made it appear that he had apologized to the House for his behavior. Adams, of course, had done no such thing — nor was he likely to. He then asked to speak in his own defense, a privilege granted reluctantly, and delivered a stinging and far-ranging speech.

He accused the House members of denying the right of petition for political reasons, an act "no despot, of any age or clime, has ever denied . . . to the poorest or the meanest of human creatures. . . . When the principle is once begun of limiting the right of petition, where would it stop? . . . The honorable gentleman makes it a crime because I presented a petition which he affirms to be from colored women, which women were of infamous character, as the honorable gentleman says — prostitutes, I think the gentleman said."

"I did not say they were prostitutes," Patton called out. "They are free mulattoes."

Adams continued: "The word 'woman' is an expression much dearer to my heart than that of 'lady'. I thought the honorable gentleman had said they were 'infamous'. I shall forever entertain the proposition that the sacred right of petition, of begging for mercy, does not depend on character any more than it does on condition. It is a right that cannot be denied to the humblest, to the most wretched."

"I have not said that I know those women," Patton protested.

Adams turned on him coolly. "I am glad to hear the honorable gentleman disclaim any knowledge of them, for I had been going to ask, if they were infamous women, then who is it that had made them infamous? Not their color, I believe, but their masters!" Adams drew himself up and attacked. "I have heard it said in proof of that fact, and I am inclined to believe it is the case, that in the South there existed great resemblances between the progeny of the colored people and the white men who claim possession of them. Thus, perhaps, the charge of infamous might be retorted on those who made it, as originating from themselves."*

Adams had made a stunning and bold comment, and the *Register of Debates* recorded the turmoil: "Great agitation in the House!"

The third resolution failed to pass, a triumph for Adams, although two days later the House overwhelmingly voted the second resolution, that slaves had no right to petition.

Now, threats of assassination began arriving in Adams's mail along with the petitions. One named the day and hour he would be killed. Another was a drawing of him with a bullet hole in his head. A third depicted a raised arm and fist clutching a bowie knife, with a caption reading: "Vengeance is mine, say the South!" Although these threats troubled Adams, Louisa took them very hard. She wrote a poem called "Threats of Assassination/1839" that contained the stanza:

> *Grant, grant! O God a helping hand*
> *And save us when we call;*
> *Protect us 'gainst the murderer's hand,*
> *Support us lest we fall.*

Louisa, for this and other reasons, wanted her husband to "bring his mind to the calm of retirement," but she recognized that he thrived on the agitation of the House and on the public acclaim he had received. He himself felt keenly the need to continue in public service: "More than sixty years of incessant active intercourse with the world has made political movement to me as much a necessary of life as atmospheric air. This is the weakness of my nature, which I have intellect enough to perceive, but not energy to control. And thus while a remnant of physical power is left to me to write and speak, the world will retire from me before I shall retire from the world."

The issues before the House kept him active and creative. He tackled with vigor the question of annexing Texas — a question that struck to the core of the slavery issue. In the Republic of Texas, slavery was an established institution, and

* Bemis, *John Quincy Adams and the Union*, pp. 345–346.

when the question of annexation came before the House, it was wrapped tightly in the question of extending slavery. Petitions against annexation poured in to Adams for presentation, and he did so warmly. During the "morning hour" of the House, every day from June 16 to July 7, 1838, Adams spoke against the extension of slavery and prevented a vote on the annexation. But he raised a larger question than the expansion of slavery, one similar to the question he had raised in the Senate over the Louisiana Purchase: Could a man be transferred by treaty or agreement from one country to another?

It was a losing cause — the Mexican War would soon begin — but his countrymen began calling Adams "Old Man Eloquent." Nowhere was that eloquence more appropriate, and perhaps more needed, than during Adams's appearance in 1841 before the United States Supreme Court. In his first case before the court since 1809, Adams defended thirty-nine Africans who had been shipped as slaves on the *Amistad* for Cuba. Led by the slave Cinque, they revolted while at sea. Cinque and the slaves had hoped to sail back to West Africa, but a clever ruse by the captain had steered them instead into Long Island Sound, where they were captured. By 1841 the trial had passed through the lower courts to the Supreme Court; the question was whether to return the slaves to the slave owners in Cuba or free them.

Adams took the case reluctantly. He felt he was too old and too long out of legal practice. "The life I lead," he wrote in his diary, "is trying to my constitution. . . . My eyes are threatening to fail me. My hands tremble like an aspen-leaf. My memory daily deserts me."

But he did accept the case, and worried for weeks over his argument, which took as its final tone both a legal and personal appeal to the court. Judge Joseph Story called Adams's argument "extraordinary, for its power, for its bitter sarcasm, and its dealing with topics far beyond the record and points of discussion." In March, 1841, the court ruled that the Negroes were free. "Glorious," wrote Roger Baldwin to Adams. "Glorious not only as a triumph of humanity and justice, but as a vindication of our national character from reproach and dishonor."

Although victorious in the Supreme Court, Adams was

still fighting in the House. In 1842, he presented a petition from the citizens of Haverhill, Massachusetts, asking that, because of the issue of slavery, the Union be dissolved. The petition was satirical, but Adams was attacked by members of the House, who called again for his censure. The speeches against him went on for several days. Most eloquent was Thomas F. Marshall of Kentucky, nephew of the former chief justice of the United States (who had been appointed by John Adams). The young Marshall charged John Quincy Adams with constantly stirring up the slavery topic, and because his "conduct [was] so utterly unworthy of his past relations to the State, and his present position," called for the "severest censure."

Adams seemed to gather strength from the invective. When he had left Quincy for this session of Congress, Adams had been troubled with pimples, boils, eruptions, a catarrhal cough and pain that never lessened. But as the controversy blew, his health returned. "When they talk about his old age and venerableness and nearness to the grave," said Ralph Waldo Emerson, "he knows better. [Adams] is like one of those old cardinals, who, as quick as he is chosen Pope, throws away his crutches and his crookedness, and is as straight as a boy. He is an old roué, who cannot live on slops, but must have sulphuric acid in his tea."

Adams quickly used the Haverhill petition to speak at length on human freedom and — once again — against slavery. He rattled the House slaveholders, defied them, challenged them to try him and expel him. He even threatened them: "I have constituents to go to who will have something to say if this House expels me. Nor will it be long before gentlemen will see me here again!" Adams attacked by name and character those who had attacked him: Henry Wise was a "blood-stained man" and Tom Marshall should go home and study law "and learn a little of the rights of the citizens."

Accusations and debate raged for more than a month. Adams literally overwhelmed the southern forces, and as they tried to back away they offered to withdraw their resolution of censure if Adams would take back his petition. "No! No! I cannot do that," the old man argued. "That proposition comes to the point and issue of this whole question — that is to say, to the total suppression of the right of petition to the whole people of this Union."

Adams was enjoying himself, and the more he argued, the better he felt. On February 7, 1842, he told the Speaker of the House that he would need to continue at least another week in order to present his full defense. But, he suggested, if anyone wanted to table the censure, he would stand aside. John Minor Botts, a Virginian, quickly so moved and the censure was tabled and the House — temporarily — quieted. Before the day was out, however, Adams had presented almost two hundred more petitions, which were blocked by the Gag Rule. But he had clearly won another victory: the "trial" of Adams for censure before the House had failed, and had awakened men and women who were not abolitionists to the dangers of the Gag Rule and the possibility of its application to issues other than slavery.

Support for the rule began to fade. The margin of backing for it before congressional sessions dropped to four and then three. At the opening of the Twenty-eighth Congress, in 1845, Adams once again offered a motion to rescind the Gag Rule. On the same day, in a surprise move, the House adopted the motion, 105 to 80. Adams's eight-year battle for the right of open, free debate and for the freedom of citizen petitions to be heard before the House was over. He had won. "Blessed, ever blessed be the name of God," he wrote in his diary that night.

Even before the Gag Rule was overcome, Adams had achieved a spectacular level of public acclaim never before reached by any member of his family. Two trips confirmed his popularity. The first, to Niagara Falls in the summer of 1843, with his daughter-in-law Abigail Brooks Adams and his oldest grandson, John Quincy II, turned into a triumph of speeches and applause. It was unlike anything he had experienced, and he enjoyed it. During a train trip on August 2: "Crowds of people were assembled [along the track], received me with three cheers, and manifested a desire to see and hear me."

In late fall, Adams made another trip, this time to Cincinnati for the laying of the cornerstone at the Cincinnati Ob-

PENNSYLVANIA AVENUE, WASHINGTON, D.C.
DAGUERREOTYPE ASCRIBED TO MATHEW BRADY, 1843

THE OLD HOUSE OF REPRESENTATIVES. OIL BY SAMUEL F. B. MORSE, 1821-1822

servatory, a project he had zealously fostered for six years. In October, 1843, when he was seventy-six years old, he set out by rail and steamer for the West. Although his passage on Lake Erie went "silent and unnoticed" he made a speech in Erie, Pennsylvania, and enjoyed a torchlight procession. But it was in Ohio in December that the acclaim came. The old West owed much to John and John Quincy Adams. Some still remembered how father and son had kept Great Britain from lowering the United States boundary to the Ohio River and had blocked British efforts to insert an Indian barrier state across the land. "Blessings on thee, Patriot, Statesman, and Sage!" cheered the *Cleveland Herald*. It proclaimed the "true greatness and patriotism" of "John Adams and his illustrious son."

Adams braved the midwest winter and made speeches to crowds along the Ohio Canal as he traveled by public boat. In Akron, after a short speech, a "very pretty" young woman kissed him on the cheek. He promptly "returned the salute on the lip, and kissed every woman that followed, at which some made faces, but none refused." The activity warmed the old fellow for the rest of a snowy day. After stops at Newark and Hebron, Adams spoke in Columbus on "the subject of astronomy," which, he said, "I regard as one of the most important that can engage the attention of the human race."

At Jefferson, Springfield, Dayton and Lebanon, there were more greetings and cheering processions. He grumbled pleasantly at the adulation: "The only comfort I have is that they are intended to manifest respect, and not hatred." In Cincinnati, he rode to one speech passing under a wide banner across Sixth Street that said: "John Quincy Adams, the Defender of the Rights of Man." The next day in the rain he spoke to a plain of umbrellas at the laying of the cornerstone, and that night spoke again to two thousand at a temperance tea given by the ladies of Cincinnati. Adams walked back from the temperance meeting to his hotel through a double line of torchlights, accompanied by Judge Jacob Burnet, who owned a winery that produced more than two thousand barrels of good wine a year. Adams's learned speech the next day on the history of astronomy was twenty-five thousand words long and as awesome in its scholarship as his work on weights and measures — "a gem," Brooks Adams later called it.

Adams stayed a week in Cincinnati and turned down invitations to stay longer and to head farther West to other celebrations. He did get into Kentucky, where he was greeted by a vast crowd and bands, and where he paid tribute to "that great man, your own citizen . . . my associate and friend, Henry Clay." He stopped at Maysville, on his way home, and again praised Clay. He wrote in his diary: "And here I solemnly declare that the charges of corrupt bargaining which had been trumped up against him and me are utterly without foundation." But the pain of the remembrance lingered. The acclamation for John Quincy Adams continued through Pennsylvania. There were still battles ahead in the House but Adams savored to the end of his days that last triumphant swing around the nation he had so long served.

Death was now stalking Adams and he sensed it. On March 25, 1844, he wrote in his diary: "I approach the term when my daily journal must cease from physical disability to keep it up. . . . I rose this morning at four . . . with smarting, bloodshot eye and shivering hand. . . . My stern chase after Time is, to borrow a simile of Tom Paine, like the race of a man with a wooden leg after a horse." In July, 1846, he walked slowly to the Potomac for swims, although he found "all my station rocks occupied by young men but one." The walk and the swims were less refreshing than they had been. From this time on, he would bathe in his bedchamber, rubbing his body with a horsehair mitten and strap.

Adams now took time to enjoy his grandchildren. He and Charles Francis had slowly reconciled their differences; Charles even helped his father prepare legislation and did other work for him in the Congress. The grandchildren often tumbled about the old man's house in Quincy. He gave each an inscribed Bible. He tried to teach Louisa her alphabet, but had not the patience for it. One day in Quincy, when Henry Adams refused to go to school and stood arguing with his mother, the former president strode out of his study, took the six-year-old by the hand, and walked him not just to the school, but right to his desk. Adams was rather formal with his grandchildren; he was never called "Gramps" or even

"Granddad," but always "the President"; Louisa was always "Madam." But he was tolerant of them and fond of them all. Henry Adams later wrote about the times he "hung about the library; handled the books; deranged the papers; ransacked the drawers; searched the old purses and pocketbooks for foreign coins; drew the sword cane; snapped the travelling pistols; upset everything in the corners, and penetrated the President's dressing-closet where a row of tumblers, inverted on the shelf, covered caterpillars which were supposed to become moths or butterflies, but never did."

In November, 1847, in Boston after rising at four and bathing and rubbing with strap and mitten, John Quincy Adams went for a walk. He suddenly collapsed, and only with help got back to his son's home where he was visiting. He had suffered a slight cerebral hemorrhage, and took several weeks to recover. But he returned to Washington, and upon entering the House of Representatives, he was greeted with a standing ovation from its members. He was a patriarch, venerated by all sections of the nation he had sought to keep united, son of the Revolution who connected George Washington and the middle of the nineteenth century.

On Monday, February 21, 1848, he rode to the Capitol by carriage and took his seat in the House, where he chatted with other members. The House had under consideration a resolution calling for awarding medals to several generals who had fought in what Adams called the "most unrighteous" Mexican War. Venerated Adams surely was and stubborn to the end. When the Speaker called for ayes and noes, John Quincy Adams replied with a firm and clear "No!" He sat at his desk for a few moments, when a reporter who was watching him noticed a deep color tinging his temples. He moved his lips, as though trying to call "Mr. Speaker," but slumped to his left. A member seated near him called out in alarm: "Mr. Adams is dying!"

Quickly he was carried into the Speaker's room and laid on a sofa. Henry Clay hurried in to pay his last respects, and left weeping. Louisa came, too. In the afternoon, Adams tried to say, "Thank the officers of the House." That evening he murmured, "This is the end of earth, but I am composed."

Two days later, at twenty minutes after seven in the evening, John Quincy Adams died.

Until the twenty-fifth his body lay in state in the committee room of the House in a coffin surrounded by evergreen boughs and spring flowers. Then, at dawn, cannon boomed mournfully over the Potomac in a salute that continued until noon. "A Sage has fallen at his post," cried a notice of his funeral. Services were held in the Congress.

A week later, a congressional committee of escort took the body by railroad and boat to Massachusetts for burial. Flags along the route flew at half-mast; people stood with heads bowed as the black-draped carriage passed.

After several days of mourning, the people of Massachusetts moved the body on to Quincy. Small guns fired salutes from the top of Penn's Hill, from which John Quincy Adams and his mother had watched the Battle of Bunker Hill. Neighbors carried his remains to the Stone Temple, the family tomb, and laid him to rest beside his parents. Citizens, dignitaries and congessmen filed past the vault, and as they did so, one of the members of the congressional Committee of Escort stepped forward, and with trembling voice, said in the soft tones of the South:

"Goodbye, Old Man."

11

The Union Is Not Destroyed

[1848–1868]

*W*ITHIN ten years John Quincy Adams's seat in the U.S. House of Representatives was again held by an Adams. In 1858, his son Charles Francis was nominated and elected as the Republican candidate from the Third Massachusetts District. But this was the last elected national office any Adams would achieve, and although Charles Francis Adams would contribute to national politics and international diplomacy, the fourth generation of the Adams family was already moving toward other careers that would carry its influence into the twentieth century. For both the nation and the Adams family, therefore, the 1850's marked a time of major transition.

In 1852, Louisa Catherine Adams died. She had been a central figure in the Adams family dynasty, one who connected the time of the Revolutionary War with the early drumrolls of secession and the Civil War. Her last years were spent in "quiet and contented infirmity" in Washington with her daughter-in-law Mary Catherine. She took comfort from her books and Bible, and captivated her grandson Henry Adams, who wrote of a lady "more remote than the President, but more decorative." During visits to Quincy she "stayed much in her own room" overlooking the garden at the Old House, and appeared as "a fragile creature to a boy who sometimes brought her a note or a message, and took distinct pleasure in looking at her delicate face under what seemed to him very becoming caps." He liked "her refined figure; her gentle voice and manner," which made her a lady not of New England, but of "Washington or . . . Europe, like her furniture, and writing-desk with little glass doors above and little eighteenth-century volumes in old bindings, labelled 'Peregrine Pickle' or 'Tom Jones' or 'Hannah More.' " Henry found her "charming, like a Romney portrait . . . singularly peaceful, a vision of silver gray, presiding over her old President and her Queen Anne mahogany; an exotic, like her Sèvres china." When she died, Congress adjourned to attend her funeral, as it had her husband's. Her son Charles Francis had her remains brought to Quincy and interred in the crypt of the Stone Temple where her husband and his father and mother were buried.

Louisa Adams's husband had been a forceful spokesman against slavery. At her death, she left behind a son and four grandsons who would also battle, with pen and sword, in the cause of emancipation and freedom. For Charles Francis, the line was clear: He was committed to halt the expansion of slavery and preserve the Union. With his father, he had written antislavery legislation and opposed the admission of Texas as a slave state. In 1848, when President James Polk had refused to run for reelection, the national parties had split. The Democratic nomination had gone to Lewis Cass of Michigan, an uncompromising expansionist. The Whigs, once again rejecting Henry Clay, brought forward Zachary Taylor, a slaveholder. The antislavery electorate had no one to back.

Northern splinter groups from eighteen states met in Buffalo, New York — a cross section of disgruntled Whigs, Democrats, "Barnburners" and abolitionist Liberty Party members. They nominated Martin Van Buren for president, and Charles Francis Adams for vice-president. Their slogan was "Free soil, free speech, free labor and free men," and these Free-Soilers went out to topple Whigs and Democrats. In fact, they beat no one in any state. But the Van Buren–Adams ticket did manage to gather enough votes to swing New York, and the election, to the Whigs.

In 1850, President Taylor died in office, and Millard Fillmore took over a nation echoing to threats of secession from the South. Compromises were offered. The Union once more was preserved. But this was the last time.

Adams and other Free-Soil Party members joined abolitionists opposing the compromises. The Fugitive Slave Act was most hated. But the years of compromise, 1851–1852, marked the low point of antislavery crusaders. "The moral tone of the Free States," Adams bemoaned, "never was more thoroughly broken."

This was the calm before the storm, and Adams used it well. In 1848, he had published the fourth edition of Abigail Adams's letters, and he now undertook the voluminous task of putting together a biography of John Adams and an edition of his papers. He worked in Boston in the library of his home at 57 Mount Vernon Street, which he had bought in 1842 and used as a winter residence. His son Charles Francis Jr. remembered sunlight pouring into the library, which was "the only really desirable room in the house." Charles had "not a single pleasant recollection" of that house and instead remembered its "monotonous atmosphere of winter gloom."

Much more pleasant were the houses in Quincy, where the Adamses spent the summer, from late May to early November. There was the Old House on the Plymouth road, and in 1837 Charles Francis had a country house built on "the Hill," in what was once John Adams's cow pasture. In that house, young Charles Jr. watched his grandfather, John Quincy Adams, time the rising and setting suns with watch in hand. The child remembered that "he seemed to be always writing — as, indeed, he was. I can see him now, seated at his table in the middle of the large east room, which he used as a library, a very old-looking gentleman, with a bald head and white fringe of hair — writing, writing, writing — with a perpetual inkstain on the fore-finger and thumb of the right hand."

Charles Jr. and his brothers loved the houses in Quincy, and the village. But already in those quiet years the Quincy granite quarries were slowly carving up the area, working their "manifest injury" on the countryside. Some of the granite in those days was going to "the new hotel of Mr. Astor in New York." But for a few years more, Quincy would still be bright skies, "open windows, green fields, singing birds, the blue bay with white sails dotting it, and a distant view over a country rolling into great whale-back hills, with the State-House dome on the horizon. Boston was gloom personified — frost, snow and discomfort; short days and long school-hours; wet, cold feet and evening lessons."

John Quincy II, the oldest boy, and Charles Jr. — two "red-headed and freckle-faced urchins" — often walked to school together. They had a "very close and affectionate relationship" that lasted long after the red hair had fallen. They were both short, stocky and broad-shouldered. During this decade of transition, John moved smoothly through Harvard and into law practice. Charles, on the other hand, found the Boston Latin School "a dull, traditional lifeless day-academy in which a conventional, commonplace, platoon-front, educational drill was carried on." He did not do well, and his father soon withdrew him and had him taught by a private tutor. Charles graduated from Harvard in 1856. Henry was not far behind, graduating in 1858, and Brooks, the youngest (thirteen years younger than Charles), was the last Adams to sample the rigors of Harvard in the nineteenth century. As a lad, Brooks was "a disagreeable little sculpin" to Charles.

There was also the oldest child, Louisa Catherine Adams, called Lou. Her classic remark, "always quoted with pleasure by her brothers," according to her niece Abigail Adams Homans, was that "she would marry a blackamoor to get away from Quincy." Instead, she married Charles Kuhn, "a severe and bearded gentleman from Philadelphia," and in 1859 they moved to Italy. The other daughter, Mary, who was next to the youngest of the children, eventually married H. P. Quincy of Dedham.

While their father worked on John Adams's papers, and as national events swept toward the tranquillity of Quincy, Charles and Henry began their careers. But they were undecided about what they wanted to do. Both boys were close — they had shared living quarters off-Yard at Harvard — and shared as well anxieties and hopes about growing up and making their mark. Charles regarded life as "a sequence — one thing, accident apart, leading to another." The trick was to catch the step and move along.

In October, 1856, he entered the office of Dana and Parker to read law. He was a reluctant student for twenty months, and passed the bar, he admitted, largely because the examination consisted of one sheet of questions administered and graded by an old family friend and Quincy neighbor. At first he shared an office with John, but later took "a gloomy, dirty den in my father's building, 23 Court Street" in Boston.

Neither Charles nor John considered law their first love. John had hung out his shingle in Quincy with charming indifference. The *Quincy Patriot* carried a notice in 1858 that "John Quincy Adams may be found at his office on Mondays and Tuesdays — at such and such a time." His brother Henry described him as "the sort of fellow who could make you laugh when the ship was sinking."

John worked at law and in a few years he would move toward local politics. He also liked fishing a lot. One client, whose case was coming up in court, scurried about Quincy trying to find him. He finally located his attorney in a rowboat fishing for smelts in an isolated salt creek. Adams refused to stop fishing and hastily scribbled a note to Judge Horace Gray — who would later become an associate justice of the U.S. Supreme Court — asking that his case be held over. Judge Gray read the note, and told his clerk that Adams "had been detained on important business." In fact, John had written: "Dear Judge, For the sake of old Isaac Walton please put my case over, — the smelts are biting and I can't leave."

Charles Francis Jr. did not have his mind entirely on the law either. He was a handsome bachelor about Boston, and rather enjoyed the night life and ladies. He wrote his brother Henry: "Never since I have been in society have I seen a winter go off with such a sort of shriek & howl, so drunk with wine and excitement, so ram full of canvas-back duck & oysters, so slop up in jollity, so jam down in fatigue." The Tiger Ball, a bacchanal, was "the event of this century. . . . I assure you we all stepped round there like ram's tails in fly time. It was the grand overwhelming Waterloo victory of dancing." The ladies, reluctant at first since the Tiger Ball "is vulgar," soon enough threw off their "bonnets & cloaks" and

TOP LEFT: CHARLES FRANCIS ADAMS JR., 1855

TOP RIGHT: HENRY ADAMS, 1858

BOTTOM: BROOKS ADAMS, 1860-1865

OPPOSITE TOP: JOHN QUINCY ADAMS II, 1853

OPPOSITE BOTTOM LEFT: MARY ADAMS, 1860-1865

OPPOSITE BOTTOM RIGHT: LOUISA CATHERINE ADAMS II, 1860-1865

The fourth generation of Adamses, nurtured in Quincy and at Harvard, soon reached halfway around the world. The young men across the top (left) were all photographed during their college days. Charles Francis Adams Jr. (far left) is appropriately serious. Henry (middle) and the gaily attired John Quincy Adams II looked determined for their graduation photographs. Below, Brooks Adams (far left), a student in England, sat stiffly for his portrait. Mary Adams (middle) was photograhped in the elegant dress she wore when she was presented to Queen Victoria. Louisa Adams (left) posed during her brief years on the Continent before her tragic death.

"rushing onto the Tiger floor danced away like mad." In the late hours, Charles retired with friends "to drink brandy & waters" and then, at four-thirty in the morning, went off to finish the night "on turkey & champagne." He got home at six. On the Fourth of July, after a boat trip with four male friends to the Isle of Shoals, where the landlord of a hotel sent the boisterous lads back to Boston, Charles ended up a long night of food and wine by washing his face, "long since become about the color of a lobster, with raw whiskey."

These were days of whiskey and love. The debutantes seemed to get younger every season until they appeared to Charles to be "out of their nurseries." His classmates married, and he watched as their wives swelled with "litter" or "foal." During one barren period, however, he noted of his friends and their wives that "copulation may vigorously proceed, but assuredly conception is at a standstill."

During all this, Charles was living at home on the top floor of his father's house. When he got home late, which he did with frequency, he had to ring the bell and get his father out of bed. This sometimes prompted family discussions about expectations and lack of direction. When asked when he might settle down and marry, Charles snapped that he could not "go into the market place & buy a wife as easy as I could buy a horse. 'Go & get in love' — isn't it what I've been trying to do for two years."

In 1858, Henry Adams sailed for Europe for two years of "study." He, too, was expected to find himself, and was the first Adams to take the Grand Tour to discover his profession. Instead, he felt "under obligations and bonds for future conduct."

While Henry was abroad and Charles was ringing the bell late at night, Charles Francis Adams received both the Free-Soil and Republican nomination to the U.S. House of Representatives. The elder Adams had been in and out of politics for almost ten years, serving in the Massachusetts House (1840–1845) but losing, in 1852, a bid to regain his father's seat in the U.S. House. He became a "man of parts," and tended his accounts, served on banking and academic boards, worked on his classical studies, and mulled over his coin collection. His family was large, his estate well established, his marriage to

Abigail Brooks fortunate: her father, Peter Chardon Brooks, was at his death one of the richest men in New England. In addition, John Quincy Adams had left his son "a tolerably ample fortune." For the first time, some of the Adamses enjoyed a level of affluence never before achieved by the family.

Much of the period 1850–1858, Adams spent in historical research. In the first six years, he had brought out ten volumes of John Adams's papers. In 1856, he completed the final manuscript of the life of his grandfather. Beyond Quincy, these were years of drama and violence. The peaceful interlude from 1850 to 1854 ended with the passage of Stephen A. Douglas's Kansas–Nebraska bill, which explicitly repealed the Missouri Compromise of 1820, allowed the spread of slavery beyond the 36°30′ line in the Louisiana Territory, and opened up two new territories, Kansas and Nebraska, in which the existence of slavery would be determined by the vote of the people living there. The next day a Boston mob led by a Unitarian minister tried to prevent U.S. soldiers and a sheriff's posse from taking a fugitive slave, Anthony Burns, to a ship and forcibly returning him to his owner in the South.

Indignation over slavery was spreading, and new parties and factions forming. Free-Soilers were soon joined by the Know-Nothings, the Republicans and the anti-Nebraska Democrats. The Know-Nothings were native-born Americans who opposed the increased immigration of Irish Catholics and Germans into the country, and their anti-Catholic and antiforeign bias attracted malcontents from all the other political parties. In 1854, the Know-Nothings did well in national elections, won state elections in Massachusetts, and almost took New York. But in 1855, the party split into pro- and antislavery factions. The search began once again for a national antislavery party.

Tensions were rising in the nation. There was an outbreak of civil war in Kansas. Senator Charles Sumner of Massachusetts was beaten in the Senate chamber by an irate South Carolinian. Charles Francis Adams was elected to the Republican national convention in Philadelphia, where the "Black Republicans" put forth "Free soil, free speech, Frémont." Although John C. Frémont lost to James Buchanan, Adams and other Republicans saw that their party was fast becoming the national antislavery party they sought. The Dred Scott case in 1857 added substance to their viewpoints. Adams, the old Free-Soiler, found himself gaining popularity and strength in Massachusetts. In 1858, then, the Republicans swept the state, and Charles Francis Adams won almost twice the number of votes of his main opponent for a U.S. House of Representatives seat. In Berlin, Henry heard of his father's election and wrote his brother Charles: "The old Free Soilers, sir, are just about the winning hosses, I reckon, just now." Indeed they were.

Although Henry did not know it, his future was beginning to take shape, too. He had agreed to Charles's suggestion that he try writing since it was "certain that I shall never be a lawyer." Charles recommended that Henry read Gibbon, and when he had done so, Henry replied: "I feel much as if perhaps some day I too might come to anchor like that. Our house needs a historian in this generation and I feel strongly tempted by the quiet and sunny prospect."

In February, 1860, their father took a stand in the House against granting approval as official printer to a candidate who benefited from the spoils system. Adams smelled the political pork barrel, and fanned its fumes with his opposition. Charles, in Boston, wrote about his father's stand under the name PEMBERTON for the *Boston Advertiser*. Henry, in Europe, read the piece and wrote to Charles that he might "perhaps furnish material for a pleasant series of letters" to some newspaper. Charles, in turn, acting as Henry's agent, could entice only the proslavery *Boston Daily Courier* to run Henry's writing, and although Henry mildly objected to the paper's political bias, his first letter of this "pleasant series" appeared on April 30, 1860.

Henry sought the dramatic and picturesque. Italy seethed with its war of liberation, and Henry, leaving war coverage to reporters like Henry J. Raymond of the *New York Times*, wrote of a fortune-hunting lieutenant and Emperor Francis Joseph. King Victor Emmanuel II "looked like a very vulgar and coarse fancy man, a prize fighter, or horse jockey." Garibaldi, dictator of Sicily, "had his plain red shirt on, precisely like a fireman, and no mark of authority. His manner is, as you know of course, very kind and off-hand, without being vulgar or demagogic." Of American politics abroad, Henry wrote: "There is a general sensation or suggestion of bad Bourbon whiskey about American politics that is not pleasant. Art must exercise a refining influence, and a man who comes here to pass his life, drops Bourbon whiskey and takes to lemonade or Bordeaux at least. Americans who live abroad read the American papers with a sort of groan."

Still, as the end of his two-year holiday drew closer, Henry had failed to make his choice of profession. He felt himself, at twenty-two, "getting old and cautious," and may also have been a bit worried. Charles suggested that Henry join their father and mother in Washington. Henry grabbed at the suggestion. "I shall make up my bed in Washington, and no doubt it will be just as pleasant as anywhere else," he wrote his mother. "At all events, whether it is or not, it's the place that my education has fitted me best for, and where I could be of most use. So if Papa and you approve this course, and it's found easy to carry it out, you can have at least one of your sons always with you."

Henry was pleased at the decision. He had heard something of Washington from Charles, who although minding the family real estate and enjoying his "bachelor hall" on Mount Vernon Street in Boston, had ventured to the capital to visit his parents. He found that "Washington is a bear garden it is true and the tone of morals and manners is disgustingly low." He attended balls and wrote Henry, as older brothers will, of a worldly topic: "Now probably you don't know what a flirtation is. I didn't — in fact I never saw one except in Washington. . . . I went there green — the first time a young woman trod on my toes, as I talked to her, I drew my foot away and looked at her reproachfully. When she insisted on my holding her hand, I insisted on letting it go. When she pressed my hand in the dance, I didn't return it and only offered the end of my fingers. I came there cold & impossible and then I found it paid. They didn't understand and it bothered them and they laid themselves out to subdue me. . . . I haven't seen a Boston girl for six weeks but shall tonight, & really don't know how they'll seem — they are so very virtuous."

When not dallying with Victorian ladies, Charles Jr. was

eyeing politicians. In the summer of 1860, William H. Seward, who had been a strong candidate for the Republican nomination for president, invited Charles Francis Adams, whom he greatly admired, and his son Charles Jr. to make a swing around the country with him. During this trip, Charles Jr. was introduced by Seward to Abraham Lincoln, a small-town Illinois lawyer, whose "eye . . . never belonged to a man great in action; it is neither the quick sharp eye of a man of sudden and penetrating nature, nor the slow firm eye of one of decided will; but it is a mild, dreamy, meditative eye which one would scarcely expect to see in a successful chief magistrate in these days of the republic."

But Lincoln was the man the Republicans selected to run for president — Stephen A. Douglas was the Democratic candidate, and John C. Breckinridge the candidate of breakaway Democrats who ran on a platform of slavery and the annexation of Cuba. Henry Adams returned home in time to vote for Lincoln on November 6, 1860. His father also won reelection with sixty percent of the vote, and enjoyed a victory parade and illumination through Quincy. He confided to his diary that he had at last achieved "honorable, perhaps a high reputation for character and capacity." He had much to savor: political victory, personal wealth, and children who had grown up as "good and efficient members of society."

Henry eagerly accepted the job as his father's private secretary, and was in Washington with him for the beginning of the "lame duck" session of Congress on December 3. This was the opening day of "Secession Winter" — a great time for a journalist in the capital. Henry had made plans to be both private secretary to his father and Washington correspondent for the *Boston Advertiser*, a fact he would keep secret by writing under by-lines like "Our Own Correspondent." The study of law was quickly forgotten as the excitement of journalism took hold. "It's a great life," Henry wrote his brother Charles, "just what I wanted." Henry tasted "continual intoxication" from his work, and he did not have to search far for stories: Republican leaders like Seward, Sumner and the Know-Nothing Henry Winter Davis often relaxed in Charles Francis Adams's living room.

Henry's first dispatch from the capital to the *Advertiser*,

The second year of the Civil War had begun when Abraham Lincoln posed for this photograph by Mathew Brady or one of Brady's assistants. The anxieties and burdens of that terrible war were already marking Lincoln's face.

ABRAHAM LINCOLN. DAGUERREOTYPE BY MATHEW BRADY, 1862

dated December 7, 1860, stated that "feeling here is that nothing will do any good until secession has been tried," and some hoped it would come soon "for the country is weary of the threat." He filed regularly in the next eight weeks, but by mid-February, he was "sick" of the "hard work," and annoyed at having his broadest libels and even a whole dispatch cut by the editor in Boston. His efforts ended when the editor went to Washington and replaced him as correspondent. Henry's dispatches showed his skill at details and characterization. Burnett of Kentucky had "a voice like a bull and a face not very unlike his voice." Henry Winter Davis was caught one day, arms folded, impatiently waiting for the House to come to order, a man "rather short than tall; with a graceful figure; a finely-cut expressive face; crispy hair, closecut so as to show a finely-shaped head to the best advantage; remarkably neat and well-dressed in his round-cut English clothes."

Charles also got into print in April, 1861, with his piece "The Reign of King Cotton" for the *Atlantic Monthly*. He received $40 for the article, in which he predicted that the slave economy could be destroyed by competition and King Cotton would fall from internal chaos. The article, he later wrote, "caused me to be recognized as a young man of somewhat nebulous promise."

While his sons were writing of the struggle, Charles Francis Adams was in the thick of it. Adams and Seward, who was still a senator but soon to be the new secretary of state, sought to hold the border states in the Congress and maintain the status quo until Lincoln could take office in March. But leaders in South Carolina and other cotton states had vowed that they would secede should Lincoln be elected. There was a strong belief among the northern states that the South was bluffing, that time would heal southern discomfort. When lame-duck President Buchanan spoke to the Congress on December 3, he described the perilous situation and suggested several amendments in a spirit of compromise and moderation. The House moved to convene a special committee of one member from each state to examine Buchanan's proposals. Charles Francis was selected to represent Massachusetts on this Committee of 33, as it came to be called.

The South, perhaps rightly, saw the Committee of 33 as a

Republican attempt to stall until Lincoln took office. The committee held its first meeting on December 11. Amendments were raised and rejected, and at one point the southern members walked out — but remained listening behind closed folding doors.

On December 20, Henry Winter Davis offered a proposal that Adams described as "a cannon shot clear through the line." Davis suggested that New Mexico Territory (and, in a later proposal, Kansas) be admitted at once to statehood and that their citizens decide for themselves whether or not they wanted slavery. After assurances that slavery would never flourish in New Mexico, and feeling that the Republicans needed to make some sort of compromise, Adams supported Davis's proposal. Later, he made his own controversial New Mexico resolution, which his "staunch" Republican friends bitterly attacked even though the proposal gave no more than the South was expected to get eventually. "Is it possible," one of them wrote, "that Adams agrees to the admission of New Mexico as a Slave State? God help us, if *he* deserts us."

By the first of the year, however, it was obvious that the House Committee of 33 (and the Senate Committee of 13) would not hold the Union together whatever compromises were offered. South Carolina, on December 17, had held a convention and declared itself out of the Union. Three days later Georgia, Alabama, Florida, Mississippi, Louisiana and Texas were all meeting, and would vote themselves out by February 1, 1861. A week later, at a meeting in Montgomery, Alabama, they would declare themselves the Confederate States of America. A month before Lincoln was inaugurated, his nation had split apart. As he took office, all federal forts in the South had fallen to Confederate forces except Fort Pickens at Pensacola, Florida, and Fort Sumter, in Charleston, South Carolina.

During the spring, Adams's name had been mentioned for a cabinet post, perhaps secretary of the treasury. But there were also rumors of a diplomatic appointment, which he favored. On March 19, a telegram arrived for him in Boston which announced that Lincoln had appointed him minister to Great Britain, the third Adams to hold the post. The telegram, Charles Jr. wrote in his diary, "fell on our breakfast table like a veritable bombshell, scattering confusion and dismay. . . . My mother at once fell into tears and deep agitation; foreseeing all sorts of evil consequences, and absolutely refusing to be comforted; while my father looked dismayed. The younger members of the household were astonished and confounded."

After absorbing the shock and considering the offer, Adams accepted it and went to Washington to meet with President Lincoln. The president seemed uninterested in the new minister and his post. He listened "in silent abstraction" while Adams thanked him for the appointment, and replied: "Very kind of you to say so, Mr. Adams, but you are not my choice. You are Seward's man." Then Lincoln turned, cutting off Adams, and said, "Well, Seward, I have settled the Chicago Post Office" appointment.

Adams postponed his departure six weeks. He had to turn over his financial affairs to one of his sons. But which one? Charles Jr. was still unmarried and a spirited bachelor about Boston. Henry was going to London as his father's secretary (and again as a secret journalist). Brooks was in school. Only John Quincy II, the oldest son, was mature enough and available. The previous year he had become engaged to Fanny Crowninshield of Boston. At his father's request, he and Fanny were married quickly and went to live in the Old House in Quincy so that he could look after things.

In April, Fort Sumter was fired upon, and the Civil War began. Virginia seceded, Washington was threatened. Northern factions mended, and flags flew in the streets of Boston, young men drilled, ladies wore the colors on their dresses. On May 1, Charles Francis Adams, his wife, and their children Mary, Henry and Brooks sailed to England.

During his Washington-correspondent days, Henry had become acquainted with Henry J. Raymond, now editor of the *New York Times*. Before Henry left for London, Raymond appointed him correspondent for the *Times*, but this was a delicate assignment that required far more secrecy than the job in Washington for the *Advertiser*. In effect, Henry would be writing about events that he would be working on for the U.S. government. If discovered, he would compromise his father and perhaps discredit the whole mission with England at a sensitive time. The State Department strictly forbade "all communications with the press," and Charles Francis Adams was quick to "impress upon all the members of the Legation the importance of obeying the injunctions." He was not being facetious. Only Henry and Charles knew of Henry's double life in London as secretary and correspondent. Charles collected the fees Raymond paid his brother. And Henry shared whole days with his father at the U.S. Legation at 5 Mansfield Street. The two sometimes worked side by side in a musty study "as merry as grigs," but Henry revealed nothing.

Things were not so merry for Minister Adams, however. Upon his arrival in London, he discovered that Confederate envoys had reached the city first. Coincidently or not, Queen Victoria had issued a proclamation of neutrality, which conferred belligerent rights to the Confederate States. Adams worried that England might follow this with diplomatic recognition, which at the very least would strengthen the South's resolve to fight.

Pro-South factions were popular in England in the early 1860's. Commercial interests favored the South's attitude toward protective tariffs. Shipping interests saw in the split the ruin of American competition and hoped to obtain exclusive hold on the carrying trade with the new cotton kingdom. Besides, as Henry Adams wrote with wit, "the English mind took naturally to rebellion — when foreign."

Despite the neutrality proclamation, Minister Adams was well received by the British. He began a direct and honest, but always careful, relationship with Lord John Russell, the foreign minister. Lord Palmerston, the prime minister, was seventy-seven years old in 1861, and Adams found him "a rancorous hater of America and bent on depressing it."

The British, however, weren't always Adams's most perplexing problem. Secretary Seward, officially ensconced as secretary of state, sent off on May 21 his infamous Dispatch Number 10 which, Adams wrote in his diary, sounded as though the United States were "ready to declare war with all the powers of Europe." President Lincoln had fortunately toned the dispatch down before it was sent, and told Adams to communicate as little of it as possible. Adams wisely conveyed only its sense to Lord Russell.

When not regarding Seward carefully on the one hand,

ABIGAIL BROOKS ADAMS. PARIS, 1862

CHARLES FRANCIS ADAMS. PARIS, 1862

Adams was watching the British on the other. The English were conferring privileges on the Confederacy. British vessels brought military supplies and clothing into the South, running the northern blockade of southern ports, and southern ships sometimes flew the British flag to elude northern ships. Confederate vessels were welcomed in British ports and, as Adams rightly feared, were being outfitted far beyond the limitations set up under belligerent privileges. To make matters worse, by the end of 1861 both Britain and France needed cotton for their mills; cotton supplies in England would be gone by the end of the year.

At this time, the American minister faced his first diplomatic crisis. The British mail steamer *Trent* had been boarded on November 8, 1861, by officers and sailors of the USS *San Jacinto*, and the boarding party had taken off two Confederate diplomatic agents, James M. Mason and John Slidell. The Confederates were imprisoned, and in London the press and Lord Palmerston demanded both an apology and restoration of the prisoners. Warming to the issue, some London papers called for not just recognition of the South, but war. After two months of negotiation and consultation, the United States released the Confederates, and the end of the *Trent* affair soothed British concerns that the North might seek a quarrel. The two nations, England and the United States, eased their tensions toward one another.

Still, Minister Adams continued to press the British about outfitting Confederate ships, and on at least one occasion exchanged letters with Lord Russell, which were spiced, as Henry Adams expressed it, with "copious dashes of vinegar." Adams learned in July, 1862, that the British were outfitting a special and impressive gunship at Liverpool that was destined for the Confederate navy. He repeatedly asked the foreign ministry to seize the ship, which was designated only as the "290." Adams also sent for the USS *Tuscarora* to lie off England and intercept the 290 should she sail. Finally, after almost a year of consulting Crown law officers, the British sent instructions to the customs officials in Liverpool to detain the 290; but the ship hurriedly sailed and eluded the *Tuscarora*. It was an expensive action, for the 290 later took on British guns and supplies, and renamed the *Alabama*, began attacking Yankee

After the Confederate ship Alabama *was outfitted by the British and sailed from England, she terrorized northern shipping. Within two years, the USS* Kearsarge *caught her, and during the ensuing battle, the* Alabama's *crew was recued by the USS* Deerhound *(top, center). After the seafight, the captain and officers of the* Kearsarge *posed victoriously on deck.*

THE ACTION BETWEEN THE KEARSAGE AND THE ALABAMA, 1864

CAPTAIN WINSLOW AND THE
OFFICERS OF THE KEARSAGE
AFTER THE BATTLE, 1864

shipping. Her toll of American merchant ships and, later, her cost to British taxpayers for reparations were equally impressive.

Probably the high point of Adams's diplomacy was reached with the crisis of the Laird rams, iron-clad ships being built in Liverpool for the Confederate navy. The American minister repeatedly warned the British ministry that if the rams were permitted to sail, the American government, already threatening to resort to privateering against Confederate vessels, might challenge the British in incidents at sea. Lord Russell expressed doubt that his government had legal power to prevent the rams from leaving port. Even then, the government's seizing of the *Alexandra*, a ship being built for the Confederacy, was before the courts.

The rams were scheduled for completion in August of 1863. In an exchange of notes in early September, Adams said that if the rams sailed, "it would be superfluous in me to point out to your lordship that this is war." Adams did leave the door open to additional instructions from his government, but the firmness of his position was unmistakable. By this time, however, Britain did not want the rams to sail. The war in America had turned in favor of the North. Although the British ministry, even before it received his note, was committed to holding onto the rams, Adams's pressure over the months forced the final decision to keep the rams in port.

During 1861–1862, Henry Adams wrote dispatches every Saturday night to the *New York Times* from his two-room suite at the top floor of the U.S. Legation. He disguised his knowledge of events, not revealing the contents of Dispatch Number 10, although he had read it, and describing the number of visits between his father and the foreign minister — which he of course knew exactly — as "at least one, possibly more than one, interview." His articles were headed "Important from England," or "Matters at London," or more commonly, "Our Own Correspondent."

When Henry was not writing he was, like so many newspaper correspondents since, tasting the social life of London. Unfortunately, he found it bitter, and was repulsed by British exclusiveness and the stiffness of the levees and formal balls. A member of the U.S. Legation wrote in his diary that "as

Henry Adams says, after you have bowed to the hostess, made some original remarks to her about the weather, and looked at the family pictures, the stock of amusements is exhausted; unless you find some barbarian present with refinement enough, or, if you please, sufficient confidence in you to present you to a young lady who will talk, it is a waste of time to remain."

Henry's distaste for London society soon got him into trouble. He wrote a comparison of Manchester and London social life, which Charles offered to the *Boston Courier*. The editor of the *Courier*, proud of the success of his former correspondent, and unaware of the need for secrecy, wrote a note identifying the author of the piece. Henry was quickly in trouble on both sides of the Atlantic. London journalists picked up the article, and he was soon "sarsed through a whole column of the [London] *Times*." The attacks in the London newspaper increased, and worried him that his articles for the *New York Times* might be discovered. The attacks also hurt his ego, and he swore off journalism for a while. He wrote his brother Charles and asked him to tell Henry Raymond that "his London correspondent has stopped for a time."

The mistake didn't help Henry's pessimism. On one occasion he wrote to Charles: "I always was a good deal of a sceptic and speculator in theories and think precious small potatoes of man in general and myself in particular." He also suffered from recurring attacks of chronic dyspepsia, which tended to make him irritable; he had a bad temper. He took pepsin and cod-liver oil, and at least once sought the curative baths at Baden-Baden — as his great-grandfather had sought the waters of Stafford Springs, Connecticut.

Fortunately for his readers and his talents, Henry Adams continued writing. His major work of the period was a thirty-five-page piece for the *North American Review* on Sir Charles Lyell's tenth edition of *Principles of Geology*, a heavy tome which Henry enjoyed and reviewed well, to good notices. He received $100 for the review and became a steady contributor. His career had begun, and looking back, Henry Adams would always consider those years in London as a golden time.

The Civil War period was also a time of learning for Charles Francis Jr. His classmates from Harvard days and his other friends were enlisting, but Charles was reluctant, and wrote in 1861: "War is no plaything, and, God knows, I have no wish to trifle with it." Neither did his father want to see his son and namesake go into battle: "No man who dips his hands in this blood will remember it with satisfaction," he wrote in his diary.

But Charles was bored with dreary office work, and the feeling persisted that he was failing at the practice of law. He applied for a commission, and shortly after Christmas, 1861, became a first lieutenant in the First Regiment of Massachusetts Cavalry Volunteers. He and his unit went immediately to Hilton Head and Beaufort, South Carolina. "God! what an escape!" he wrote. "I was swept off my feet, out of my office and into the army. Educationally, and every other way, it was the most fortunate event in my life."

His father mildly disapproved of Charles's enlistment: "With abilities and character much above the average he lacks continuity of purpose. . . . He has now taken to an occupation for which he has little fitness." But, said the father of his son, "I much fear I shall never see him again." For the first year there was little to worry about. Charles wrote his father: "They talk of the horrors of war; we have made them a jest — so far. Talk of luxury — you should see our tents. Here on my table is a bundle of flowers which one of my men brought which at home would be worth yellow gold. I write on a mahogany table and behind me is a looking glass & a sofa. I sit on horsehair chairs and my feet rest upon carpets, — & all the spoil of the Philistines loaned by a paternal government to its gallant defenders."

The period of the carpeted tents soon ended. Charles and his unit rode into the battle at Antietam, which in his words was a "veritable charnel house." Strangely, Charles also wrote that he "dropped quietly asleep — asleep in the height of the battle, and between the contending armies."

The year 1863, Charles thought, was "my best period in the service." Lee, moving toward Washington through the Shenandoah Valley, sent southern cavalrymen like fingers probing to the edges of the Union armies. At Aldie near a pass in the Bull Run Mountains, the First Massachusetts found war with Virginian cavalrymen. There were bloody charges and

Charles Francis Adams Jr. (far right), who served with the First Massachusetts Cavalry, began the Civil War with the glorious feeling "I would not have missed it for anything." By 1864, when this picture was taken, Petersburg was about to fall and Adams's feelings had begun to change. In August of 1865, ill and tired, he concluded: "We were sick of the whole thing!"

DETAIL: CAPTAIN CHARLES FRANCIS ADAMS JR. AT PETERSBURG, 1864. FROM A DAGUERREOTYPE BY TIM O'SULLIVAN

A photograph from the steeple of Bethesda Church, near Cold Harbor, Virginia, caught General Ulysses S. Grant and his staff during a momentous decision: to fight or not to fight. Grant, just outside the circle of church pews, leans over to consult a map and perhaps listen to a fresh report from a newly arrived officer (with sword). Soldiers of the Third Division of the First Army Corps pass in the rear; some stop and watch curiously. Grant decided to fight, and the Battle of Cold Harbor took place on June 3, 1864.

GENERAL GRANT MAKING THE DECISION
TO FIGHT AT COLD HARBOR,
JUNE 3, 1864. DAGUERREOTYPE BY
TIM O'SULLIVAN

countercharges, and 154 of the First's officers and men fell, killed, wounded or taken prisoner. The remnants went on to Gettysburg, but stayed out of the main battle.

When the First reenlisted, Charles Adams went home on leave to Boston with them in 1864. There were official tributes and praise from relatives at family gatherings. But best of all was one quiet day, perhaps alone, when he "walked over the house and sat and smoked a cigaret and drank a glass of my old whiskey in the old familiar rooms." During the same leave, Charles sailed to England to visit his family. London he found "a big and formal Boston," but Paris was "for pleasure, the whole air is full of it." The Parisian women were beautiful and lively, and he reluctantly ended four days in that city with "one more dinner with Burgundy, and started for London smiling and happy with wine."

In five weeks he was back with the First and the Union army. Charles and Company D were transferred to General Meade's and General Grant's headquarters. During the Wilderness campaign, he wrote, "Grant smoked and whittled all the time and he is the coolest man I ever saw." Charles admired the general and thought that he had "all the simplicity of a very great man, of one whose head has in no way been turned by a rapid rise. A very approachable man, with even, unaffected manners, neither stern nor vulgar."

In 1864, Massachusetts began filling its military quotas by recruiting black soldiers. The Fifth Regiment of cavalry consisted of blacks from Canada or those brought north from the South. In July, 1864, Charles became a lieutenant colonel in the Fifth Massachusetts. By modern standards, he wasn't very enlightened about the black men who served under him. He thought the enlistment of blacks would ensure "the freedom and regeneration of the African race." But he also thought the "nigs," as he called them, docile and lacking in initiative, although skillful as workmen and possessing "an immeasurable capacity for improvement. . . . I have little hope for them in their eternal contact with a race like ours."

Colonel Adams soon led his black troops into "burning Richmond at the moment of its capture . . . the one event which I should most have desired as the culmination of my life in the army." And so it was. Adams had been ill during

Charles Francis Adams Jr. led his troops of the Fifth Massachusetts Cavalry into Richmond, Virginia, "at the moment of its capture." The city had been largely destroyed by artillery shelling and fire.

his last two years of service; he had had dysentery, malaria and jaundice. He took opium and quinine, went on sick leaves, but continued to suffer. In August, 1865, he was discharged as a brevetted brigadier general — and weighed just 130 pounds.

His service had begun with elation. After his first day of fighting, he wrote: "I would not have missed it for anything . . . the sensation was glorious. Without affectation it was one of the most enjoyable days I ever passed." But the war quickly lost such romantic flavor. Charles reacted to the surrender at Appomattox: "We were so sick of the whole thing! . . . The life had become hateful." In London, his father rejoiced: "Thanks be to God. This deplorable war seems to have come to an end and the Union is not destroyed and emancipation is undoubtedly attained."

Charles Francis Jr. thought, in retrospect, that he had learned much from his army experiences. As he had said in 1864, the men were better than the officers. He had renewed faith in democracy and mankind. War, in effect, had taught him about the promise of peace. He had gained poise and confidence from command. But he had also seen "the old family traits" as reflected in the opinions of his men, who thought him "cold, reserved, and formal. They feel no affection for me, but they believe in me, they have faith in my power of accomplishing results and in my integrity."

During the war, Charles had visited his sister Louisa in Newport, Rhode Island. There he met Mary Hone Ogden, and "with her I was charmed, — as pretty as a French picture." Matchmakers were at work, of course, and soon Charles wrote that "Miss Ogden . . . runs through my head infernally. She persuades me that my sensibilities are not dead but sleeping! Hora! I'm not played out." During a sick leave, Charles visited Mary again, and although properly surrounded by chaperones, recalled: "A pleasant night of waking dreams suggestive of perennial youth." In February, 1865, he slipped away from John's house in Boston and went to Newport, where he and Mary became engaged. In November, they were married. One of the ladies in his old circle of Washington friends said of the match: "He found the one woman of his generation fit to marry him, so beautiful, so self-possessed, so nearly his equal in every way." Charles and Mary — the Aunt Minnie of later diaries — sailed for Europe in 1866. Now, as he later wrote, he would search for his life's work — "catch the step."

Charles Francis Sr.'s career as a diplomat in London was calm during its last few years. He vacationed with his family in Wales and enjoyed the seashore. He briefly rented the house in Ealing, where he had lived as a boy fifty years before. He turned more of his attention to his youngest children, Brooks and Mary, and worried about their health and education. In April, 1868, longing for home, he wrote Secretary Seward asking that his resignation be accepted. The London *Times*, an old antagonist, praised his "wise discretion and cool judgment." Other ministers and diplomats publicly acclaimed his skill: Adams had never, said one, been "in a passion and never in a panic," although he had seen enough "to have excited a man of less governed temper."

The century was fast moving toward its end. Charles Francis Adams, politician, businessman, diplomat, was ready for a little peace in Quincy. His children, as he had previously remarked, were a pleasure. John, the lawyer, was also a politician. Louisa and Mary were joys, and Brooks was maturing quickly. Charles Jr. — well, Charles would find something. And Henry had already learned a lesson basic to his work. "After all," he told a friend, "writing is only half the art; the other being erasure. No one can make any real progress that doesn't practice the latter as vigorously as the first."

As John Adams had said, he had studied war and politics so his descendants could study art and history. With war ended, the Adamses turned, as their great-grandfather intended, to these pursuits.

12

Catching the Step

[1868–1886]

*O*N a hot July evening in 1868, Charles Francis Adams and his family disembarked from Europe in New York City. Adams's return to the United States after seven years as minister to Great Britain went largely unnoticed. Even in Massachusetts, only a few prominent men gave him public recognition, and the *Boston Advertiser* merely printed a perfunctory notice. At home in Quincy, Adams hoped to settle down to a "very charming quiet life."

His sons were already deeply involved in the nation's reconstruction following the Civil War. The oldest, John Quincy II, who had been a staunch supporter of Lincoln, had become so angered by the Republican Party's handling of the South that he bolted to the Democrats. Like other political moves by the Adamses, his change of party was made solely from moral motives. His daughter Abigail Adams Homans wrote that "his gesture of resigning however ill-advised, was very characteristic of his independent spirit, nor would he have hesitated if he had been able to foresee that in so doing he lost any chance of political preferment."

John Quincy II had no way of knowing that the Democrats would be out of power until 1884, and by that time, Abigail later wrote, her father had "lost his youthful zest." Although still politically popular, he turned down appointments to foreign missions and cabinet posts made by President Cleveland. He became, like his father, "too set in his ways. . . . It was indolence too . . . and a desire to be left alone."

Here again was the strange Adams characteristic of seeking political office — he even on occasion became angry when it was not offered or attained — and yet refusing to engage in the tough give-and-take of politics. And while an Adams of an early time could afford to remain above political campaigning, John Quincy II could no longer do so in 1867, when he ran for governor of Massachusetts and lost. Politics in America was changing fast — like the voters and the politicians.

And yet there was the family's moral imperative to seek office. As he watched the horror of Reconstruction spread throughout the South, John Quincy II began to realize the need to strengthen the new Democratic Party. "My grandfather," he said, "used to predict that when the great slavery struggle which he saw impending closed, there must come a great constitutional party or anarchy."

The prescience of his grandfather appeared accurate in 1867. Almost four million blacks had been freed by the Emancipation Proclamation or the Thirteenth Amendment. By March of that year, thousands of northern carpetbaggers and southern freed blacks replaced the local government officials in the South. Military tribunals replaced civil courts, the state legislatures of the old Confederacy were weakened, and an army of twenty thousand men, aided by black militia, occupied the land. Radical Republicans in the government sought to punish the South even more, and from 1868 to 1877, they controlled in varying degrees each state in the region. Every state administration of the Confederacy was soon characterized by extravagance and corruption. State treasuries were looted, and taxes and debts increased. Officials bought votes, judicial decisions, franchises, whole elections. The public debt of most southern states doubled and sometimes quadrupled: a saturnalia in Louisiana drained off some

$26 million in five years and rang up the state's debt to more than $40 million.

Corruption was by no means peculiar to the South. New York State and the federal government were bloated with it. But the South could be rebuilt only through borrowing capital from the North, and the rates of interest were ruinous. Despite the obstacles to rebuilding, the former Confederate states did undertake such reforms as tax-supported public education, abolition of imprisonment for debt, broadened franchise — all of which were badly needed. Yet northern critics harped on the corruption and debt, and doubted openly whether blacks were capable of participating in democratic government. As a result of the prejudice, the blacks were written off and a white government in the South received northern acquiescence — the tragedy of Reconstruction.

The outrages of the carpetbagger and the scalawag were soon matched by the terror of the Klan. By 1870, the Ku Klux Klan had spread from Pulaski, Tennessee, into the Deep South, and Klan members and the Knights of the White Camelia challenged the Radical Republican political power at its source by attacking blacks and carpetbaggers.

Troubled by these events, John Quincy II began building the "great constitutional party" his grandfather envisioned. Although he was the only Adams to bolt to the Democrats, he was not the only Adams concerned about Reconstruction. Henry wrote: "I tell you frankly, that when I think of the legislation since last year, my blood boils." Yet however opposed the Adamses may have been to slavery in the abstract, none of them expressed specific concern for the fate of the emancipated blacks or for the development of their capacities for citizenship. Between 1867 and 1871, John Quincy II represented Quincy in the state legislature and ran unsuccessfully for governor of Massachusetts. In July, 1868, at the time his parents were settling in after their return to the United States, young Adams received one vote for his nomination as the Democratic Party candidate for president.

He knew that the Democrats were a minority and success at any level would be difficult. But he believed, like his forefathers, in minority political efforts and regarded their existence and the political fights they stimulated as vital to democracy. He had written his father in London: "I am fond of a shindy and I like a minority." His daughter added: "He seems positively to have reveled in lost causes." When the elder Adams tried to console him, John replied: "As to the trouble, pain, and expense of my politics I hope that you do not think that I did it for a reward. I do trust that you know me to be sincere when I say that I do not wish, and would shun, any political honors. Once and for all understand me — do — when I assure you on my honor, that absurd as it may look, I took my line last fall solely from a sense of duty and because I felt that the time demanded that an insignificant person like myself do his little d——est."

In 1868, to carry his party and its ideas into the South, John Quincy II accepted an invitation from the Democratic Committee of South Carolina to speak at Columbia and Charleston. His speeches were a strange mixture of conciliation and lecture, and fitted the tone of exhortation that one Adams or another had sounded since 1776. He introduced himself to the audience as "the grandson of the earliest opponents of your peculiar institutions, an ardent supporter of Lincoln in the active prosecution of the war, and as one who hailed with gratitude the abolition of slavery." Stunned, his audience sat silent, and he challenged them by asking if any would call for restoring slavery, for renewing the rebellion or continuing coercive legislation. Who among them, he asked, would restrain free speech?

He prodded them, and ended up by recalling the old close associations between Massachusetts and South Carolina that had been torn apart during the last two decades. "Let us forgive and forget," he said. "With slavery its cause let our feelings cease. Let good will and brotherly love cast out all bitterness and let us all hasten the day when South Carolina and Massachusetts may stand once more, hand in hand under the old roof tree and under the old flag. . . . I am deeply and seriously impressed with the difficulties under which you labor and the dangers which threaten our system of government." Adams called on them to join in "calm, earnest, patient, honest effort" to restore "the Constitution and the Union." Here was the echo of his great-grandfather and grandfather: "Independence and Union Forever!"

This, then, was the politics of the Adamses when Henry Adams set off for Washington in October, 1868, at the age of thirty. His father noted sadly that he would miss Henry, his European companion, "every day and every hour of the rest of my life. . . . Nobody has known so much of me, as he." Henry was an ambitious journalist, and like his brothers John and Charles, filled with ideas of reform. In fact, he and Charles were soon to join forces as pioneer muckrakers, and as they would both discover, corruption spread outward from Washington, often on railroad tracks.

One of President Grant's weaknesses was his failure to understand government finances. Some $400 million greenbacks were still in circulation after the war, the currency was not legal tender for all purposes, and it was uncertain that the government would redeem any of it for gold. In September, 1869, two notorious speculators, Jay Gould and James Fisk, tried to take advantage of the fluctuation in money and corner the gold market. They had help from members of Grant's administration, including people close to the secretary of the treasury. The price of gold plunged from 162 to 135, and on September 24, "Black Friday," Wall Street brokers faced ruin. The government had to bail them out by dumping $4 million in gold on the market.

By the time "Black Friday" crashed around Gould and Fisk and the men of the Erie Railroad, Henry and Charles were already hard at work. Henry was collecting evidence for his article "The New York Gold Conspiracy." He had also become interested in the "rings" of lobbyists in the Congress and he wanted to find out just how traders like Fisk and Gould profited by currency speculation. He soon discovered plenty of muck to rake. "These fields," he wrote Charles, "are gloriously rich and stink like hell." When Henry did the research for his article "American Finance, 1865–1869" for the *Edinburgh Review*, he found "the whole revenue system a mass of corruption."

In Washington, he was fast earning a reputation as a "clear and forcible writer, [perhaps] at times a little too forcible," according to his brother Charles. They both used the press to attack and reform. Henry thought that the American public should understand "how dramatic and ar-

OVERLEAF

*When the golden
spike was driven into
the last rail at
Promontory, Utah,
on May 10, 1869, the
locomotives of the
Union Pacific (right)
and the Central
Pacific (left) were
moved forward until
their cowcatchers
touched. The nation
was spanned by rail.
Railroad men, dusty
and sunburned,
christened the two
engines with wine and
shared a bottle of
champagne. The chief
engineers shook
hands: Grenville M.
Dodge (right) of the
Union Pacific and
Samuel S. Montague
(left) of the Central
Pacific. The railroads
widely publicized
their feat by
distributing copies of
a poster announcing
the "great event"
and promising four
days to San Francisco
in "luxurious cars &
eating houses."*

tistically admirable a conspiracy in real life may be, when slowly elaborated from the subtle mind of a clever intriguer, and carried into execution by a band of unshrinking scoundrels." His "Gold Conspiracy" piece did just that, and was also deliciously libelous.

James Fisk, said Henry Adams, "was coarse, noisy, boastful, ignorant; the type of young butcher in appearance and mind." Jay Gould had "a reminiscence of the spider in his nature. He spun huge webs, in corners and in the dark, which were seldom strong enough to resist a serious strain at the critical moment." Adams called Gould "an uncommonly fine and unscrupulous intriguer, skilled in all the processes of stock gambling, and passably indifferent to the praise and censure of society."

Meanwhile, Charles had also completed investigative work on the American railroads, and was hard at work on "Railroad Inflation." After the war, he had made up his mind to devote fifteen years "to making my way into a position." Politics might have been one choice, but he felt he had no aptitude. "I lack magnetism frightfully, & have no facility of doing the right thing at the right time. I am frightfully deficient in tact; I never can remember faces or names, and so I am by nature disqualified. I never could be a popular man." Instead, as he wrote in his *Autobiography*, "I endeavored to strike out a new path and fastened myself, not, as Mr. Emerson recommends, to a star but to the locomotive-engine. I made for myself what might be called a specialty in connection with the development of the railroad system."

It was a wise and perspicacious choice. By 1860, there were 30,626 miles of railroad track east of the Mississippi, 1,264 of them in Massachusetts alone. Between 1865 and 1873, the number more than doubled, to 70,000; by 1887, it would more than double again, to 157,000. By 1900, the amount of track in the United States would exceed that of Europe. Railroad expansion, begun in the 1840's, reached across the continent by 1869 and touched the life of every American, from Wall Street to the mineral mines of the Far West. The railroads were fast-growing, big, rich and corrupt — an ideal field for a reform-minded Adams.

Charles thought that he could win a post with the rail-

GREAT EVENT POSTER ANNOUNCING THE COMPLETION
OF THE FIRST TRANSCONTINENTAL RAILROAD

CEREMONY AT THE DRIVING OF THE GOLDEN SPIKE AT PROMONTORY, MAY 10, 1869

roads by writing about them. At the same time, he would be educating himself and putting his name before the public and the railroadmen. In April, 1867, the *North American Review* published "The Railroad System," in which Charles enthused about the "application of steam to locomotion" as "the most tremendous and far-reaching engine of social revolution which has ever either blessed or cursed the earth."

He also attacked the railroads, and "incessantly" pestered Henry for "documents especially about railway matters and nice bits of corruption." Charles was a good investigative reporter, one who used newspaper files and made contact with participants. His best work, "A Chapter of Erie," showed that the labor paid off. He considered it "the hardest piece of work I ever did . . . very good! Much better than I thought."

"Erie" detailed the attempt by Commodore Vanderbilt, president of the New York Central, to gain control of the Erie. Vanderbilt was opposed by Jay Gould, Daniel Drew and James Fisk, and the two powerful forces battled on Wall Street. Vanderbilt tried to buy a majority of the Erie stock, but the Erie managers kept producing so much of it that he couldn't keep up. Adams exposed the stock manipulations and the bribery of state officials.

Both Charles and Henry, with their writing and investigations, had concluded that such financial maneuvers were bringing "Caesarism into corporate life." Measuring the corruption around them, and foreseeing the temptations of the next one hundred years, Henry had written: "The belief is common in America that the day is at hand when corporations far greater than the Erie — swaying power such as has never in the world's history been trusted in the hands of mere private citizens, controlled by single men like Vanderbilt, or by combinations of men like Fisk, Gould, and Lane, after having created a system of quiet but irresistible corruption — will ultimately succeed in directing government itself."

The railroad and the telegraph companies were already concentrating power in a few hands. Charles wrote "The Government and the Railroads" for the *North American Review*, and followed it up in April, 1871, with "An Erie Raid," in which he attacked railroad management. In September Charles and Henry jointly published their book *Chapters of Erie and Other Essays,* which included Henry's "The Legal Tender Act" and "The New York Gold Conspiracy." The book was a hard-hitting indictment of corruption among American industrialists.

Charles Adams's journalism, by this time, had finally gotten him into railroading. In a two-part article in the *North American Review* in 1868, Adams had made suggestions for the establishment of regulatory commissions, and the next year he was pleased to note that the Massachusetts legislature had passed "my railroad commissioners bill." Charles worked every influence he had, and in June, 1869, he was appointed to the Massachusetts Railroad Commission. "The preliminary struggle was . . . over," he later wrote in his *Autobiography.* "The way was open before me. At last I had worked myself into my proper position and an environment natural to me."

Within two years, he was chairman of the commission and hard at work regulating the Massachusetts lines. He had faith in his own ability to guide the railroads and in "the general supremacy of an enlightened public opinion" – a measure perhaps of his naiveté. Public opinion, in fact, counted for little. The era of "laissez-faire" was just beginning, and the railroads were determined to stay unregulated. They issued free passes to politicians and paid the campaign expenses of candidates who wanted to keep them running – and their taxes low – at any cost. Adams soon found himself trying to work around the Massachusetts governor, who was "so slow and tired that I can't do business with him," and the State House, "where business is flapping around in its usual loose way & it remains to be seen how far we can influence it." After six months he found the commissioner's task "simply execrable; it destroys all one's nerves."

The panic of 1873 brought with it a public reaction against the full-steam-ahead railroads. The regulation of tariffs and services followed, and special railroad commissions were set up, modeled on Adams's Massachusetts Railroad Commission. He had struggled for a standard system of books and accounts for the railroads; for seniority, dismissal arbitration, and insurance against death or disability from sickness or accident for the workers. He prepared a report on safety:

the trains were hand-braked in each car; the wooden stock often telescoped upon collision and burst into flames from the stove heaters and open-flame lighting; wooden railroad bridges sometimes gave way; hand-coupling maimed employees. Adams pushed for braking trains from the locomotive — the lack of such braking had caused the Revere crash of 1871, when twenty-nine were killed and fifty-seven injured; for the construction of railroad cars so they would not telescope; and for the use of candles or fluids that would not ignite at less than three hundred degrees in the passenger cars. Despite some successes, Adams found the commission work "wearisome." He resigned in 1879 and accepted an offer from the railroading genius Albert Fink. He would serve on the three-man board of arbitration overseeing the railroad trunk lines that ran from the East Coast to the Middle West. It was a major step for Adams, and after a walk in the Quincy woods, he took it. His work entailed traveling frequently to western shipping centers and meeting many kinds of railroad men.

At this same time, he began building a personal fortune in investments and real estate. "My future," he had once written, "must be business and literature," and indeed that was the direction he took. He had now "caught the step" in journalism and railroading, and was heading toward the presidency of the Union Pacific Railroad and into battle with his old foe Jay Gould.

While Charles and Henry Adams employed journalism to expose injustices and to reform industry and government, their father turned his back on reform politics. The revolt against the corruption of the Grant administration had made reformers bold. In May, 1872, the Liberal Republican Party held a convention in Cincinnati that attracted a wide spectrum of reformers, a number of free-traders like Horace Greeley, and eastern conservatives who supported Charles Francis Adams as a candidate.

Adams, out of retirement from diplomacy and back in the thick of things, was home between phases of negotiations in Europe, and his sons, it is certain, fully informed him of conditions in America. It was a heady time of transcontinental railroads and industrial revolution. There was more money in circulation than at any other time in the nation's history. The per capita wealth of the North, the 1870 census showed, had doubled in the past decade. Opportunities for making a great deal of money appeared limitless. Millionaires sprang up across the land, and their names became synonymous with their industries: Morgan and Cooke, Vanderbilt and Gould, Armour and Swift, McCormick and Pillsbury. But there was pain with the treasure: defalcations, bankruptcies, stock-watering schemes, wildcat investments. Speculators flocked to oil wells, gold and silver mines, and railroad construction — speculation was almost safe since the railroads were unregulated. By 1873, sensational corruption was uncovered in the Grant administration: the Navy Department selling business to contractors; the secretary of the navy making hundreds of thousands during his tenure; the Interior Department working hand-in-wallet with land speculators; the treasury "losing" $450,000; the U.S. minister to England associated with the Emma Mine swindle; the U.S. minister to Brazil defrauding the Brazilian government of $100,000 and fleeing to Europe (the U.S. government refunded the money). In 1874–1875, the newly elected Democrats unpeeled further fraud in the Treasury and War departments, and exposed a "Whiskey Ring" in St. Louis that systematically cheated the federal government of millions in taxes on liquors. Even the secretary of war got caught selling trading posts in the Indian Territory.

On September 17, 1873, the failure of the banking house of Jay Cooke and Company tumbled other banks along Wall Street as if they were dominoes. The New York Stock Exchange closed its doors for several days. A panic became a long-term depression.

Only the railroads held firm. With the Pacific Railway bill of 1862 the federal government had begun the practice of giving land directly to the railway corporations for construction of tracks. The Union Pacific averaged $16,000 a mile from the government, and obtained some 20,000,000 acres of public lands along its rights-of-way. In all, the federal government handed out to the railroads 158,293,377 acres of land — of which 44,000,000 was later declared forfeit.

CARTOON OF JAMES FISK. FROM "PUNCHINELLO," AUGUST 20, 1870

*James Fisk, the
notorious financier
and Wall Street
speculator, battled
for control of com-
panies and men. With
Jay Gould, Fisk tried
to corner the national
market in gold, and
turned a tidy profit
struggling with
Vanderbilt over the
Erie Railroad. In this
cartoon (left), Fisk
performs a neat
balancing act with
his many acquisitions.*

The railroads sold the lands but retained mineral and timber rights — an extremely lucrative holding. In fact, land grants to both the Union Pacific and the Central Pacific more than covered the legitimate costs of building the lines. (Moreover, the government got back more than it gave away by having its freight and employees travel for half fare.)

Here, too, as Henry and Charles Adams pointed out, corruption thrived. During 1872, wholesale corruption was discovered on the Union Pacific. The company's investors, in an attempt to divert construction profits to themselves, had organized a construction company, the Crédit Mobilier of America, and had persuaded the head of Union Pacific to award it rich contracts. The effect was to put the Union Pacific on the edge of bankruptcy, while Crédit Mobilier paid dividends to its investors of 348 percent in one year. To dissuade Congress from investigating, the Union Pacific directors placed Crédit Mobilier stock in the hands of key congressmen — James A. Garfield of Ohio, Oakes Ames of Massachusetts, James Brooks of New York — and even of Vice-President Schuyler Colfax. Little wonder that when Charles Adams came into the Union Pacific he found the corporation in "a shocking bad way."

Reform, then, should have been a major issue of the 1872 presidential elections. When the Liberal Republicans met in Cincinnati in May of 1872, any one of a half-dozen men might have taken the prize. Charles Francis Adams, the son and grandson of presidents, was the most obvious choice. He had served his nation well as minister to England during the critical Civil War years. But he was, at the very moment, sailing with Brooks Adams back to Europe to negotiate with the British in Geneva on certain matters that had remained un-settled after the Civil War, among them the claims made for damages incurred by the Confederate warships *Alabama*, *Shenandoah* and *Florida*.

In Cincinnati, meanwhile, swarms of politicians joined the Liberal Republicans, but they sought this new alliance as a tool to power not to reform. Adams's supporters contended that Greeley and his backers had climbed on board solely to battle President Grant; reform was secondary to them. Greeley announced that he "felt it in his bones" that Grant could be thrown out. Adams's backers attacked Greeley's commitment as "scatterbrained." On the other side, Adams's opponents thought he represented "too much of the anti-popular element — the sneering and sniffling element."

Like his forebears, Adams remained aloof from the election process. He wanted to feel, as John Adams and John Quincy Adams had felt, that the nomination had come unsolicited and without political compromise. Instead of taking part in the Cincinnati convention and his own political campaign, he chose to sail to Europe. If the "unequivocal call" should come, he told supporters, he would then consider it.

It never came. At one point Adams had been thought a sure winner. But as the balloting proceeded, he faded, and by the sixth ballot there was a strong movement to Greeley. Adams, just arrived in London, heard the news from a stranger, who rushed up and told him that Greeley had been nominated. Adams felt only relief.

By the end of August in Geneva, negotiations were almost settled. Adams had smoothed over an obstacle concerning claims by making a bold move. He had approached the British directly rather than through the arbitration proceeding. After some jockeying, both sides had agreed to $15.5 million in payment by the British for damages caused by the *Alabama*. Adams was credited with saving the negotiations. Lord Tenterden's report to the British cabinet noted Adams's "dignity, tact, self-command and moderation."

When Adams returned to the United States there was mention of a cabinet post or the Senate. In 1875, admirers pushed him for governor of Massachusetts, and in 1876, the centennial year, he was suggested as a presidential candidate. He ran for governor but lost, partly because, again, he took no interest in the campaign. The day after he was nominated, he left Massachusetts with his family for Philadelphia to see the exposition and did not return until late September.

For the next decade, he prepared his father's diary, which was published in 1874–1877 in twelve volumes as the *Memoirs of John Quincy Adams*. He was seventy in 1876, and his health was failing rapidly. But he still studied the classics for an hour a day and worked over his coin collection. He attended meetings of the Harvard Overseers and, in 1877, went

By his seventieth year, Charles Francis Adams had finished editing
the twelfth and final volume of his father's diary. A work of thirty
years had ended. Both politics and editorial pressures lay behind him.
He retired to Quincy, where he and his wife, Abigail Brooks Adams,
settled into a peaceful routine in their old age. For a few more years,
Adams continued his daily hour of classical study, mulled over his
coin collection, and kept up his diary. Domestic squabbles offered
some relief from the pattern. Charles and Abigail did not get along
with Marian Hooper Adams, Henry's wife, who caught traces of their
sourness in this photograph. At one point, the elder Adamses actually
stopped seeing her. It is interesting to compare the three pairs of
portraits of Charles and Abigail: the oils on page 321, the photographs
on pages 360-361 and this one. They span an adult lifetime from early
marriage to old age. As the Adamses declined, they sometimes
traveled to New York for Abigail's medical examinations and to
Saratoga Springs for treatment. Charles's keen mind, however,
degenerated totally at the end.

CHARLES FRANCIS ADAMS AND ABIGAIL BROOKS ADAMS SEATED OUTSIDE
THE OLD HOUSE IN QUINCY. PHOTOGRAPH BY MARIAN HOOPER ADAMS

to the anniversary of the Free Soil convention in Buffalo. Gradually, however, his memory failed. He was unable to work, and finally gave up keeping his diary after fifty-five years. But no matter how his mind slipped, Adams never lost touch with his upbringing: he always rose whenever his wife entered the room. He died on November 21, 1886. He had long shunned the public, and his wish to be left alone was respected after his death. He received little obituary or public notice.

His sons, meanwhile, carried on. Henry had left Washington to become an assistant professor of medieval history at Harvard. He had agreed to a five-year contract that paid $2,000 a year; with his private investments and, in 1871, the editorship of the *North American Review,* he could count upon an income of just $6,000 a year. A bouncy and irreverent professor, he gave nine lectures a week. He was fond of saying, "I am a professor of history in Harvard College, but I rejoice that I never remember a date." He told his students in more serious moments: "Whatever else you do, never neglect trying a new experiment every year."

At Harvard Adams met Marian Hooper, a bright woman of twenty-eight. They fell in love, and were engaged in February of 1872. "Socially," he wrote to a friend, "the match is supposed to be unexceptionable. She is certainly not handsome; nor would she be quite called plain, I think. . . . She talks garrulously, but on the whole pretty sensibly. She is very open to instruction. *We* shall improve her. She dresses badly. She decidedly has humor and will appreciate our *wit.* She has money enough to be quite independent. She rules me as only American women rule men, and I cower before her. Lord! how she would lash me if she read the above description of her!"

Henry and Marian were married the following June in a private ceremony performed by one of Henry's book reviewers who also happened to be a clergyman. Since Henry saw a chance for "medieval work in France and Germany," they went to Europe on their honeymoon; as usual, Henry was "deadly sick" on crossing. He read "history in German" and renewed old friends. Marian wrote to her father, "Henry is utterly devoted and tender," and Henry assured his father-

Marian Hooper was a reluctant subject for the camera, and this tintype is thought to be the only photograph taken of her. She was out riding at Beverly Farms in 1869, about three years before she married Henry Adams.

OVERLEAF
During their honeymoon to Europe, Henry and Marian Hooper Adams visited England. Henry, the bald-headed chap in the photograph at left, struck a pose with some friends on a ancient stairway in Wenlock Abbey. On the Nile, Adams enjoyed the comforts of the dahabeah Isis *(right) while touring Egypt. Marian refused to appear in either photograph.*

MARIAN HOOPER ADAMS. TINTYPE TAKEN AT BEVERLY FARMS, MASSACHUSETTS, 1869

HENRY ADAMS AND HIS FRIENDS ON THE RUINED STAIR OF
WENLOCK ABBEY, ENGLAND, 1873

HENRY ADAMS ON THE DAHABEAH "ISIS," DECEMBER, 1872

in-law that Marian had "gained flesh and strength, so that she is in better condition, I think, than I have ever known her to be." Neither mentioned that during their visit to the temple of Karnak on the Nile, Marian had suffered from a deep depression. They returned to Boston in August of 1873, "bobbing up on this side of the ocean, like a couple of enthusiastic soap bubbles."

Back at Harvard, Henry lectured twelve hours a week, and recruited writers like James Russell Lowell, Henry James and Francis Parkman for the *North American Review*. All were friends and all contributed. But the *Review* was losing money; it had only four hundred subscribers. In 1874, Brooks Adams, who had been recently admitted to the Massachusetts bar, wrote for the July issue "The Platform of the New Party," which echoed brothers Henry and Charles and their theme of an "invisible government" that existed outside the elected government and controlled the country. But the help from friends was not enough. In 1875, after a quarrel with the publisher over other matters, Henry resigned as editor.

He turned to his writing — two novels were taking shape — and lectured in 1876 on the primitive rights of women, a topic that as he grew older became increasingly interesting to him and formed a section of his autobiography, *The Education of Henry Adams*. He had been influenced by John Stuart Mill, an early champion of women's rights, and his concern was, perhaps, spurred by the tragic and wasteful death in 1870 of his sister, Louisa, from gangrene after an accident in Italy. But though he was intellectually aroused, he was never moved to embrace the crusaders of the 1870's — Susan B. Anthony, Elizabeth Cady Stanton, Lucretia Mott — or the National American Woman Suffrage Association.

In the spring of 1877, L. Lawrence Gallatin asked Adams to write a biography of his father, the late Albert Gallatin, and gave Adams access to his father's papers, which were kept in Washington. Although Adams was already at work on his magnum opus, the nine-volume *History of the United States of America During the Administrations of Jefferson and Madison*, he looked on the offer as providential. He very much wanted to undertake the biography for its own sake, but it would also give him the opportunity to do extended and much-needed research in Washington for the *History*. He accepted with enthusiasm and resigned from Harvard.

He and Marian were happy to leave Boston. Washington, they thought, would offer them excitement, and Henry looked forward to a prolonged period of hard work and good times. He wrote to a friend: "If I felt a perfect confidence that my history would be what I would like to make it, this part of life — from forty to fifty — would be all I want." Adams soon settled into his research for both projects. He thrived in Washington. For forty years he lived on Lafayette Square just to the north of the White House across Lafayette Park. He and Marian first rented the house at 1501 H Street, but within two years moved to 1607. Their home was soon filled with watercolors and carefully selected paintings by young American artists, and with oriental rugs, Japanese vases and bronzes.

Some of these furnishings and others were paid for by generous Christmas checks from Marian's father, Dr. Robert Hooper. She used one of them to buy a section of woods near their farm at Beverly Farms in Massachusetts — land that Henry had hoped someday to give her himself. In fact, Henry soon found himself competing with Dr. Hooper for his wife's love and attention. Dr. Hooper visited his "Clover" and her husband in Washington every spring, and Marian wrote him at least one long letter every Sunday. Father and daughter enjoyed the summers together while Henry worked. Still, the results of Dr. Hooper's contributions gave both the Adamses much pleasure. "We strut about as if we were millionaires," wrote Marian. "Henry says for the first time in his life he feels like a gentleman."

She found life so pleasant that she wished old age and death were "myths." She feared a lingering death. "I cannot understand why the Episcopalians pray to be delivered from 'sudden death.' " She went on to say that she and Henry had decided that when they died they would be buried in Washington and "not expressed to Boston like canned terrapin."

The social life in Washington, then a city of about 150,000, was especially congenial to the Adamses. Marian pulled Henry away from his desk for gatherings — her small frame belied immense energy. Their circle of friends, in Wash-

ington, Boston and abroad, included John Hay, Oliver Wendell Holmes, Jr., Henry James, John La Farge, Edith Wharton, Stanford White, Clarence King, John Fiske, William James, and William Dean Howells, among others. Marian charmed them all. Henry James wrote: "We never knew how delightful Henry was till he lost her; he was so proud of her that he let her shine as he sat back and enjoyed listening to what she said and what others let her say."

In 1878, Henry joined the newly formed Cosmos Club, where he went for Monday nights of small talk with the nation's leading politicians and intellectuals. He and Marian also had their own small group, the Five of Hearts, that met regularly for five years, and included John Hay and his wife and Clarence King. All of them wrote and gossiped to one another. King, Carl Schurz, and Henry Cabot Lodge also frequently joined congressmen at the Adamses' for dinner, especially during the Christmas holidays. On one occasion, the Adamses traveled with the British minister Sir Edward Thornton and his distinguished entourage for ten days to Niagara Falls. They sang English ballads. Henry went on a wild sleigh ride and "shinnied" up huge icicles. They jollied away hours with whist and poker and singing songs with lyrics like "Give my chewing gum to sister, I shall never want it more."

Marian rented a piano and had her music sent from home. The Washington dogcatcher carried off Henry's favorite, Boojum, who was quickly retrieved. Marian wrote a humorous little piece about the episode from Boojum's point of view. Earlier she had written that their household was like a "Noah's ark" — two of a kind — with "Henry and I, 2, 2 dogs . . . 2 horses, 2 women servants, 2 men servants."

Henry's work went well. By 1879, he thought he could profit from "a winter in Spain and Paris, and a spring in London . . . to study the diplomatic correspondence of the three governments in regard to America, during the time of Napoleon, from 1800 to 1812." His two-volume biography of Albert Gallatin was finished and in press, and his first novel, *Democracy*, had been sent off to his editor, Henry Holt. Marian had read the manuscript and made suggestions; she knew who the characters really were. *Democracy* was a solid effort, although one critic later labeled it only "clever"; the *Saturday Review* called it a masterpiece.

The Adamses' European trip was a charmed adventure. Marian won new friends with her American slang ("the inside track" was one of her phrases) and such colorful descriptions as "fat, rosey, placid, torpid like a feather bed." Henry, wearing what Marian called the "cloak of historian," followed the diplomatic trails to archives in Madrid, Paris and London.

London was, as always, pleasant. Henry James, self-exiled from the United States, became a constant companion, and often kept the Adamses up beyond midnight. Marian wrote in her diary that they could not understand why James had left the United States and become "a man without a country." She thought it "high time Harry James was ordered home by his family. He is too good a fellow to be spoiled by injudicious old ladies in London." In her opinion James should settle in Cheyenne and "run a hog ranch. . . . He had better not hang around Europe much longer if he wants to make a lasting literary reputation."

Robert Browning was an acquaintance who, Henry wrote, carried "the intellectual apathy in his face of a chronic diner out [who] talked incessantly in a voice like steel." They encountered Matthew Arnold almost weekly, and although they encouraged him and helped him plan an American tour they noted that he had a tendency to be too facile and "slop over." They also sought out the London art critic and poet Francis Turner Palgrave, and the sculptor Thomas Woolner. Both Palgrave and Woolner helped them collect new watercolors and drawings, and Woolner, a pre-Raphaelite poet, got them into the new Grosvenor Gallery, "a refuge for the Pre-Raphaelites," where they met all sorts of "queer and pleasant folk" at "tea fights."

By the summer of 1880, after six intense months, Marian thought she and Henry were "pretty well dinnered out." They left Europe, she wrote, with "no more regret than on finishing a pleasant story."

Back in Washington their lives once more centered around collecting art and Henry's writing. Marian bought two unusual portraits by Joshua Reynolds for their home — although Henry disliked portraits — and they inherited a

Teniers and obtained several Boningtons from Woolner in London. There were also works by Constable and Turner. Both Adamses frequently sought the advice of art critics and friends like John La Farge, and at one point the art critic of the *New York World* spent two hours in their home admiring their watercolors. A wealthy neighbor on Lafayette Square, after eyeing their collections with a cool appraisal, told Marian: "My dear, I dislike auctions, but I mean to go to yours after you die."

By the end of 1882, Henry wrote his friend John Hay that he was "grinding out history with more or less steadiness." But he complained, "I am very irritable and several gentlemen who have been dead these fifty years, are catching singular fits in Hell on account of my dyspepsia." Adams, now almost fifty, was pacing himself: "I am working very hard to get everything out of my brain that can be made useful. If my father is a test, I can count on twenty years more brain, if the physical machine holds out."

In the summers, Henry Adams secluded himself in a playhouse that he had had built for his nieces in the woods at Beverly Farms. There he pounded his typewriter, according to Marian, "like a belated beaver, from nine to five every day, garbling the history of his native land as run by antediluvian bosses." His second novel, *Esther*, was nearing completion, and would be published anonymously in 1884. It would sink without a trace — although later scholars would pick through it for reflections on Marian's life — and Adams would write Holt: "So far as I know, not a man, woman or child has ever read or heard of Esther. . . . My inference is that America reads nothing — advertised or not — except magazines."

Marian meanwhile studied photography, which she found "very absorbing," and became a skilled amateur. She took portraits of John Hay, George Bancroft and other friends, posing them in the Adams parlor, and her work was much admired in Washington. Later in 1883, Henry and Marian planned to build a house on the corner of H and 16th streets. With John Hay, they bought the entire corner property, which they divided. The Adamses hoped to spend $30,000 on a "square brick box with flat roof — pine finish," which would have fireplaces in every room and not be de-

LAFAYETTE STREET, WASHINGTON, D.C. PHOTOGRAPH BY MARIAN HOOPER ADAMS, 1883

REBECCA LODGE AT OLD SWEET SPRINGS, VIRGINIA. PHOTOGRAPH BY MARIAN HOOPER ADAMS, 1885

pendent upon steam heat. H. H. Richardson was the architect, a large, blustery and expensive man. Progress on the house was slow, and Marian had at least a year in which to scramble around on the scaffolding taking photographs.

The year 1885 began with much promise: the new house was under construction; Henry had all but completed his study of the second Jefferson administration for the *History*, and the manuscript was being read by friends. But in March, Dr. Hooper, who suffered from angina pectoris, began slowly dying. Marian's worst fear was being realized. She hurried to his bedside, and for a month watched his painful decline.

Henry detested being left alone. The threat of Marian's "nervous seizures" or depressions had subsided, and Henry had become less protective of her, and far more dependent on her. In 1883, at his urging, she had traveled by herself to New York to visit friends, their first separation since 1872. Henry was lost without her. He and Marian were so of a mind that they often spoke of "we" when voicing opinions. The fact that they could have no children, a secret sorrow, reinforced their closeness. Yet when Marian stayed at her father's bedside, Henry's letters were not loving and concerned but coolly businesslike: he listed the day's work; the business of the new house; dinner with Hay; visits to the dentist. It was almost as though he were angry at her absence.

Dr. Hooper died on April 13, 1885. Marian was stricken. Her grief for her father seemed stronger than her love for her husband. Henry took her to Old Sweet Springs, West Virginia, for her health, and they went on long horseback rides into the mountains. Instead of renting their place at Beverly Farms, they went there to rest and work. But depression was engulfing Marian Adams, and when they returned to Washington, Henry wrote their friends: "We lead a quiet and very retired life at present as my wife goes nowhere." The depression continued and she sank into a condition that the historian Ernest Samuels labeled "manic-depressive psychosis."

On Saturday, December 6, 1885, Marian Adams sat alone in her bedroom at her desk writing to her sister: "If I had one single point of character or goodness I would stand on that and grow back to life." Downstairs, Henry prepared to go for a walk, but a visitor called to see Marian. He went upstairs to his wife's bedroom, and found her on the floor, dead. Although the newspapers at first gave the cause of death as "paralysis of the heart," it was painfully clear to Henry what had happened. Marian, his companion and source of joy, had swallowed potassium cyanide — a poison she had used in her photographic work.

His first response was to withdraw from life. He refused to see his friends and stayed alone in his house; neighbors occasionally glimpsed him at one of the windows. He later wrote of those days as "the awful horror of solitude." When Marian's relatives and Charles Adams arrived he told them that he had "also died to the world," that he "had got out of life all the pleasure it had to give. I admit that fate at last has smashed the life out of me; but for twelve years I had everything I most wanted on earth."

Prolonged mourning was in fashion during this part of the nineteenth century: Queen Victoria had her dead husband's clothes laid out every evening before dinner; Dante Gabriel Rossetti buried all of his unpublished manuscripts with his wife's body. Henry Adams, too, entered a long period of exaggerated mourning. He learned to master the letter of condolence to others as he nurtured his grief. His novel *Esther* took on in retrospect the tone of a memorial to Marian, and the publisher inquired if it might be reissued. Henry vowed that he cared "more for one chapter, or any dozen pages of *Esther* than for the whole history." Yet he would not reissue it under his name. His *History*, he insisted, belonged to the "*me* of 1870, a strangely different being from the *me* of 1890." Even his autobiographical *Education* was silent about his married life; there is no mention of Marian or the marriage.

In the last days of 1885, Adams moved alone into the new house on H Street. He sent Marian's two Joshua Reynolds portraits to the Corcoran Gallery and gave some of her jewelry to a neighbor to wear to "remind you of her." The next spring, he left Washington on a long journey to the Far East. Earlier he had written to a friend: "You will understand as I do that my only chance of saving whatever is left of my life can consist only in going straight ahead without looking behind."

13

My Course Is Well Enough Marked Out

[1886-1900]

*H*ENRY ADAMS and his friend John La Farge set out from Boston for the Far East in the directors' private car of the Union Pacific Railroad. It was a luxurious beginning, especially for La Farge. He had spent the day "dodging creditors and sheriffs . . . and trying to borrow a few thou' right and left wherewith to paint Japan red." In San Francisco, they sailed for the Orient "gay as petrels," although Henry was soon seasick and pestered by "four female missionaries" who "sing and talk theology, two practices I abhor."

Henry read works on Buddhism and pondered the Eastern religions and mysticism. La Farge sketched. They visited the shogun shrine at Nikko and the holy city of Kyoto. The shadow of sadness was never far, and one of Henry's diary entries read: "Today, and for more than a year past, I have been and am living with not a thought but from minute to minute." His words were not entirely accurate. For almost a year he had been planning a memorial to Marian that would convey both deep sorrow and the mysticism of Buddhism.

Back home, after an eighteen-day voyage during which

he was well enough to smoke his cigars, Adams began looking for a sculptor. He settled on Augustus Saint-Gaudens to carve the statue — a mysterious, veiled figure of a faceless woman — and on the architect Stanford White to construct the foundation and pedestal. To pay for the work Adams "sold at a sacrifice two thirds of all the railroad stock I still own, and am beginning to provide twenty thousand dollars for Saint-Gaudens and Stanford White."

At the same time, he resumed his historical research and writing. He wanted to finish his *History of the United States*, and applied himself to it during the summer in the deep quiet of the Stone Library behind the Old House in Quincy. His niece Abigail remembered him working there with his two Skye terriers, Marquis and Possum. He wore white linen suits, kept his papers very neat, and wrote in "large careful handwriting." During the summer of 1887, he employed a stenographer to speed him along, a "vile modern innovation" that, he feared, might "spoil my work" (it did not).

By 1888 the section of the *History* dealing with the Madison administrations was ready for preliminary reading by friends, among them John Hay and Carl Schurz, and the final volumes were published in January, 1891. The work was widely anticipated but it enjoyed only a limited readership. Its value as technical history was noted by the prestigious *Guide to Historical Literature*, which called it "one of the very best pieces of work American historians have produced."

In Washington, although he never went out socially, Adams was often attended by nieces in residence and more guests than he wished: "My breakfast table is crowded to suffocation and famine," he complained. He decorated his house at 1603 H Street with new pieces of art, and the rooms, said a friend, were "full of strange trophies of Japan." John Hay, who lived next door, frequently dropped by for chats; he was a superb storyteller, to Henry's delight.

At this time Cecil Spring Rice joined the circle of Adams's friends. He was a British diplomat, just twenty-eight, and Adams, who was then forty-seven, found him "an intelligent and agreeable fellow" with "creditable wits" and "mad, of course, but not more mad than Englishmen should be." Spring Rice thought Adams "queer to the last degree; cynical, vindictive, but with a constant interest in people, faithful to his friends and passionately fond of his mother and of all little children ever born; even puppies."

Henry was especially fond of two-year-old Martha Cameron, whose mother was a close friend. He stuffed Martha with treats and love, and when she was old enough, he kept an elaborate dollhouse for her behind a sliding panel in his study. Henry wrote Martha letters and confessed in his diary that "by dint of incessant bribery and attention [I] have quite won her attachment so that she will come to me from anyone. She adores Del Hay's pigeons, and takes a fearful joy in visiting Daisy in my stables. Her drawer of chocolate drops and ginger-snaps; her dolls and picture books, turn my study into a nursery."

Spring Rice found the whole Adams family "as odd as can be. They are all clever, but they all make a sort of profession of eccentricity. . . . Two of them were arguing. One said, 'It seems to me I am the only one of the family who inherits anything of our grandfather's manner.' 'But you dissipated your inheritance young,' answered the other."

As the *History* drew toward completion, Henry contemplated another trip to the Far East. He studied Chinese, and thought of going to China and solving "the tantalizing 'Asiatic mystery.' " He intended to start in the South Pacific, and then follow the medieval route of Marco Polo from China through India to Europe. In preparation he began outfitting himself for two years in the South Seas, and beyond. He talked La Farge into going with him, although La Farge had no money and had to work in a frenzy to try to finish his commissions of stained glass and paintings. It would be a trip of adventure and art (both of them would paint). They started out in high enthusiasm, and Adams wrote to his niece Mary Hooper, a watercolor artist herself, that La Farge had exclaimed during the train ride to San Francisco: "*By Jove* and *Adams, look at that!* and *Just see the color of that pig-stye,* or *Now we're getting into yellow again,* or *What is the color of that sky,* just when I think it's pure cobalt, and he sees sixteen different shades of red in it."

Off they sailed, with Adams cheering jovially: "Here goes, then, for Polynesia."

When not working in Washington, Henry Adams enjoyed writing at his desk at Beverly Farms (right). Marian Adams caught him in this informal pose, pen in hand, inkwells open. After Marian's death, Henry commissioned Augustus Saint-Gaudens to sculpt the hooded figure (below). The work, titled Grief (or Henry's preference, Peace of God), stands in Rock Creek Cemetery, Washington, D.C.

"GRIEF," THE ADAMS MEMORIAL. BRONZE BY AUGUSTUS SAINT-GAUDENS, 1891

HENRY ADAMS. PHOTOGRAPH BY MARIAN HOOPER ADAMS

In the spring of 1884, Charles Francis Adams Jr. assumed the presidency of the Union Pacific Railroad. The Union Pacific, like the New York Central and the Pennsylvania, was one of the largest corporations in America. Charles Adams commented: "We have some forty organizations of which I am president, I think." The government had granted the Union Pacific and the Central Pacific two charters, in 1862 and 1864, that made them the eastern and western links respectively of the transcontinental railroad system. The government also gave the Union Pacific rights to public lands along its route, and the UP, like other railroads, issued bonds using the lands as security. The government also loaned the UP $27 million for thirty years at 6 percent interest, and the railroad did not have to pay any interest or principal until the land matured. It was not surprising that investors scrambled to purchase UP stock.

When Oakes Ames of Massachusetts (with others) got caught in the Crédit Mobilier scandal, he sold out his UP holdings to the powerful railroad financier Jay Gould. Gould soon cornered 100,000 shares of UP stock. By 1875 his holdings were so large that he was able to appoint his own board of directors and to begin paying 8 percent dividends. He was, in effect, paying himself.

The Crédit Mobilier scandal, however, brought congressional investigation of the Union Pacific, and in 1878, Congress passed the Thurman Act, which declared that UP must pay the government 25 percent of its net earnings every year until its $27 million loan was repaid. If UP defaulted, it could not pay dividends. Congress also authorized the appointment of a railroad commissioner to examine all the land-grant railroad accounts.

In 1870, Adams had begun traveling into the West every year on business — a practice he would continue annually until 1890. He visited the Mountain States in 1876 and the Pacific Coast in 1878. Sometimes the trips lasted several months and covered tens of thousands of miles. They were dull and fatiguing, and Adams's diary was studded with comments on his having to kill "a lonely evening at a typical place of provincial amusement" by playing poker or suffering through a "little humorous" local orchestra, as he did in Detroit. He wrote of the dreariness of train travel across "that great, fat uninteresting West": "Passed the day in the C. B. & Q. cars running on a rainy day through monotonous Illinois — newspapers, cigars, a glass of spirits now and again, talk, sleep, bad meals, and the Senate report on transportation wore away the day."

He began investing in the parts of the country he visited and in the stock of local corporations. In 1869, his income had been just $5,000 a year, "if indeed it was quite that much," but he soon found that his family name was a decided asset in borrowing money. By the time he was appointed to the railroad commission, he was investing through Nathaniel Taylor, in whose Boston office Adams heard "all kinds of good things flying around loose."

As a railroad man, he admired the air brake, and met an inventor named George Westinghouse who had a good one for sale. Adams bought stock, and by the 1890's had $225,000 sunk in the Westinghouse Company. He also bought stock in the UP and other railroads — the Chicago, Burlington and Quincy; the Atchison, Topeka and Santa Fe; the Denver and Rio Grande. But he made the most money in Kansas City real estate at a time when that town was expanding as a major rail and cattle center.

Adams had first gone to Kansas City in 1869. Before the Civil War, the town had been called Westport Landing and was "a forbidding spot on the southern bank of the Missouri consisting of a few warehouses, planters' dwellings, and negro shanties, scattered loosely along the river levee, with a tavern for its most permanent feature. A mere steamboat stopping-place."

Not for long. In 1865, the Pacific Railroad crossed Missouri from St. Louis to Kansas City, and the Eastern Division of the Union Pacific was building track out from there to the Rockies and beyond. Between 1860 and 1870, the population of Kansas jumped almost 240 percent, and during the decade of the 1870's it jumped again by 173 percent.

A new cattle kingdom was growing from Canada to Texas on the Great Plains, and in the 1870's men like Philip D. Armour began making fortunes by packing meat in Kansas City. Charles Adams already owned seven hundred shares of the company that owned the Kansas City stockyards, and took a keen interest in it. In 1875, he became president of the company and began expanding and rebuilding it. He wrote in his *Autobiography* that in that year the stockyards had $100,000 in capitalization and grossed "perhaps" $20,000 a year. He and the stockyard managers built the business up "stage by stage" in "a broad, liberal spirit," and by 1900 the stockyards' capitalization was $10 million and the business was grossing $1.2 million annually. Adams's interest in the stockyards never waned; the yards were the cornerstone of his finances. He watched over them like a hen over golden eggs. One of his diary entries states: "Saw in the paper that Kanzas [sic] City is under water — save the Cattle Yards!"

Adams also made a habit of buying land at some of the developing centers and potential terminal points he had discovered while traveling. The West was filling with cattle and railroads, and he was smart enough to see this and invest accordingly. His plan was "buying, selling, improving." He invested in Fort Worth and San Antonio, Texas; Denver, Salt Lake City, Portland, Seattle; Lewiston, Idaho; Helena, Montana; and Spokane Falls, Washington, where he found a "boom in mines and doing business under canvas."

His best investment, however, was in Kansas City, Kansas. In 1879, he bought land there for $150 to $200 an acre (land was selling across the Missouri River in Kansas City, Missouri — "it seemed miles away" — for $1,000 an acre). Adams and another partner put up $300,000, formed a real estate company, built a steel bridge across the river and opened the town to development. A remarkable land boom took off, and Adams's real estate company paid 40 percent dividends for the year ending June 30, 1885. In 1886, it paid twelve monthly dividends of 10 percent each. By 1900, when its assets were divided, they amounted to more than 400 percent on the original capital.

Not every investment went up. Adams had bad luck with mines. He put money into the Calumet and Hecla copper mine in Michigan, but failed to sell at the peak and moaned: "I have missed a great coup in Calumet. I feel bad." He would feel worse. In the 1880's, he got caught in the "enormous speculative craze" for silver mines. He lost money in Leadville, Colorado, and in 1881 "took a gamble" on Robinson Consolidated by buying a thousand shares at $4.80 a share. The stock tumbled and he sold out at a loss, accepting it as "the price of my emancipation from all faith in mining stocks."

He bought and he borrowed. In 1871, he had a floating debt of $50,000; by 1881, his debt reached $200,000 and continued to grow until the end of the decade, when he owed more than a million and was paying between $45,000 and $60,000 a year in interest charges. He sometimes turned to members of his family for money to invest. During the panic of 1873, he confessed that he "paid the penalty of carrying too much sail in money matters, being compelled to pay 7% for 6 mos. on $16,000 notes — not pleasant but wholesome — my father endorsed my note and that is the last business transaction on my account I ever propose to have with him."

John Quincy II and Brooks were also talked into lending him money and signing notes — only Henry seems to have escaped — and Brooks signed as much as $26,000 over to Charles, and argued about it for years. For this and other reasons Charles generally referred to his brother as "that crank Brooks."

Even with other people's money, Charles Adams was a cautious investor. He sought advice from knowledgeable friends and seldom acted hastily. He was acquainted with geologists and engineers, and liked to walk any land he bought. He made vain resolutions like that in April, 1874: "Here I stop! Cash or nothing."

In the end, Charles Adams won. He was an original and successful capitalist, who started with $5,000 in 1870 and by the 1880's was grossing annually about $125,000. His assets reached almost $3 million. His borrowing he held to one third of his assets. By 1890, he owned a seaside home in Minot, Massachusetts, a country place in Quincy, and a Boston townhouse on Commonwealth Avenue with La Farge stained glass. He bought paintings "lavishly," and Francis D. Millet, an American painter, was a close friend. When Adams's holdings tumbled in value, as they did occasionally, he would almost invariably buy a painting, a strange response to the pain of financial loss.

"I have all I want," he said in the great capitalist's cry, "and I want a great deal."

He believed that "mere wealth will not enable a man to

accomplish much; but it is a most powerful spring-board. . . .
I am received with deference and listened to with acceptance;
— I can dictate my own terms. It becomes a question of ability,
emphasized by wealth. I could do more for my own success by
getting rich than by slaving my life away in mere political
action. This I failed to appreciate twenty years ago. . . . I
want wealth as the spring-board to influence, consideration,
power, and enjoyment." In his time, Charles Adams would
have all four, and he would discover that just as the pursuit of
wealth made other men ruthless, the drive for power corrupted
him. But unlike the capitalists of his day, he recognized his
moral failure.

In 1878, as he was traveling through the monotonous
prairie states, Adams read in a newspaper that his friend, Carl
Schurz, then secretary of the interior, had gotten him appointed as one of five governmental directors of the Union
Pacific. Adams accepted, served a year, and learned at first
hand the breadth and strength of the railroad. With an investor's eye, he concluded that "there was not a more valuable
railroad property in existence or one with greater latent power
of development." Adams bought 2,500 shares, and in a letter
to the *Boston Advertiser* urged that others buy, too.

On March 7, 1883, Union Pacific stockholders elected
him to their board of directors. The company was already on
financial hard times: it had been in litigation with the government for almost a decade. Its earnings were falling sharply: its
stock dipped from 85 ⅝ in February of 1884, to 33 ¼ in May.
Adams acted as intermediary between the railroad and a
Senate committee; part of the price for compromise was his
election as president of the railroad.

Adams "went on deck" as the president of UP on June
24, 1884, and made his headquarters in the Boston office. He
long maintained that he had been "forced" into the presidency.
To take it, he later said, he had to sacrifice his "private business, literary work, leisure and comfort."

Adams was soon embroiled in a major power play. The
Union Pacific had four corporate centers: Boston, New York,
Washington and Omaha. Boston interests controlled one third
of the UP board of directors, and they included F. L. Ames,
nephew of Oakes Ames and a friend and neighbor of Adams's,

who held $5 million in UP stock and bonds; and Ezra Baker, who bored Adams "nearly to extinction" with his "snarling criticisms" and "senility," but who held almost ten thousand shares.

Opposing the Boston interests were the New York stockholders, led by Jay Gould and Russell Sage. Adams thought Gould "an infernal scoundrel, a moral monstrosity, but he is astonishingly quick!" Worse, Adams was considered by some stockholders to be "the mere nose of wax, the poor figurehead," that is, the front man for Gould. It was not a title he could cherish, and despite Adams's efforts at conciliation, Gould withdrew. The New York financier sold his UP stock and piously stated that he thought it best for the Union Pacific "to have a large scattered ownership . . . through the different States." But Gould would not sit idly by, and began building up his other railroad holdings while Adams put the Union Pacific through several management purges and hired easterners and Harvard men, whom he called "my kids."

After his battle with Gould, Adams lobbied for the railroad against the federal government, "the most hopeless and repulsive work in which I ever was engaged." A government director of the road considered the Union Pacific "a perfect and absolute monopoly," and UP was entangled with almost every federal agency, from the attorney general to the Department of the Interior (General Land Office). Adams also battled with Congress, "that incapable and mischievous body," and as a result, in the 1885–1886 sessions alone, twenty-six bills and resolutions specifically concerning the UP were introduced in the House or Senate.

At one point, three commissioners were appointed to "investigate the books, accounts, and methods of the Pacific railroads." As the work of the commission got under way, Adams thought one staff member "a reptile" and the rest "bores, schemers, etc." Although the majority report favored Adams, the commission's minority report, written by Governor R. E. Pattison, said that Gould and Adams "showed an entire disregard of sound principles of trade." Adams called Pattison's report "the dyspeptic utterances of an untruthful, dishonest, political crank."

Union Pacific was having trouble paying off its debt as

JAY GOULD. CARTOON BY F. OPPER, 1882

Jay Gould toppled a great many companies and small investors during his wild speculations. Not all his schemes were legal, but then neither were those of his opponents. This cartoon shows Gould, a smiling bowler with diamond buttons on his trousers, scattering hapless tenpins with "trickery" and "false reports" along Wall Street.

required by the Thurman Act. Its dividends were being curtailed and investor confidence in its stock was waning. Adams decided to ask Congress to pass a bill that would ease the terms of repayment or write off the debt altogether. He had chosen a poor time to ask for favors: the 1880's had produced the first attacks on monopolies and the practice of laissez-faire, which encouraged them. Popular sentiment pushed state legislatures to consider antitrust laws. By 1890, the platforms of both major political parties pledged them to oppose trusts and monopolies, and the Sherman Anti-Trust Act was passed. When Adams went to Washington, the railroads (and other corporations) had just been dealt a blow with the passage of the Interstate Commerce Act of 1887. This act specifically prohibited "pooling" (gentlemen's agreements to hold prices and divide up business), rebates, and higher charges for short hauls than for long. The act provided that all charges should be "reasonable and just," and required that the railroads (and other shippers) post their tariffs for the public. To supervise enforcement, the act established the first regulatory agency in the history of the republic, the Interstate Commerce Commission.

But this laissez-faire period was also a time of corporate defiance, when John D. Rockefeller shopped around for the most lenient state in which to license his Standard Oil Company (and found New Jersey). The business ethos called for beating your competitor by any means available or joining together with him to beat everyone else. Accordingly, Adams had erred by not crushing Gould when he could and by failing to buy Congress or the political parties.

Now, in 1888, to get the bill he wanted for Union Pacific's relief, Adams went to Washington. Adams and Ames agreed, this being a presidential election year, to "contribute" $50,000 to the chairmen of both the Republican and Democratic parties: $20,000 immediately, the rest when the UP bill got through Congress and the president. One chairman assured Adams: "I can get your bill passed if any man can, and you can rest assured, if I can't get it passed it cannot be passed."

Adams attempted to make other payoffs. Senator P. B. Plumb of Kansas proved to be an obstacle, and Adams — by his own account — at first thought to please the senator by building a railroad station at Lawrence, Kansas, and even leasing a local railroad to Plumb's constituents. Plumb wasn't moved. According to Adams, he wanted more — $50,000 to be exact — and even then the incredible right not to vote for the bill. Plumb never got the $50,000. "I was willing enough," said Adams, "to fling the dirty dog his bone, provided I could do so in safety" after the bill was passed.

Another barrier was Senator George F. Edmunds of Vermont, who as chairman of the Senate Judiciary Committee could "bushwhack" UP legislation. Edmunds, Adams thought, was "the most thoroughly corrupt and dishonest, and the most insidiously dangerous man, when balked of his bribes, that there is today in Washington." He was also "fond of his whiskey bottle." Union Pacific sought to put him on retainer. Adams and Ames made the campaign contributions to each party, and Adams said "we would soon in this way learn what political influence money could buy."

It bought nothing. The Union Pacific funding bill was "thrown out" in 1889. But the mystery of why Adams, the political reformer, allowed himself to take part in what he called the "most extraordinary and discreditable negotiation" remained. He showed little, if any, remorse. In a self-serving statement, he reflected on his failure at corrupting politicians: "I simply don't know how to go to work. Not that I am above it; I'm not. I would have bought Plumb, just as I would have bought a horse or a hog, and there would to me have been a perfect and intense satisfaction in slipping the dollars into the greedy hands of the Vermont immaculate; but simply it wasn't in me to do it. And I knew it and they knew it, and they dispised and hated me accordingly."

Unsuccessful in Washington, Adams sought to expand his railroad operations in the field. Union Pacific was strong west of Omaha. To the east, however, other railroads cut into UP's traffic and territory. UP had no Chicago connection, and in 1889 Adams negotiated an alliance with the Chicago and Northwestern for reciprocal use of tracks. He wrote that "the two companies became in all essential . . . respects one company. They will protect and sustain each other and, in case of attack, make common cause." With the Kansas Pacific merger (achieved under Gould's regime), Union Pacific controlled a

In 1876, both Charles Francis Adams Jr. and his wife, Mary Ogden Adams, sat for their portraits by Francis Millet. Charles thought his had a "tremendous likeness" and said of his wife's: "Millet painting Minnie and getting along well."

TOP: CHARLES FRANCIS ADAMS JR.
OIL BY FRANCIS MILLET, 1876

BOTTOM: MARY OGDEN ADAMS.
OIL BY FRANCIS MILLET, 1876

wide section of the American West, from Chicago to the coast.

The alliance angered the other railroads. Gould and his investment group had put together a conglomerate that, by 1900, promised to control 16,074 miles of main track from St. Louis and Kansas City to the Rio Grande, and from St. Louis on the Missouri Pacific across Kansas into central Colorado. To the east, Gould was linked with eastern railroads by means of the Wabash Railroad, which ran to Toledo.

Adams's alliance with the C & NW (and the Kansas Pacific) threatened Gould's system, for Jay Gould, as one associate joked, "always claimed all the territory there is within 1,000 miles of his road." Gould's obvious countermove was to regain control of the Union Pacific. Adams defied him: "April, 1890 – Rumors that Gould is making a drive at me – let him drive!"

Gould's task was formidable. One third of Union Pacific's $60 million in stock was held in New England and another one third abroad. To corner enough to kick Adams out would be almost impossible. Gould would have to wait patiently for Adams to make a mistake.

As the president of UP, Adams had at first moved cautiously. In August, 1886, he had managed to settle the road's floating debt: "went into town and paid off the last U.P. note and gave clerks a half holiday. . . . Today was memorable." His board of directors, however, was soon pressing him to borrow more money to finance expansion, especially for the purchase of the Oregon Railroad and Navigation Company. The corporation's finances, already under strain, weakened further; in 1890, Adams was carrying $14 million in short-term notes. "I had failed to market $6,000,000 of O. R. & N. Co. advances and $3,000,000 of equipment bonds and I had failed to secure the $2,000,000 of new money which would have enabled me to sell the bonds. My budget was askew. It fell like a house of cards."

The Union Pacific faced bankruptcy. Adams needed $4 million fast, and turned to his traditional backers, Kidder, Peabody, which tried to obtain a loan by selling sterling through the Barings (at twelve percent per year). But the Barings were on the slippery edge of bankruptcy themselves because of losses in Argentina. Adams got nothing. Morgan also turned Union Pacific down, and the Chicago and Northwestern, despite vows to make "common cause" in times of trouble, refused to help Adams. As his options narrowed, the only escape became increasingly obvious: Gould.

Ames and Adams made an appointment and went to New York to see the "little wizard." Adams paused long enough to buy "an engraving of Meissonier's '1814,' it being suggestive of my recent and present experience." Adams found Gould "quiet, small, furtive," and told him "my credit, position and responsibility have been undermined and I could no longer carry the load and he must carry it. He assented." Adams told Gould that he would call a directors meeting and turn over Union Pacific to him. "There being nothing more for me to do there, I got up to go. . . . Gould showed me out. As we formally shook hands, the little man seemed to look smaller, meaner, more haggard and livid in the face and more shriveled up and ashamed of himself than usual: — his clothes seemed too big for him, and his eyes did not seek mine, but were fixed on the upper buttonhole of my waist-coat. I felt as if in my hour of defeat, I was overawing him, — and, as if he felt so, too."

Adams knew it was time to withdraw and "meditate the fact of failure." He knew what to do: "The only true course is to bow like a gentleman, quietly pass in your chips, and leave the table. The man, who under such circumstances hangs around the table, proving to others how it ought to have resulted otherwise, is a bore, as well as an ass." Adams thought about his qualities as a railroad executive. He had planned well, he concluded. "My mind was active enough and my plan of operations and scheme of development was well devised, well thought out, and wholly practicable." Later he added: "My ideas were right but I did not hold to them. . . . I was weak of will."

Gould "was gunning for me," Adams concluded, "and he . . . dropped me." While Adams was still president, he noted: "I lack combativeness. I get into a fight easily enough: but, being in it, I lack desperate courage. . . . I fail because I cannot make up my mind on the instant and my reserves are not at my command." There was, of course, the element of

Charles Francis Adams Jr. did well as the first
capitalist of the Adams family. His living style
soon reflected his success. He and Mary Ogden
Adams (Minnie) bought the elegant house
(left, top) on President's Hill in Quincy. Inside
was a large, formal, oak-paneled dining room
with portraits of Abigail and John Adams on
either side of the fireplace. The sitting room
(left, bottom) was more cluttered and featured
the portrait of Minnie by Millet over the mantel.

THE PRESIDENT'S HILL HOUSE, QUINCY, BUILT BY CHARLES
FRANCIS ADAMS JR.

THE SITTING ROOM, PRESIDENT'S HILL HOUSE

THE DINING ROOM, PRESIDENT'S HILL HOUSE

Gould's revenge for Adams's replacing him in the directorate in 1885, and perhaps for *Chapters of Erie*. But basically the error was, as Adams would later write about a much smaller failure: "Expansion and debt."

On November 26, 1890, Adams wrote in his diary: "To-day ceased to be Pres't of Union Pacific and so ended my life of railroad work. . . . Gould, Sage and the pirate band were scrambling on deck at 10." Jay Gould remained a director of Union Pacific until his death in 1892. The next year, as UP's debts mounted and the country was swept by financial panic, Union Pacific went into receivership.

As Charles Adams was heading home to Quincy in defeat, Henry Adams was sailing to Polynesia in victory. His *History* was behind him, finished in 1888, and he could look forward to several months of painting watercolors in Tahiti. From there he would go on to Europe and compile a scrapbook on his architectural interests.

During the first few years of the last decade, while Henry traveled or wrote, the other brothers lived near one another in Quincy and Boston. Henry saw much of his brothers during the 1890's, especially Brooks, a man in his forties, whom Henry found "a strong writer and vigorous thinker who irritated too many Boston conventions ever to suit the atmosphere." Brooks said of himself: "I am a crank, very few people can endure to have me near them," and "as soon as I join a group of people they all melt away and disappear." But Henry admired him more than the other brothers did, perhaps because, as Henry said, Brooks was "a kind of exaggerated *me*."

John Quincy II, meanwhile, had set up a "gentleman's farm" on Mount Wollaston close to the sea. In 1870 Charles had built a fashionable and expensive home on what was called President's Hill in Quincy. Brooks lived in the Old House during the summer, and rented a house in Boston for the winter. He loved the Old House, and had taken it over when his mother died in 1889. At that time, he also decided to marry and consulted Mrs. Cabot Lodge for suggestions about who the bride should be. Mrs. Lodge suggested her sister, Evelyn Davis. Brooks courted the lady and became engaged to her as the whole family looked on in disbelief. At one point, after the engagement, John Quincy II got dressed up and announced to the others: "I am now going to pay my respects to the unfortunate lady who says that she is going to marry my brother Brooks."

Marry him she did. The couple settled into the Old House, and Brooks restored the garden according to an original plan. The brothers all continued their writings and took various locations in Quincy in which to work. Abigail Adams Homans, the daughter of John Quincy II, recalled her uncles as always writing: "Uncle Charles in a nice square house just below his own on President's Hill, which he had bought to provide space for his books and to insure him peace from the distractions of a growing family, which he called the 'Annex.' Uncle Henry when he was in Quincy commanded undisputed possession of the Stone Library, while Uncle Brooks reigned in John Adams's study on the second floor of the Old House."

Abigail's father never seemed to write at all, and when she asked him why her uncles were always writing, he told her, "I suppose it amuses them." Her father, Abigail said, told her he had done all his writing when he was young, and "had nothing more to say now."

The second Cleveland administration was two months old when the panic of 1893 began. A long agricultural depression, strikes, the silver policy of the government, and the loss of overseas markets, among other causes, hurt commerce and industry and the railroads dependent upon them. The Reading Railroad failed early in the spring. In July, the Erie failed. Then the Northern Pacific, the Union Pacific, and the Santa Fe all went into receivership. Banks called in loans, and in July alone commercial failures reached $73 million; some fifteen thousand businesses failed in that one year, and 158 national banks. Henry Adams wrote of Boston financiers: "Men died like flies under the strain and Boston grew suddenly old, haggard, and thin."

All of the Adamses were financially overextended except Henry. Brooks, "who was a nervous creature with little self-control," according to his niece, hurriedly wired Henry to come home from Europe to bolster the family with his wise advice — and available credit. Henry arrived, and helped out, and then held long conversations with Brooks about social revolution, which Brooks found helpful since he was writing *The Law of Civilization and Decay*. Brooks picked Henry's brains until Henry, exhausted by his brother's persistence, left for the World's Fair in Chicago. There he discovered the "delights" of the Dynamo. John "wilted" under the panic of 1893, while Charles claimed that he "had never lost a night's sleep over the panic." And as things eased, some of the Adamses, like other Americans, followed Henry and "packed up our troubles and made for Chicago, too."

No World's Fair could hide the basic changes taking place in America, changes that were being felt in Quincy. For one thing, during the 1880's more than five million immigrants entered the United States from Europe. Another three and a half million came in during the 1890's, and nearly nine million would enter during the first decade of the twentieth century. Immigrants competed for jobs, and labor tried to organize to gain security and work. This led to strikes. The Knights of Labor took on the railroads in 1885, and in 1890 there were more strikes than in any other year of the nineteenth century. And as a growing and restless labor force confronted a fat and paternalistic management used to having its way, violence erupted. The stage was set for political revolt, and the Populists in 1892 won a million popular votes in the presidential election, and 22 electoral votes. In 1894, the Populists rolled up 1.5 million votes during the congressional elections.

This was the time of Edward Bellamy's novel *Looking Backward*, and Jacob Riis's shocking story of slum life, *How the Other Half Lives*. The qualities of both — the search for utopia, the reality of life — permeated America in the 1890's. The influx of foreigners searching for the American promise washed into the quiet retreat of Quincy, too. The town's granite quarries brought change. Although the Adamses and the Quincys had welcomed the quarries in the 1830's, and invested in them, by 1888 the quarries were moving nearer President's Hill. The Irish laborers came not by streetcar or rail from Boston, but by foot from the rank poverty of the "Catholic villages" nearby.

John and Charles Adams sought to hold back the industrialization of Quincy and the laborers. They believed, as their fathers had, in the "beneficience of government by the best people." They both had served long and hard in the town meetings. John was the moderator for two decades. Charles had been elected a town committeeman fifteen consecutive times and, he noted with pride, "at least three times won the largest number of votes passed for any candidate." But the town hall in 1888 was filling with a restless throng of men of "noticeably low type, — young, vulgar, badly dressed, of the hoodlum type." These workingmen now held the political power of Quincy, not the Adamses, who had been the town's "bosses" for almost a century. In a way, the change reflected what was happening outside Quincy as well. By 1887, the local workers, pushed by the Knights of Labor, were working their will upon the town meeting, and John and Charles knew that their "connection with town affairs was ended." As Charles put it, "John and I thought it was high time for us to haul out."

With the political change in the town, the quarrying continued, and land developers began to cut the farmland into house lots, "which are hawked about by the vulgarest kind of speculators. . . . Poor, cheap houses are being built under the eaves of the old mansion." Quincy was becoming a "mining camp . . . cursed with the stone industry."

The same industrialization was affecting much of Boston and its environs, and in 1892, the Massachusetts General Court authorized a commission of three to suggest the "advisability of laying out ample open spaces" in the area. Charles Adams served on this commission and helped write its report, which called for establishing a metropolitan park commission to preserve "open spaces for exercise and recreation." Adams headed the second commission, and in 1894, $500,000 was spent on wide boulevards connecting the communities and another $500,000 for open spaces along the Charles River.

But in May, 1893, Charles was through with Quincy. He bought 320 acres of land near Lincoln, west of Boston along Fairhaven Bay, where he could "feel and smell and taste the country, the sunshine, the stillness, the unbroken view." He built a new home, and wrote: "Early one Monday morning in the latter part of November, 1893, I mounted my horse at the door of my house on the hill at Quincy — the sun being hardly above the horizon of the distant sea-line in the nipping atmosphere — and rode over to Lincoln. I have not passed a night at Quincy since."

So it was that only two members of the Adams family remained in Quincy. Then, in 1894, John Quincy II died. Charles and his wife were vacationing in Europe, and hurried home for the funeral. He and John had been close these last few years, although Charles thought his brother "lacked persistence and will" and "curiously wanted in the spirit of adventure and desire of novelty . . . thus, he systematically narrowed himself down and rusted."

Charles and John had sailed sloops or schooners around Boston Bay, sometimes stopping on one of the islands where they could make chowder. Charles loved the sea, and in the summer in North Scituate he swam every day. Swimming was his favorite activity, and he had taken "one of my headers" in the Adriatic, the Pacific, at Yosemite Valley. Around Boston, he swam until late September. Abigail, his niece, remembered seeing him "as he used to stand on a cold September morning gazing out at a gray sea while pensively rubbing his bald head and happily murmuring, 'My God, how dreary!'" He also took up bicycling and enjoyed riding or hiking where the land was still untarnished by advancing industrialization.

After John's death, Charles wrote: "I am in my sixtieth year. I must be up and doing, — and doing persistently, systematically, constantly. I have but ten years left." He became the family historian for the fourth generation, and also watched the family finances. His own prosperity gradually returned during the first decade of the twentieth century as his western real estate holdings paid off. Of all the Adamses of the fourth generation, Charles had engaged life the fullest. He reflected: "I have seen much of life and affairs, — mixed largely with men and events; — traveled much, and taken my full share in the great game."

The other brothers, by choice or fate, withdrew. Brooks alone remained in Quincy. He and Henry traveled, and were in Paris together near the end of the century. Brooks had brought Evelyn, his wife, and Abigail, his niece, to Paris, where they met Henry, who was writing and living in an apartment near the Bois. Henry's most lasting writing — *Mont Saint-*

Michel and Chartres and *The Education of Henry Adams* —
still lay ahead of him. He showered Evelyn and Abigail with
gifts and attention, and when he found out that Abigail, then
a teenager, loved marrons glacés for breakfast, he bought them
for her, and exclaimed: "Is there anything short of a camel
that can touch the digestion of a growing girl?"

Like a confection, the old century — the Adams century
— melted away. Henry prepared to go to Egypt with his friend
John Hay, the new American ambassador to the court of St.
James's, an appointment which John Adams was the first to
hold. The news of the sinking of the *Maine* in Havana harbor
hardly stopped them. Back home, Sousa's *Stars and Stripes Forever!* summoned young American boys to war with Spain. It
would be — thankfully — a short one. Commodore Dewey
sailed into Manila Bay and, without losing a man, reduced the
Spanish fleet to junk. Teddy Roosevelt and his horseless
Rough Riders fought in Cuba. Old nineteenth-century an-
tagonisms and Manifest Destiny were settled. The muscle of
the coming twentieth century was flexed. As John Hay wrote
home to Roosevelt: "It has been a splendid little war." And so
the new century began.

Brooks loved the Old House and stayed in it until his death
in 1927. He was proud of the restored garden, and Henry's
share of the old family portraits remained. The Old House,
the portraits, were but a fraction of the legacy and record of
the four generations of Adamses. In their letters and diaries,
which they kept faithfully, in their books and ledgers, each
generation of this most historic American family recorded its
witness of history. It was as though for almost two hundred
years they had taken upon themselves the burden of being ob-
servers as well as participants.

They were, from first to last, historians and journalists,
watching and writing and interpreting for future generations.
They documented in clear and objective prose the birth of
their nation. Although they served it as diplomats, presidents,
congressmen, and cabinet secretaries, they always found time
to write in their diaries and copy letters. One reason John
Quincy Adams thought Henry Clay's late-night card parties
so exasperating was that as an Adams he had to fulfill the ob-

The Old House (left) in Quincy retains today its eighteenth-century lines and charm. It was a retreat and source of pride for four generations of the Adams family. The Stone Library on the grounds still contains the family's vast collection of books and other materials, overseen by a portrait of John Adams as president. The library was built by Charles Francis Adams, and there he began the editing of his father's diary.

LEFT: THE OLD HOUSE
IN QUINCY

RIGHT: THE STONE
LIBRARY NEAR
THE OLD HOUSE

ligation of his writing before he could enjoy the attractions of Ghent. The Adams women, too, took up the pen and added their special perceptions to the record.

The Adamses were men and women of persistence, vision, intelligence. They were also mule-stubborn, disciplined, tyrannical, rebellious. They were flawed: some of their children grew up to alcoholism and suicide. Their tempers were legend into the fourth generation. Abigail Adams Homans said she "never remember[ed] seeing Uncle Henry in a temper — indeed, he said that a temper fit gave him a bilious attack — but his brothers, Charles and Brooks, could produce, when provoked, quite appalling ones."

The family temper grated other men and women, and sometimes made delicate political maneuvering difficult if not impossible. The Adamses were for many reasons misunderstood and disliked, unappreciated by the American people they thought they were serving. Adams men considered themselves hereditary statesmen, who appealed to morality and reason and were aristocrats and dreamers; each carried the peculiar notion that he had the vision for America.

The Adamses were aware of the judgment of future generations and anxious about it. On September 20, 1824, John Quincy Adams reflected: "I walked in the burying-yard, and viewed the granite tombstones erected over the graves of my ancestors by my father. Henry Adams, the first of the family, who came from England; Joseph Adams, Sr., and Abigail Baxter, his wife; Joseph Adams, Jr., and Hannah Bass his second wife; John Adams, Sr., my father's father, and Susannah Boylston, his wife. Four generations, of whom very little is known than is recorded upon these stones. There are three succeeding generations of us now living. Pass another century, and we shall all be mouldering in the same dust, or resolved into the same elements. Who then of our posterity shall visit this yard? And what shall he read engraved upon the stones?"

The diaries and letters and books and ledgers would assure that legacy, although the four brothers of the last generation, said Abigail Adams Homans, were "a little afraid of the papers." They contained the bright and the dark sides of the family: elections, appointments, writings, a scandal, suicides, alcoholism; the victories and the disappointments. The four

Adamses had heated arguments about what should be done with the piles of documents in the old Stone Library. At one point, after days of debate and rage, John Quincy II lost his patience and said, "Come on Charles, let's burn the damn things."

Luckily, they didn't. In 1905, a manuscript trust was established, and in 1956 the papers were deeded to the Massachusetts Historical Society for preservation. By 1959, all of the Adamses' diaries, letters, and other records were safely on microfilm and available to scholars.

These documents reveal much about our nation and this unique family, and through them runs a continuing love of the land they reached by perilous journey and which they served for four generations. If there is a continuing thread between the Adamses it is the land and the seasons. Charles Francis Jr., like his forefathers, lived with the seasons and worried about his hay crops and droughts much as John Adams had. Like John Quincy Adams, Charles planted trees for future generations and loved walking among them, cutting, pruning, transplanting. Even the family seal contained a deer, water and a pine tree. And after a day of transplanting in 1875, Charles wrote: "What a good time — this is worth living for." Not a generation of Adamses would have disagreed.

They made mistakes; they missed opportunities like everyone else. They stood aloof from the changing country. But the Adamses also left their mark on America's first one hundred and fifty years. They were sought after, elected, chosen, listened to; they gave advice, governed, negotiated, pushed, cajoled, and wrote about the major issues of this nation.

They gave much to the land and to its people. They dug and planted, nurtured and pruned. And what resulted was an America far larger, stronger, better than what it would have been without them.

Selected Bibliography

Adams, Abigail. *Letters of Mrs. Adams, the Wife of John Adams.* Introduction by Charles Francis Adams. Boston: Little, Brown, 1840.

———. *New Letters of Abigail Adams, 1788–1801.* Edited by Stewart Mitchell. Boston: Houghton Mifflin, 1947.

Adams, Brooks. *America's Economic Supremacy.* New York: Macmillan, 1900.

———. *The Emancipation of Massachusetts* (1887). Boston: Houghton Mifflin, 1962.

———. *The Gold Standard: An Historical Study.* Washington, D.C.: Harman, 1897.

———. *The Law of Civilization and Decay: An Essay on History* (1895). New York: Random House, Vintage Books, 1955.

———. *The New Empire* (1902). New York: Bergman, 1969.

Adams, Charles Francis. *The Diary of Charles Francis Adams.* 6 vols. Vols. 1–2 edited by Aïda and David Donald; vols. 3–6, by Marc Friedlaender and L. H. Butterfield. Cambridge, Mass.: Harvard University Press, 1964–1974.

———. *The Life of John Adams.* Begun by John Quincy Adams; completed by Charles Francis Adams. 2 vols. Philadelphia: Lippincott, 1871. Also published as vol. 1 of *The Works of John Adams* (1856).

Adams, Charles Francis, Jr. *An Autobiography* (1916). New York: Russell & Russell, 1968.

————, and Henry Adams. *Chapters of Erie and Other Essays* (1871). Ithaca, N.Y.: Cornell University Press, Great Seal Books, 1956.

Adams, Henry. *The Degradation of the Democratic Dogma* (1919). New York: Harper & Row, 1969.

————. *Democracy* (1880). Introduction by Ernest Samuels. Garden City, N.Y.: Doubleday, 1961. Published with *Esther* in 1 vol.

————. *The Education of Henry Adams: An Autobiography* (1918). Boston: Houghton Mifflin, 1961.

————. *Esther* (1884). Introduction by Ernest Samuels. Garden City, N.Y.: Doubleday, 1961. Published with *Democracy* in 1 vol.

————. *The History of the United States of America During the Administrations of Jefferson and Madison* (1889–1891). Edited by Ernest Samuels. Chicago: University of Chicago Press, 1967.

————, and Charles Francis Adams Jr. *Chapters of Erie and Other Essays* (1871). Ithaca, N.Y.: Cornell University Press, Great Seal Books, 1956.

Adams, John. *The Adams-Jefferson Letters.* Edited by Lester J. Cappon. 2 vols. Chapel Hill: University of North Carolina Press, 1959.

————. *Diary and Autobiography of John Adams* (1961). Edited by L. H. Butterfield and others. 4 vols. New York: Atheneum, 1964.

————. *The Earliest Diary of John Adams.* Edited by L. H. Butterfield and others. Cambridge, Mass.: Harvard University Press, 1966.

————. *Familiar Letters of John Adams and His Wife Abigail Adams During the Revolution* (1876). Edited by Charles Francis Adams. Freeport, N.Y.: Books for Libraries Press, 1970.

————. *Legal Papers of John Adams.* Edited by L. K. Wroth and H. B. Zobel. 3 vols. Cambridge, Mass.: Harvard University Press, 1965.

————. *Letters of John Adams, Addressed to His Wife.* Edited by Charles Francis Adams. Boston: Little, Brown, 1841.

————. *The Works of John Adams* (1850–1856). Edited by Charles Francis Adams. 10 vols. Boston: Little, Brown, 1956.

Adams, John Quincy. *The Diary of John Quincy Adams, 1794–1845*. Edited by Allan Nevins. New York: Ungar, 1951.

———. *Life in a New England Town: 1787, 1788. Diary of John Quincy Adams, While a Student in the Office of Theophilus Parsons at Newburyport*. Introduction by Charles Francis Adams Jr. Boston: Little, Brown, 1903.

———. *Memoirs of John Quincy Adams, 1795–1848* (1874–1877). Edited by Charles Francis Adams. 12 vols. Freeport, N.Y.: Books for Libraries Press, 1969.

———. *The Writings of John Quincy Adams*. Edited by Worthington C. Ford. 7 vols. New York: Macmillan, 1913–1917.

Adams, Louisa Catherine (Mrs. John Quincy Adams). "Narrative of a Journey from St. Petersburg to Paris." With a foreword by Brooks Adams. *Scribner's Magazine* 34 (October, 1903): 449–464.

Adams Family Correspondence. Edited by L. H. Butterfield and others. 4 vols. Cambridge, Mass.: Harvard University Press, 1963–1973.

Bemis, Samuel F. *John Quincy Adams and the Foundations of American Foreign Policy*. New York: Knopf, 1949.

———. *John Quincy Adams and the Union*. New York: Knopf, 1956.

Butterfield, L. H. "Tending a Dragon Killer." *Proceedings of the American Philosophical Society*, 118 (April, 1974): 165–178.

Charles, Joseph. *The Origins of the American Party System*. New York: Harper, 1961.

Chinard, Gilbert. *Honest John Adams* (1933). Boston: Little, Brown, 1964.

Cochran, Thomas Childs, and William Miller. *The Age of Enterprise: A Social History of Industrial America*. New York: Harper, 1961.

Dangerfield, George. *The Awakening of American Nationalism, 1815–1828*. New York: Harper & Row, 1965.

———. *The Era of Good Feelings*. New York: Harcourt, Brace, 1952.

Duberman, Martin B. *Charles Francis Adams, 1807–1886*. Boston: Houghton Mifflin, 1961.

Ford, Worthington C., ed. *A Cycle of Adams Letters, 1861–1865*. 2 vols. Boston: Houghton Mifflin, 1920.

Homans, Abigail Adams. *Education by Uncles*. Boston: Houghton Mifflin, 1966.

Howe, John B. *The Changing Political Thought of John Adams*. Princeton, N.J.: Princeton University Press, 1966.

Kirkland, Edward C. *Charles Francis Adams Jr., 1835–1915: The Patrician at Bay*. Cambridge, Mass.: Harvard University Press, 1965.

Kramer, E. F. "John Adams, Elbridge Gerry and the Origins of the XYZ Affair." *Essex Institute Historical Collections*, 94 (January, 1968): 57–58.

Maclay, Edgar S., ed. *The Journal of William Maclay, U.S. Senator from Pennsylvania, 1789–1791*. New York: Boni, 1927.

McMaster, J. B. *History of the People of the United States, from the Revolution to the Civil War*. New York: Farrar, Straus, 1964.

"Mrs. John Quincy Adams' Ball, 1824." *Harper's Bazar*, 4 (March 18, 1871): 116–168.

Nichols, Roy F. *The Disruption of American Democracy*. New York: Macmillan, 1948.

Oliver, Andrew. *Portraits of John and Abigail Adams*. Cambridge, Mass.: Harvard University Press, 1967.

———. *Portraits of John Quincy Adams and His Wife*. Cambridge, Mass.: Harvard University Press, 1970.

Samuels, Ernest. *Henry Adams: The Middle Years*. Cambridge, Mass.: Harvard University Press, 1958.

———. *The Young Henry Adams*. Cambridge, Mass.: Harvard University Press, 1948.

Sibley, John L., and Clifford K. Shipton. *Biographical Sketches of Graduates of Harvard University in Cambridge, Massachusetts*. Cambridge, Mass.: Harvard University Press, 1873–.

Smelser, Marshall. *The Democratic Republic, 1801–1815*. New York: Harper & Row, 1968.

Smith, Page. *John Adams*. 2 vols. Garden City, N.Y.: Doubleday, 1962.

Stampp, Kenneth M. *The Era of Reconstruction, 1865–1877*. New York: Knopf, 1965.

Copyright Acknowledgments

Picture Credits

Chapter 1

[5] *top:* Courtesy of the Worcester Historical Society; photo © Fernand Bourges, Time-Life Picture Agency. [5] *bottom:* Courtesy of the Massachusetts Historical Agency. [9] Courtesy of the Massachusetts Historical Society. [12-13] Courtesy of the American Antiquarian Society, Worcester, Mass. [17] *both:* Courtesy of the Massachusetts Historical Society. [20] Courtesy of the Massachusetts Historical Society. [24] Colonial Williamsburg Photograph. [27] Courtesy of the American Antiquarian Society, Worcester, Mass. [28-29] Courtesy of The Henry Francis du Pont Winterthur Museum. [31] The I. N. Phelps Stokes Collection of American Historical Prints, Prints Division, New York Public Library. [32] *top:* Courtesy of the American Antiquarian Society, Worcester, Mass. [32] *bottom:* The L. L. Bean Collection. [33] Courtesy of the Museum of Fine Arts, Boston; deposited by the City of Boston. [39] Courtesy of The Henry Francis du Pont Winterthur Museum.

Chapter 2

[43] Courtesy of the Museum of Fine Arts, Boston; bequest of Winslow Warren. [44] Courtesy of the Museum of Fine Arts, Boston; gift of Joseph W., William B., and Edward H. R. Rever (*top*); by subscription and Francis Bartlett Fund (*bottom*). [47] Adams National Historic Site, U.S. Department of the Interior, National Parks Service, Quincy, Mass.; photo courtesy of Charles Eames. [51] The John Carter Brown Library, Brown University. [59] *top:* Colonial Williamsburg Photograph. [59] *bottom:* Rare Book Division, New York Public Library; Astor, Lenox and Tilden Foundations. [62-63] *all:* The I. N. Phelps Stokes Collection of American Historical Prints, Prints Division, New York Public Library. [66] Washington-Curtis-Lee Collection, Washington and Lee University; photo courtesy of Thomas C. Bradshaw II. [69] The I. N. Phelps Stokes Collection of American Historical Prints, Prints Division, New York Public Library. [70-71] Courtesy of The National Gallery of Art, Washington; gift of Edgar William and Bernice Chrysler Garbisch. [81] Courtesy of the Massachusetts Historical Society. [82] Courtesy of Kennedy Galleries, Inc.

Chapter 3

[88] *top left:* New York Public Library. [88] *left above and below:* Courtesy of The Adams Papers. [88] *bottom:* Adams National Historic Site, U.S. Department of the Interior, National Parks Service, Quincy, Mass. [91] Courtesy of the Musée de Blérancourt, France; photo by Linda Bartlett, Photo Researchers. [96] *top:* Picture Collection, New York Public Library; *bottom:* Metropolitan Museum of Art, gift of William H. Huntington, 1883; photo courtesy of Charles Eames. [98-99] Courtesy of The Papers of Benjamin Franklin, Yale University; photo courtesy of Charles Eames. [103] Courtesy of The Adams Papers. [106-107] *top:* Royal House Archives, The Hague; *bottom:* Collection of the Municipal Archives of The Hague. [107] *top:* Courtesy of the New-York Historical Society. [111] Courtesy of The Henry Francis du Pont Winterthur Museum. [115] Courtesy of the Harvard University Portrait Collection; bequest of Ward Nicholas Boylston, 1828.

Chapter 4

[126] Courtesy of the National Gallery of Art, Washington; Andrew W. Mellon Fund. [130] *top:* Courtesy of the Trustees of the British Museum; *bottom:* Prints Division, New York Public Library. [131] Prints Division, New York Public Library. [133] Courtesy of the New York State Historical Association, Cooperstown; photo courtesy of the White House. [134] *both:* Adams National Historic Site, U.S. Department of the Interior, National Parks Service, Quincy, Mass. [138] Collection of Charles Francis Adams; photo courtesy of the Smithsonian Institution, National Portrait Gallery. [144] *top:* The I. N. Phelps Stokes Collection of American Historical Prints, Prints Division, New York Public Library; *bottom left:* New York Public Library; *bottom right:* Courtesy of the Massachusetts Historical Society.

Chapter 5

[158] Adams National Historic Site, U.S. Department of the Interior, National Parks Service, Quincy, Mass. [161] *top:* The I. N. Phelps Stokes Collection of American Historical Prints, Prints Division, New York Public Library; *bottom:* Picture Collection, New York Public Library. [167] Prints Division, New York Public Library. [174] Courtesy of Fanny C. Mason. [175] Courtesy of the Museum of Fine Arts, Boston; bequest of Charles Francis Adams.

Chapter 6

[182] Courtesy of the Massachusetts Historical Society. [193] *top:* Picture Collection, New York Public Library; *bottom:* Culver Pictures. [195] Prints Division, New York Public Library. [199] Adams National Historic Site, U.S. Department of the Interior, National Parks Service, Quincy, Mass. [206] *both:* Adams National Historic Site, U.S. Department of the Interior, National Parks Service, Quincy, Mass. [211] *top:* From the Collections of the Library of Congress; *bottom:* The I. N. Phelps Stokes Collection of American Historical Prints, Prints Division, New York Public Library.

Chapter 7

[219] Courtesy of the Smithsonian Institution, National Portrait Gallery (*top*) and National Collection of Fine Arts (*bottom*). [226] *top:* Courtesy of the American Philosophical Society; *bottom left:* Courtesy of the Academy of National Sciences, Philadelphia; photo courtesy of Charles Eames; *bottom right:* Courtesy of the American Philosophical Society; photo courtesy of Charles Eames. [233] *both:* Picture Collection, New York Public Library. [242] From the Collections of the Library of Congress. [243] *top:* The Anne S. K. Brown Military Collection, John Carter Brown Library, Brown University; *bottom:* The I. N. Phelps Stokes Collection of American Historical Prints, Prints Division, New York Public Library. [246] Courtesy of the Museum of Fine Arts, Boston; M. and M. Karolik Collection.

Chapter 8

[257] Courtesy of the New-York Historical Society. [268] The I. N. Phelps Stokes Collection of American Historical Prints, Prints Division, New York Public Library. [270] From the Cochran Collection, Philipse Manor State Historic Site, Taconic State Park and Recreation Commission, New York State Office of Parks and Recreation. [273] Courtesy of the Smithsonian Institution, National Collection of Fine Arts. [279] Courtesy of the American Antiquarian Society, Worcester, Mass.

Chapter 9

[288–289] Courtesy of the Historical Society of Pennsylvania. [293] Courtesy of the Smithsonian Institution, National Collection of Fine Arts. [296]

Adams National Historic Site, U.S. Department of the Interior, National Parks Service, Quincy, Mass. [302–303] From the Collections of the Library of Congress. [307] Courtesy of the Smithsonian Institution, from the Harry T. Peters "America on Stone" Lithograph Collection. [311] *both:* Courtesy of Elinor N. Johnston.

Chapter 10

[321] *both:* Adams National Historic Site, U.S. Department of the Interior, National Parks Service, Quincy, Mass. [324] Culver Pictures. [325] Courtesy of the Museum of Fine Arts, Boston; M. and M. Karolik Collection. [329] Courtesy of the New-York Historical Society. [336] From the Collections of the Library of Congress. [337] In the Collection of the Corcoran Gallery of Art. [340] Metropolitan Museum of Art, gift of I. N. Phelps Stokes, Edward S. Hawes, Alice Mary Hawes, Marion Augusta Hawes, 1937.

Chapter 11

[348] *top, both:* Courtesy of the Harvard University Archives; *bottom:* Adams National Historic Site, U.S. Department of the Interior, National Parks Service, Quincy, Mass. [349] *all:* Adams National Historic Site, U.S. Department of the Interior, National Parks Service, Quincy, Mass. [355] From the Collections of the Library of Congress. [360–361] *both:* Adams National Historic Site, U.S. Department of the Interior, National Parks Service, Quincy, Mass. [363] *both:* Culver Pictures. [367, 368–369] *all:* From the Collections of the Library of Congress. [371] Valentine Museum, Richmond, Va.

Chapter 12

[380–381] *both:* Courtesy of the Union Pacific Railroad Company. [386] Culver Pictures. [389–400] *all:* Courtesy of the Massachusetts Historical Society.

Chapter 13

[406] Culver Pictures. [407] Courtesy of the Massachusetts Historical Society. [414] Culver Pictures. [417] *both:* Adams National Historic Site, U.S. Department of the Interior, National Parks Service, Quincy, Mass. [420–421] *all:* Courtesy of the Society for the Preservation of New England Antiquities. [428–429] *both:* Adams National Historic Site, U.S. Department of the Interior, National Parks Service, Quincy, Mass.; photo on 428 © Robert Kelly, Time–Life Picture Agency.

Index

Page numbers in italics refer to illustrations.

to Europe (1880), 398; and his wife's death, 401–402; trips to the Far East, 403, 405; commissions memorial by Saint-Gaudens, 403, 405; later years, 404–405, 422, 423–424, 426, 427, 430

WRITINGS: articles for Boston newspapers, 352–353, 354, 356; review of Lyell's *Principles of Geology*, 365; articles on currency speculation, 378–379; *Chapters of Erie and Other Essays* (with CFA Jr.), 382–383, 422; biography of Albert Gallatin, 394–395, 397; *The Education of Henry Adams*, 394, 402, 427; *Democracy*, 394, 397–398; *Esther*, 394, 399, 402; *History of the United States During the Administrations of Jefferson and Madison*, 394–395, 401, 402, 404, 405, 422; *Mont Saint-Michel and Chartres*, 426–427

Adams, John: birth and family background, 4; as schoolteacher, 6–7; law studies and practice, 10–11, 14–15, 21, 30, 34; courtship of Hannah Quincy, 15–16; courtship of Abigail Smith, 18–19; marriage, 21; early political activities, 21, 23; opposes Stamp Act, 30; selectman of Braintree, 30, 34; defends John Hancock, 35; defends the *Pitt Packet* crew, 36; recognized as a patriot, 36–37; defends British soldiers after the Boston Massacre, 40; abandons politics and visits Stafford Springs, 48; moves back to Boston, 49; attacks Crown payment of judges' salaries, 49–50; and the impeachment of Chief Justice Oliver, 50; delegate to the First Continental Congress, 54–60; NOVANGLUS articles, 61; delegate to the Second Continental Crongess, 61, 64, 65, 68, 72–73, 78; nominates Washington as commander in chief, 67; and the Declaration of Independence, 78–80, 81; and the king's clemency offer, 84–85; as head of Board of War and Ordance, 86; commissioner to France (1777), 87, 89–90; drafts Mass. constitution, 93; negotiator of peace with England, 93, 95, 100–101, 105, 108–110, 112–113; negotiates loans and commercial treaty with the Dutch, 102, 104–105, 114, 151; minister to Great Britain, 117–118, 123, 125, 127; audience with George III, 120–123; friendship with Jefferson, 119, 136–137; and the framing of the Constitution, 153–154; elected vice-president, 156–157; as president of the Senate, 157, 159–160, 171; denounced as a monarchist, 163–164, 166, 178; dissension with Jefferson, 164–166, 213–214; re-elected, vice-president, 169; in the 1796–97 campaign, 178–179; elected president, 180; inaugurated, 183–185; attacked by the press, 184, 187, 190; and U.S. relations with France, 185–186, 195–196, 198, 200–205; defense measures, 196; and the Alien and Sedition acts, 197–198; changes from bellicosity to search for peace, 198, 200–205; and schism in the Federalist Party, 203, 205, 207–208; judicial appointments, 213–214; supports JQA on embargo, 234; and his grandchildren, 251; reconciliation with Jefferson, 253–254; in old age, 253, 272; death, 295; CFA's biography of, 345

PERSONAL DATA: character and temperament, 6, 7 (Franklin's assessment), 8, 100, 110, 112, 155 (Jefferson's assessment); portraits, *9*, *107*, 114, *115*, 116, 132, *182*; appearance, 10, 116 (CFA's description); courtroom style, 15; amorous disposition, 16; failings as a diplomat, 100, 101–102; quality of mind, 221 (Louisa Adam's description)

OPINIONS ON: diary writing, 4, 6–7; lawsuits in Braintree, 15; growing revolutionary fervor, 26, 30, 36–37; on the fickleness of Hancock, 46; the Boston Tea Party, 52–53; New York City, 56–57; Boston's superiority to Philadelphia, 60; the battles of Lexington and Concord, 61; John Dickinson, 72; the Olive Branch petition, 72–73; his children's education, 74; Abigail's pleas for rights for women, 77; insufficient pay as delegate to Congress, 87; administration of ships, 89; ministers vs. commissioners, 90; French enthusiasm for the U.S., 95; Paris, 101; Robert R. Livingston's rebuke, 112–113; English vs. American manure, 133; a Harvard education, 142; form of address for the president of the U.S., 157, 159; on Washington as president, 160; presidential power, 163; monarchy 164; *vox populi*, 171; diplomacy, 172; the Alien and Sedition acts, 198, Aaron Burr, 213

WRITINGS: his diary and correspondence, 4–5, 7; *Autobiogrphy*, 16, 79–80; "A Dissertation on the Canon and the Feudal Law," 23; memorial against the closing of the courts, 30; "Braintree Instructions," 30; protest against seizure of the *Liberty*, 35; protest against British offenses in Boston, 37; articles on Crown payment of judges' salaries, 49–50; articles on events leading to the First Continental Congress, 64; *Thoughts on Government*, 75; "Peace Journal," 110, 112, 117; *A Defence of the Constitutions of Government of the United States of America*, 150, 178; *Discourses on Davila*, 163–164, 166, 178

Adams, John, II (2d son of JQA), 227, 250, 251, 253, 271, 272, 304; marriage, 298–299; children, 299; brush with the press, 300–301; portrait of, 272, *311*; death, 322

Adams, John Quincy (1st son of JA): birth, 34; to France with JA (1778), 87; schooling in Europe, 92, 100, 102, 104; to England with JA (1779), 93; secretary to Francis Dana, 104; joins JA in The Hague, 113; attends Harvard, 119, 139–142; law studies, 142–143; social life, 143–144; love for Mary Frazier, 145, 190; minister to the Netherlands, 171–173, 176–177, 189; engagement and marriage, 177, 190–191, 216–218; attacked by the press, 188, 190; minister to Prussia, 190–192, 218; financial troubles, 221; enters politics, 222; as senator, 222, 227–229; accepts Harvard professorship, 229; protests British impressment and supports nonimportation, 231–232; breaks with Federalists, 232, 234; minister to Russia, 235–238; and the Treaty of Ghent, 238–241, 244; minister to Great Britain, 250–251; appointed secretary of state, 251; income and responsibilities as secretary of state, 254–256; and U.S. foreign policy, 258–265; and the acquisition of the Floridas, 259–265; and settlement of U.S. western boundaries, 264; policy of non-intervention and noncolonization, 273–274; against proposed alliance with England, 274, 276; and 1824 campaign, 277, 280–282; elected president, 282; inaugural address, 283; first annual message to Congress, 284–285; his plans for the U.S. opposed, 285; refuses to indulge in patronage, 286; troubles with Congress, 286–287; and loss of trade with the West Indies, 290–291; and the Treaty of Indian Spring, 291–292; and the Tariff of Abominations, 292, 294; and JA's death, 295; family life, 297–300; and the Jarvis incident, 301; response to adversity, 302, 304–305; defeated by Jackson, 306, 308, 309; and his son George's death, 310, 312, 314; retirement to Quincy, 315–316; as congressman, 316–320; views on nullification, 318; "Independence and Union" speech, 318–319; and his son John's death, 322; his fight against the Gag Rule, 322–328, 330–332, 334–335; and the annexation of Texas, 332–333; wins the *Amistad* case, 333; defeats his censure, 334–335; national acclaim for, 335, 338–339; death, 339, 341–342; his fortune, 351

PERSONAL DATA: portraits, *88, 175, 219, 270, 340*; his reading, 189; character and temperament, 216–217, 227–228; social shortcomings, 267–268; as a parent, 268, 271; CFA Jr.'s recollection of, 345

OPINIONS ON: U.S. relations with England, 177–178; his marriage, 217; politics, 221–222; Monroe's cabinet, 256, 258; the Missouri Compromise, 266; his mother, 272; Calhoun's conduct in the Senate, 287, 290; treatment of the Indians, 292; the birth of his namesake, 320; his need to engage in politics, 332

WRITINGS: remembrance of Bunker Hill, 68; in defense of JA (PUBLICOLA articles), 165; in support of Washington (MARCELLUS and COLUMBUS articles), 172; *Report on Weights and Measures,* 254; debate with Calhoun (PATRICK HENRY articles), 287–288

Adams, John Quincy, II (1st son of CFA), 320, 358; education, 346; law practice, 347; portrait of, *349;* bolts to the Democratic Party, 374–377; and loans to CFA Jr., 411; Mount Wollaston home, 422; and the industrialization of Quincy, 424–425; death, 426; and the family papers, 431

Adams, Louisa Catherine Johnson (wife of JQA), 177, 190–192, 227; portraits of, *174, 272, 273;* on court life in Berlin, 191–192; character and temperament, 216, 217–218, 299, 301–302; first meeting with the Adams family, 218, 220–221; opinion of JA, 221; journey from Russia to Paris, 244–245, 247–250; and Washington etiquette, 266–268; and the ball for Jackson, 277–278, *279,* 280; on her son John's marriage, 299; and her son George's death, 314; and her husband's public service, 316, 322; death, 343–344

Adams, Louisa Catherine, II (1st dau. of CFA), 320, 346, *349,* 372

Adams, Marian Hooper (wife of Henry Adams), 390–391, 395, 397–399, 401–404

Adams, Mary (2d dau. of CFA), 320, 346, 349, 358, 373

Adams, Mary Catherine Hellen (wife of JA II), 297–299, 309, 343

Adams, Mary Louisa (1st dau. of JA II), 299

Adams, Mary Ogden (wife of CFA Jr.), 372–373, *417*

Adams, Samuel, 23, 33, 40, 50n, 54, 90

Adams, Sarah Smith (wife of Charles Adams), 177, 189

Adams, Susanna (dau. of JA), 34

Adams, Susanna Boylston (dau. of Charles Adams), 189

Adams, Thomas Boylston (3d son of JA), 49, 86n, 143–144, 168, 173, 191, 218, 221, 255

Adams, William (British lawyer), 239

Agg, John, 277–278, 280

Alexander I, tsar of Russia, 236, 272, 273, 274

Allen, Ethan, 64

Ambrister, Robert C., 261, 263

American Anti-Slavery Society, 323, 327

Ames, F. L., 412, 415, 416, 419

Ames, Fisher, 196, 227, 234

Ames, Oakes, 387, 408, 412

Anthony, Susan B., 394

Arbuthnot, Alexander, 261, 263

Armour, Philip D., 385, 409

Arnold, Benedict, 64, 94

Arnold, Matthew, 398

Articles of Association, 57

Articles of Confederation, 124

Astor, John Jacob, 152

Aurora (General Advertiser), 173, 176, 178, 183, 187–188, 190

Bache, Benjamin Franklin, 92, 173, 176, 187, 190, 197

Baker, Ezra, 413

Baldwin, Roger, 333

Bancroft, George, 399

Bank of the United States, 317

Barbour, James, 284, 291

Bayard, James A., 238, 244

Beaumarchais, Pierre-Augustin Caron de, 95

Berkeley, George C., 230–231

Bernard, Sir Francis, 35–36

Binns, John, 306

Bird, Savage & Bird, 221

Blount, William, 187

Blyth, Benjamin, *9, 20*

Bonington, Richard Parkes, 399

Boston Advertiser, 354, 356

Boston Daily Courier, 352, 365

Boston Gazette, 23

Boston Massacre, the, 38, 40

Boston News Letter, 73

Boston Tea Party, 52–53

Botts, John Minor, 335

Bowdoin, James, 54, 148

Brattle, William, 49

Braxton, Carter, 80

Breckinridge, John C., 354

British East India Company, 50, 52

Brooks, Abigail. *See* Adams, Abigail Brooks
Brooks, James, 387
Brooks, Peter Chardon, 351
Brown, Mather, *132, 134, 135, 136, 138*
Browning, Robert, 398
Buchanan, James, 351, 356
Burgoyne, John, 94–95
Burke, Edmund, 55, 64
Burnet, Jacob, 338
Burns, Anthony, 351
Burr, Aaron, 152, 212–213
Bute, Lord, 22
Butler, John, 85

Calhoun, John C., 256, 259, 276, 285–287, 328
Callender, James, 197–198
Cameron, Martha, 405
Canning, George, 272, 274–276
Carmathen, Lord, 120–121, 125, 127
Cass, Lewis, 344
Castlereagh, Lord, 238, 263, 272, 274–275
Catherine II, empress of Russia, 97
Chambers, John, 328
Cincinnati Gazette, 306
Cinque (West African slave), 333
Civil War, 358–359, 362, 364–366, 370, 372
Clay, Henry: peace commissioner at Ghent, 238–241, 244; political career, 256, 258, 262, 264, 280–282, 284, 286; duel with John Randolph, 287; and Jackson's inauguration, 309; rejected by Whigs, 344
Clayton, Augustus Smith, 319
Clark, Susan B., 295
Clark, William, 227
Cleveland, Grover, 375
Cleveland Herald, 338
Clinton, De Witt, 282
Clinton, George, 166, 169
Cobbett, William, 187
Colfax, Schuyler, 387
Columbian Centinel, 165, 190
Common Sense (Paine), 42, 75
Condorcet, marquis de, 95
Confederate States, 357, 359, 362, 364
Congress of the Confederation, 152–153
Constable, John, 399
Continental Congresses. *See* First *and* Second Continental Congress
Constitution, the federal, 153–155
Cooke, Jay, 385
Cooper, Thomas, 197, 294
Copley, John Singleton, *33, 43, 44,* 61, 113–114, *115,* 116, *175*
Cornwallis, Lord, 104–105
Cranch, Richard, 16, 18
Crawford, William H., 256, 258, 261, 280–282
Crédit Mobilier of America, 387, 408
Crowell, John, 291
Crowninshield, Benjamin, 256
Crowninshield, Fanny. *See* Adams, Fanny Crowninshield
Cushing, Thomas, 46, 54

Dana, Francis, 93, 104
Davie, William R., 203, 205
Davis, Evelyn. *See* Adams, Evelyn Davis
Davis, Henry Winter, 354, 356–357
Dawes, William, 61
Daws, Tom, 21
Day, Luke, 148
Deane, Silas, 79, 86, 89–90, 95
Declaration of Independence, 80–81, 83
Definitive Treaty of Peace, 112–113
Dickinson, John, 68, 72–73, 80–81
Dolph, Eliza, 313–314
Douglas, Stephen A., 351, 354
Drayton, William, 319
Dred Scott case, 352
Drew, Daniel, 382
Dudley, Joseph, 23
dueling, 287n, 301
Dunmore, John Murray, earl of, 75, 146

Edmunds, George F., 416
Ellsworth, Oliver, 203, 205
Emancipation Proclamation, 375
embargo of 1807, 231–232, 234
Emerson, Ralph Waldo, 334
Erving, George W., 263, 265
Eustis, William, 222

Farmer, Miles, 313–314
Fenno, John, 187, 190
Ferdinand VII, king of Spain, 265, 275
Field, Joseph, 14
Fillmore, Millard, 345
Fink, Albert, 384
First Continental Congress, 54–55, 57, 58, 60
Fisk, James, 377–379, 382, *386*
Fiske, John, 397
Fitch, Samuel, 23
Fitsherbert, William, 109
Fox, Charles James, 105
Franklin, Benjamin: his opinion of JA, 7; and the king's clemency offer, 84–85; and the Olive Branch petition, 72; commissioner to France, 87, 89–90; reception by the French, 96; portraits of, *96, 98–99;* feud with JA, 102; and peace negotiations, 104–105, 108–109
Franklin, William Temple, 140
Frazier, Mary, 145, 191
Free Soil Party, 344–345, 351, 390
Frémont, John C., 351
French Revolution, 163, 166, 170
Fugitive Slave Act, 345

Gadsden, Christopher, 54
Gage, Thomas, 53–54, 61
Gag Rule (Twenty-first Rule), 323–335
Gallatin, Albert, 196–197, 224, 237–238, 244, 265, 290–291, 394, 397
Gallatin, L. Lawrence, 394
Gambier, Lord, 239
Garfield, James A., 387
Garibaldi, Giuseppe, 352–353
Garrison, William Lloyd, 323

Leonard, Daniel, 61
Leopard-Chesapeake incident, 230–231
Lewis, Meriwether, 227
Liberty Boys of 1776, 163
Lincoln, Abraham, 354–355, 358–359, 374, 377
Lincoln, Bela, 16
Livingston, Philip, 56
Livingston, Robert R., 81, 112, 225
Lloyd, James, Jr., 234
Lodge, Mrs. Cabot, 422
Lodge, Henry Cabot, 397
London Chronicle, 23
Louis XVI, king of France, 90, 96–97, 169
Louisiana Purchase, 225, 227, 260–261, 264
Low, Issac, 46
Lowell, James Russell, 394

Maccarty, Thaddeus, 7
McCormick, Cyrus H., 385
McHenry, James, 183, 207
Mackenzie, Stuart, 22
Maclay, William, 159–160
McLean, John, 286
Madison, James, 148, 152, 153, 166, 224; on JA's temper, 196; and the Sedition Act, 198; friendship with JQA, 232, 235
Marshall, John, 186, 213
Marshall, Thomas F., 334
Mason, Alice, *206*
Mason, James M., 362
Massachusetts Constitutional Convention, 93
Massachusetts Railroad Commission, 383–384
Meade, George C., 370
Mechanics Free Press, 306
Mechanics' Union of Trade Associations, 305–306
Meissonier, Jean Louis Ernest, 419
Mexican War, 333
Mifflin, Thomas, 166, 169
Mill, John Stuart, 394
Millet, Francis D., 411
Mills, Elijah H., 267
Missouri Compromise, 265–266, 351
Molasses Act of 1733, 25
Monroe, James, 181, 186–187, 225, 231; appoints JQA secretary of state, 251; his cabinet, 258, 261; and Jackson's Seminole campaign, 259–260, 261; and recognition of South American states, 273; annual message to Congress (1823), 276–277
Monroe, Mrs. James, 267
Monroe Doctrine, 259, 274, 276–277
Moore, Thomas, 228, 299
Morgan, J. P., 385
Morris, Robert, 81, 124
Mott, Lucretia Coffin, 394
Murray, William Vans, 186, 201–204

Napoleon, 205, 232
National American Woman Suffrage Association, 394
National Gazette, 166
National Journal, 301
Naturalization Act of 1789, 197
New England Anti-Slavery Society, 323

newspapers, 184, 187, 188, 191, 197–198. *See also* names of papers
New York Journal, 166, 168
New York Times, 358
North, Lord, 22, 37, 97, 105
North American Review, 365, 382–383, 390
Northwest Ordinance, 147
nullification, doctrine of, 317
Nullification Ordinance, 319–320

Observations on Modern Gardening (Whately), 136–137
Ogden, Mary Hone. *See* Adams, Mary Ogden
Olive Branch petition, 68, 72–73
Oliver, Peter, 50
Onís y Gonzales, Luis de, 260–264
Oswald, Richard, 105, 109
Otis, James, Jr., 11, 21, 25–26, 30, 36

Paine, Robert Treat, 54
Paine, Thomas, 42, 75, 124, 164–165
Palgrave, Francis Turner, 398
Palmerston, Lord, 359, 362
Panton, Henry Gibson, 36
Parkman, Francis, 394
Parsons, Theophilus, 142–143, 235
patronage, 286, 308
Pattison, R. E., 413
Patton, John Mercer, 330–331
Philadelphia Democratic Press, 306
Pickering, Timothy, 183, 186–187, 204, 207–208, 222
Pillsbury, John S., 385
Pinckney, Charles C., 185–186, 194
Pinckney, Henry Laurens, 323, 326–327
Pinckney's Treaty of 1795, 225, 259
Pitcairn, John, 61
Pitt, William, 26, 64, 125, 287n
Pitt Packet incident, the, 36
Plumb, P. B., 415–416
Plumer, William, 235
Polk, James K., 317, 326–327, 344
Porcupine's Gazette & Daily Advertiser, 187
Prat, Benjamin, 11, 14, 21
press. *See* newspapers
Preston, Thomas, 38, 40
Prospect before us, The (Callender), 197–198
Putnam, James, 10–11

Quadruple Alliance, 272, 273, 274–275
Quartering Act, 53
Quincy, H. P., 346
Quincy, Hannah, 14–16
Quincy, Josiah, 15–16, 40
Quincy, Samuel, 11, 14
Quincy Patriot, 347

railroads. *See* Adams, Charles Francis, Jr.; Union Pacific Railroad
Randolph, Edmund, 160
Randolph, John, 282, 286–287, 290, 294
Raymond, Henry J., 352, 358
Reconstruction, 374–376